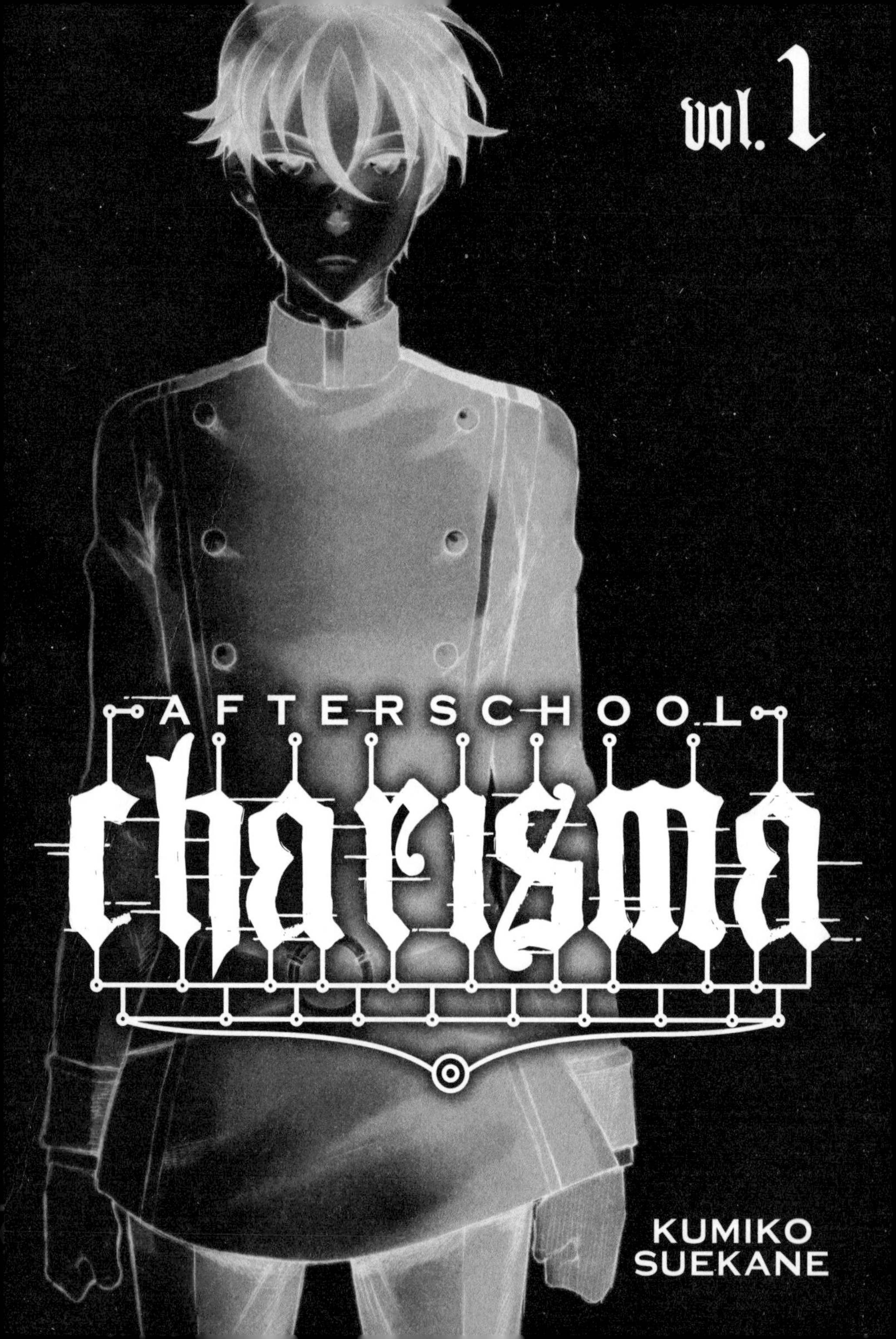
vol. 1
AFTERSCHOOL
Charisma
KUMIKO
SUEKANE

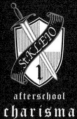

St.KLEIO

1

afterschool
charisma

c o n t e n t s

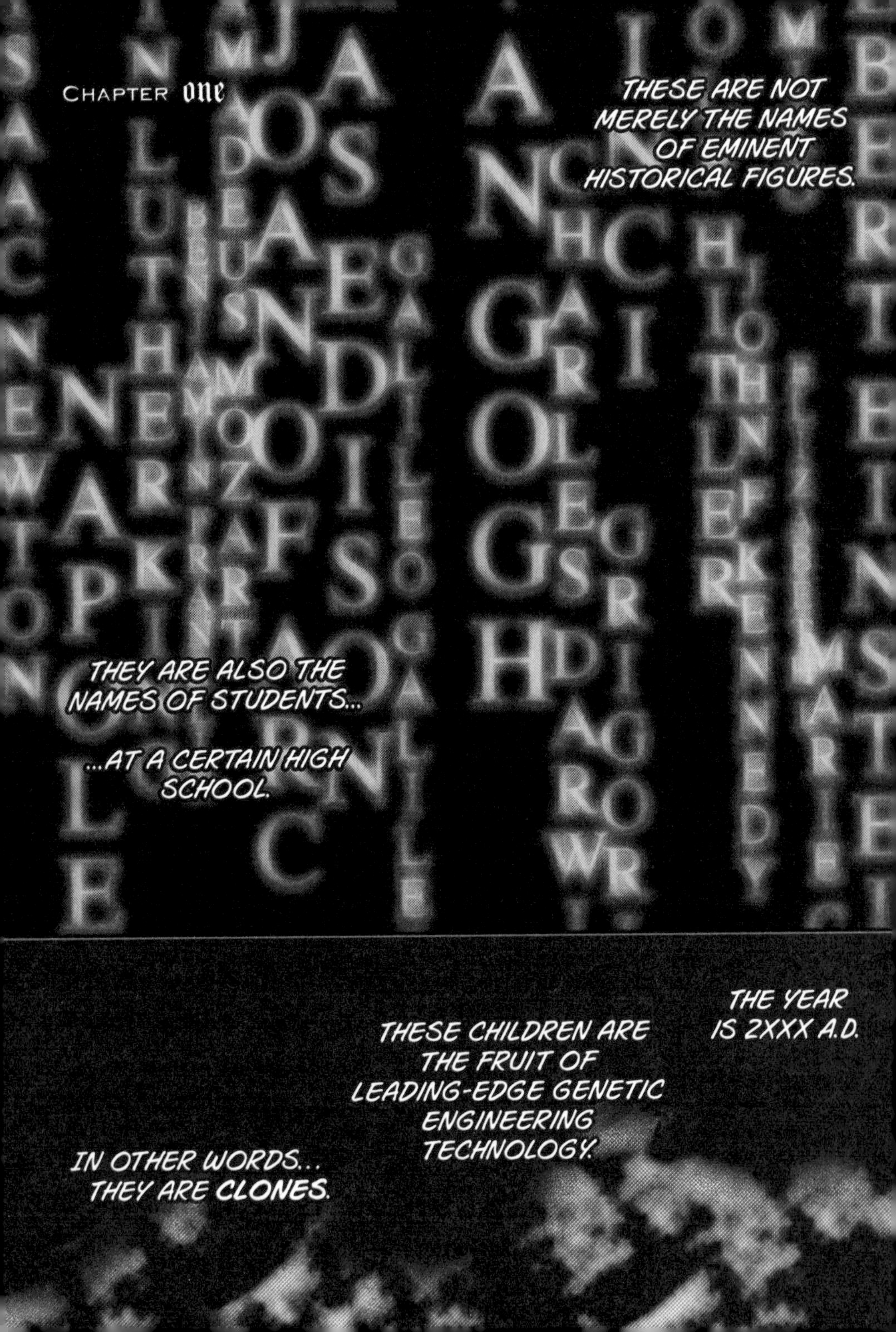
Chapter one
THESE ARE NOT MERELY THE NAMES OF EMINENT HISTORICAL FIGURES.
THEY ARE ALSO THE NAMES OF STUDENTS...
...AT A CERTAIN HIGH SCHOOL.
THE YEAR IS 2XXX A.D.
THESE CHILDREN ARE THE FRUIT OF LEADING-EDGE GENETIC ENGINEERING TECHNOLOGY.
IN OTHER WORDS... THEY ARE **CLONES**.

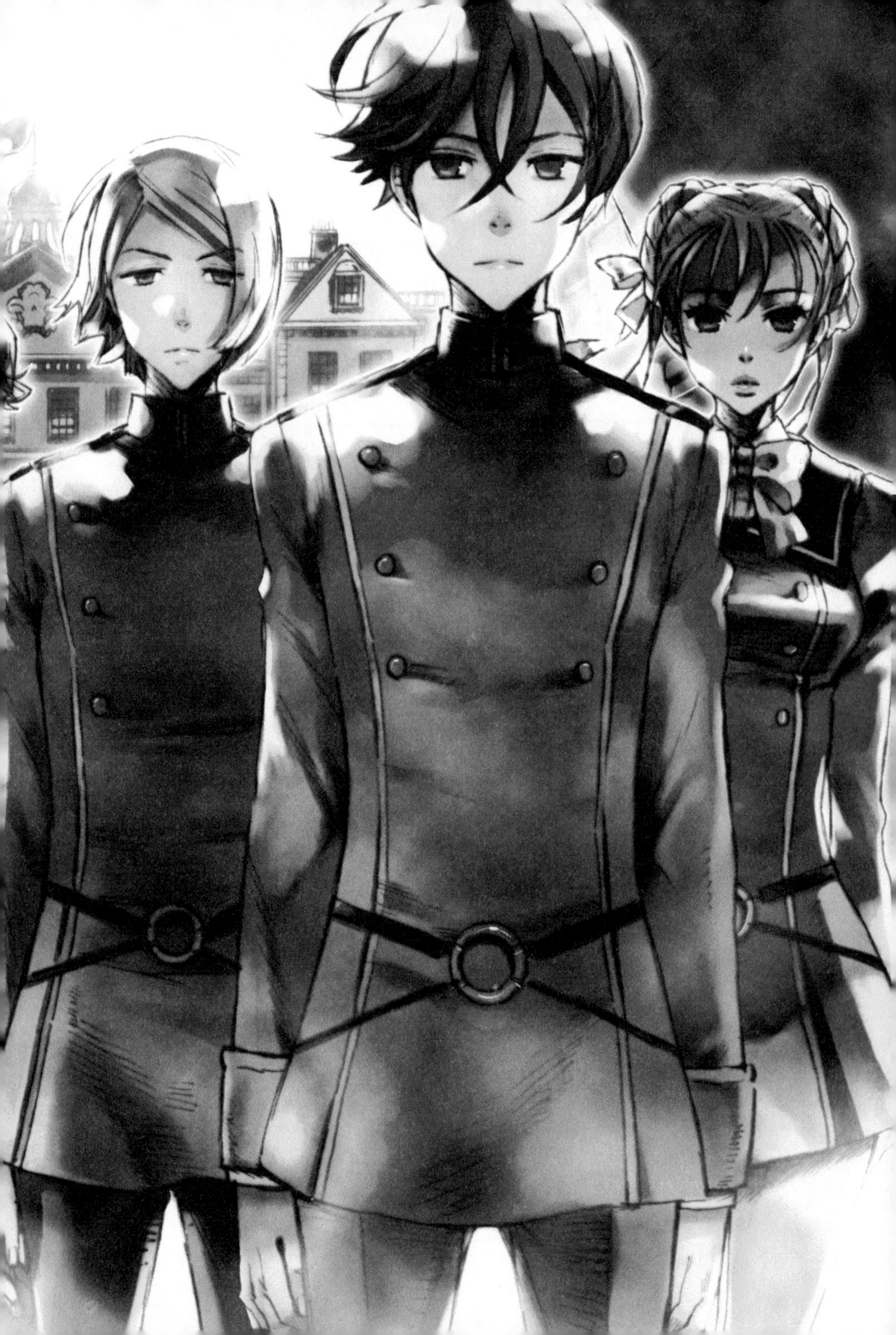

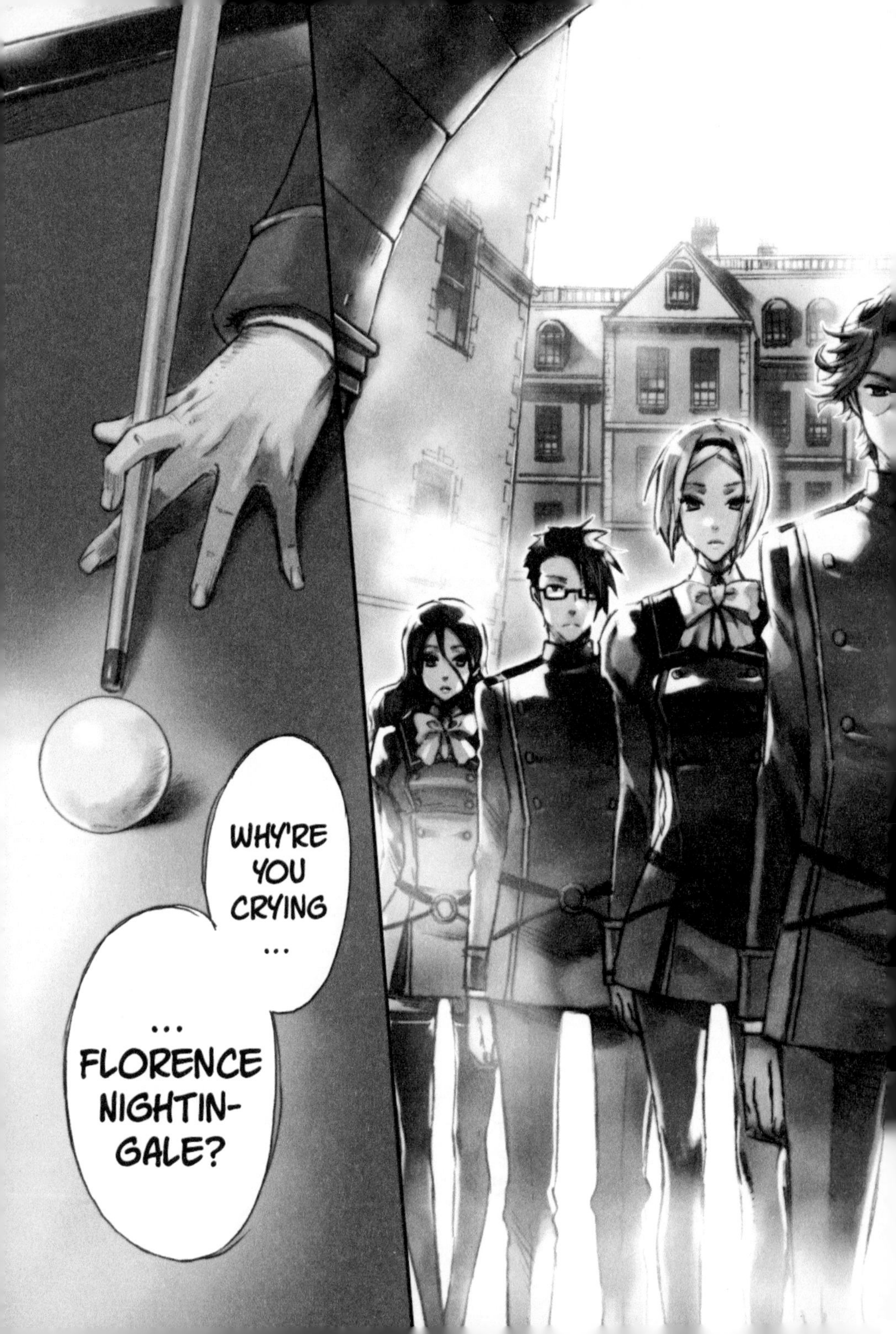
WHY'RE YOU CRYING ...
... FLORENCE NIGHTIN-GALE?

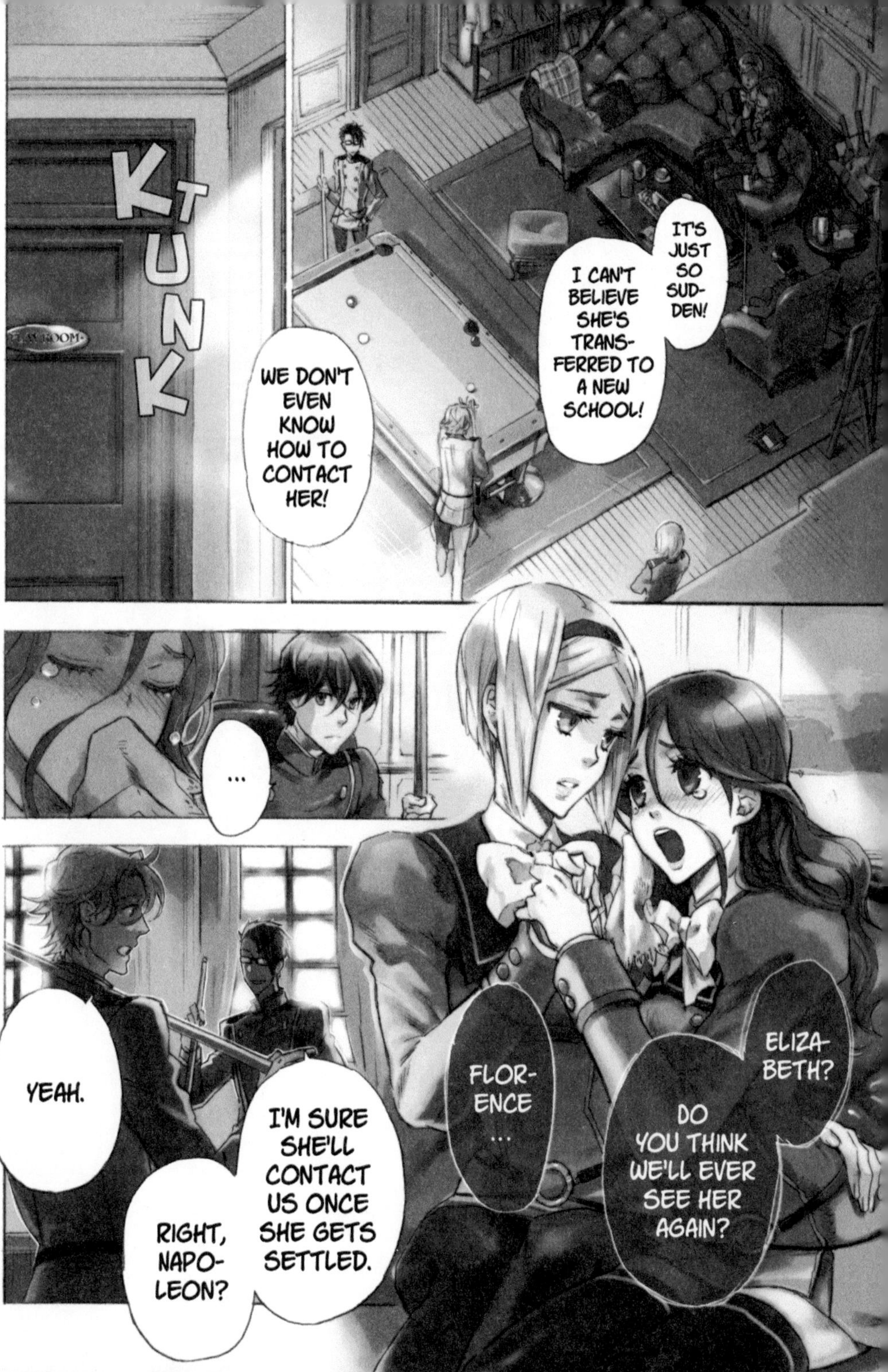
IT'S JUST SO SUDDEN!
I CAN'T BELIEVE SHE'S TRANSFERRED TO A NEW SCHOOL!
WE DON'T EVEN KNOW HOW TO CONTACT HER!
KTUNK
ELIZABETH?
DO YOU THINK WE'LL EVER SEE HER AGAIN?
FLORENCE...
...
I'M SURE SHE'LL CONTACT US ONCE SHE GETS SETTLED.
RIGHT, NAPOLEON?
YEAH.

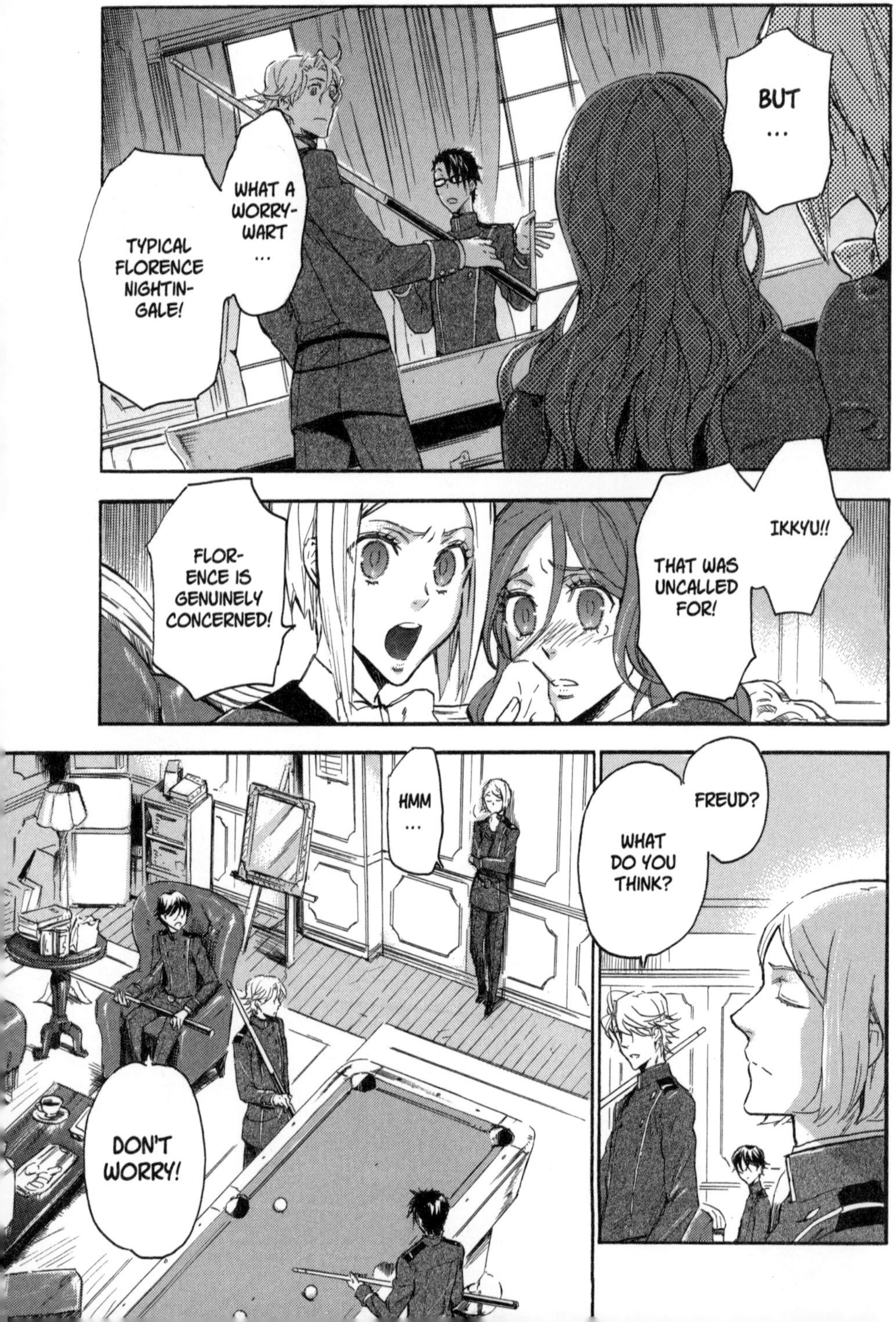
BUT ...
WHAT A WORRY-WART ...
TYPICAL FLORENCE NIGHTIN-GALE!
IKKYU!!
THAT WAS UNCALLED FOR!
FLOR-ENCE IS GENUINELY CONCERNED!
FREUD?
WHAT DO YOU THINK?
HMM ...
DON'T WORRY!

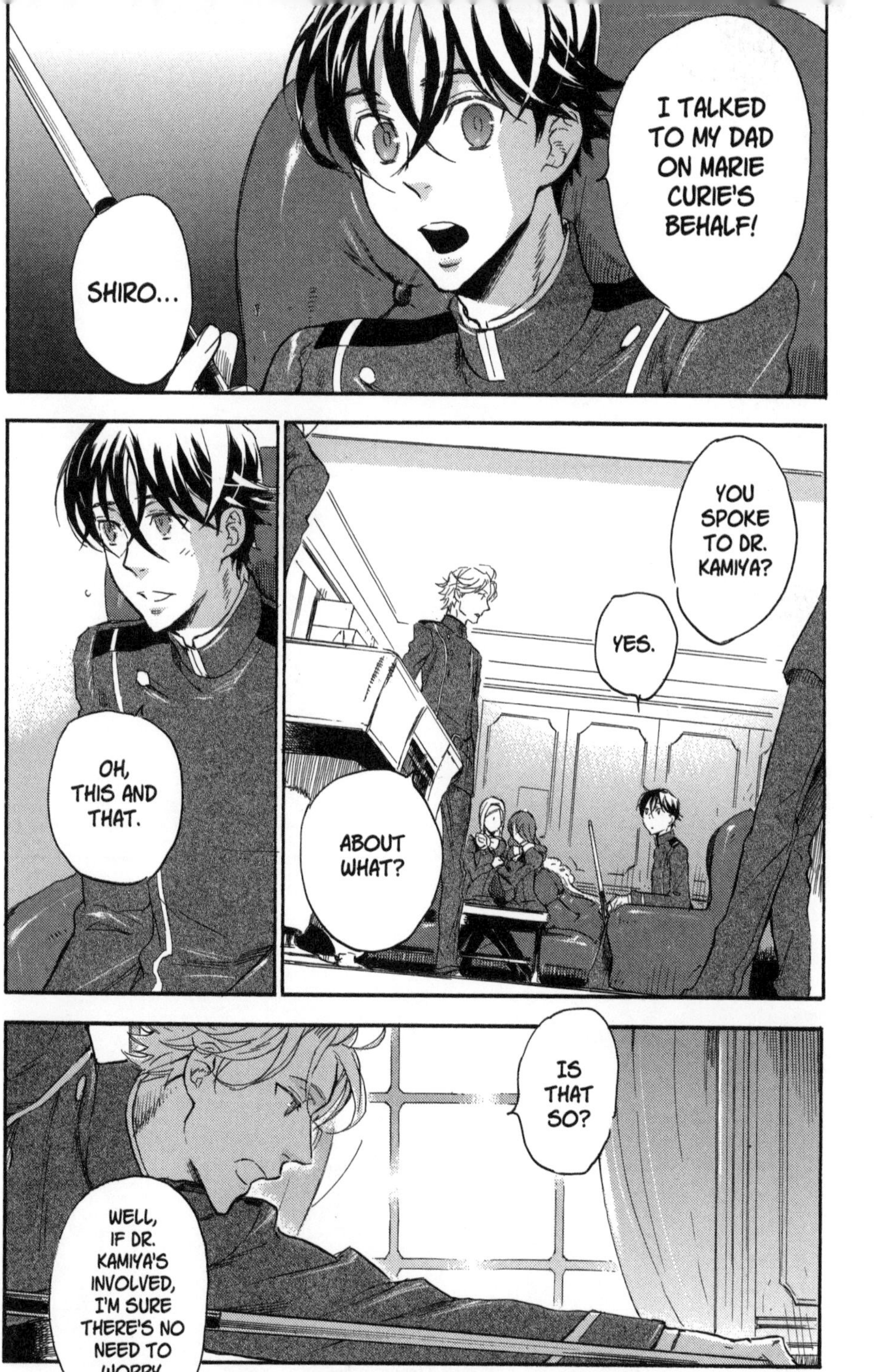
I TALKED TO MY DAD ON MARIE CURIE'S BEHALF!
SHIRO...
YOU SPOKE TO DR. KAMIYA?
YES.
ABOUT WHAT?
OH, THIS AND THAT.
IS THAT SO?
WELL, IF DR. KAMIYA'S INVOLVED, I'M SURE THERE'S NO NEED TO WORRY.

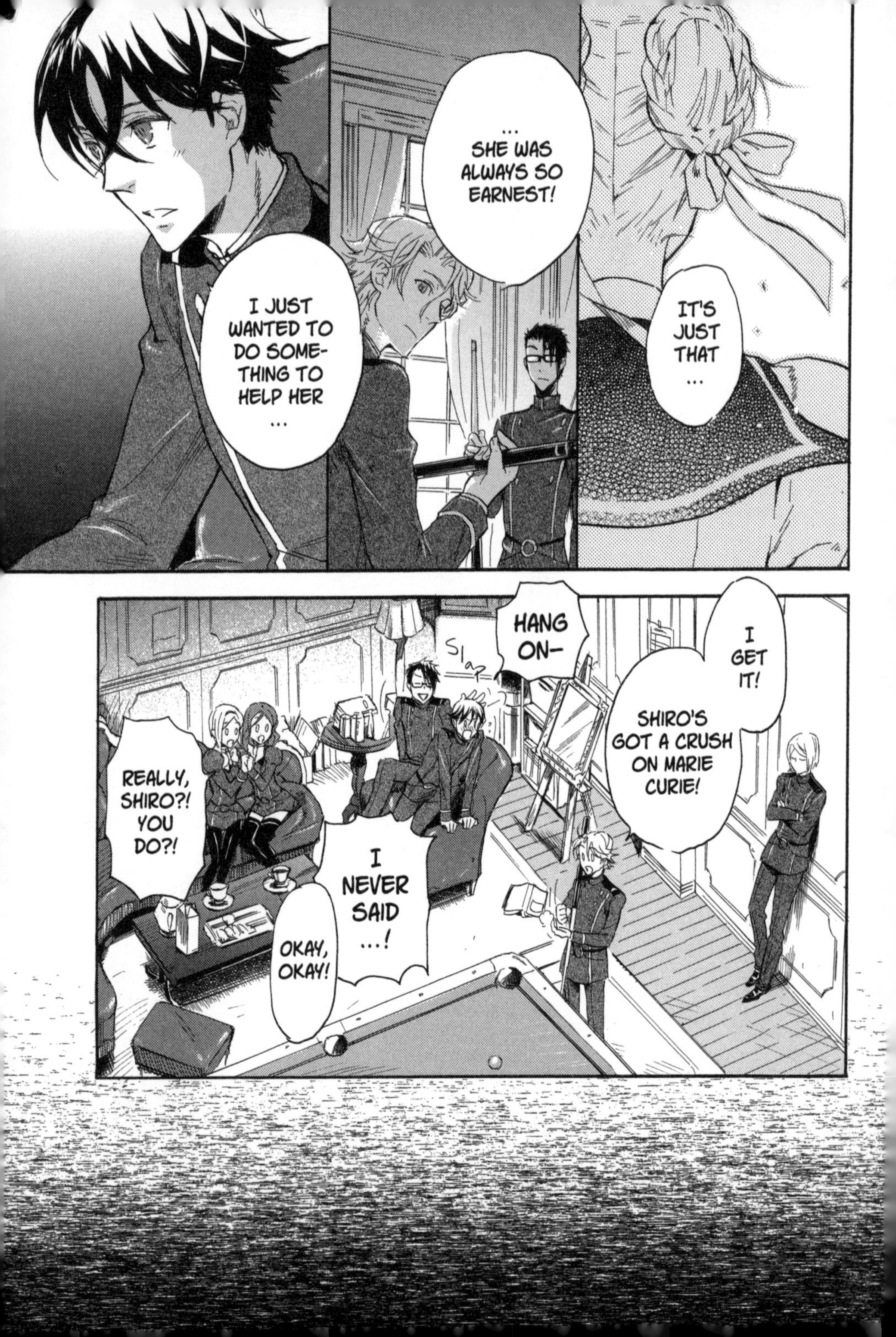
IT'S JUST THAT ...
... SHE WAS ALWAYS SO EARNEST!
I JUST WANTED TO DO SOME-THING TO HELP HER ...
I GET IT!
SHIRO'S GOT A CRUSH ON MARIE CURIE!
HANG ON-
Slap
I NEVER SAID ...!
OKAY, OKAY!
REALLY, SHIRO?! YOU DO?!

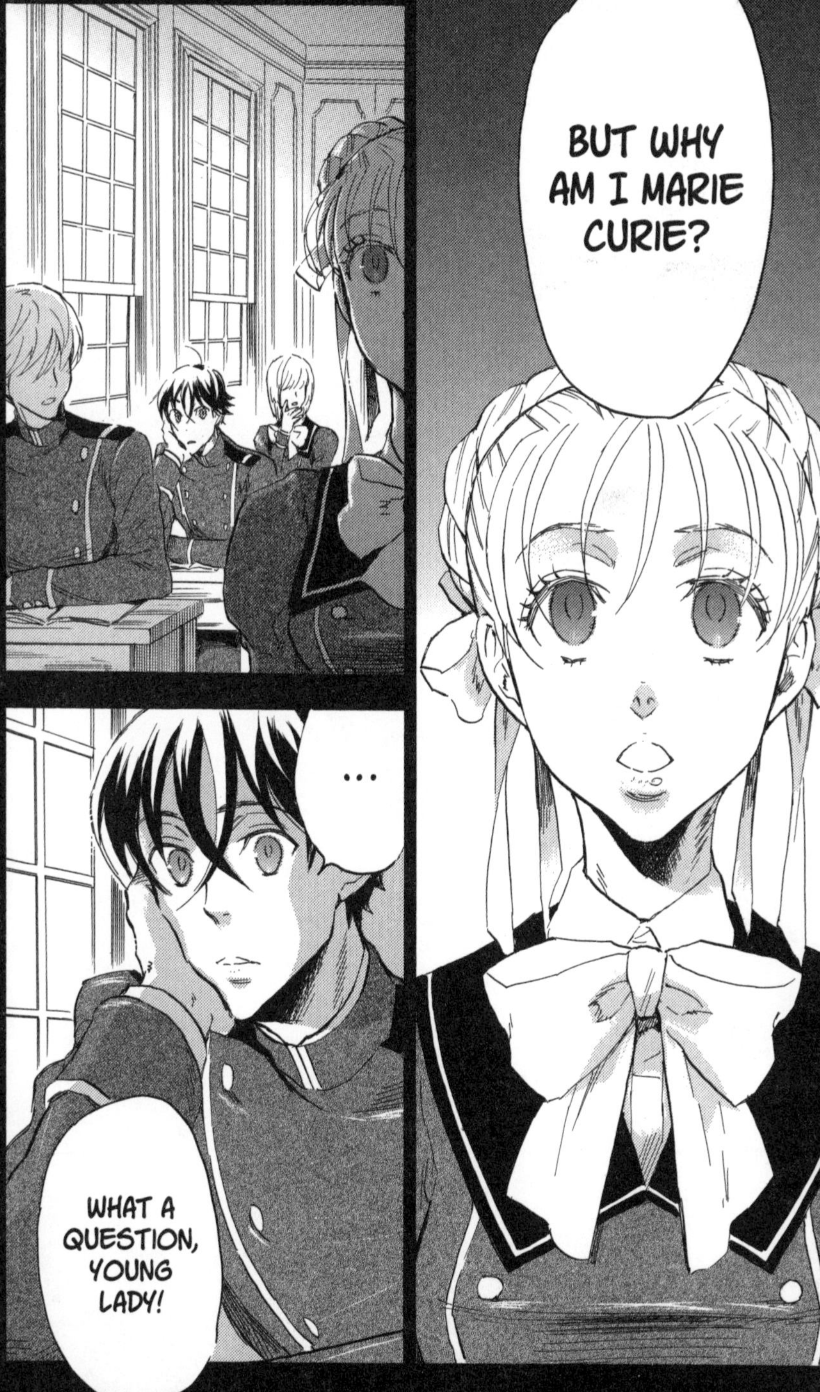
BUT WHY AM I MARIE CURIE?
...
WHAT A QUESTION, YOUNG LADY!

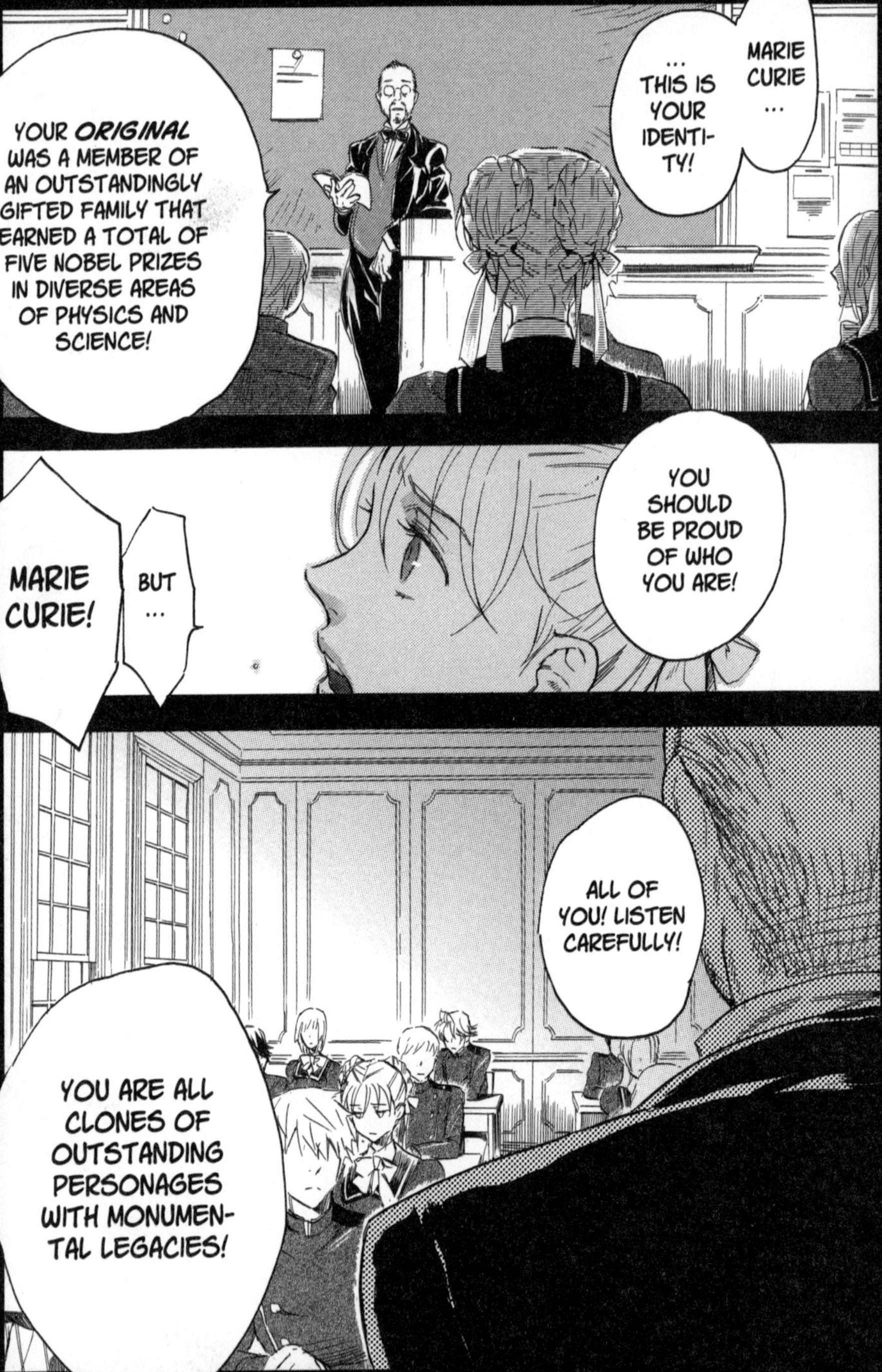
MARIE CURIE ...
... THIS IS YOUR IDENTITY!
YOUR ORIGINAL WAS A MEMBER OF AN OUTSTANDINGLY GIFTED FAMILY THAT EARNED A TOTAL OF FIVE NOBEL PRIZES IN DIVERSE AREAS OF PHYSICS AND SCIENCE!
YOU SHOULD BE PROUD OF WHO YOU ARE!
BUT ...
MARIE CURIE!
ALL OF YOU! LISTEN CAREFULLY!
YOU ARE ALL CLONES OF OUTSTANDING PERSONAGES WITH MONUMENTAL LEGACIES!

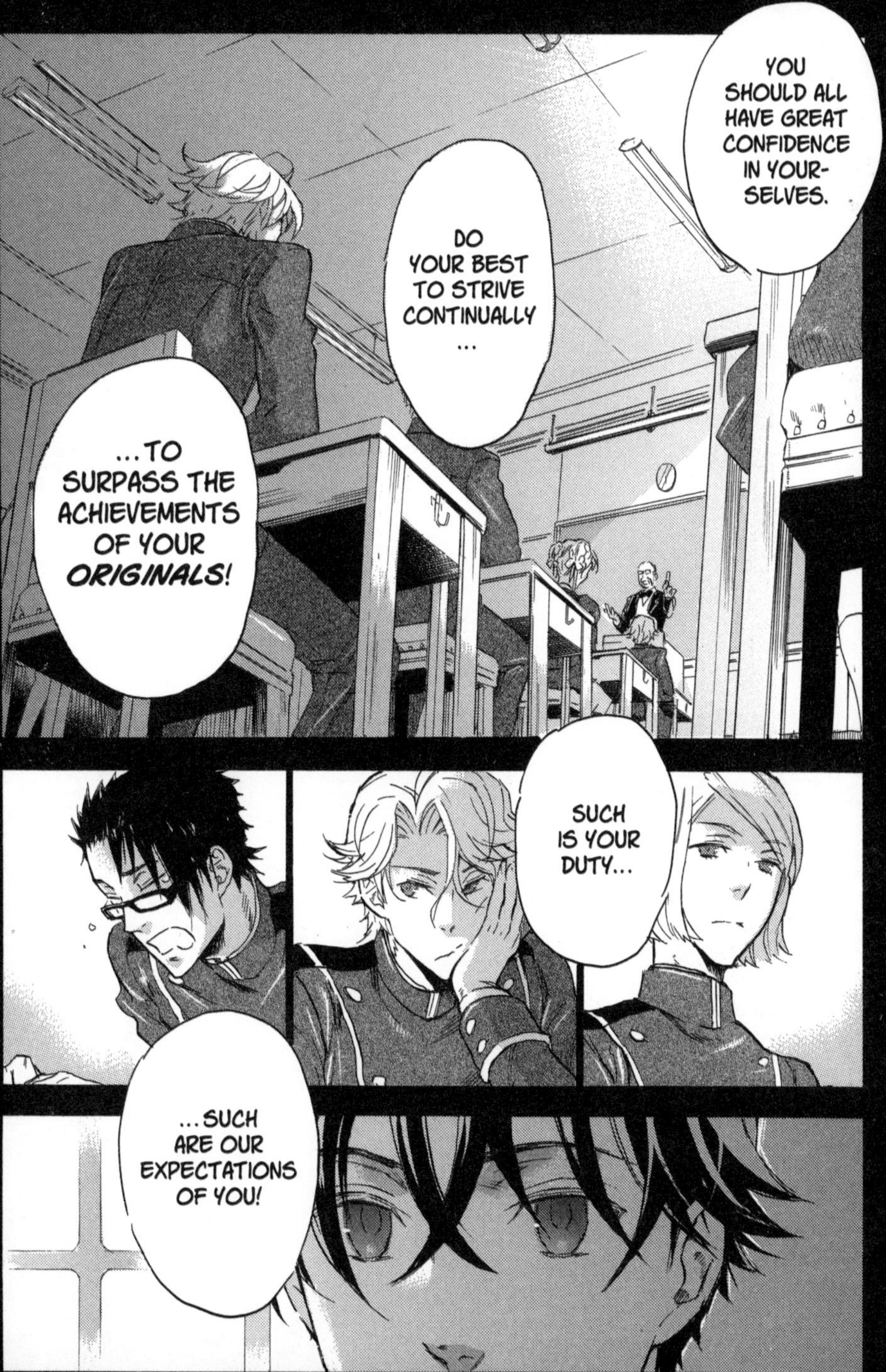
YOU SHOULD ALL HAVE GREAT CONFIDENCE IN YOURSELVES.
DO YOUR BEST TO STRIVE CONTINUALLY ...
...TO SURPASS THE ACHIEVEMENTS OF YOUR *ORIGINALS*!
SUCH IS YOUR DUTY...
...SUCH ARE OUR EXPECTATIONS OF YOU!

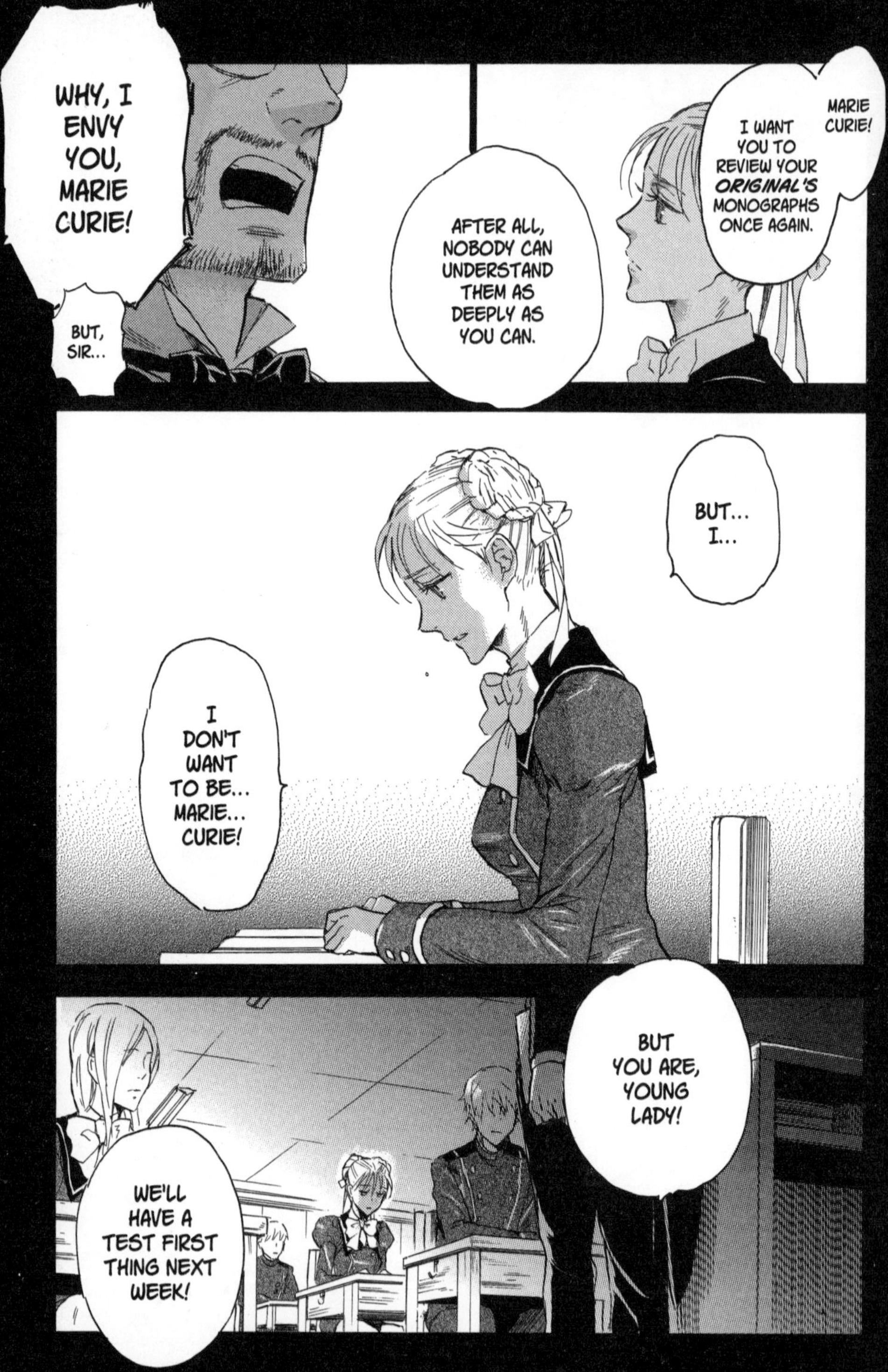
MARIE CURIE!
I WANT YOU TO REVIEW YOUR ORIGINAL'S MONOGRAPHS ONCE AGAIN.
AFTER ALL, NOBODY CAN UNDERSTAND THEM AS DEEPLY AS YOU CAN.
WHY, I ENVY YOU, MARIE CURIE!
BUT, SIR...
BUT... I...
I DON'T WANT TO BE... MARIE... CURIE!
BUT YOU ARE, YOUNG LADY!
WE'LL HAVE A TEST FIRST THING NEXT WEEK!

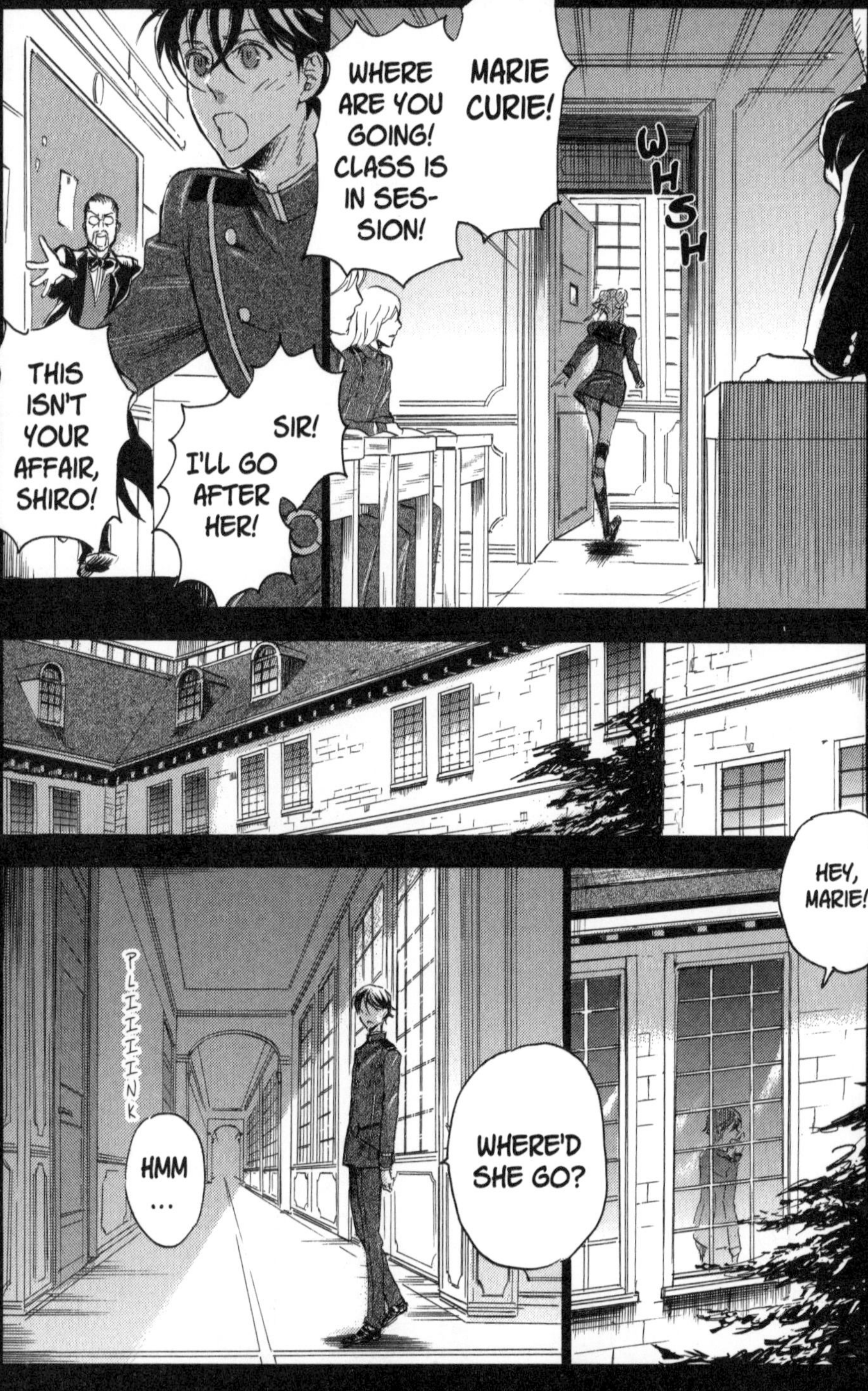
MARIE CURIE!
WHERE ARE YOU GOING! CLASS IS IN SES-SION!
WHSH
SIR! I'LL GO AFTER HER!
THIS ISN'T YOUR AFFAIR, SHIRO!
HEY, MARIE!
WHERE'D SHE GO?
PLIIIIINK
HMM ...

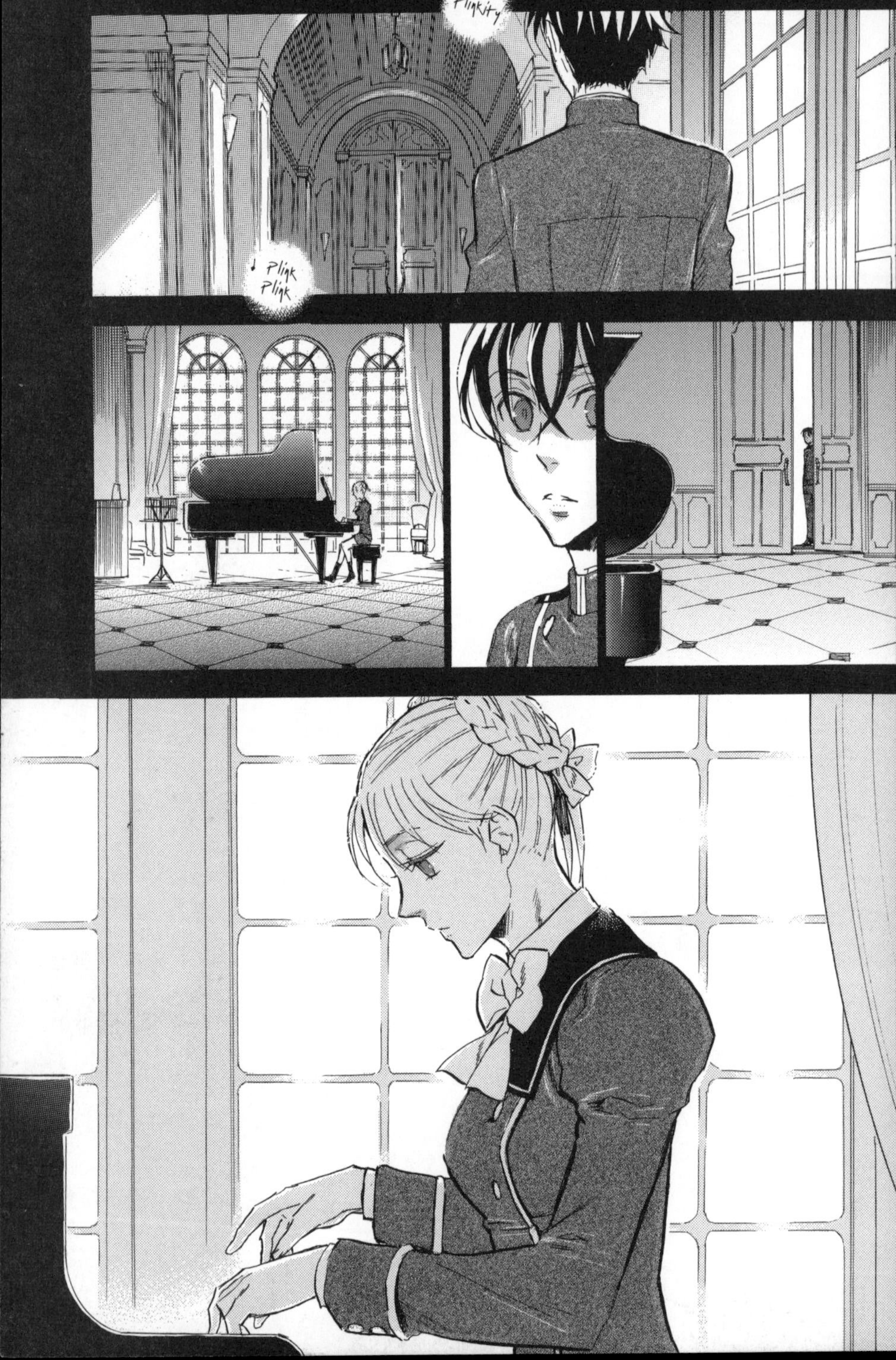
Plinkity
♩ Plink
Plink

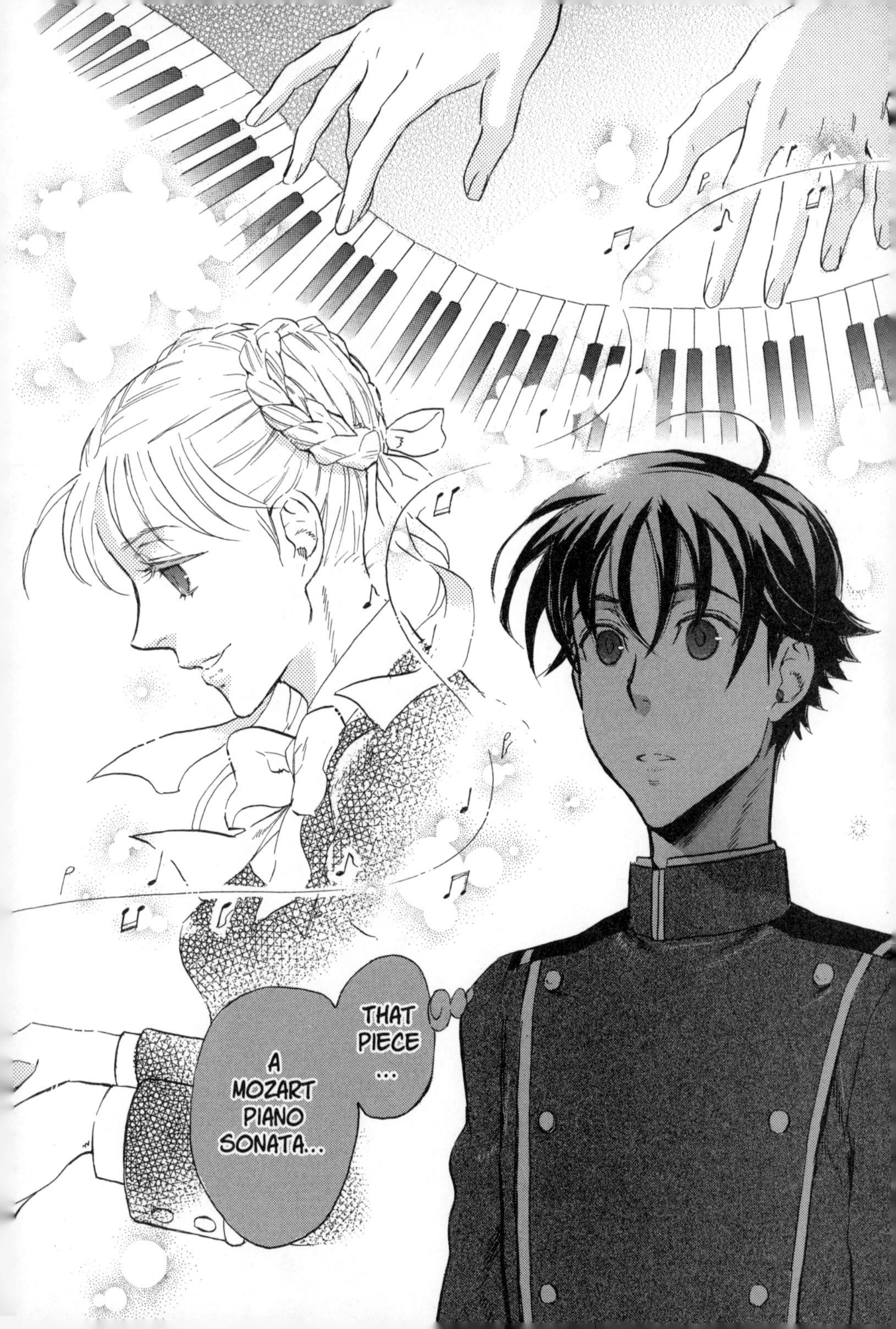
THAT PIECE...
A MOZART PIANO SONATA...

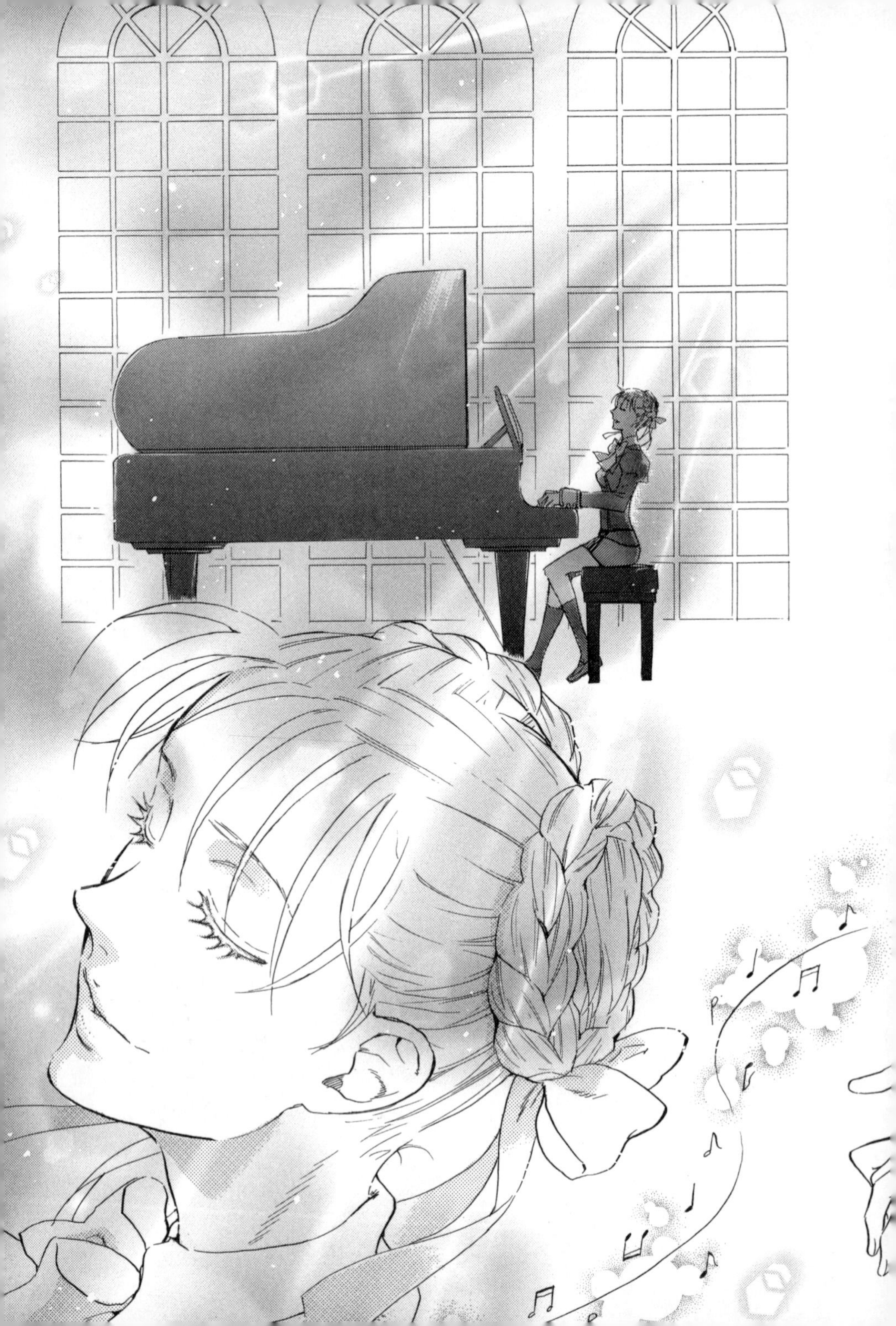

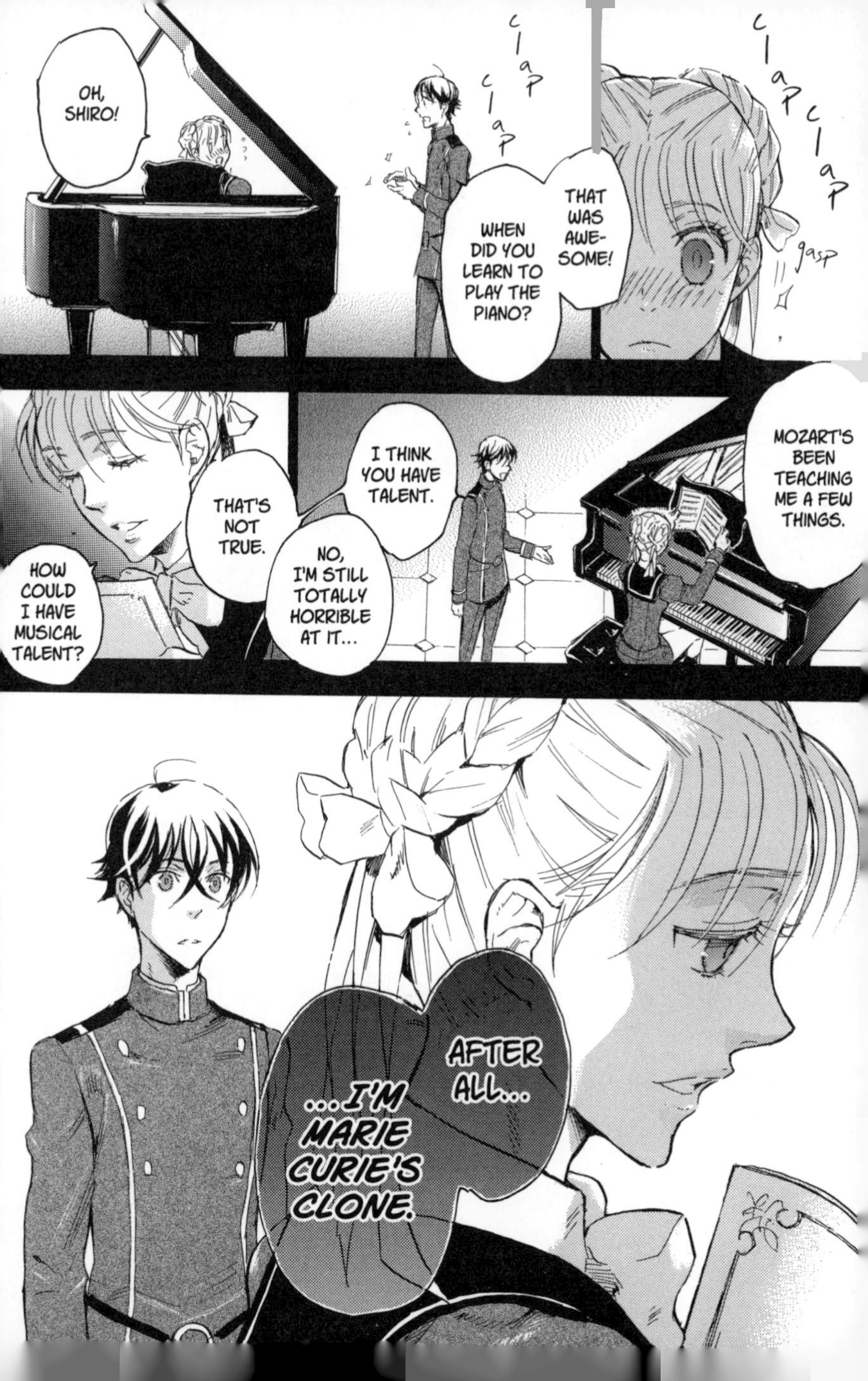
clap clap
gasp
clap clap
THAT WAS AWESOME!
WHEN DID YOU LEARN TO PLAY THE PIANO?
OH, SHIRO!
MOZART'S BEEN TEACHING ME A FEW THINGS.
I THINK YOU HAVE TALENT.
NO, I'M STILL TOTALLY HORRIBLE AT IT...
THAT'S NOT TRUE.
HOW COULD I HAVE MUSICAL TALENT?
AFTER ALL...
...I'M MARIE CURIE'S CLONE.

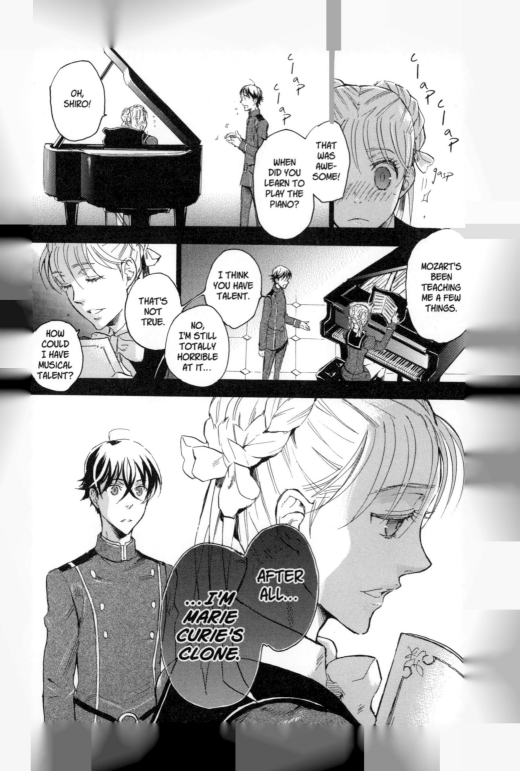

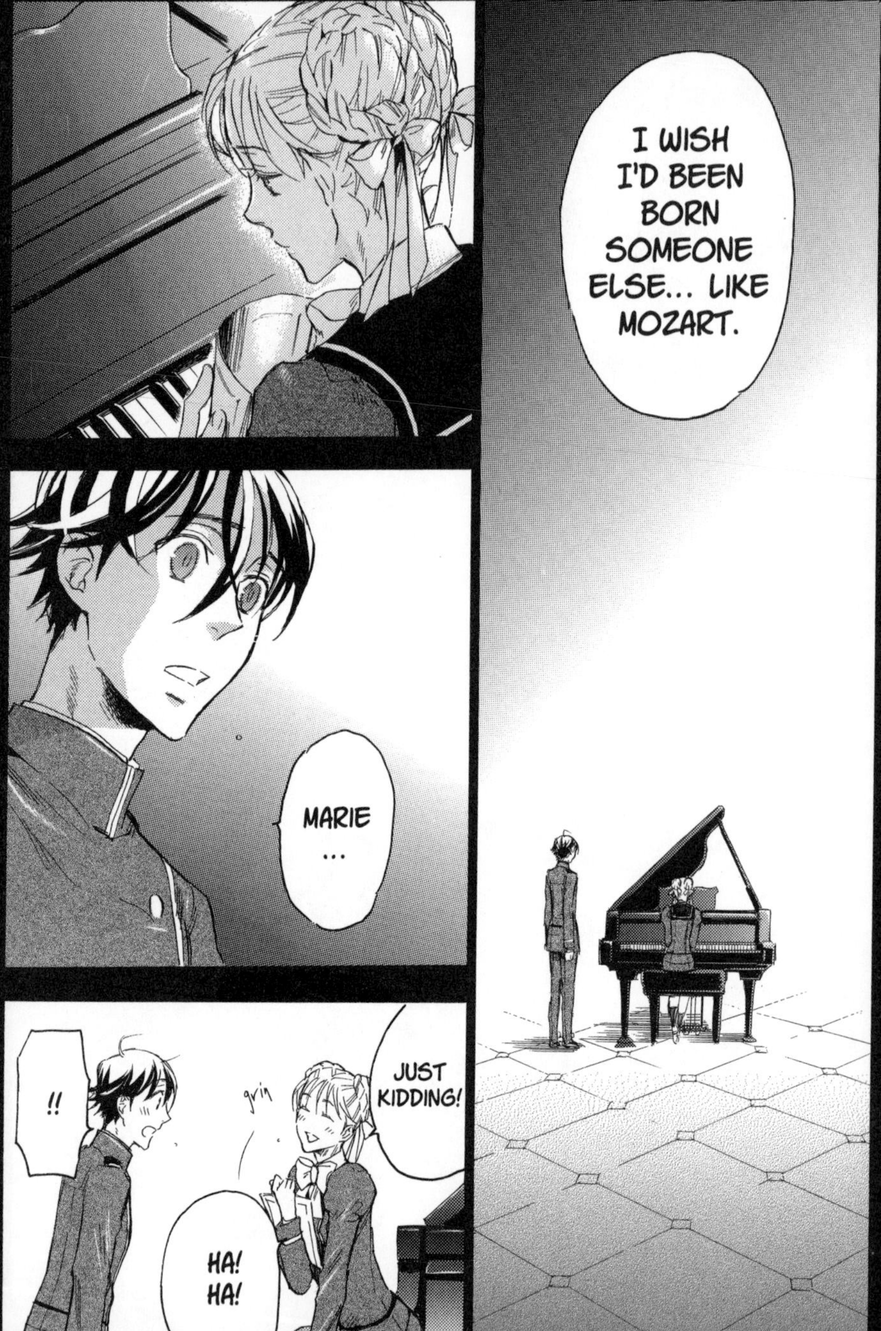
I WISH I'D BEEN BORN SOMEONE ELSE... LIKE MOZART.
MARIE ...
JUST KIDDING!
!!
grin
HA! HA!

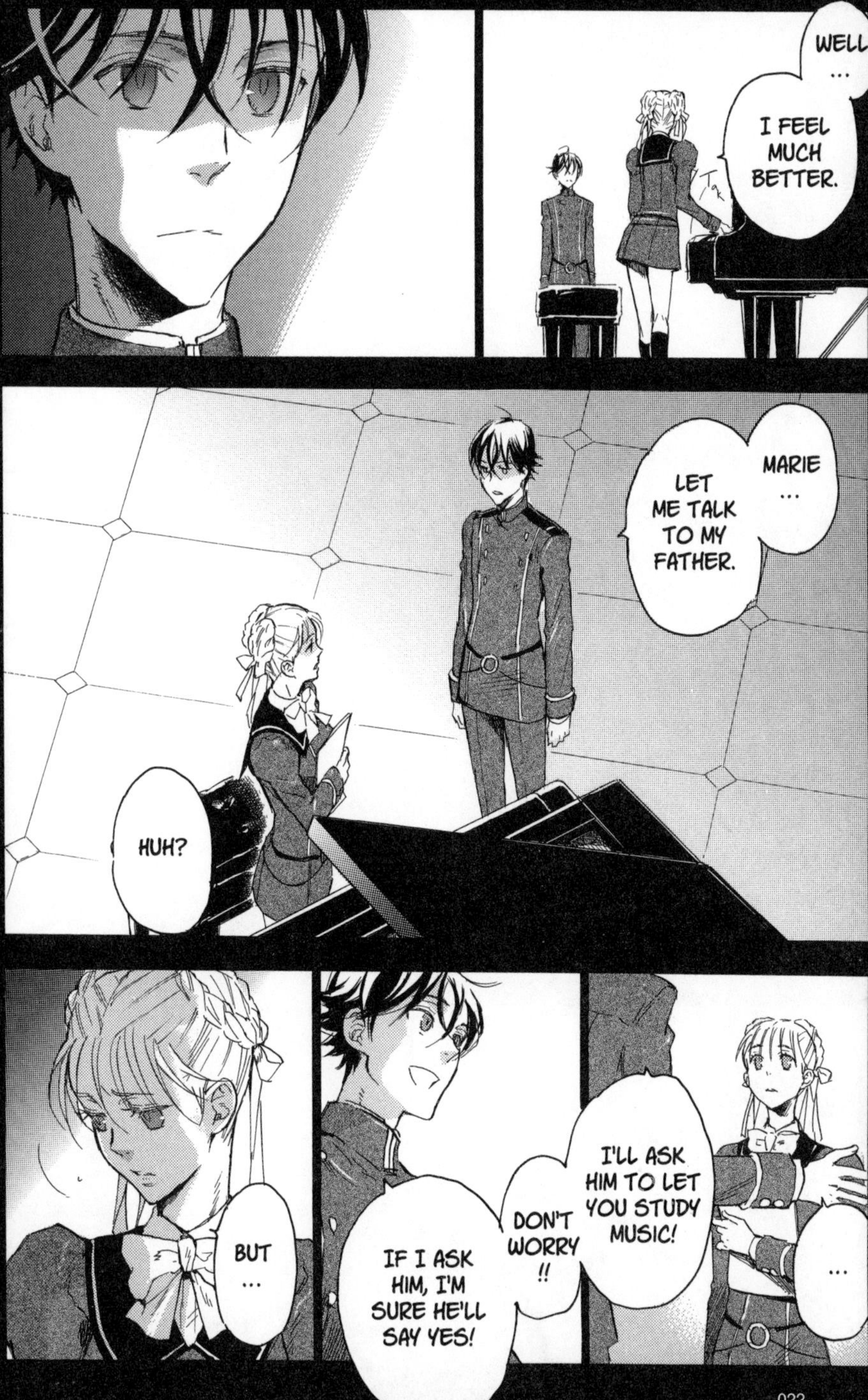
WELL ...
I FEEL MUCH BETTER.
MARIE ...
LET ME TALK TO MY FATHER.
HUH?
...
I'LL ASK HIM TO LET YOU STUDY MUSIC!
DON'T WORRY !!
IF I ASK HIM, I'M SURE HE'LL SAY YES!
BUT ...

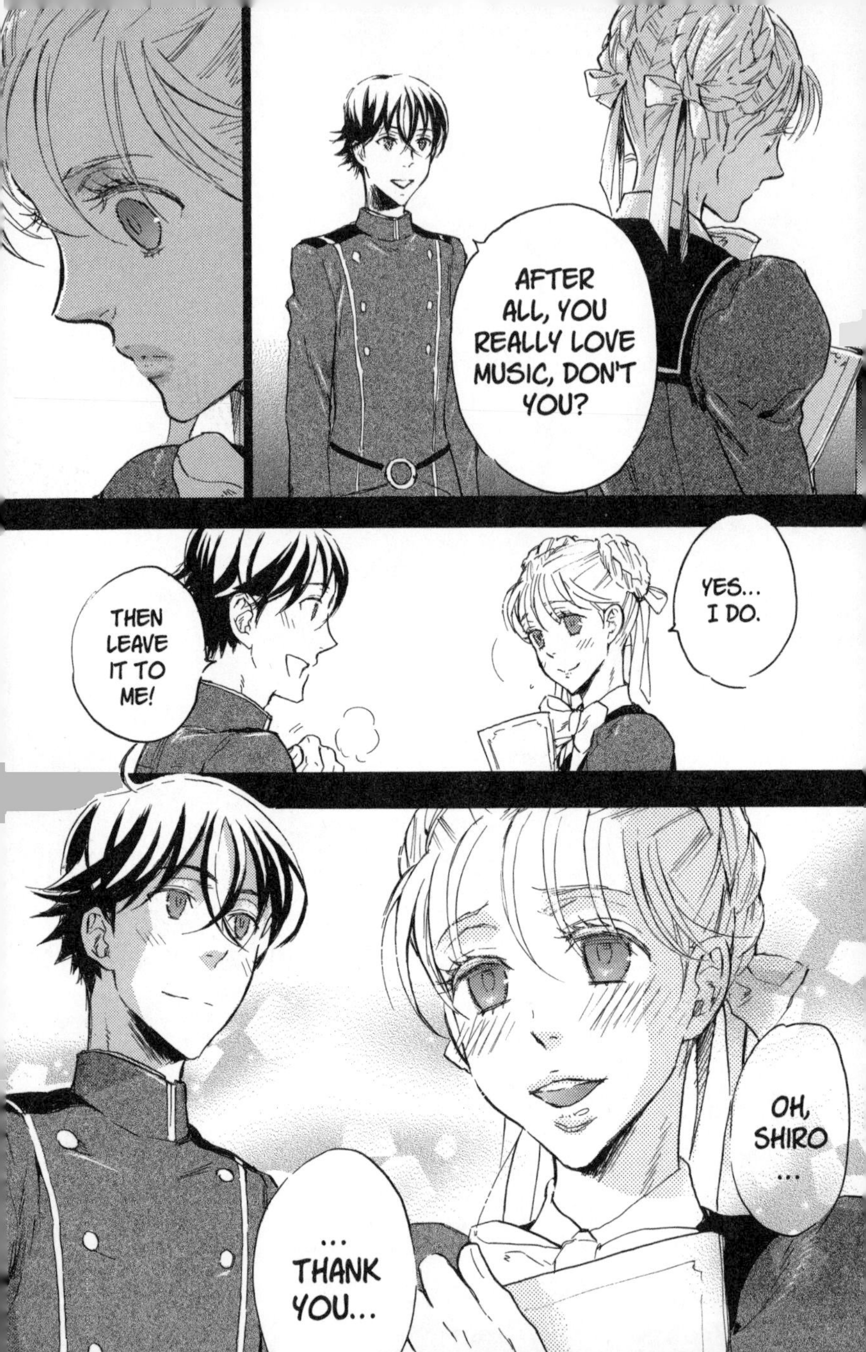
AFTER ALL, YOU REALLY LOVE MUSIC, DON'T YOU?
YES... I DO.
THEN LEAVE IT TO ME!
OH, SHIRO...
...THANK YOU...

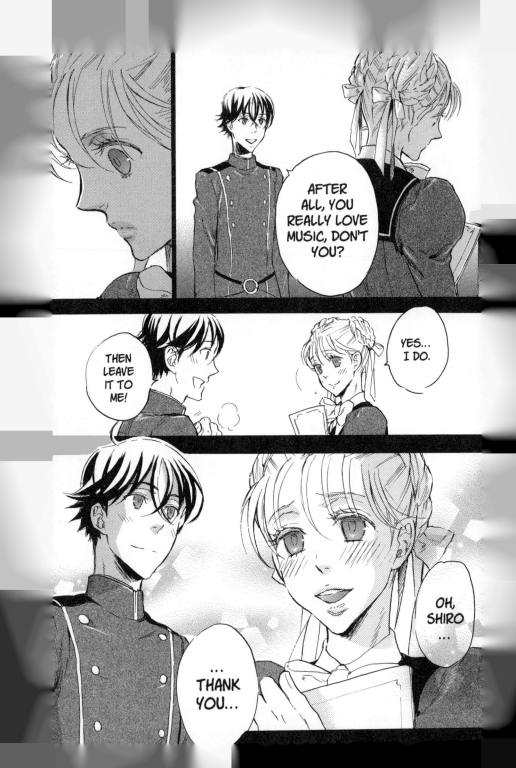

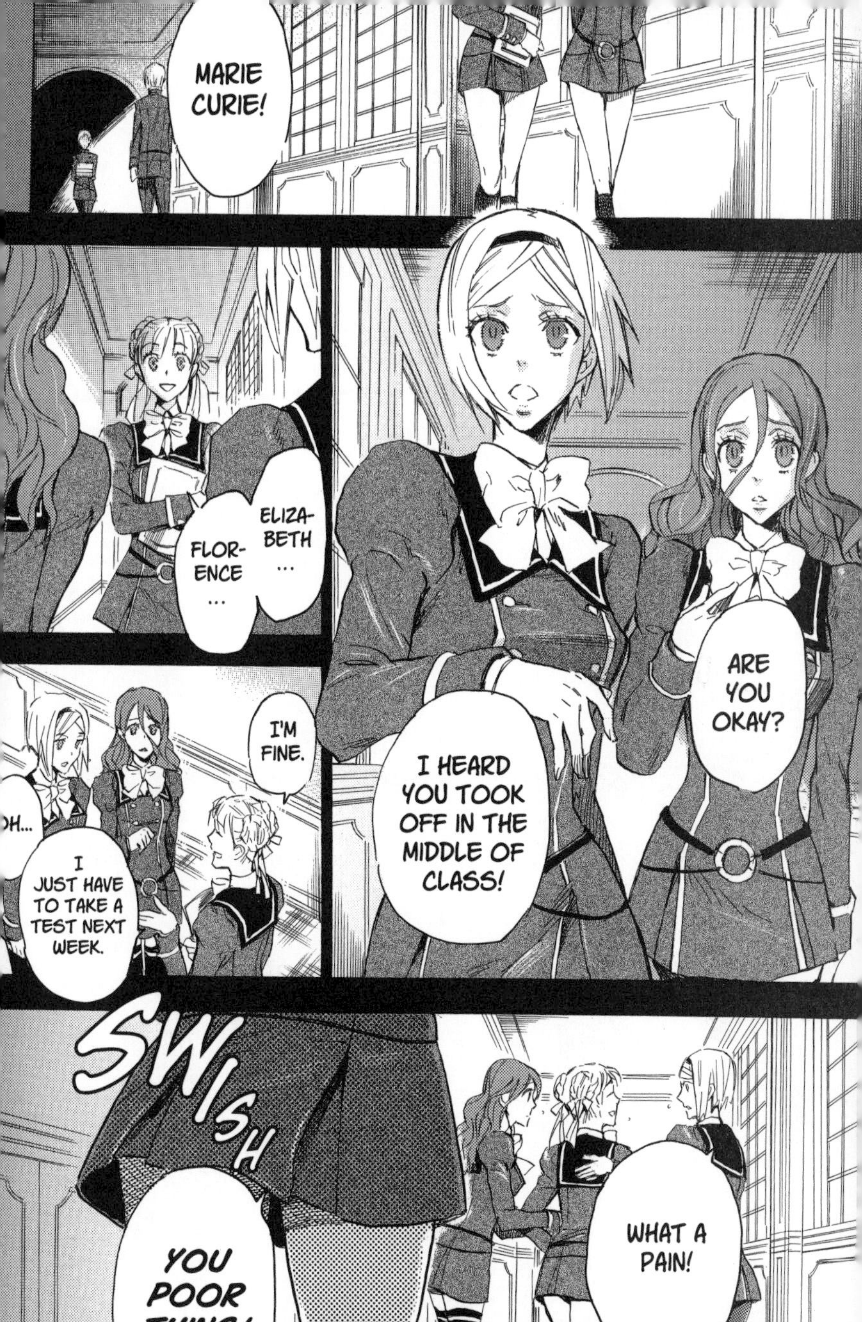
MARIE CURIE!
ARE YOU OKAY?
I HEARD YOU TOOK OFF IN THE MIDDLE OF CLASS!
ELIZA-BETH...
FLOR-ENCE...
I'M FINE.
OH...
I JUST HAVE TO TAKE A TEST NEXT WEEK.
SWISH
WHAT A PAIN!
YOU POOR THING!

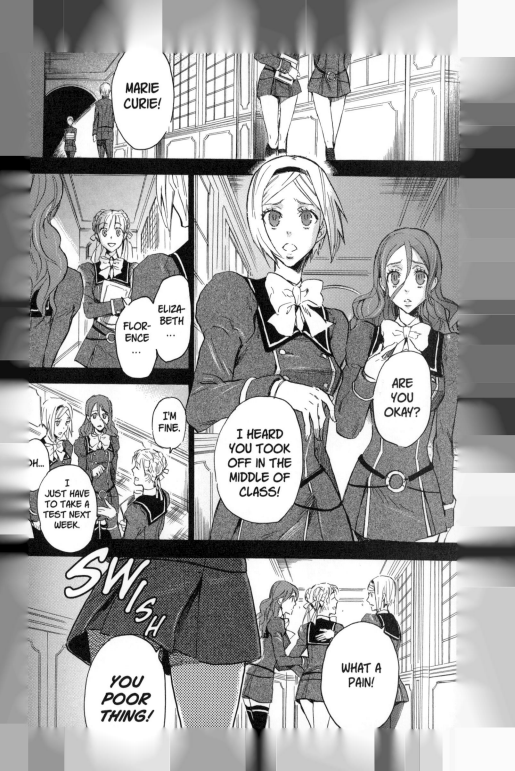

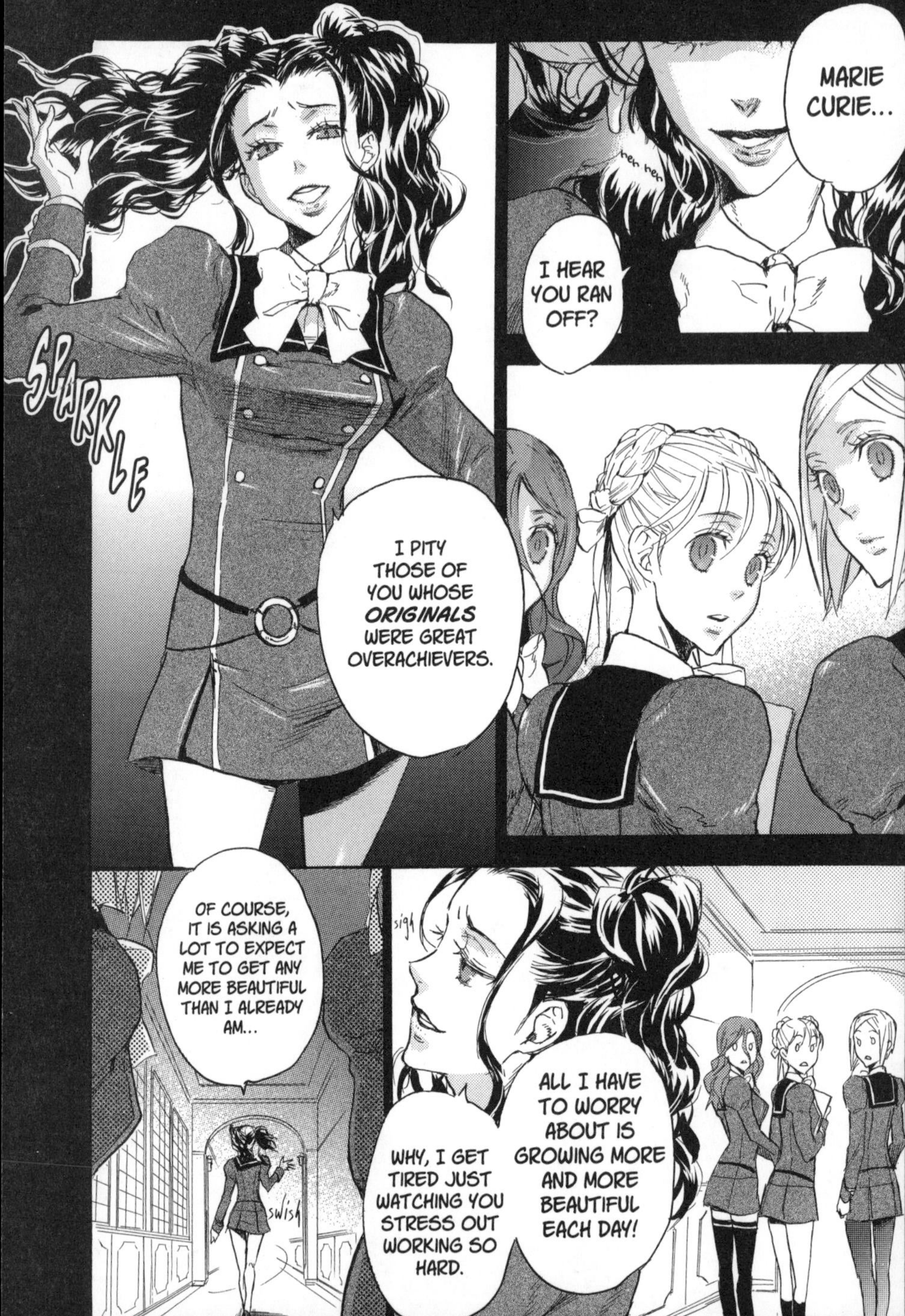
MARIE CURIE...
heh heh
I HEAR YOU RAN OFF?
SPARKLE
I PITY THOSE OF YOU WHOSE ***ORIGINALS*** WERE GREAT OVERACHIEVERS.
sigh
ALL I HAVE TO WORRY ABOUT IS GROWING MORE AND MORE BEAUTIFUL EACH DAY!
WHY, I GET TIRED JUST WATCHING YOU STRESS OUT WORKING SO HARD.
OF COURSE, IT IS ASKING A LOT TO EXPECT ME TO GET ANY MORE BEAUTIFUL THAN I ALREADY AM...
swish

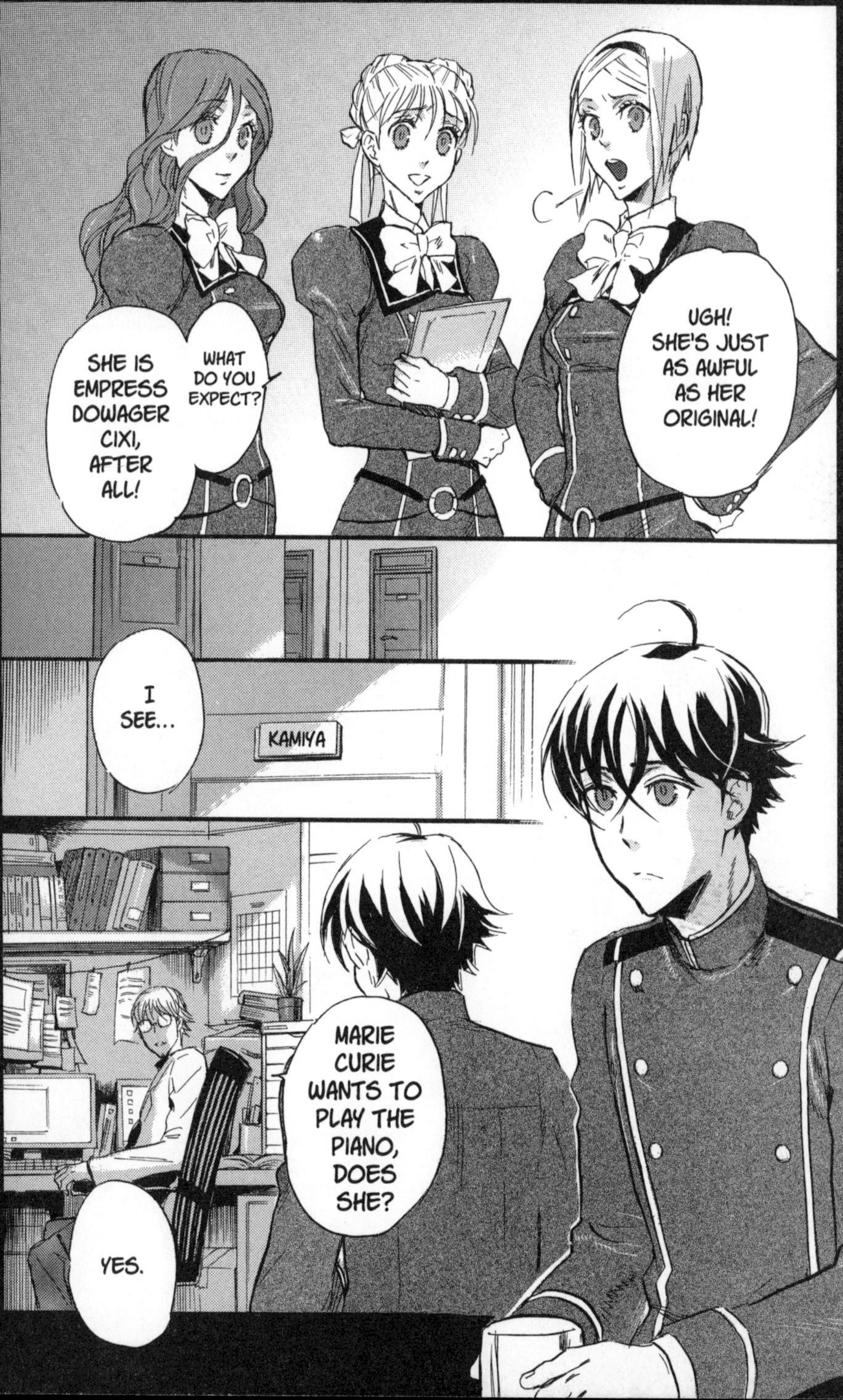
UGH! SHE'S JUST AS AWFUL AS HER ORIGINAL!
WHAT DO YOU EXPECT?
SHE IS EMPRESS DOWAGER CIXI, AFTER ALL!
KAMIYA
I SEE...
MARIE CURIE WANTS TO PLAY THE PIANO, DOES SHE?
YES.

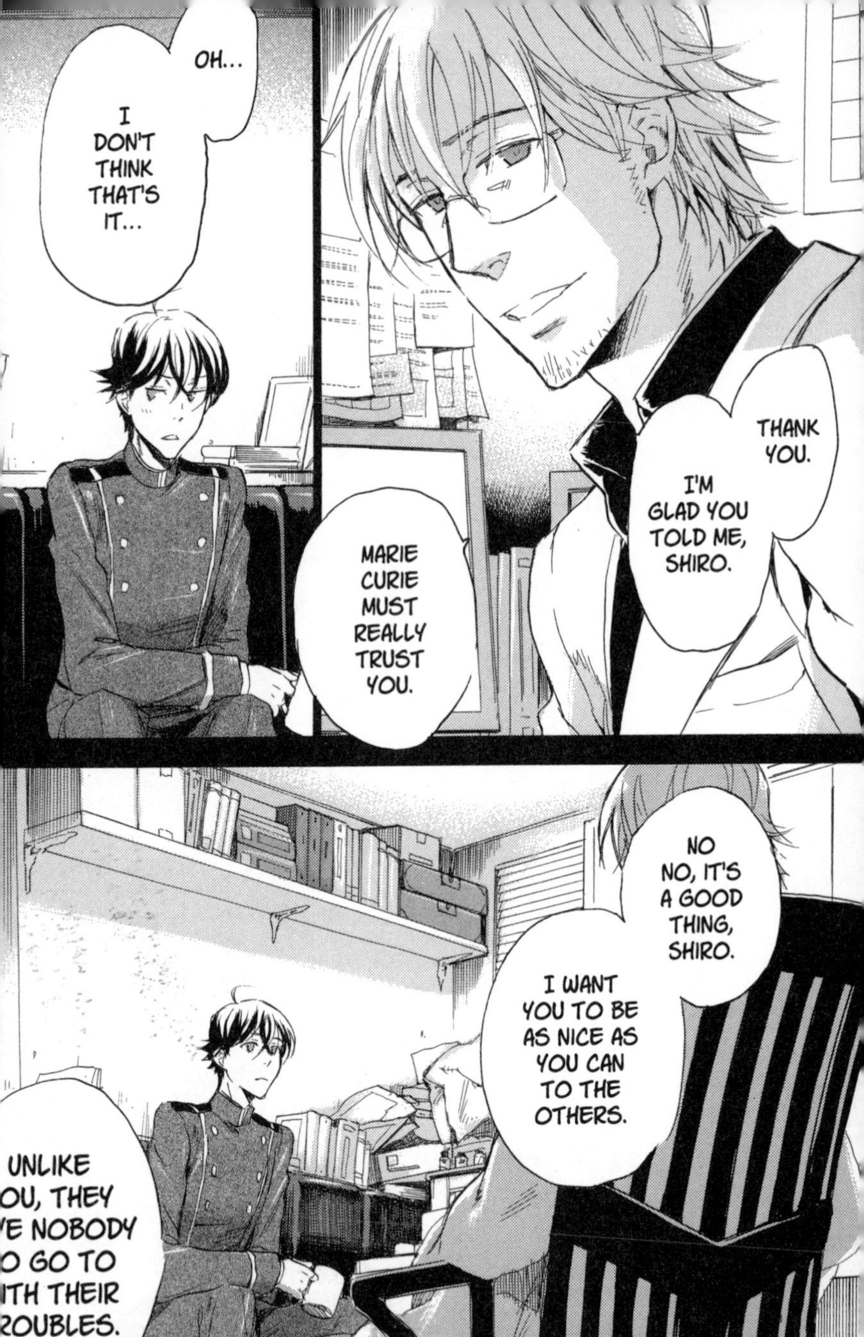
THANK YOU.
I'M GLAD YOU TOLD ME, SHIRO.
MARIE CURIE MUST REALLY TRUST YOU.
OH...
I DON'T THINK THAT'S IT...
NO NO, IT'S A GOOD THING, SHIRO.
I WANT YOU TO BE AS NICE AS YOU CAN TO THE OTHERS.
UNLIKE OU, THEY 'E NOBODY O GO TO ITH THEIR ROUBLES.

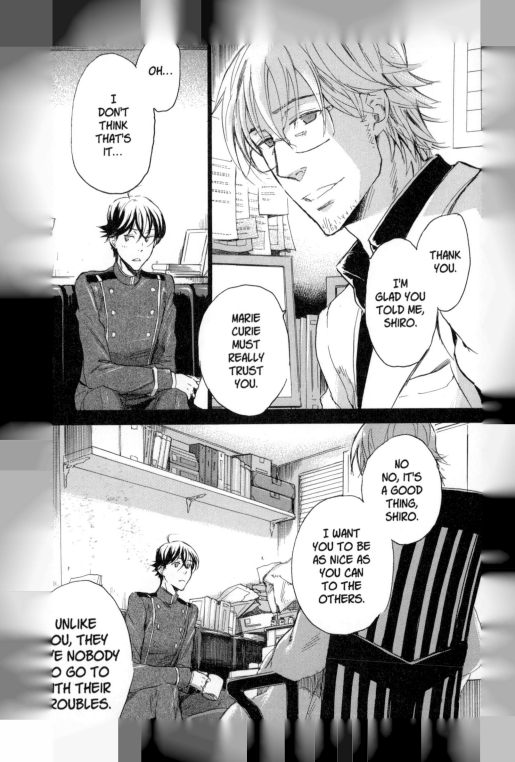

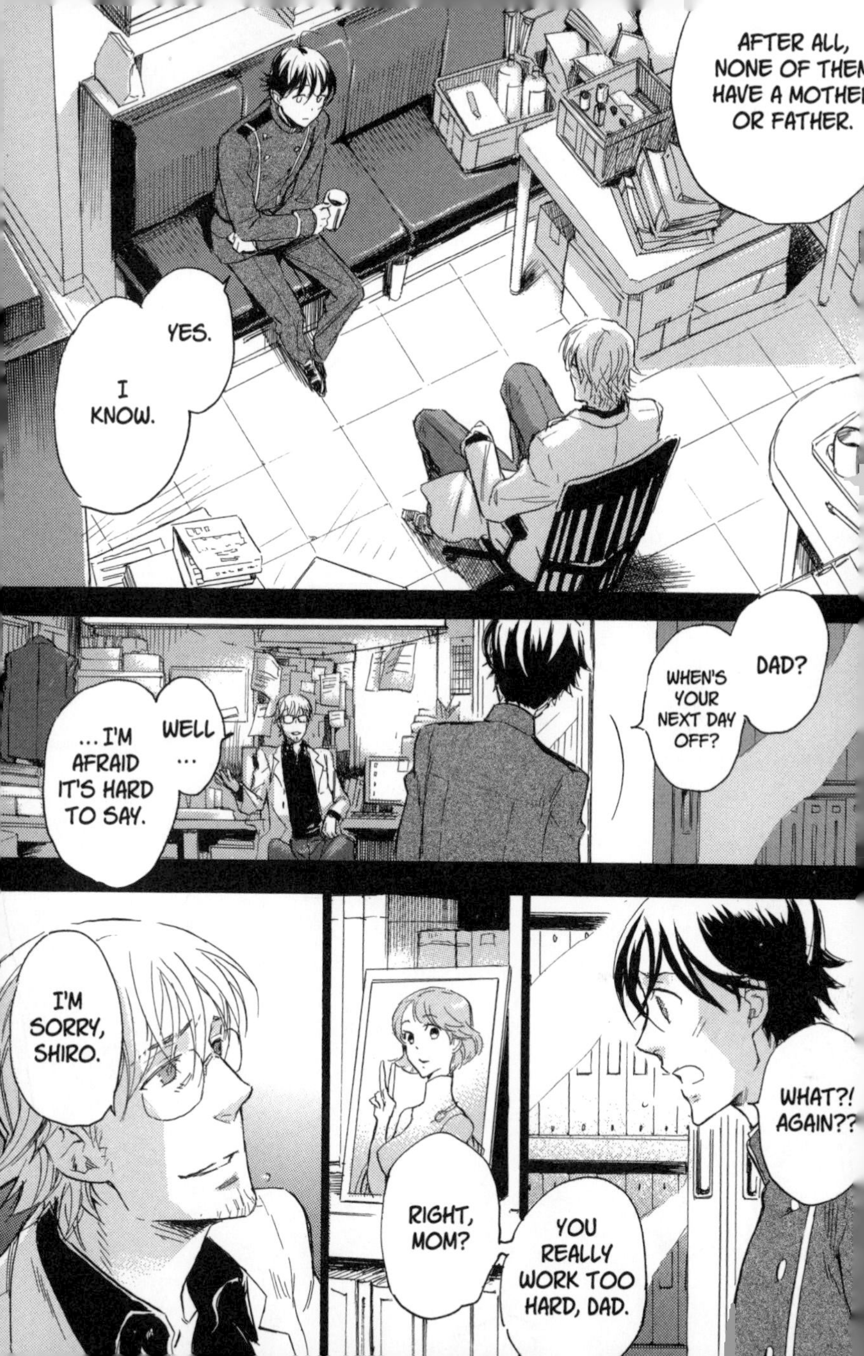
AFTER ALL, NONE OF THEM HAVE A MOTHER OR FATHER.
YES.
I KNOW.
DAD?
WHEN'S YOUR NEXT DAY OFF?
WELL ...
... I'M AFRAID IT'S HARD TO SAY.
WHAT?! AGAIN??
YOU REALLY WORK TOO HARD, DAD.
RIGHT, MOM?
I'M SORRY, SHIRO.

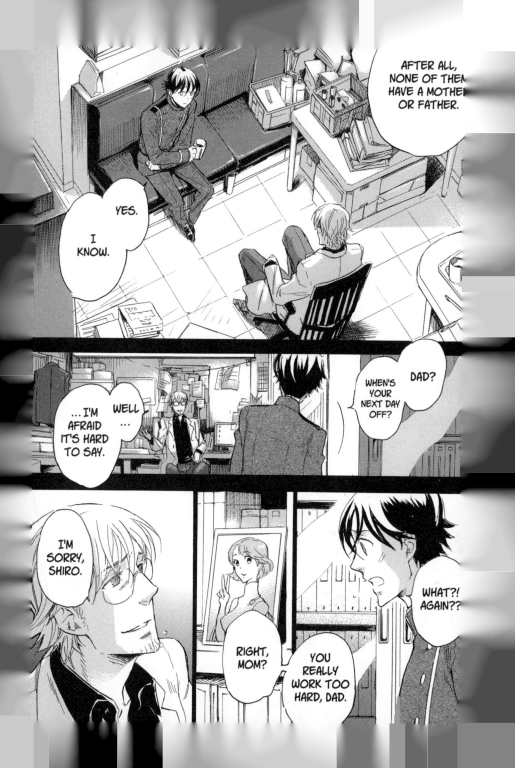

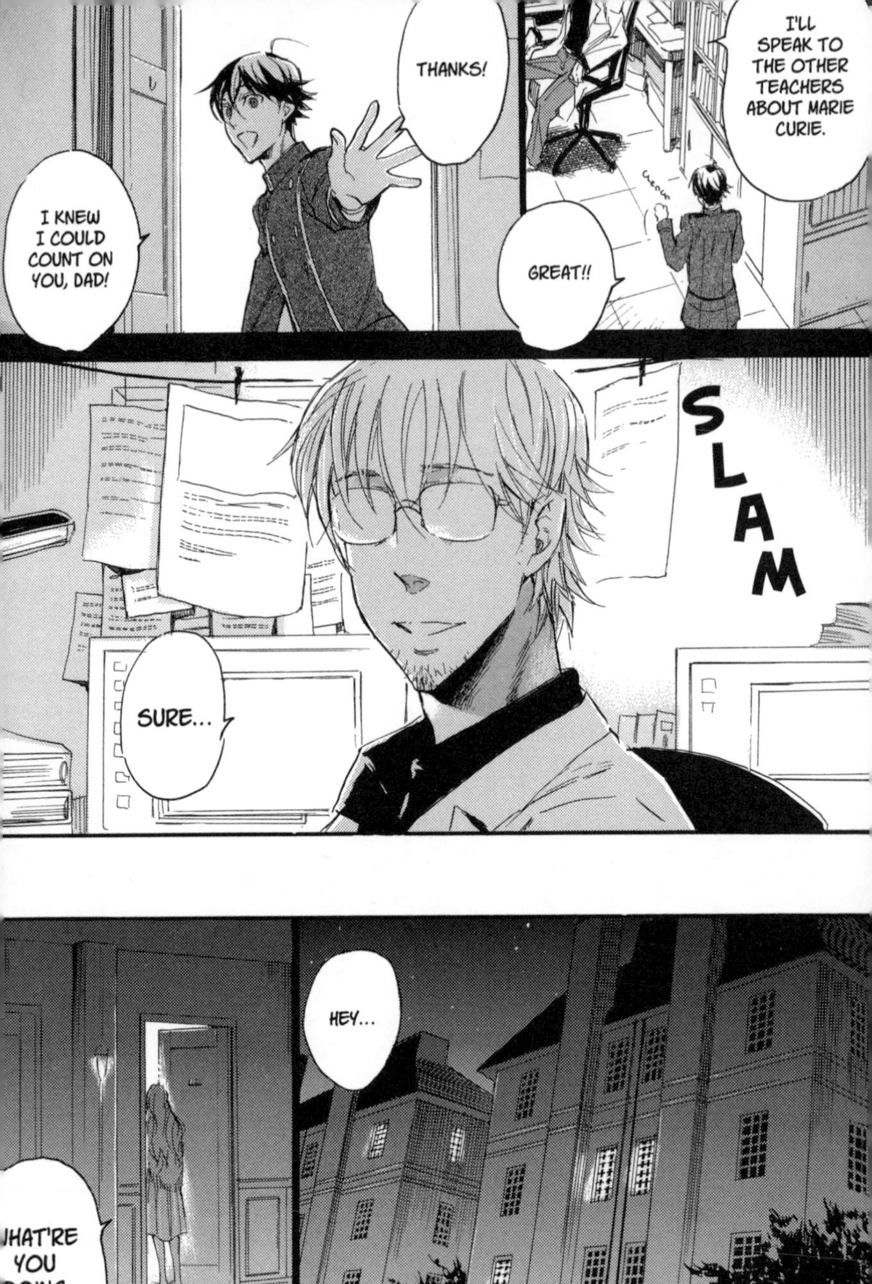
I'LL SPEAK TO THE OTHER TEACHERS ABOUT MARIE CURIE.
GREAT!!
THANKS!
I KNEW I COULD COUNT ON YOU, DAD!
SLAM
SURE...
HEY...
WHAT'RE YOU DOING UP SO LATE?

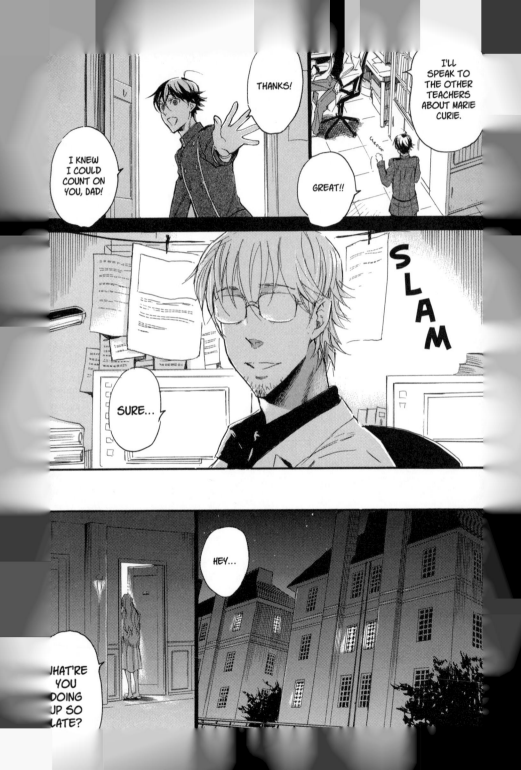

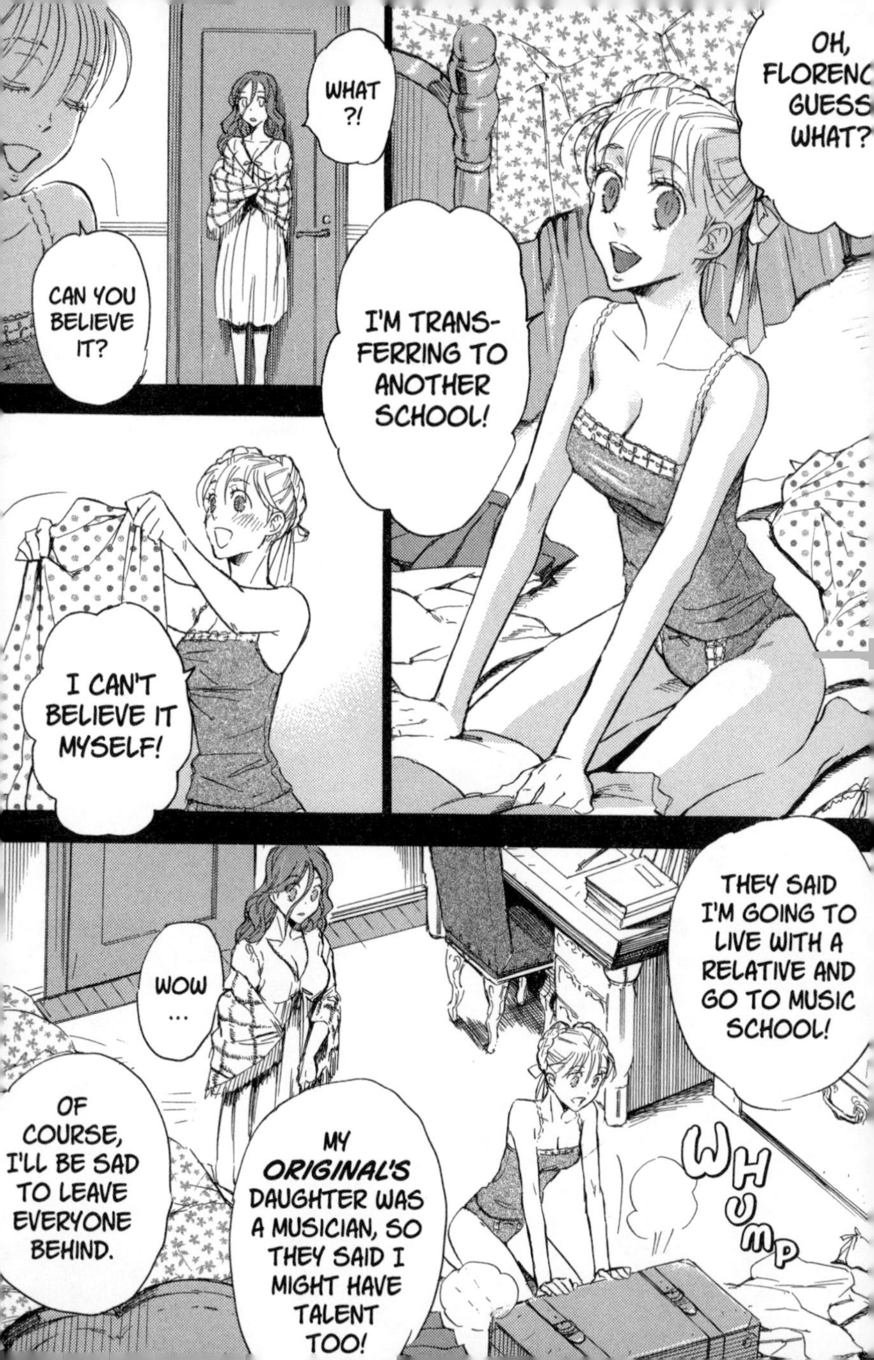
OH, FLORENC GUESS WHAT?
I'M TRANS-FERRING TO ANOTHER SCHOOL!
WHAT ?!
CAN YOU BELIEVE IT?
I CAN'T BELIEVE IT MYSELF!
THEY SAID I'M GOING TO LIVE WITH A RELATIVE AND GO TO MUSIC SCHOOL!
WHUMP
WOW ...
MY ORIGINAL'S DAUGHTER WAS A MUSICIAN, SO THEY SAID I MIGHT HAVE TALENT TOO!
OF COURSE, I'LL BE SAD TO LEAVE EVERYONE BEHIND.

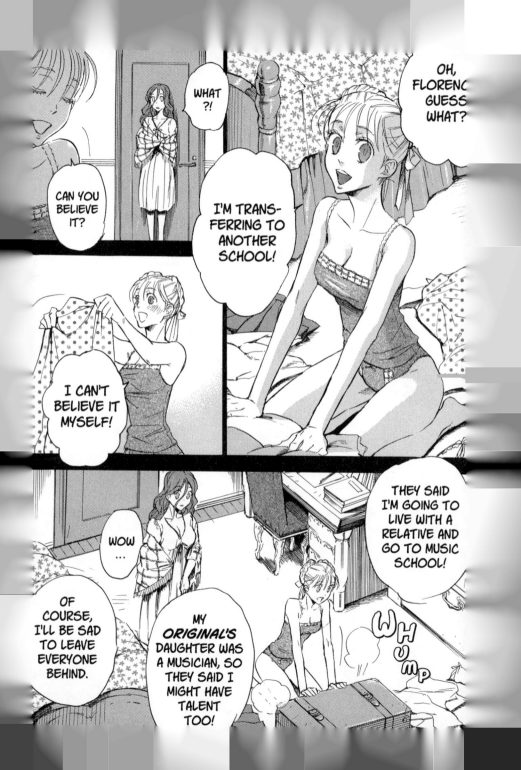

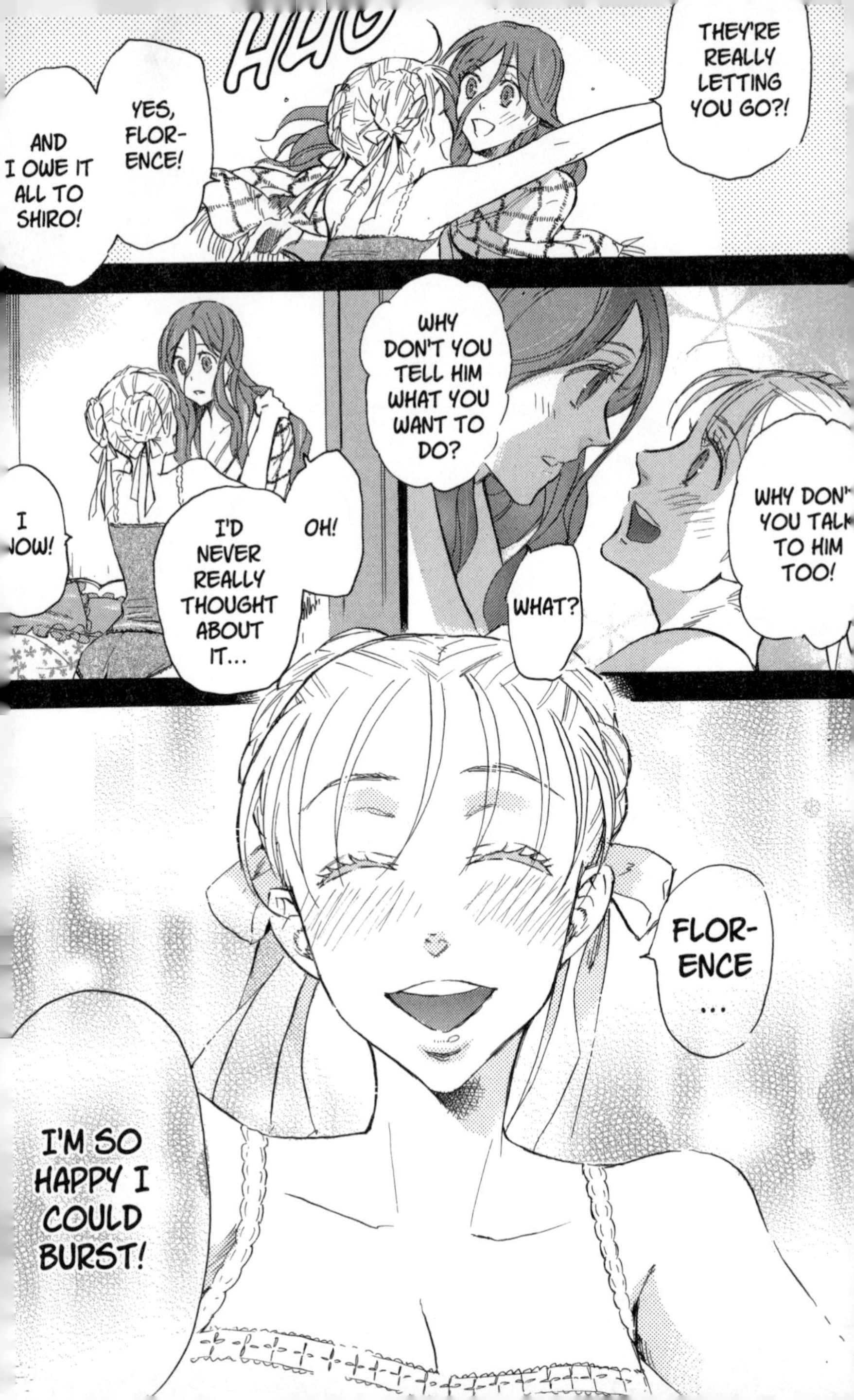
THEY'RE REALLY LETTING YOU GO?!
HUG
YES, FLOR-ENCE!
AND I OWE IT ALL TO SHIRO!
WHY DON' YOU TALK TO HIM TOO!
WHAT?
WHY DON'T YOU TELL HIM WHAT YOU WANT TO DO?
OH!
I'D NEVER REALLY THOUGHT ABOUT IT...
I NOW!
FLOR-ENCE...
I'M SO HAPPY I COULD BURST!

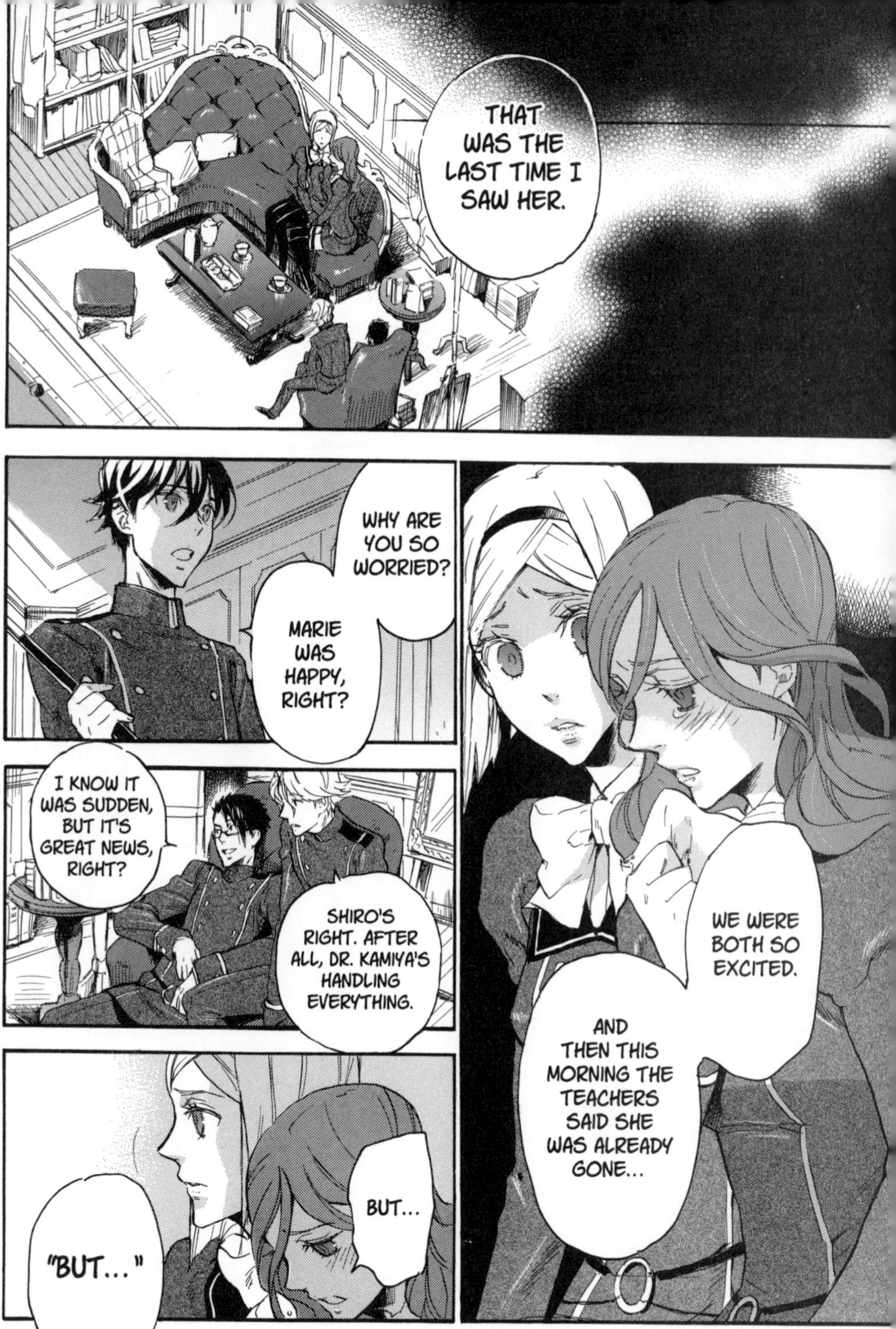
THAT WAS THE LAST TIME I SAW HER.
WE WERE BOTH SO EXCITED.
AND THEN THIS MORNING THE TEACHERS SAID SHE WAS ALREADY GONE...
WHY ARE YOU SO WORRIED?
MARIE WAS HAPPY, RIGHT?
I KNOW IT WAS SUDDEN, BUT IT'S GREAT NEWS, RIGHT?
SHIRO'S RIGHT. AFTER ALL, DR. KAMIYA'S HANDLING EVERYTHING.
BUT...
"BUT..."

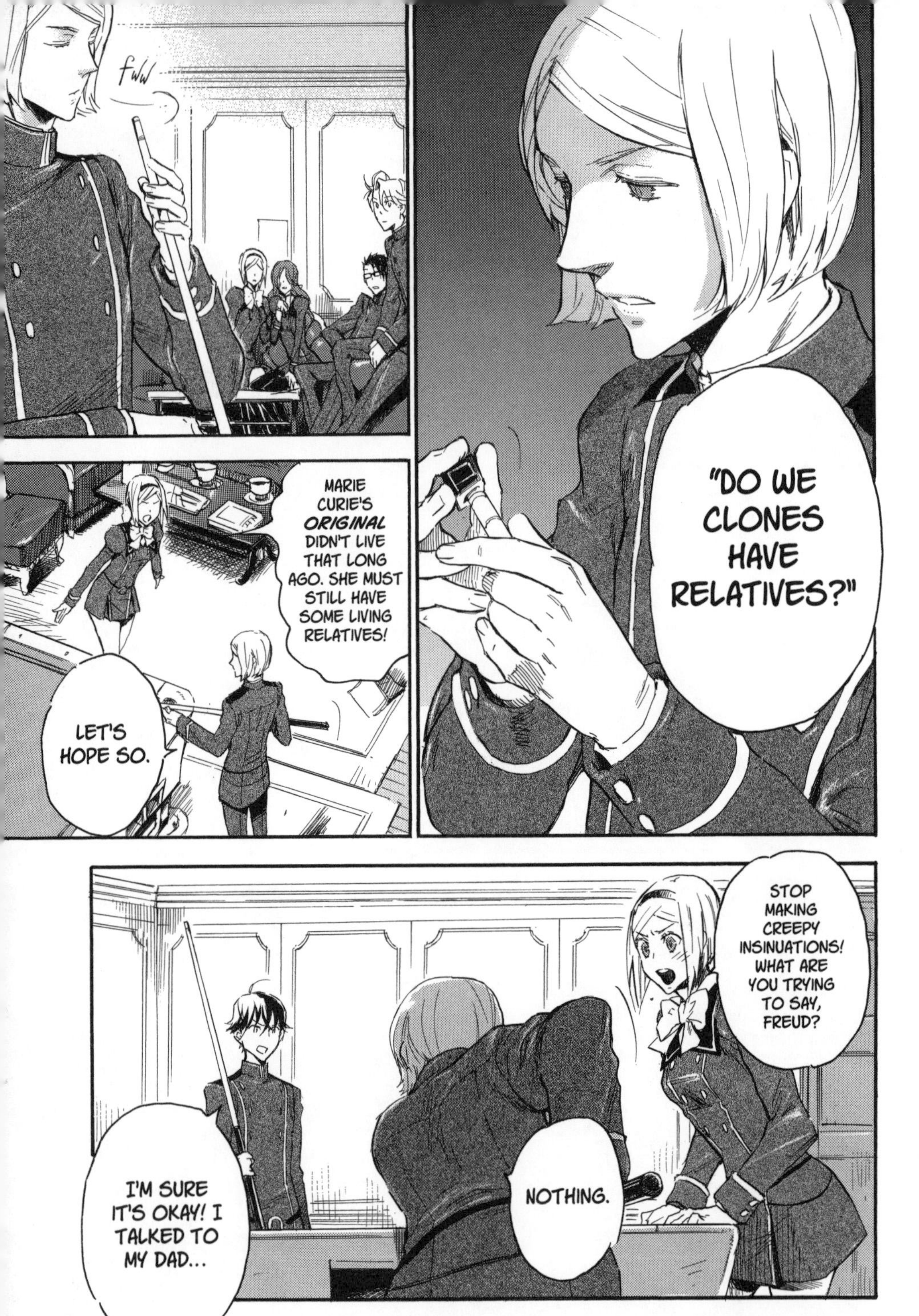
"DO WE CLONES HAVE RELATIVES?"
fww
MARIE CURIE'S ***ORIGINAL*** DIDN'T LIVE THAT LONG AGO. SHE MUST STILL HAVE SOME LIVING RELATIVES!
LET'S HOPE SO.
STOP MAKING CREEPY INSINUATIONS! WHAT ARE YOU TRYING TO SAY, FREUD?
NOTHING.
I'M SURE IT'S OKAY! I TALKED TO MY DAD...

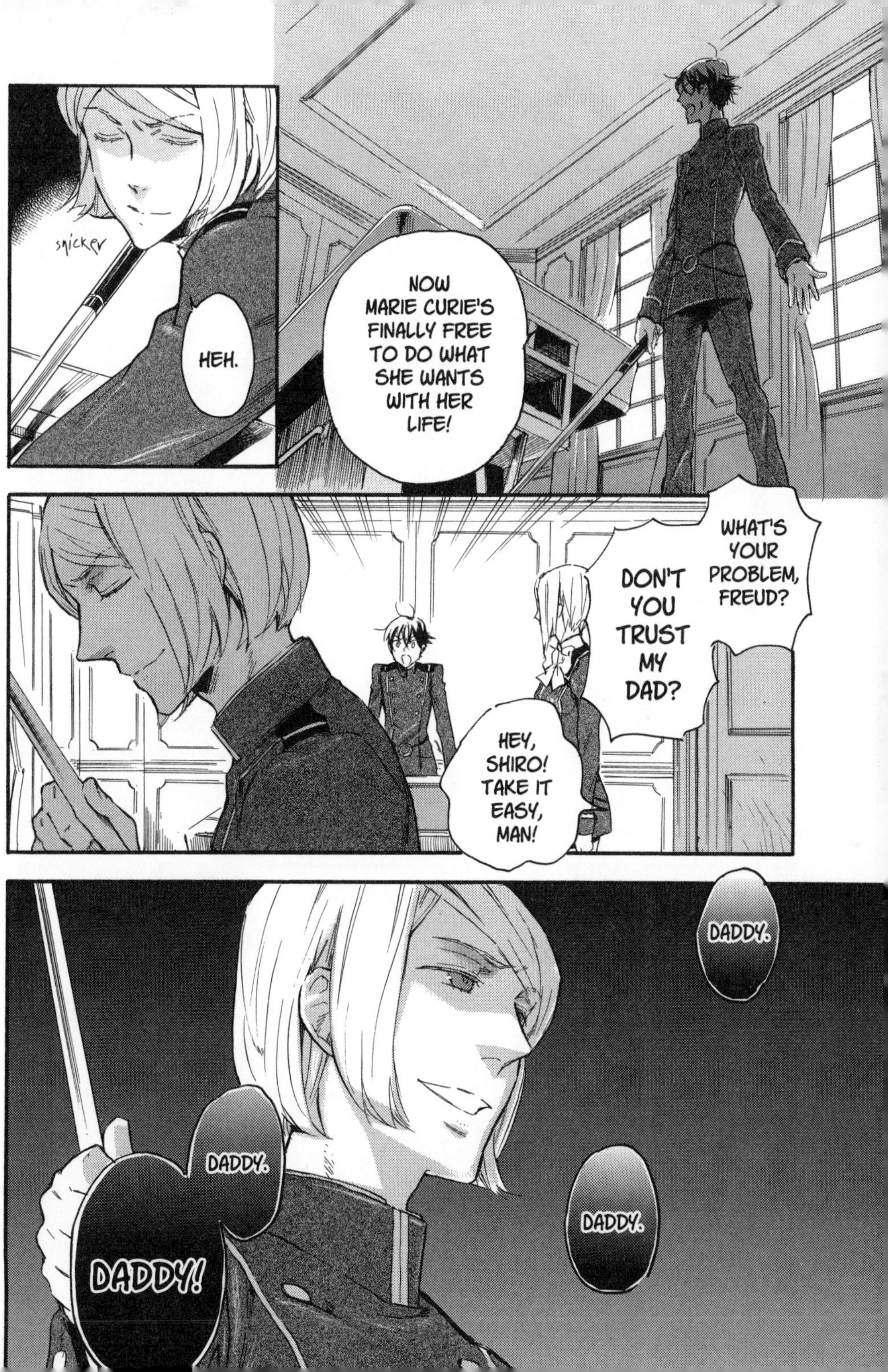
NOW MARIE CURIE'S FINALLY FREE TO DO WHAT SHE WANTS WITH HER LIFE!
snicker
HEH.
WHAT'S YOUR PROBLEM, FREUD?
DON'T YOU TRUST MY DAD?
HEY, SHIRO! TAKE IT EASY, MAN!
DADDY.
DADDY.
DADDY.
DADDY!

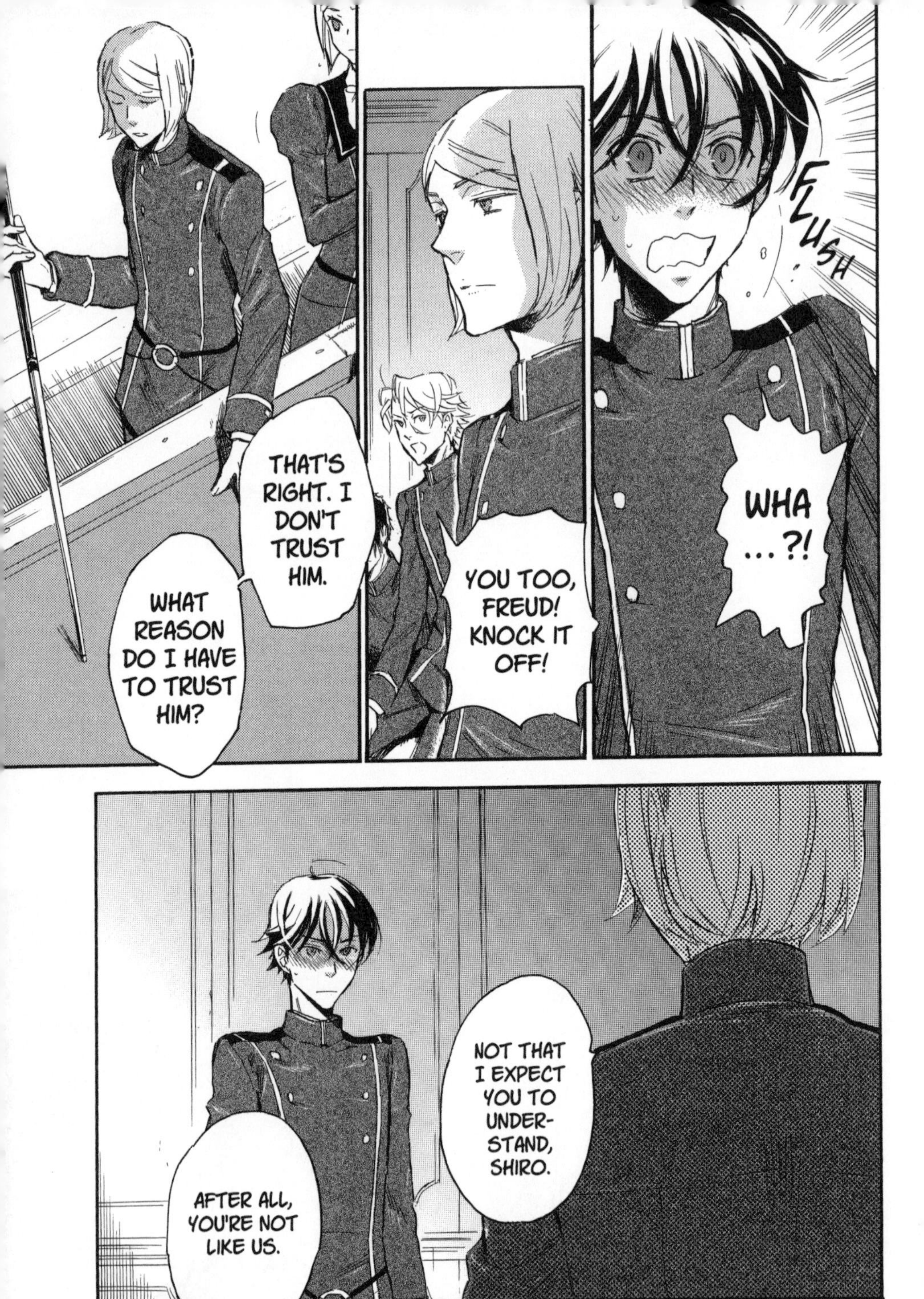
FLUSH
WHA ...?!
YOU TOO, FREUD! KNOCK IT OFF!
THAT'S RIGHT. I DON'T TRUST HIM.
WHAT REASON DO I HAVE TO TRUST HIM?
NOT THAT I EXPECT YOU TO UNDER-STAND, SHIRO.
AFTER ALL, YOU'RE NOT LIKE US.

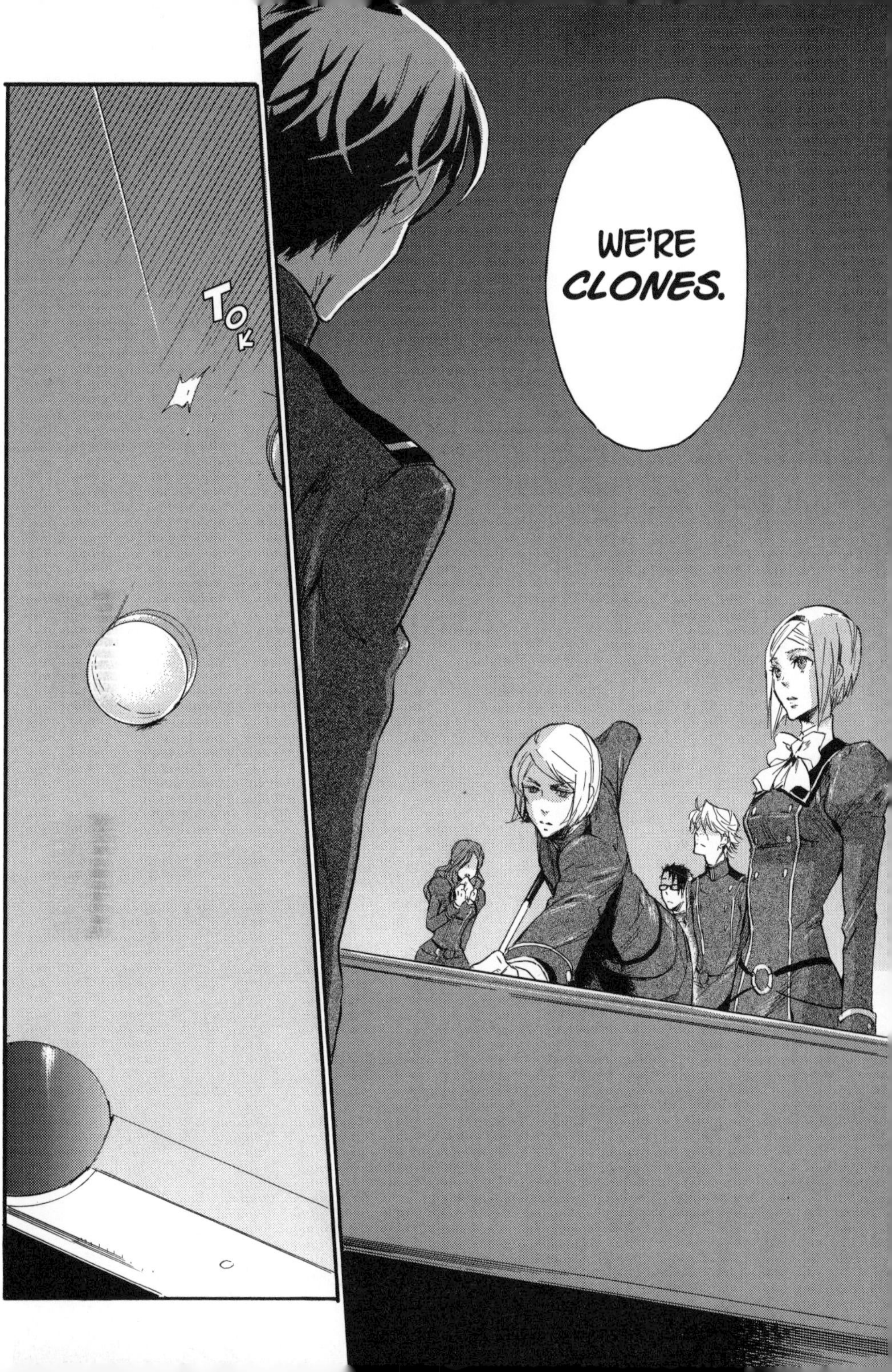
WE'RE CLONES.
TOK

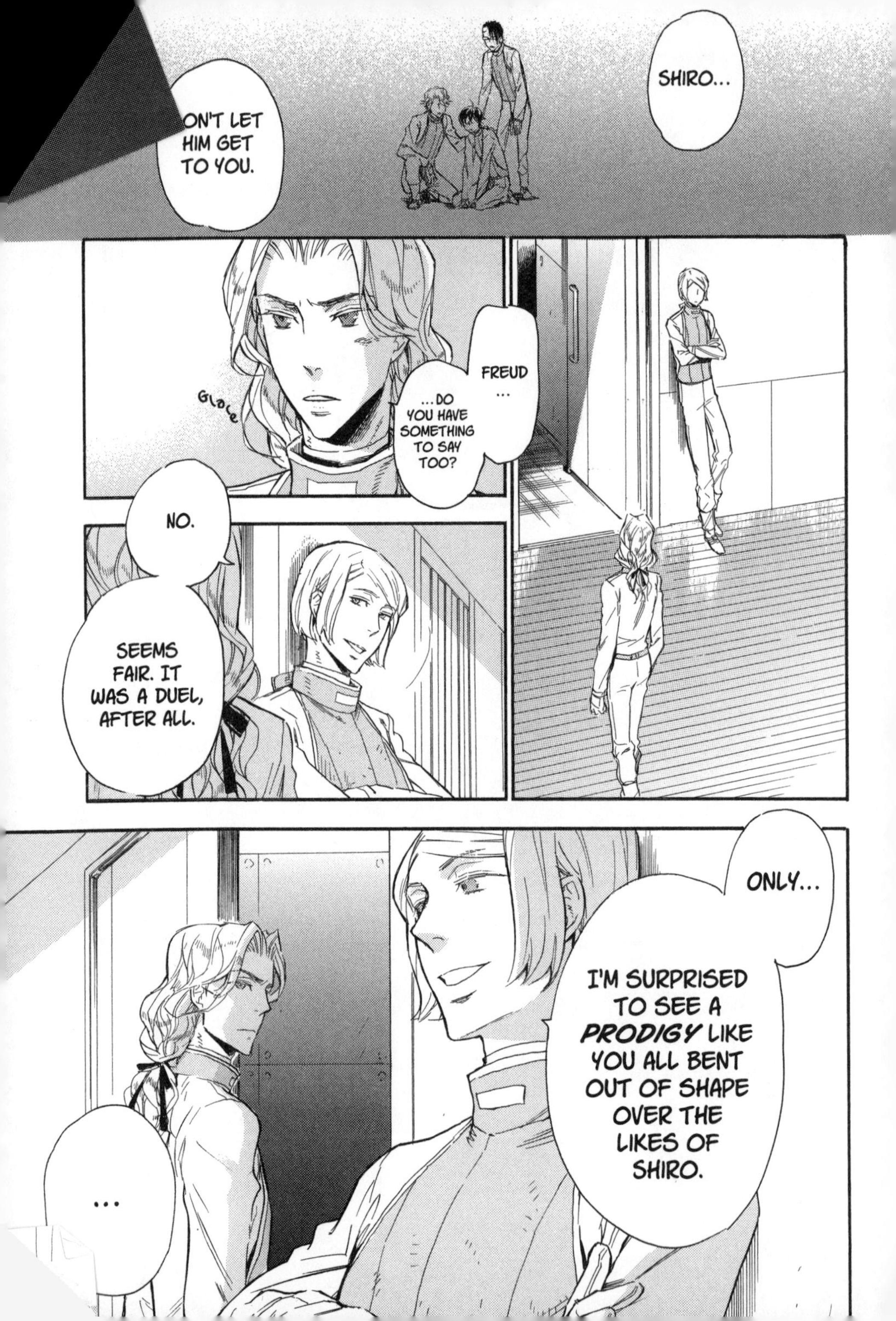
SHIRO...
ON'T LET HIM GET TO YOU.
FREUD ...
...DO YOU HAVE SOMETHING TO SAY TOO?
GLARE
NO.
SEEMS FAIR. IT WAS A DUEL, AFTER ALL.
ONLY...
I'M SURPRISED TO SEE A *PRODIGY* LIKE YOU ALL BENT OUT OF SHAPE OVER THE LIKES OF SHIRO.
...

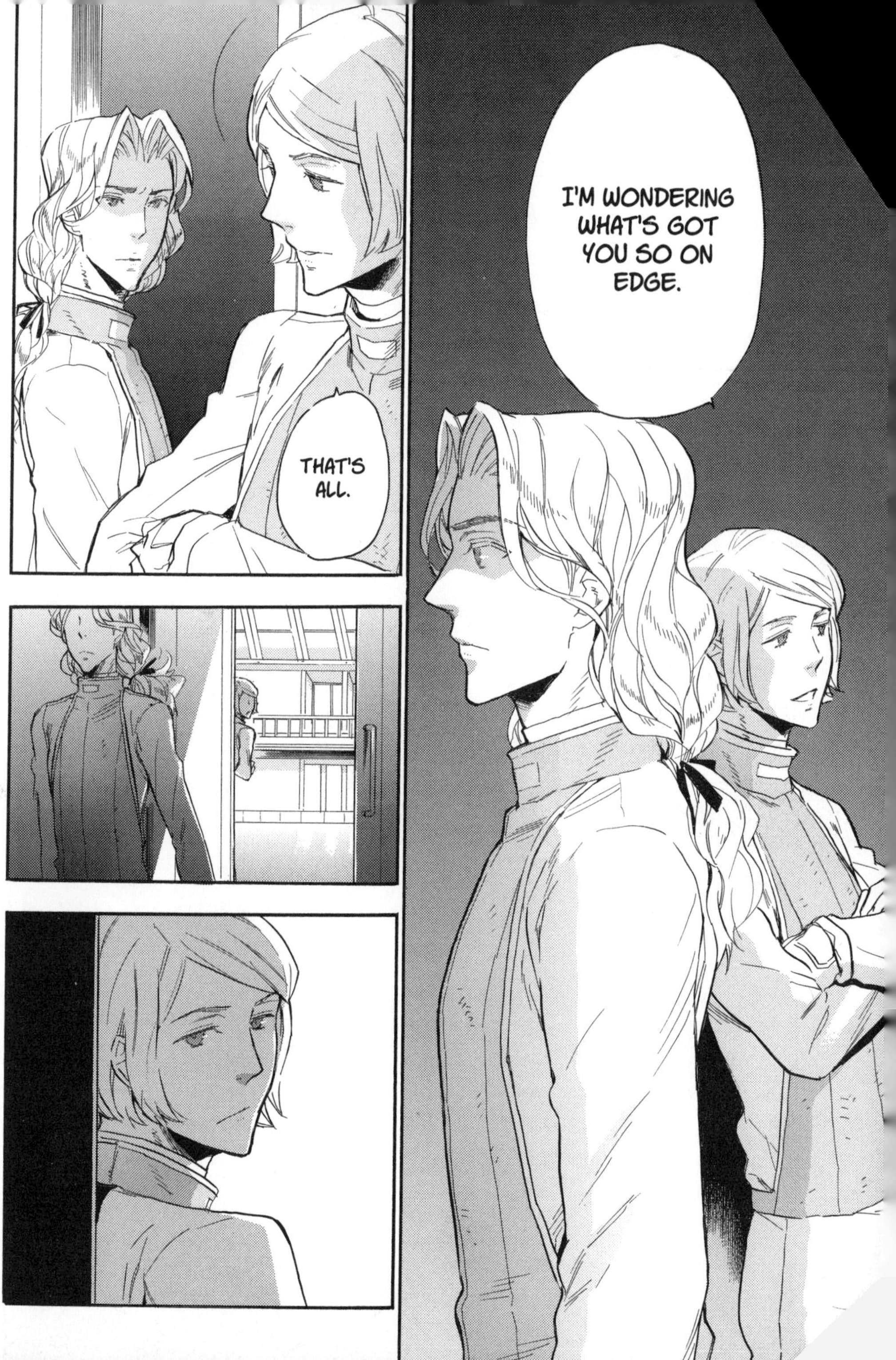
I'M WONDERING WHAT'S GOT YOU SO ON EDGE.
THAT'S ALL.

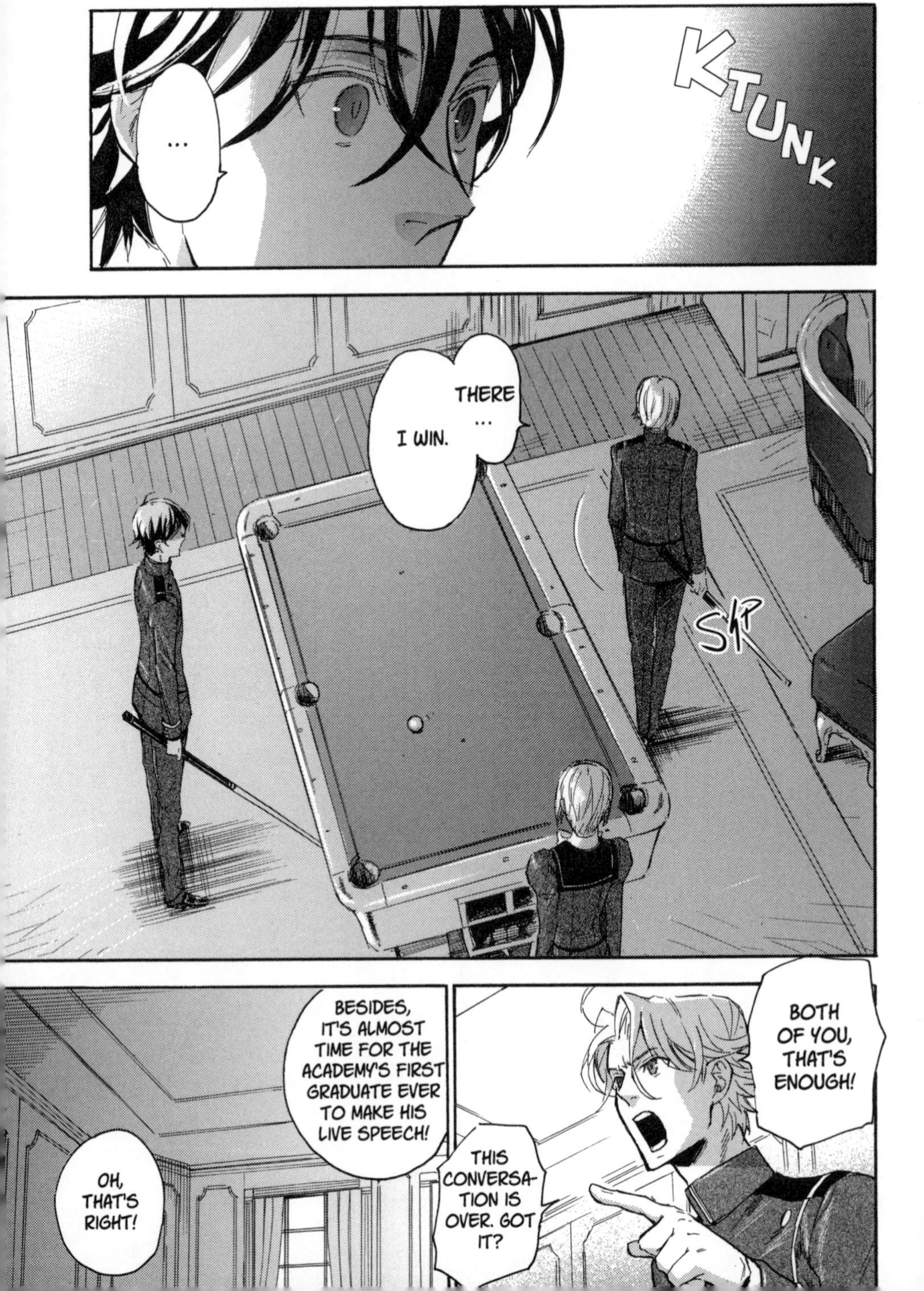
KTUNK
...
THERE ... I WIN.
SKP
BOTH OF YOU, THAT'S ENOUGH!
THIS CONVERSA-TION IS OVER. GOT IT?
BESIDES, IT'S ALMOST TIME FOR THE ACADEMY'S FIRST GRADUATE EVER TO MAKE HIS LIVE SPEECH!
OH, THAT'S RIGHT!

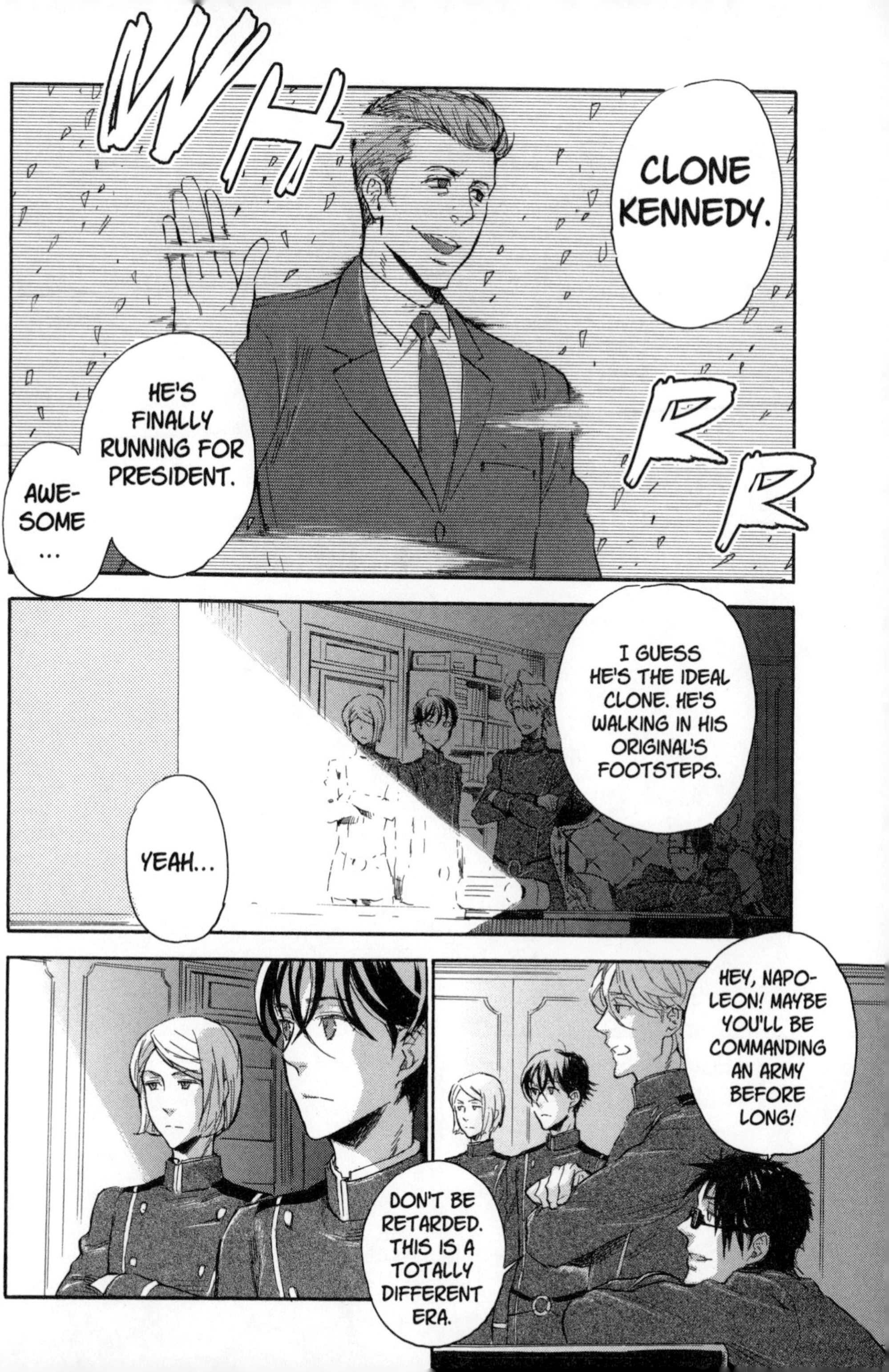
WHRR
CLONE KENNEDY.
HE'S FINALLY RUNNING FOR PRESIDENT.
AWE-SOME...
I GUESS HE'S THE IDEAL CLONE. HE'S WALKING IN HIS ORIGINAL'S FOOTSTEPS.
YEAH...
HEY, NAPO-LEON! MAYBE YOU'LL BE COMMANDING AN ARMY BEFORE LONG!
DON'T BE RETARDED. THIS IS A TOTALLY DIFFERENT ERA.

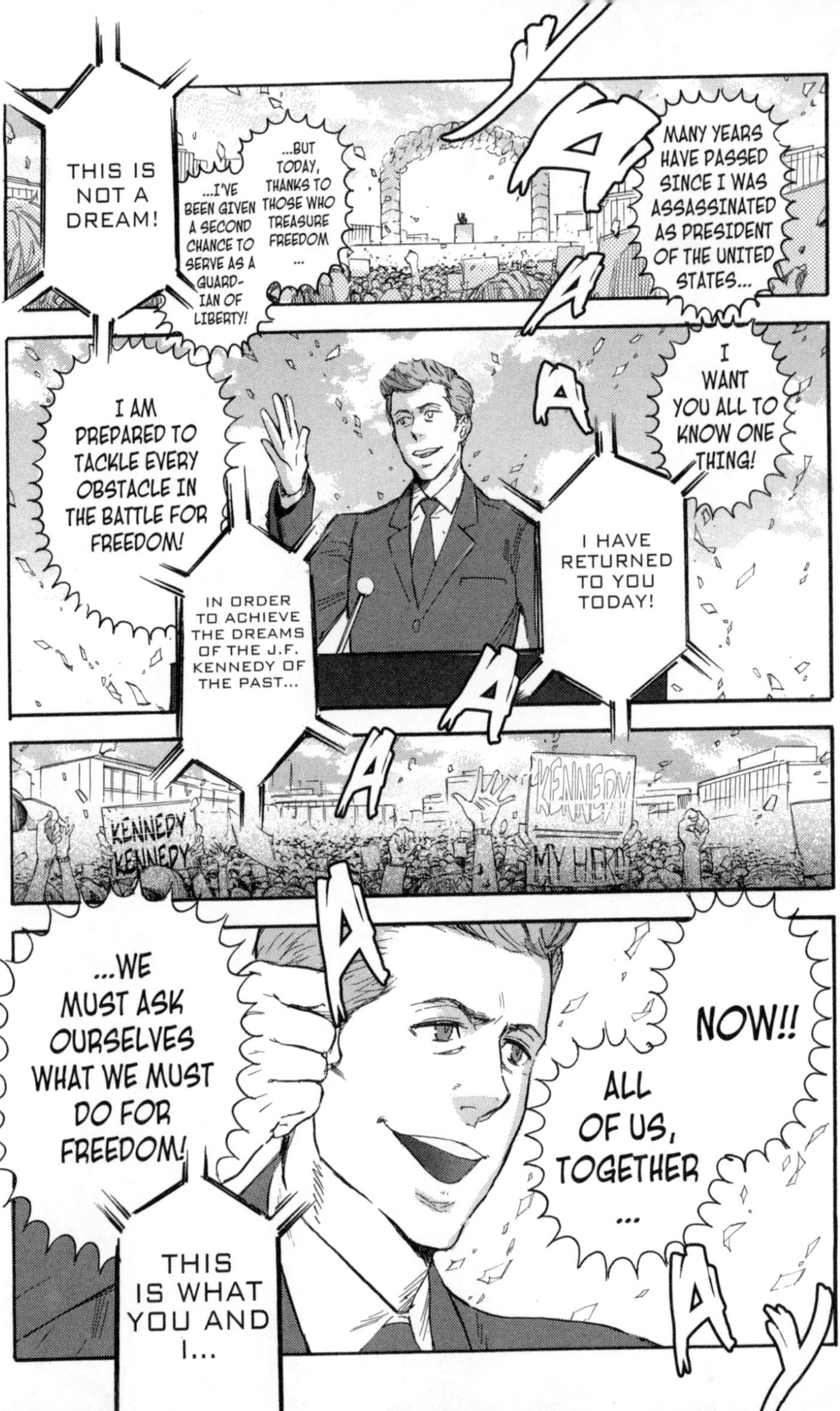
YAAAAAAAY
MANY YEARS HAVE PASSED SINCE I WAS ASSASSINATED AS PRESIDENT OF THE UNITED STATES...
...BUT TODAY, THANKS TO THOSE WHO TREASURE FREEDOM ...
...I'VE BEEN GIVEN A SECOND CHANCE TO SERVE AS A GUARD-IAN OF LIBERTY!
THIS IS NOT A DREAM!
I WANT YOU ALL TO KNOW ONE THING!
I HAVE RETURNED TO YOU TODAY!
IN ORDER TO ACHIEVE THE DREAMS OF THE J.F. KENNEDY OF THE PAST...
I AM PREPARED TO TACKLE EVERY OBSTACLE IN THE BATTLE FOR FREEDOM!
KENNEDY
MY HERO
KENNEDY KENNEDY
NOW!!
ALL OF US, TOGETHER ...
...WE MUST ASK OURSELVES WHAT WE MUST DO FOR FREEDOM!
THIS IS WHAT YOU AND I...

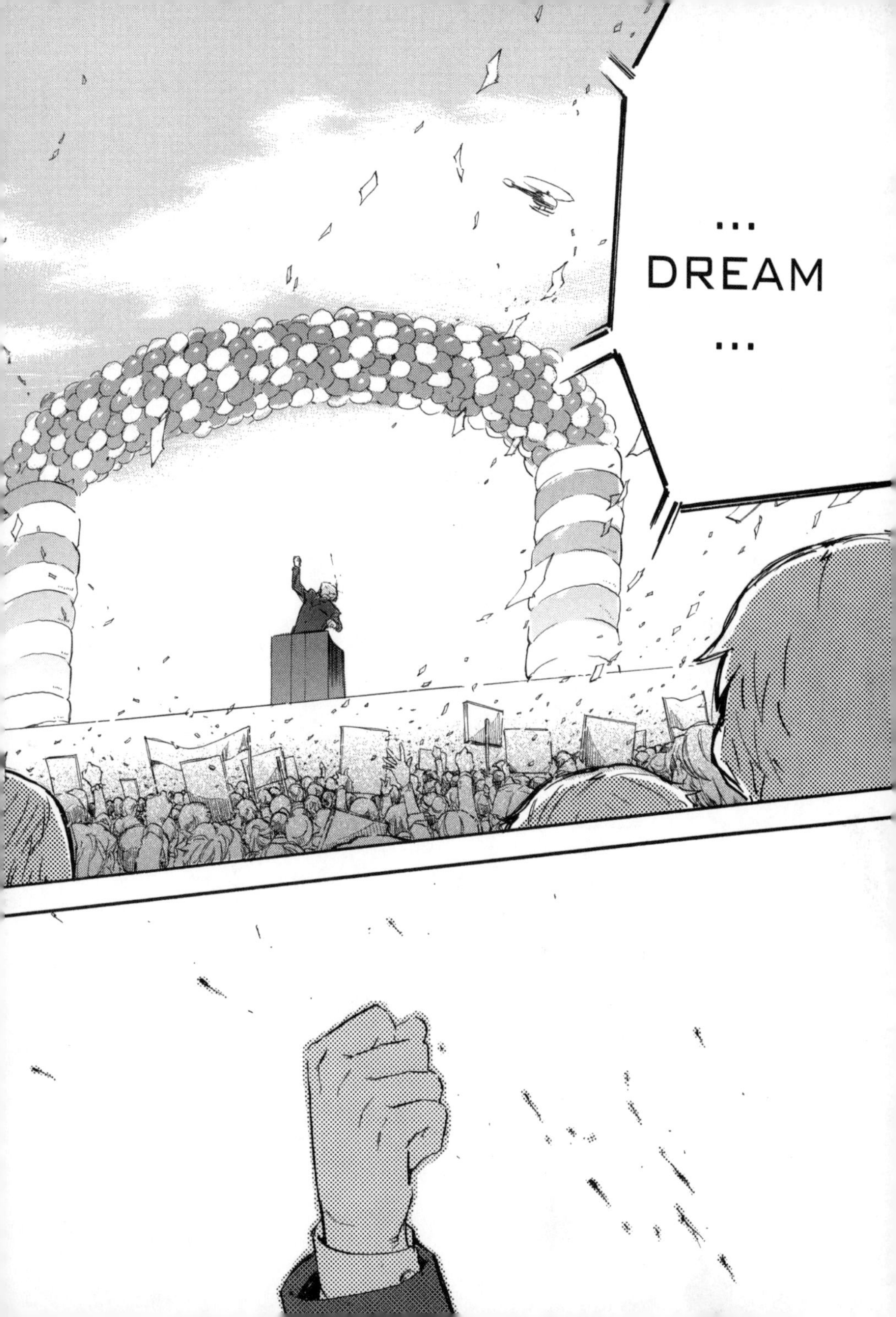

...
DREAM
...

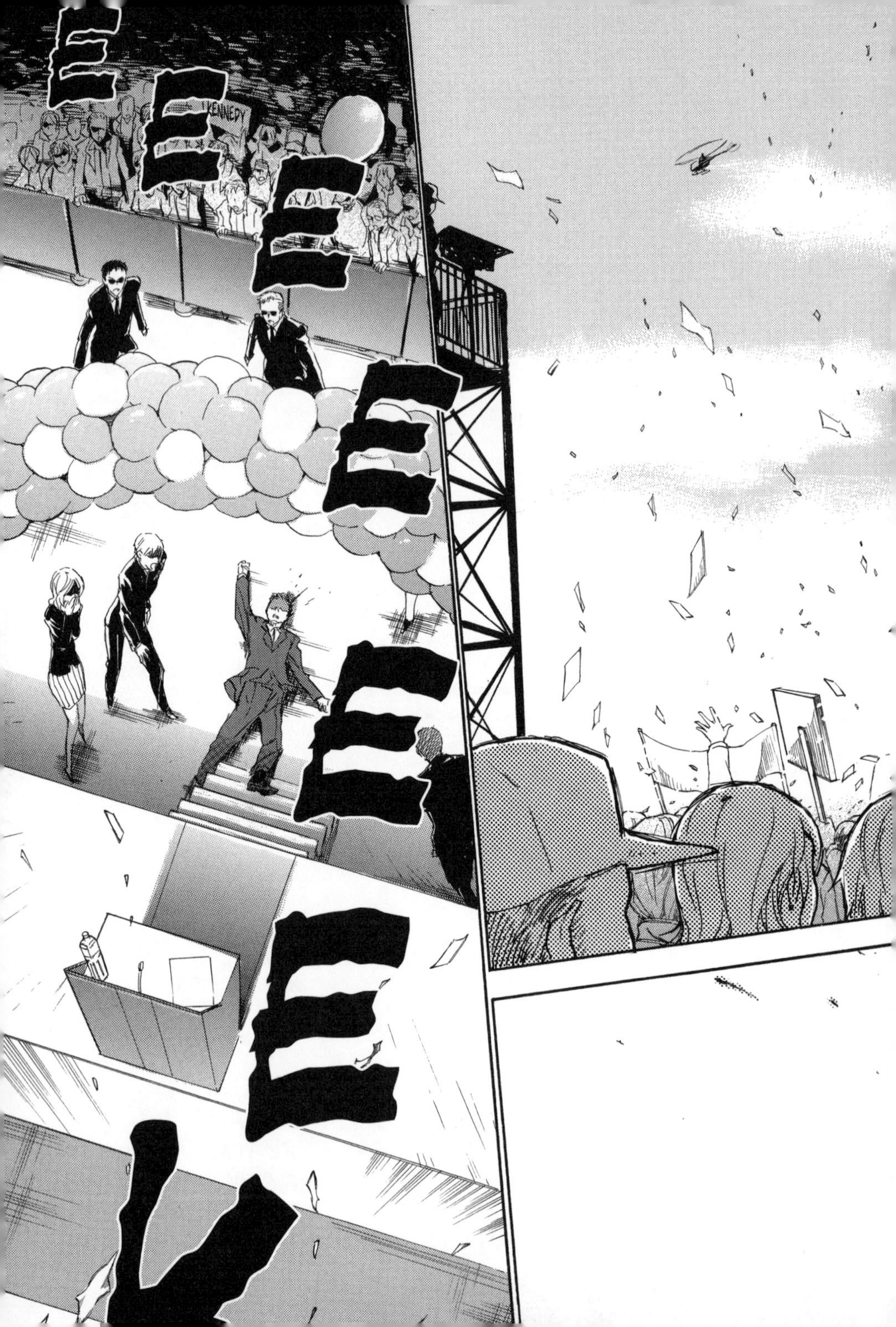
KENNEDY

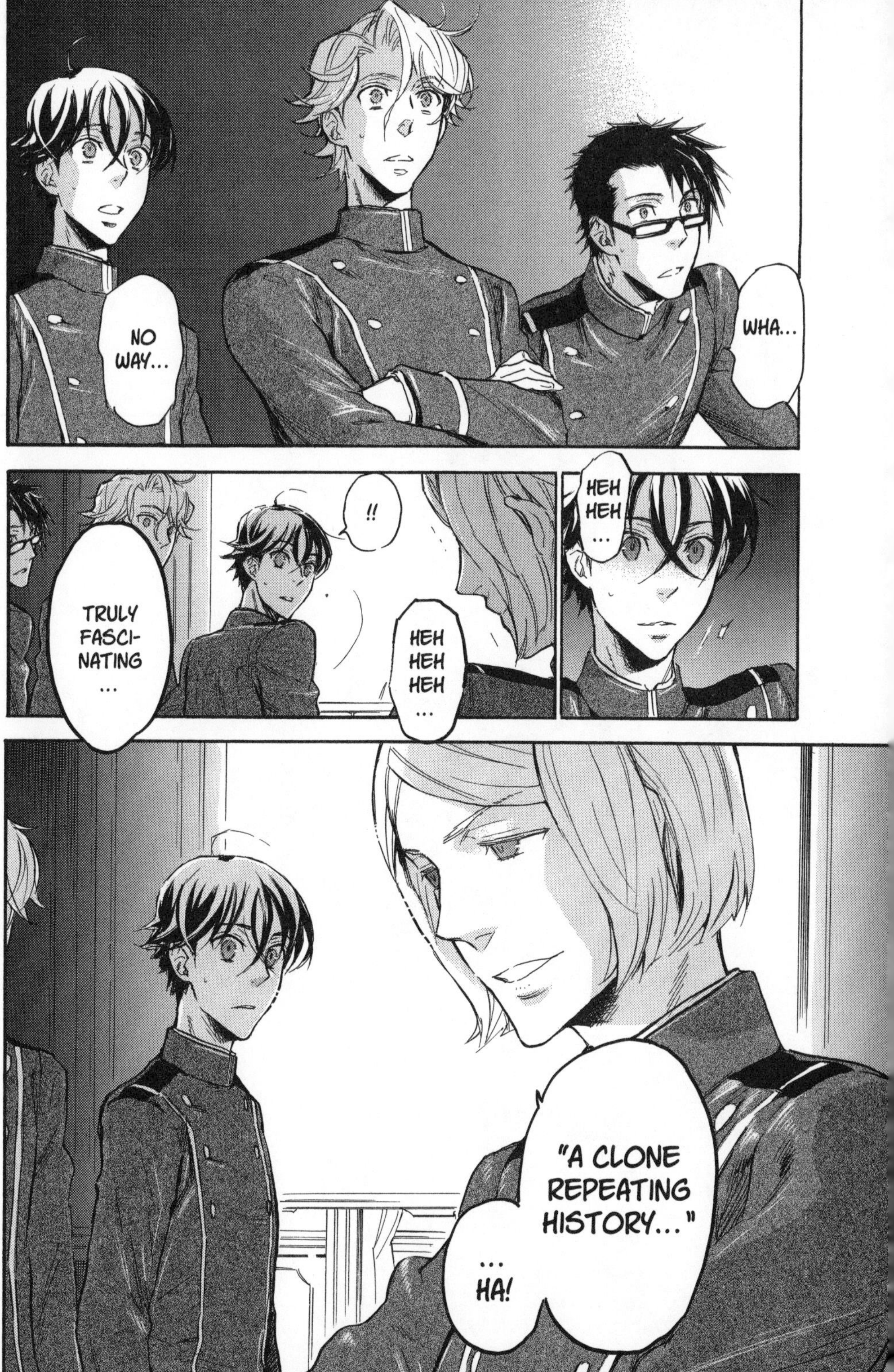
WHA...
NO WAY...
HEH HEH ...
!!
HEH HEH HEH ...
TRULY FASCI- NATING ...
"A CLONE REPEATING HISTORY..."
... HA!

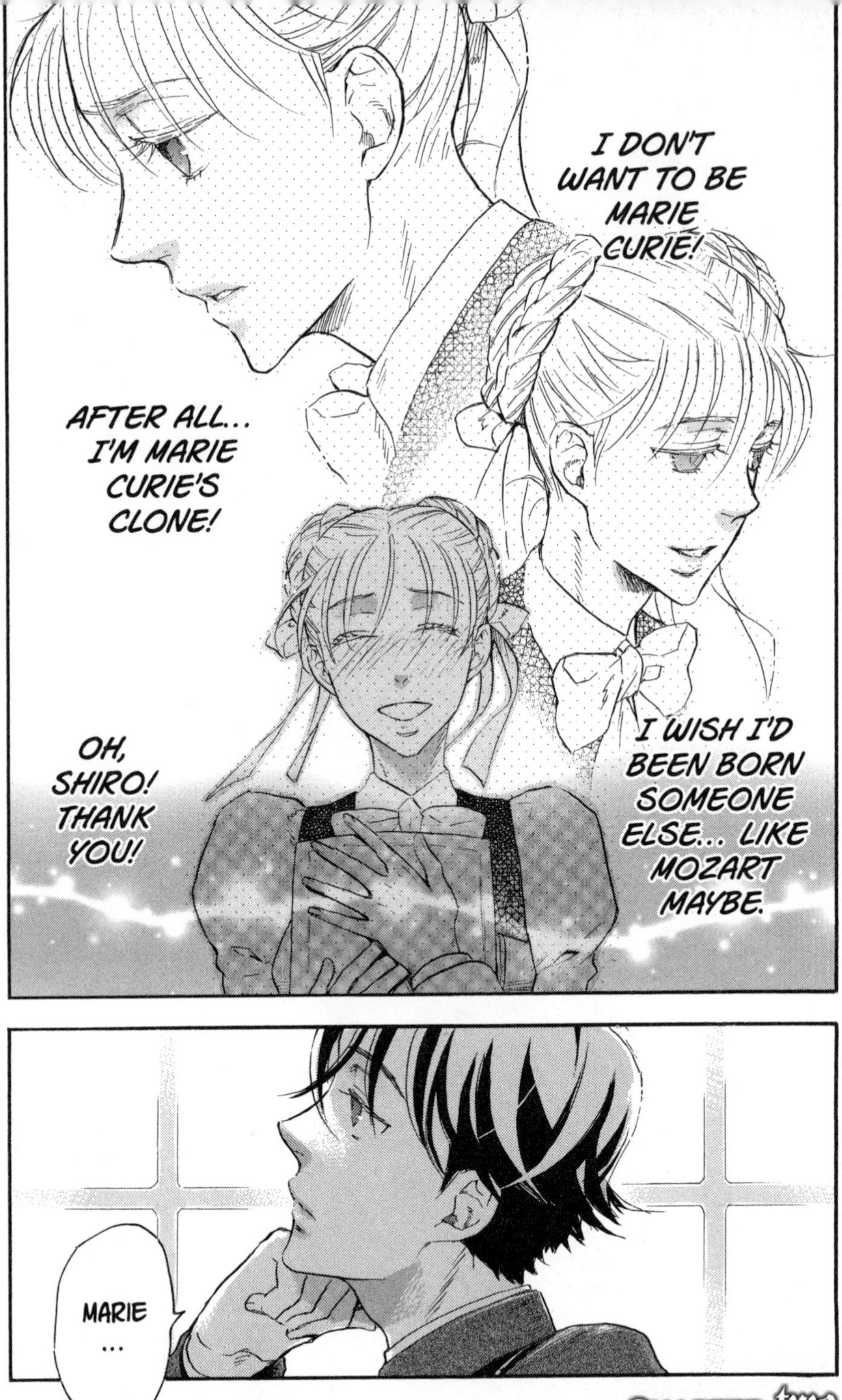
I DON'T WANT TO BE MARIE CURIE!
AFTER ALL... I'M MARIE CURIE'S CLONE!
I WISH I'D BEEN BORN SOMEONE ELSE... LIKE MOZART MAYBE.
OH, SHIRO! THANK YOU!
MARIE ...

CHAPTER two

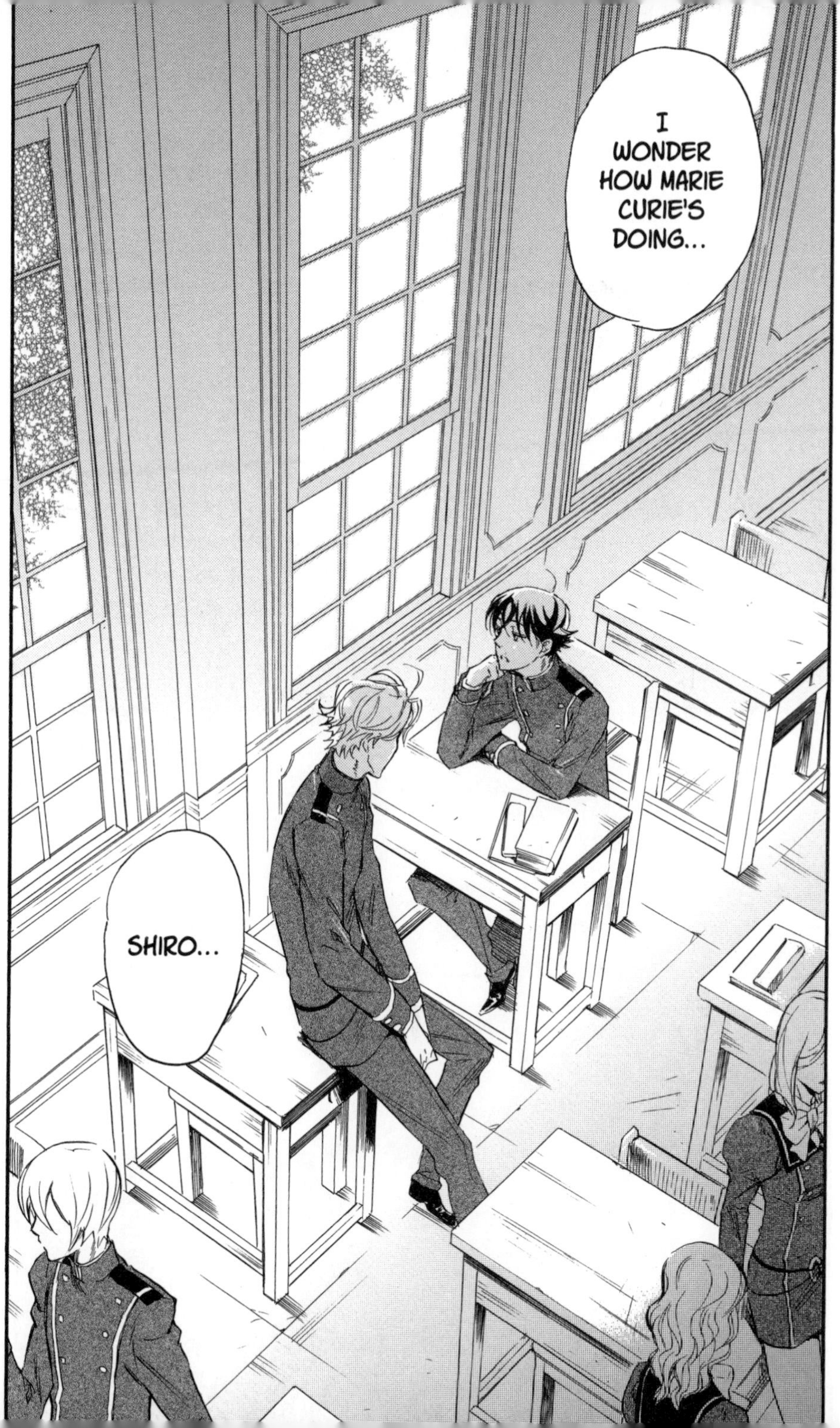
I WONDER HOW MARIE CURIE'S DOING...
SHIRO...

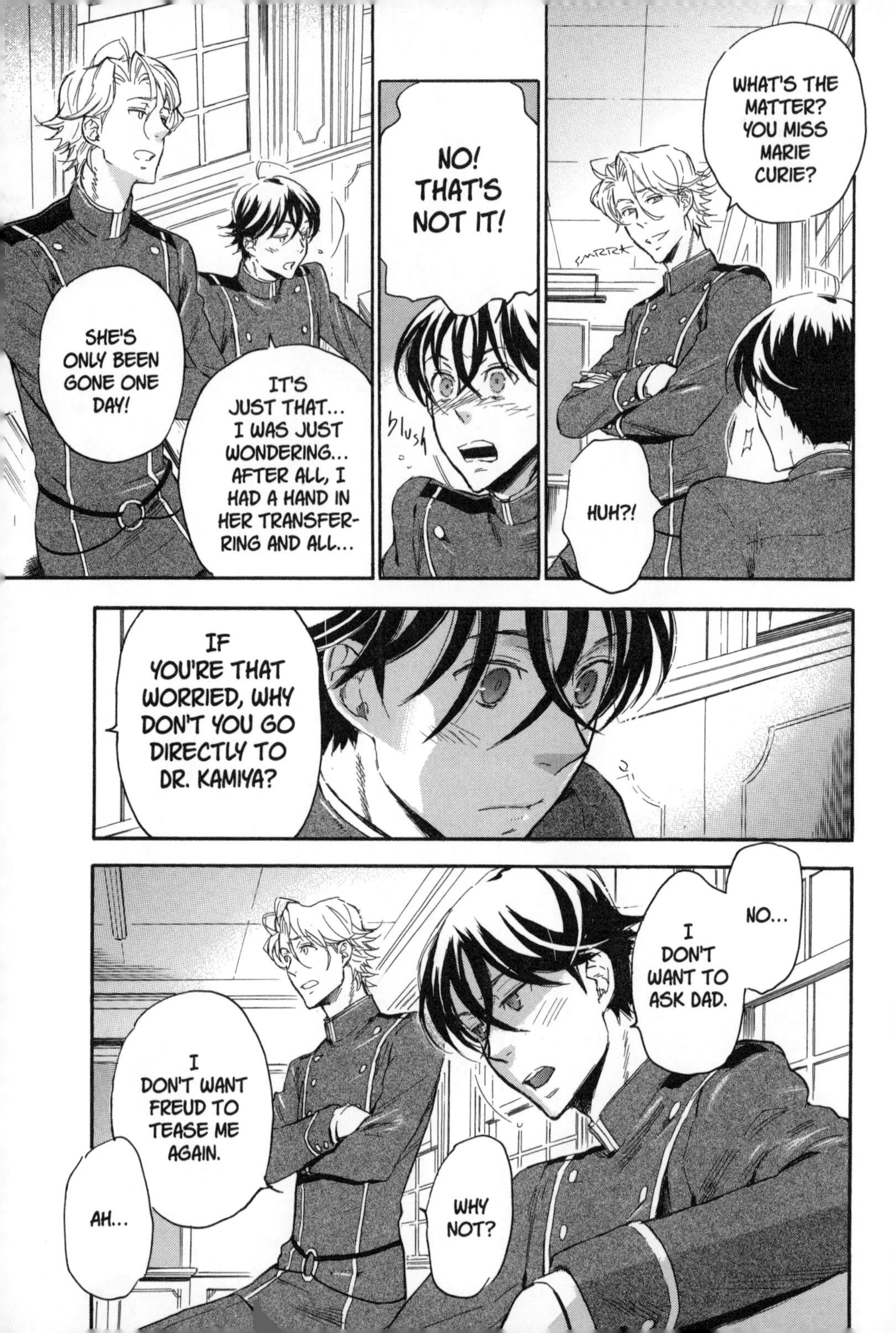
WHAT'S THE MATTER? YOU MISS MARIE CURIE?
SMRRK
HUH?!
NO! THAT'S NOT IT!
blush
IT'S JUST THAT... I WAS JUST WONDERING... AFTER ALL, I HAD A HAND IN HER TRANSFERRING AND ALL...
SHE'S ONLY BEEN GONE ONE DAY!
IF YOU'RE THAT WORRIED, WHY DON'T YOU GO DIRECTLY TO DR. KAMIYA?
NO...
I DON'T WANT TO ASK DAD.
WHY NOT?
I DON'T WANT FREUD TO TEASE ME AGAIN.
AH...

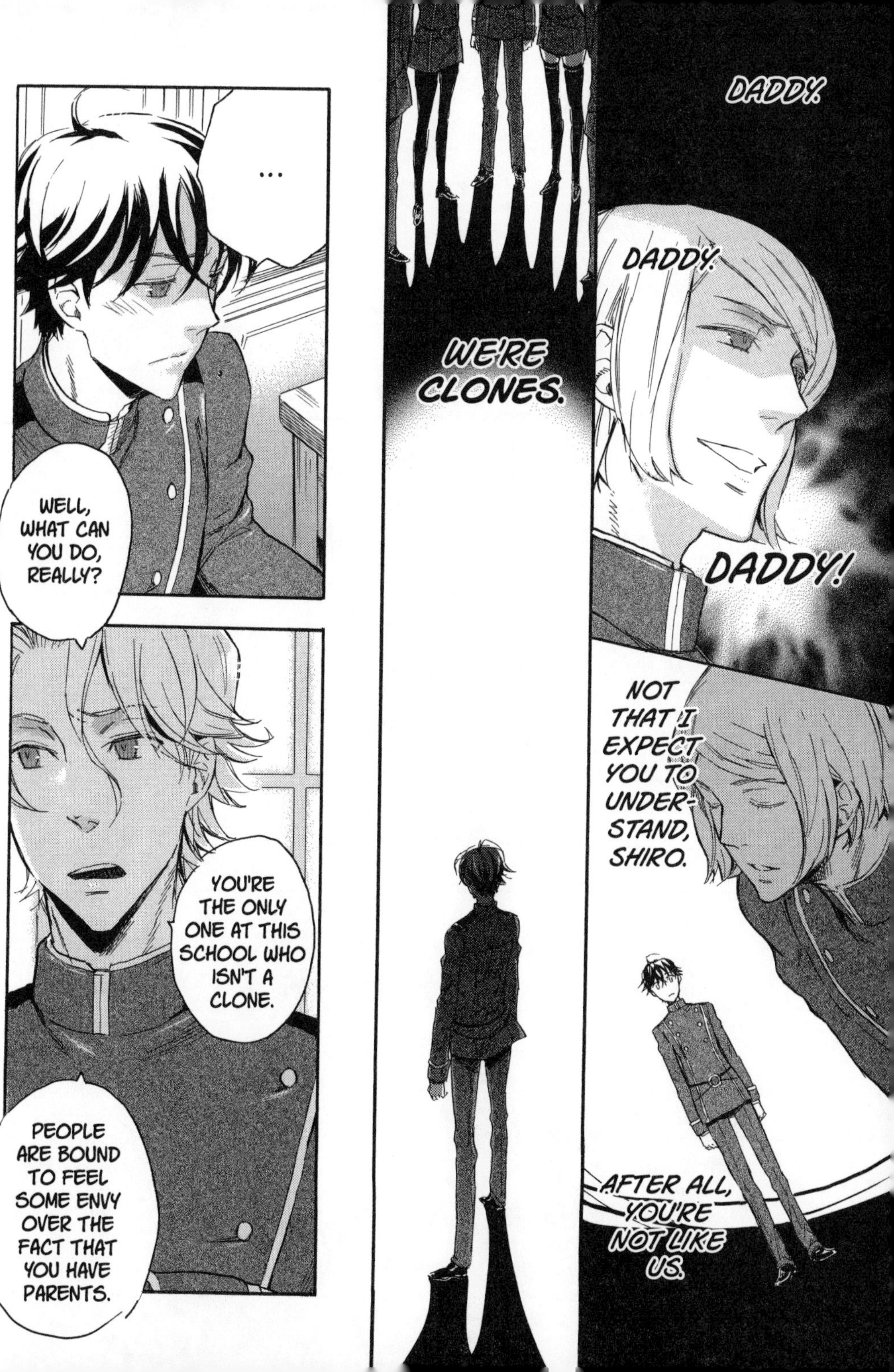
DADDY.
DADDY.
WE'RE CLONES.
DADDY!
NOT THAT I EXPECT YOU TO UNDER-STAND, SHIRO.
AFTER ALL, YOU'RE NOT LIKE US.
...
WELL, WHAT CAN YOU DO, REALLY?
YOU'RE THE ONLY ONE AT THIS SCHOOL WHO ISN'T A CLONE.
PEOPLE ARE BOUND TO FEEL SOME ENVY OVER THE FACT THAT YOU HAVE PARENTS.

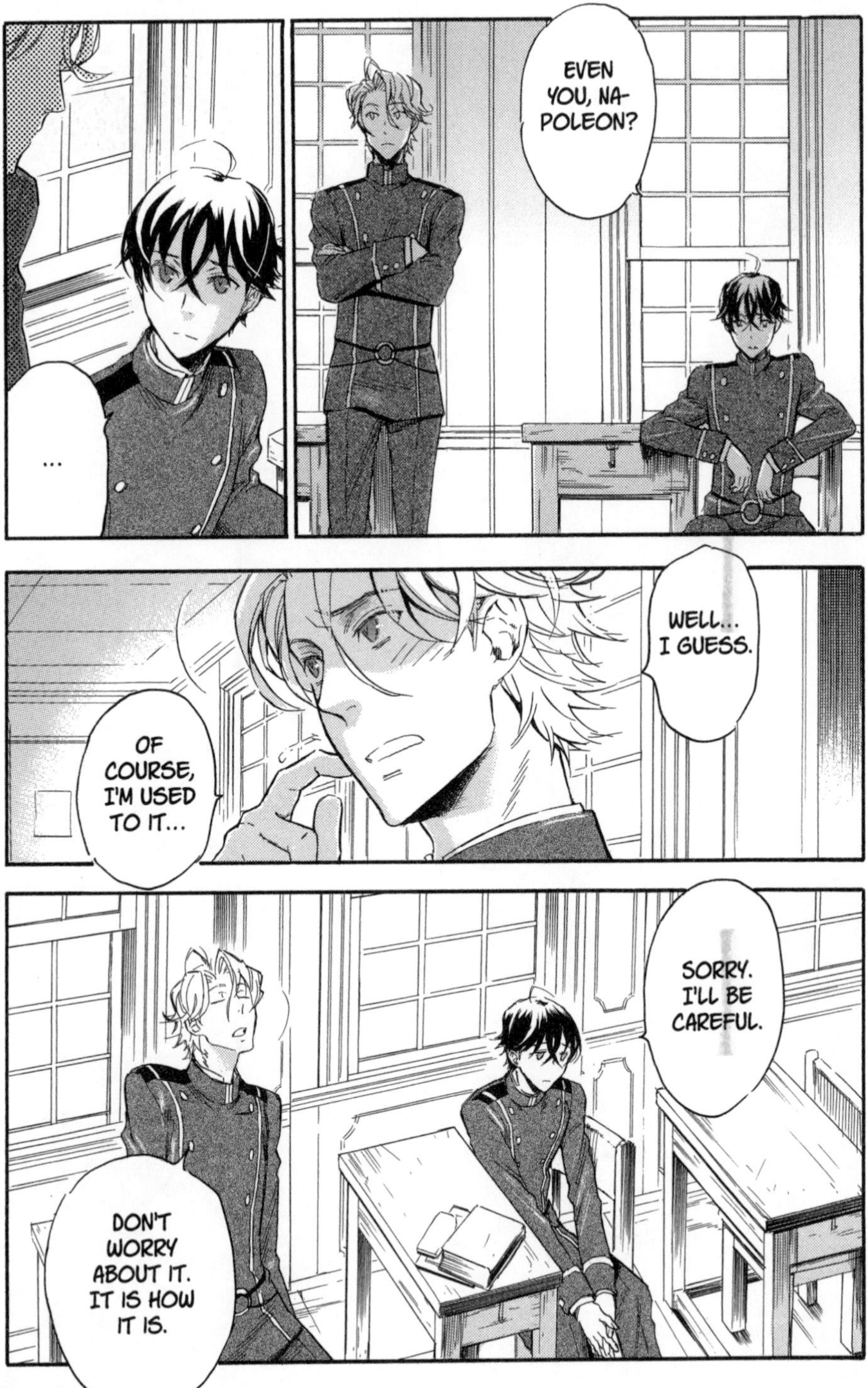
EVEN YOU, NA-POLEON?
...
WELL... I GUESS.
OF COURSE, I'M USED TO IT...
SORRY. I'LL BE CAREFUL.
DON'T WORRY ABOUT IT. IT IS HOW IT IS.

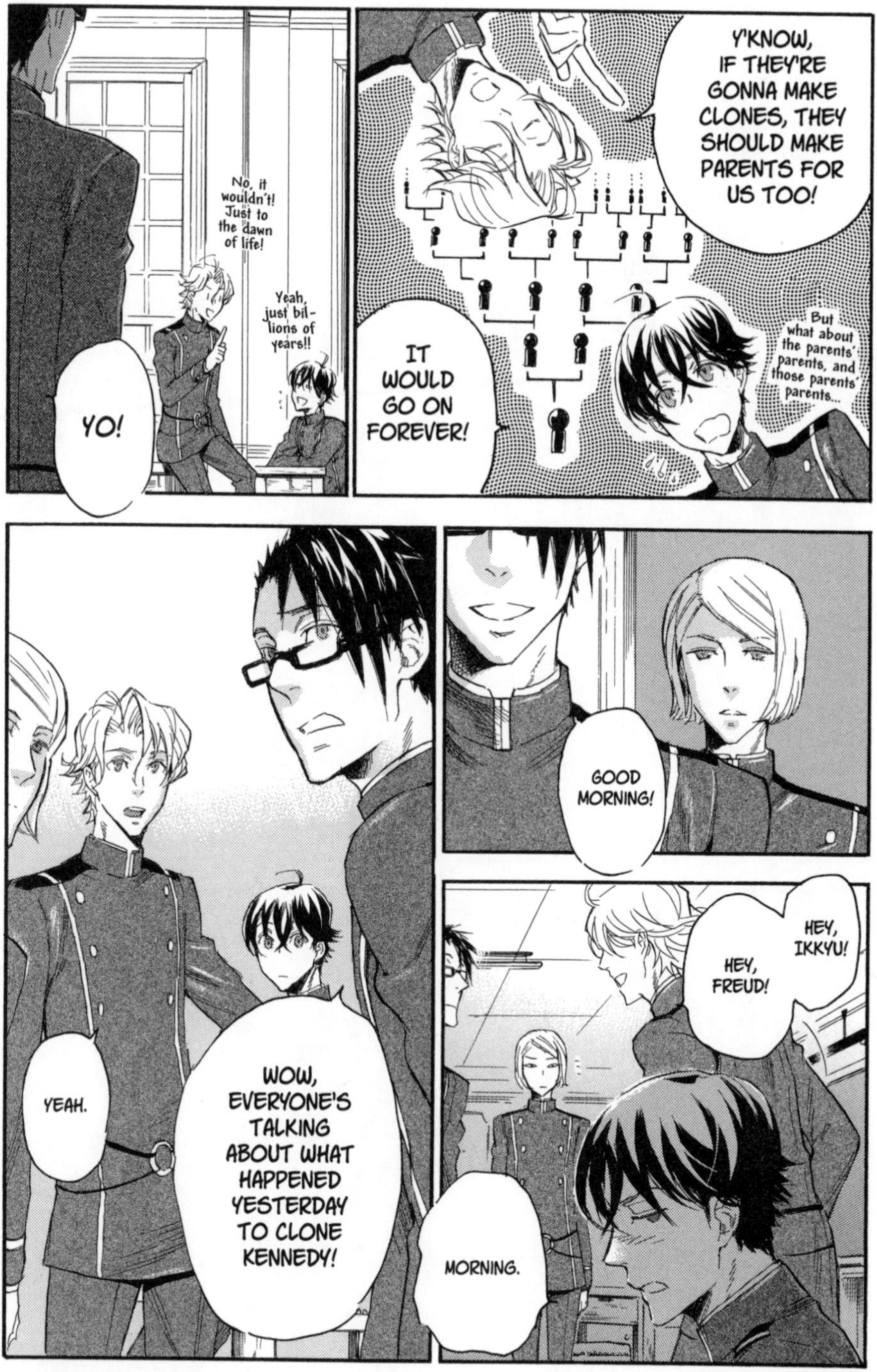
Y'KNOW, IF THEY'RE GONNA MAKE CLONES, THEY SHOULD MAKE PARENTS FOR US TOO!
But what about the parents' parents, and those parents' parents...
IT WOULD GO ON FOREVER!
No, it wouldn't! Just to the dawn of life!
Yeah, just bil-lions of years!!
YO!
GOOD MORNING!
HEY, IKKYU!
HEY, FREUD!
MORNING.
WOW, EVERYONE'S TALKING ABOUT WHAT HAPPENED YESTERDAY TO CLONE KENNEDY!
YEAH.

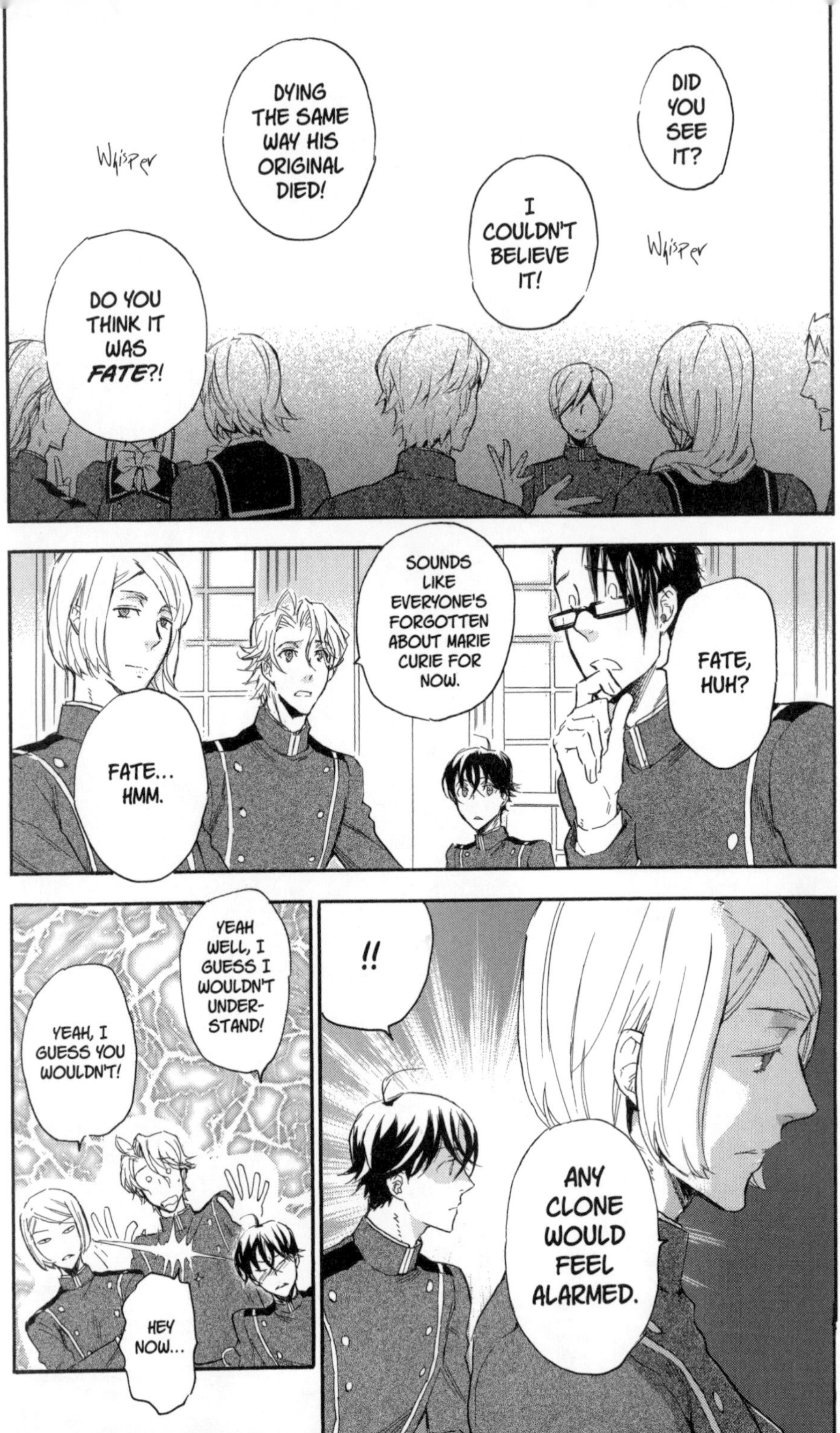
DID YOU SEE IT?
I COULDN'T BELIEVE IT!
Whisper
DYING THE SAME WAY HIS ORIGINAL DIED!
Whisper
DO YOU THINK IT WAS *FATE*?!
FATE, HUH?
SOUNDS LIKE EVERYONE'S FORGOTTEN ABOUT MARIE CURIE FOR NOW.
FATE... HMM.
!!
ANY CLONE WOULD FEEL ALARMED.
YEAH WELL, I GUESS I WOULDN'T UNDER-STAND!
YEAH, I GUESS YOU WOULDN'T!
HEY NOW...

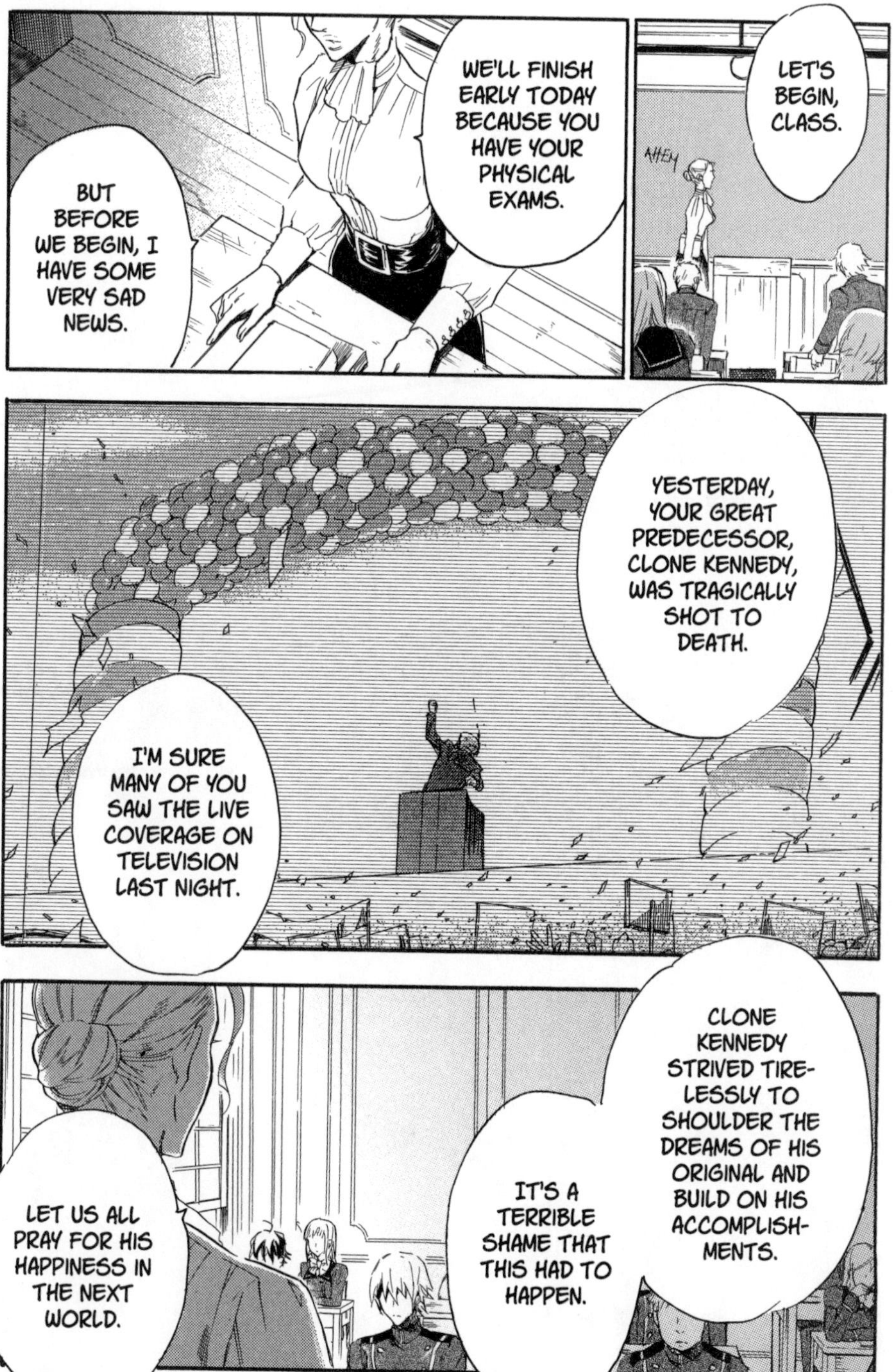
AHEM
LET'S BEGIN, CLASS.
WE'LL FINISH EARLY TODAY BECAUSE YOU HAVE YOUR PHYSICAL EXAMS.
BUT BEFORE WE BEGIN, I HAVE SOME VERY SAD NEWS.
YESTERDAY, YOUR GREAT PREDECESSOR, CLONE KENNEDY, WAS TRAGICALLY SHOT TO DEATH.
I'M SURE MANY OF YOU SAW THE LIVE COVERAGE ON TELEVISION LAST NIGHT.
CLONE KENNEDY STRIVED TIRE-LESSLY TO SHOULDER THE DREAMS OF HIS ORIGINAL AND BUILD ON HIS ACCOMPLISH-MENTS.
IT'S A TERRIBLE SHAME THAT THIS HAD TO HAPPEN.
LET US ALL PRAY FOR HIS HAPPINESS IN THE NEXT WORLD.

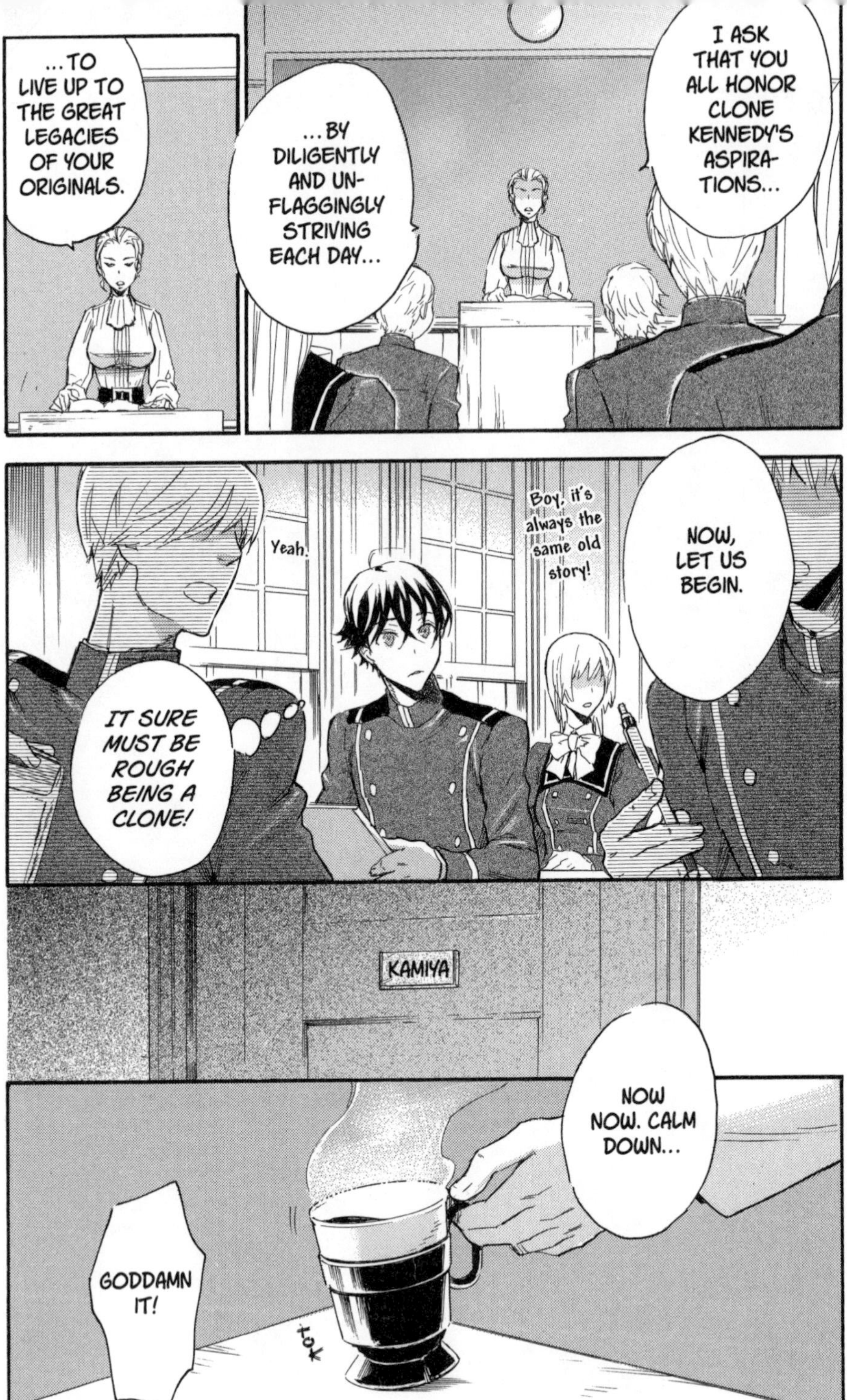
I ASK THAT YOU ALL HONOR CLONE KENNEDY'S ASPIRA-TIONS...
...BY DILIGENTLY AND UN-FLAGGINGLY STRIVING EACH DAY...
...TO LIVE UP TO THE GREAT LEGACIES OF YOUR ORIGINALS.
NOW, LET US BEGIN.
Boy, it's always the same old story!
Yeah.
IT SURE MUST BE ROUGH BEING A CLONE!
KAMIYA
NOW NOW. CALM DOWN...
GODDAMN IT!
TOK

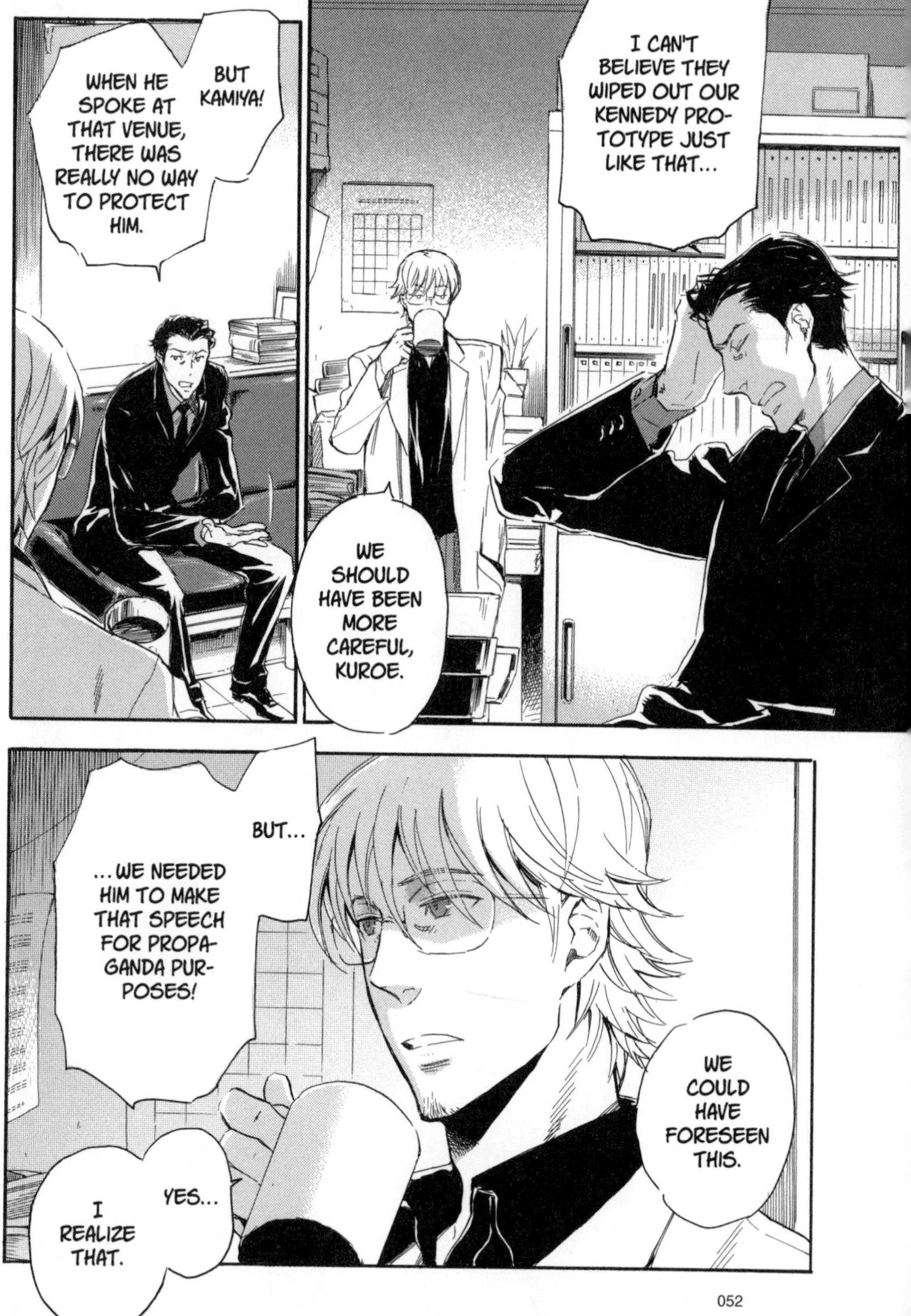
I CAN'T BELIEVE THEY WIPED OUT OUR KENNEDY PROTOTYPE JUST LIKE THAT...
WE SHOULD HAVE BEEN MORE CAREFUL, KUROE.
BUT KAMIYA!
WHEN HE SPOKE AT THAT VENUE, THERE WAS REALLY NO WAY TO PROTECT HIM.
BUT...
...WE NEEDED HIM TO MAKE THAT SPEECH FOR PROPAGANDA PURPOSES!
WE COULD HAVE FORESEEN THIS.
YES...
I REALIZE THAT.

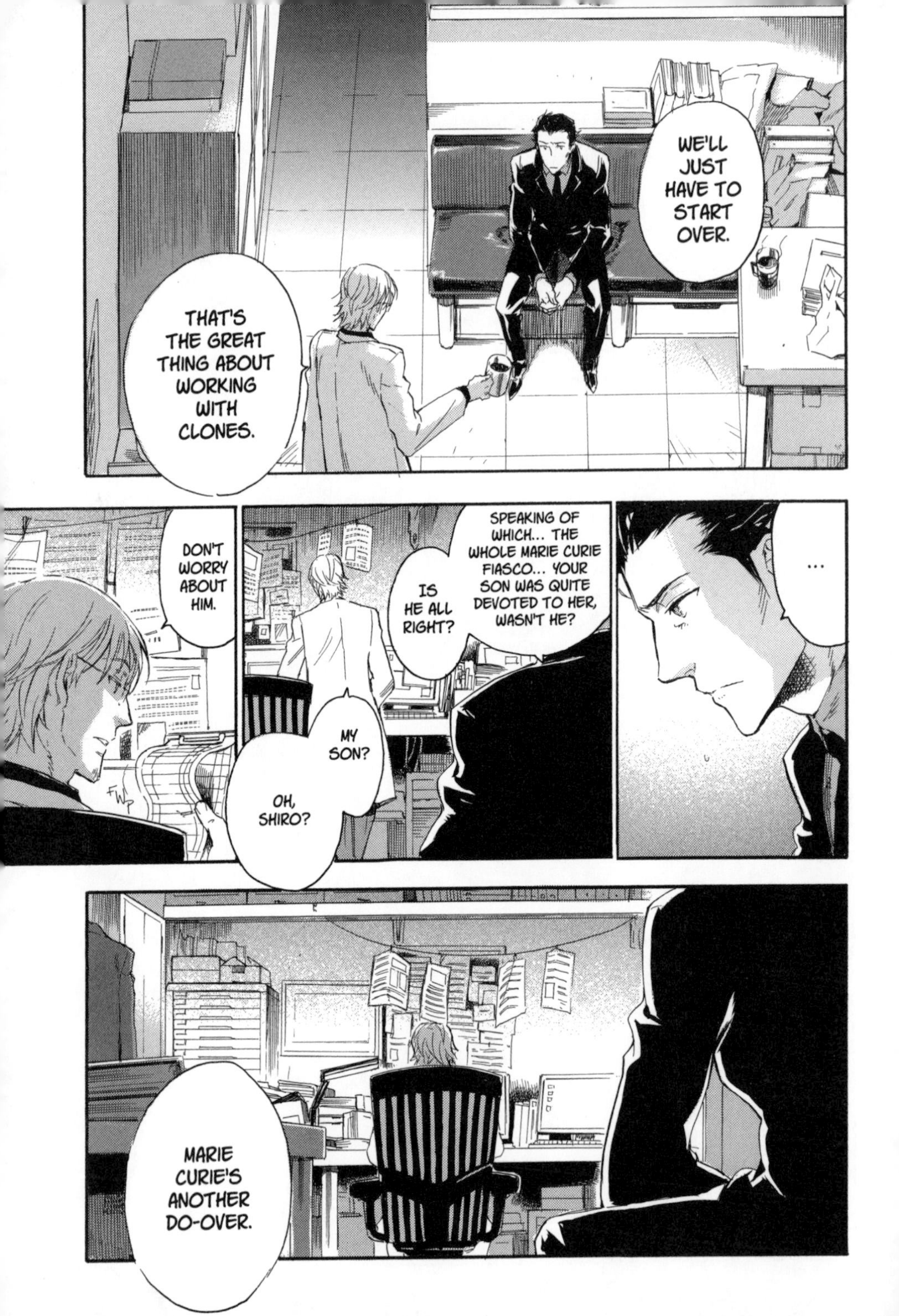
WE'LL JUST HAVE TO START OVER.
THAT'S THE GREAT THING ABOUT WORKING WITH CLONES.
...
SPEAKING OF WHICH... THE WHOLE MARIE CURIE FIASCO... YOUR SON WAS QUITE DEVOTED TO HER, WASN'T HE?
IS HE ALL RIGHT?
MY SON?
OH, SHIRO?
DON'T WORRY ABOUT HIM.
FWP
MARIE CURIE'S ANOTHER DO-OVER.

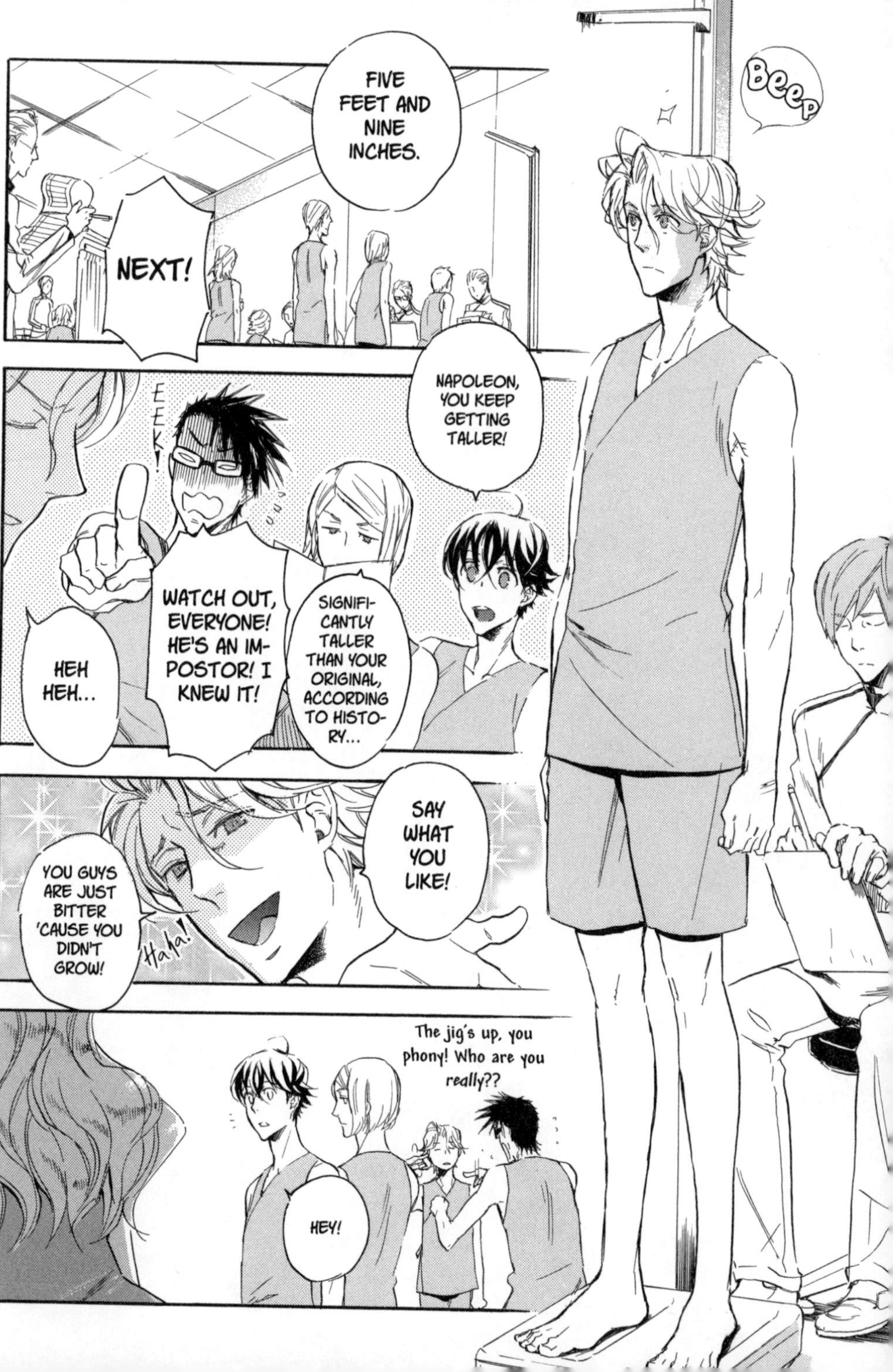
Beep
FIVE FEET AND NINE INCHES.
NEXT!
NAPOLEON, YOU KEEP GETTING TALLER!
EEK!
SIGNIFICANTLY TALLER THAN YOUR ORIGINAL, ACCORDING TO HISTORY...
WATCH OUT, EVERYONE! HE'S AN IMPOSTOR! I KNEW IT!
HEH HEH...
SAY WHAT YOU LIKE!
YOU GUYS ARE JUST BITTER 'CAUSE YOU DIDN'T GROW!
Haha!
The jig's up, you phony! Who are you really??
HEY!

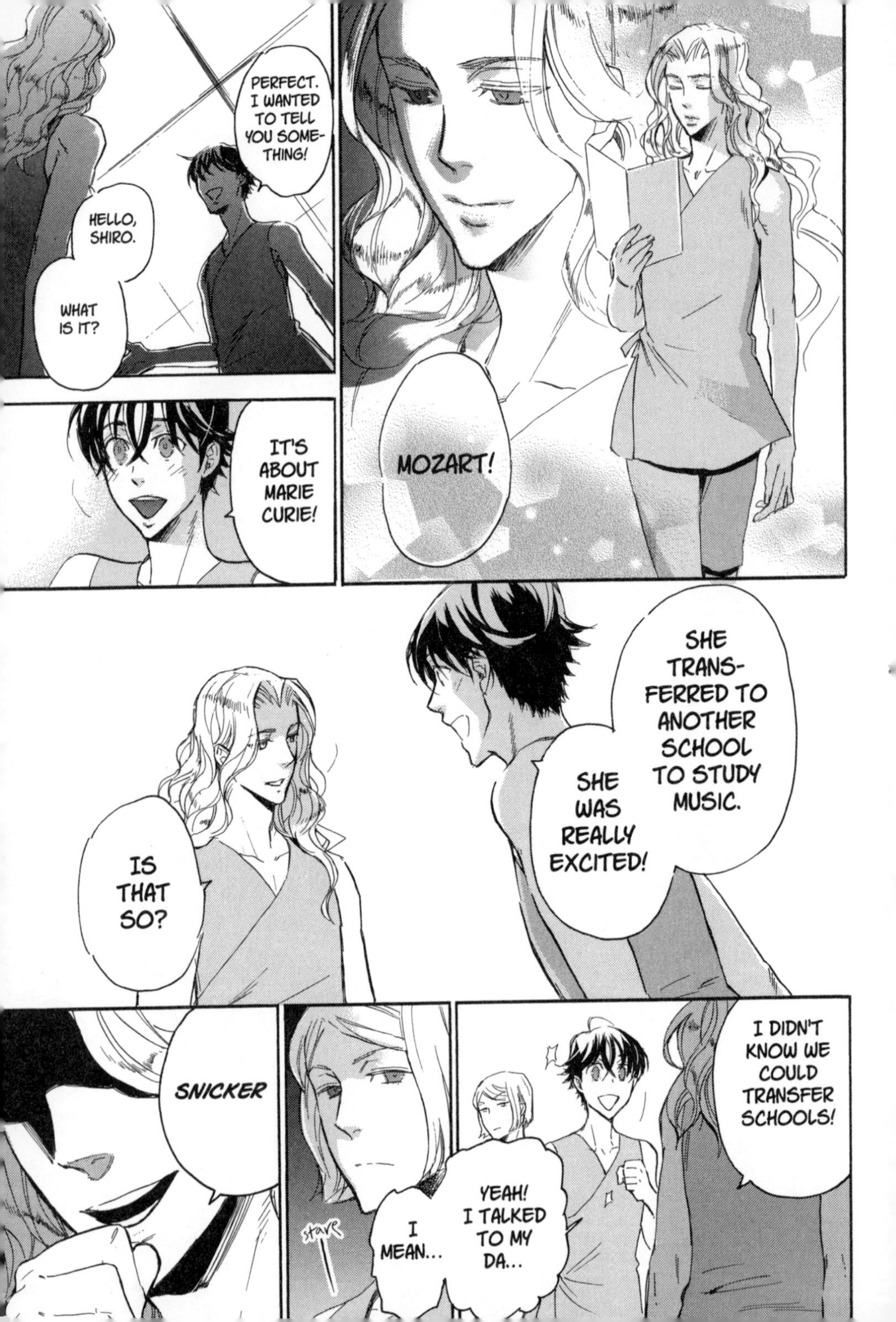
MOZART!
PERFECT. I WANTED TO TELL YOU SOME-THING!
HELLO, SHIRO.
WHAT IS IT?
IT'S ABOUT MARIE CURIE!
SHE TRANS-FERRED TO ANOTHER SCHOOL TO STUDY MUSIC.
SHE WAS REALLY EXCITED!
IS THAT SO?
I DIDN'T KNOW WE COULD TRANSFER SCHOOLS!
YEAH! I TALKED TO MY DA...
I MEAN...
stare
SNICKER

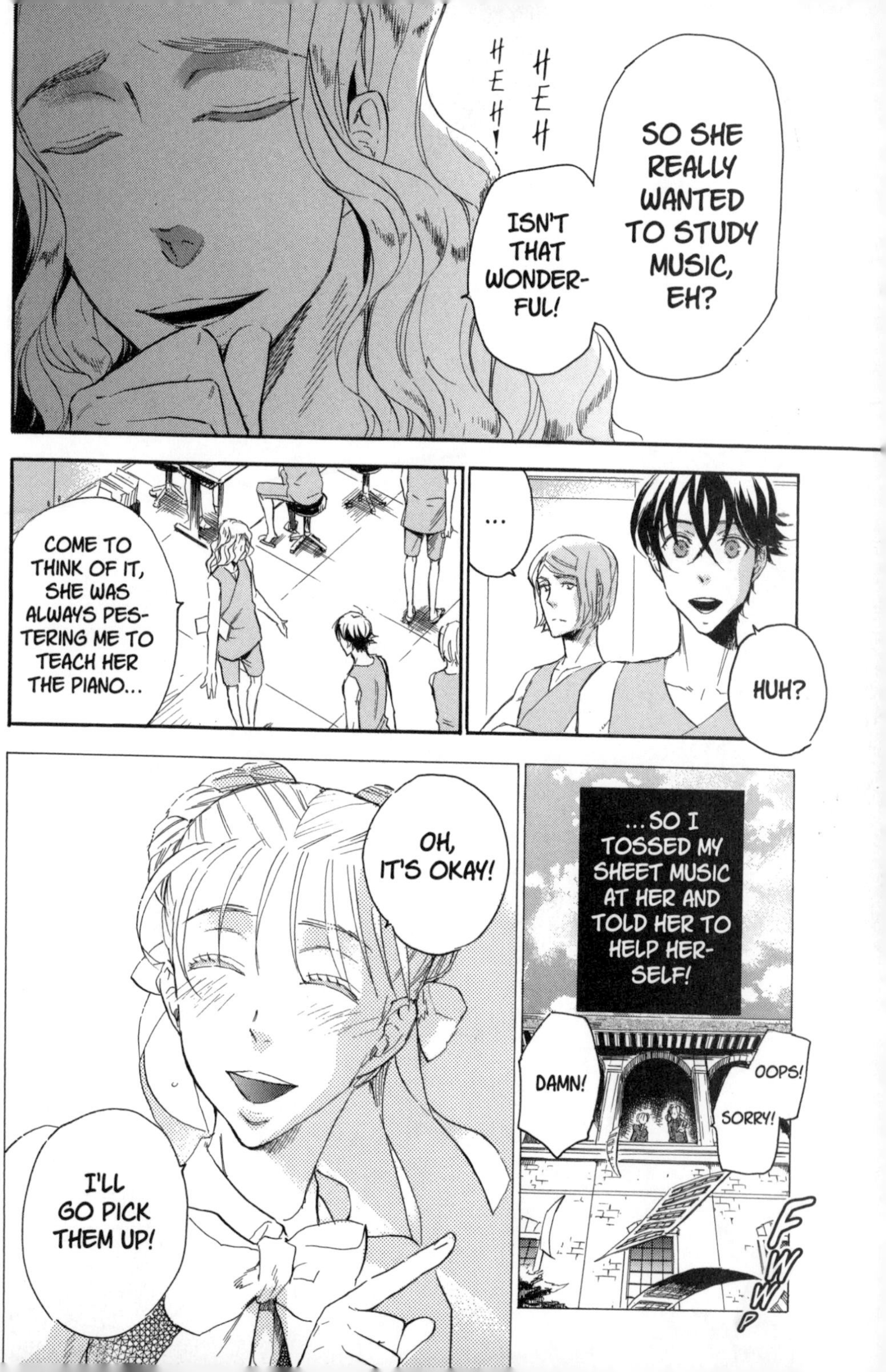
SO SHE REALLY WANTED TO STUDY MUSIC, EH?
HEH HEH
HEH!
ISN'T THAT WONDERFUL!
...
HUH?
COME TO THINK OF IT, SHE WAS ALWAYS PESTERING ME TO TEACH HER THE PIANO...
...SO I TOSSED MY SHEET MUSIC AT HER AND TOLD HER TO HELP HERSELF!
OOPS!
SORRY!
DAMN!
FWWP
OH, IT'S OKAY!
I'LL GO PICK THEM UP!

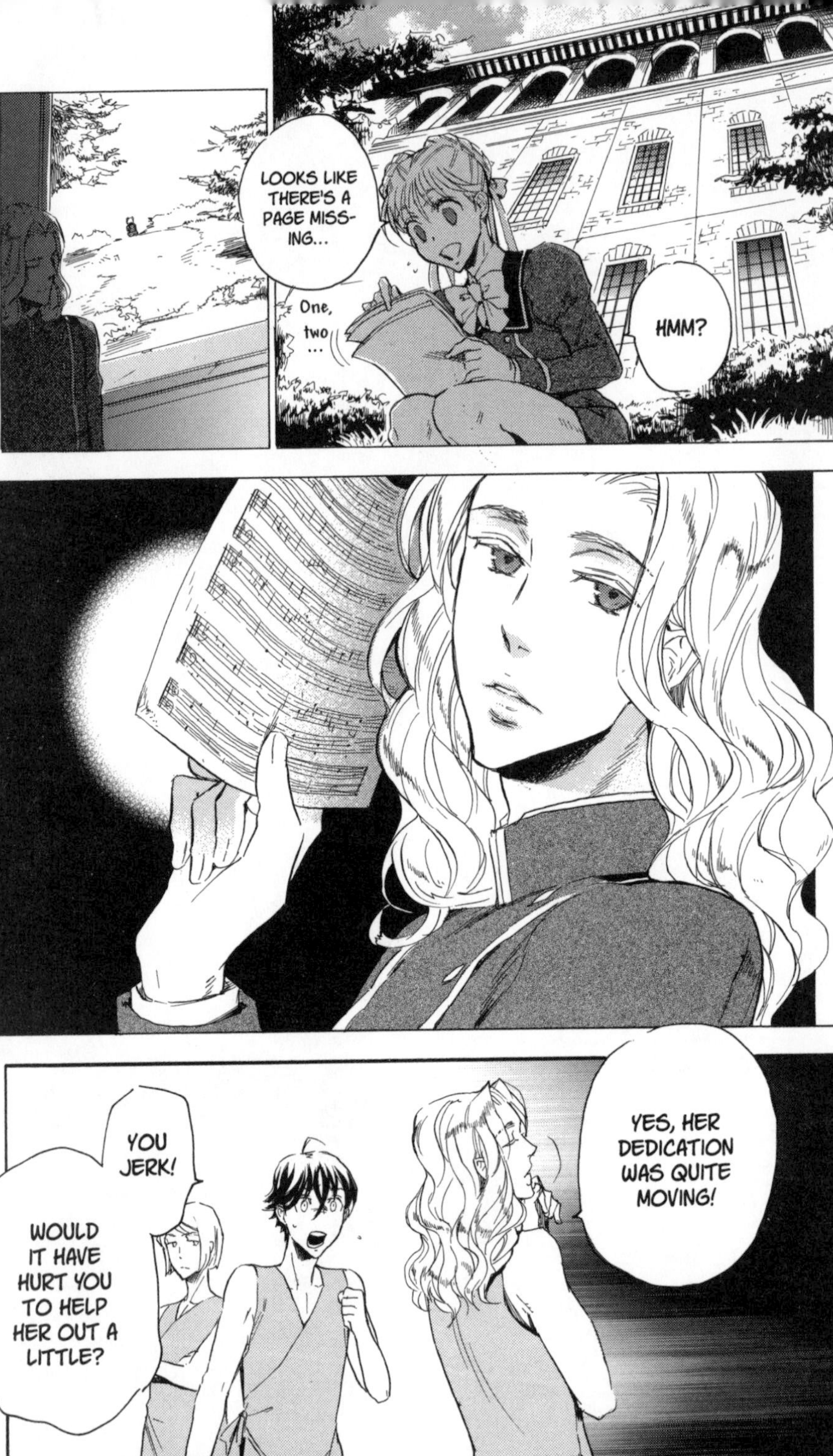

LOOKS LIKE THERE'S A PAGE MISSING...
One, two ...
HMM?
YES, HER DEDICATION WAS QUITE MOVING!
YOU JERK!
WOULD IT HAVE HURT YOU TO HELP HER OUT A LITTLE?

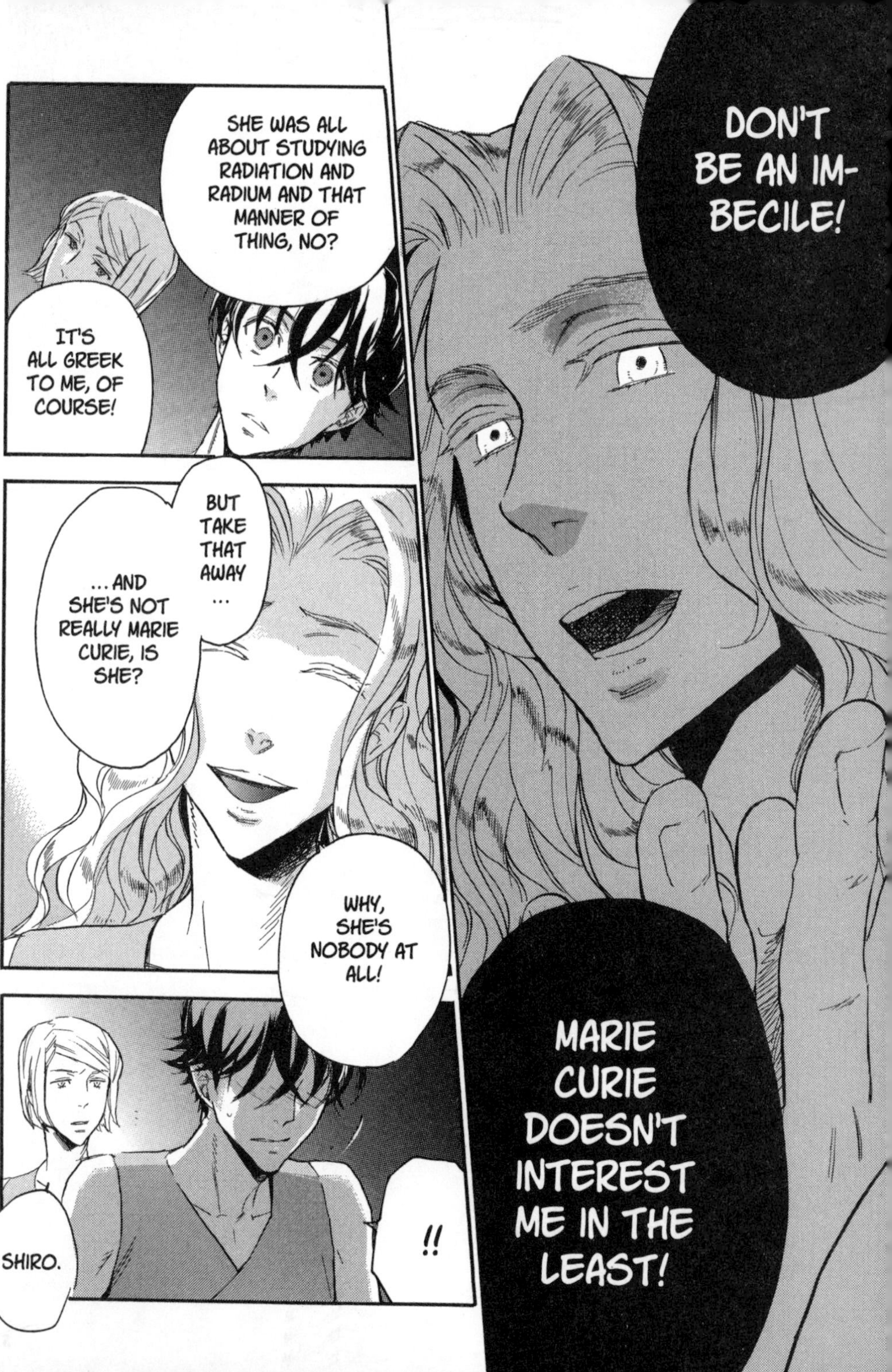
DON'T BE AN IM-BECILE!
MARIE CURIE DOESN'T INTEREST ME IN THE LEAST!
SHE WAS ALL ABOUT STUDYING RADIATION AND RADIUM AND THAT MANNER OF THING, NO?
IT'S ALL GREEK TO ME, OF COURSE!
BUT TAKE THAT AWAY ...
... AND SHE'S NOT REALLY MARIE CURIE, IS SHE?
WHY, SHE'S NOBODY AT ALL!
!!
SHIRO.

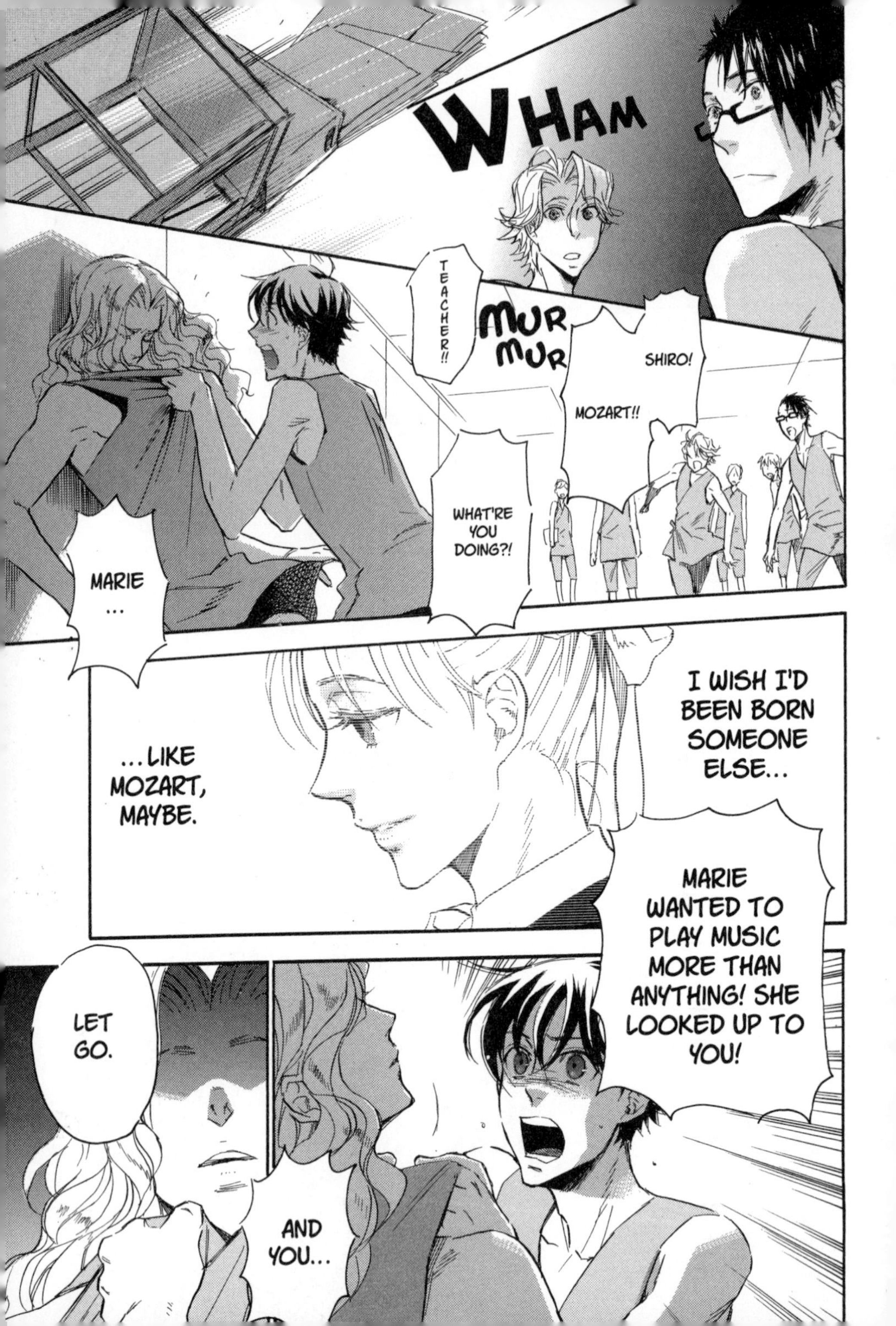
WHAM
MUR MUR
SHIRO!
MOZART!!
WHAT'RE YOU DOING?!
TEACHER!!
MARIE...
I WISH I'D BEEN BORN SOMEONE ELSE...
...LIKE MOZART, MAYBE.
MARIE WANTED TO PLAY MUSIC MORE THAN ANYTHING! SHE LOOKED UP TO YOU!
LET GO.
AND YOU...

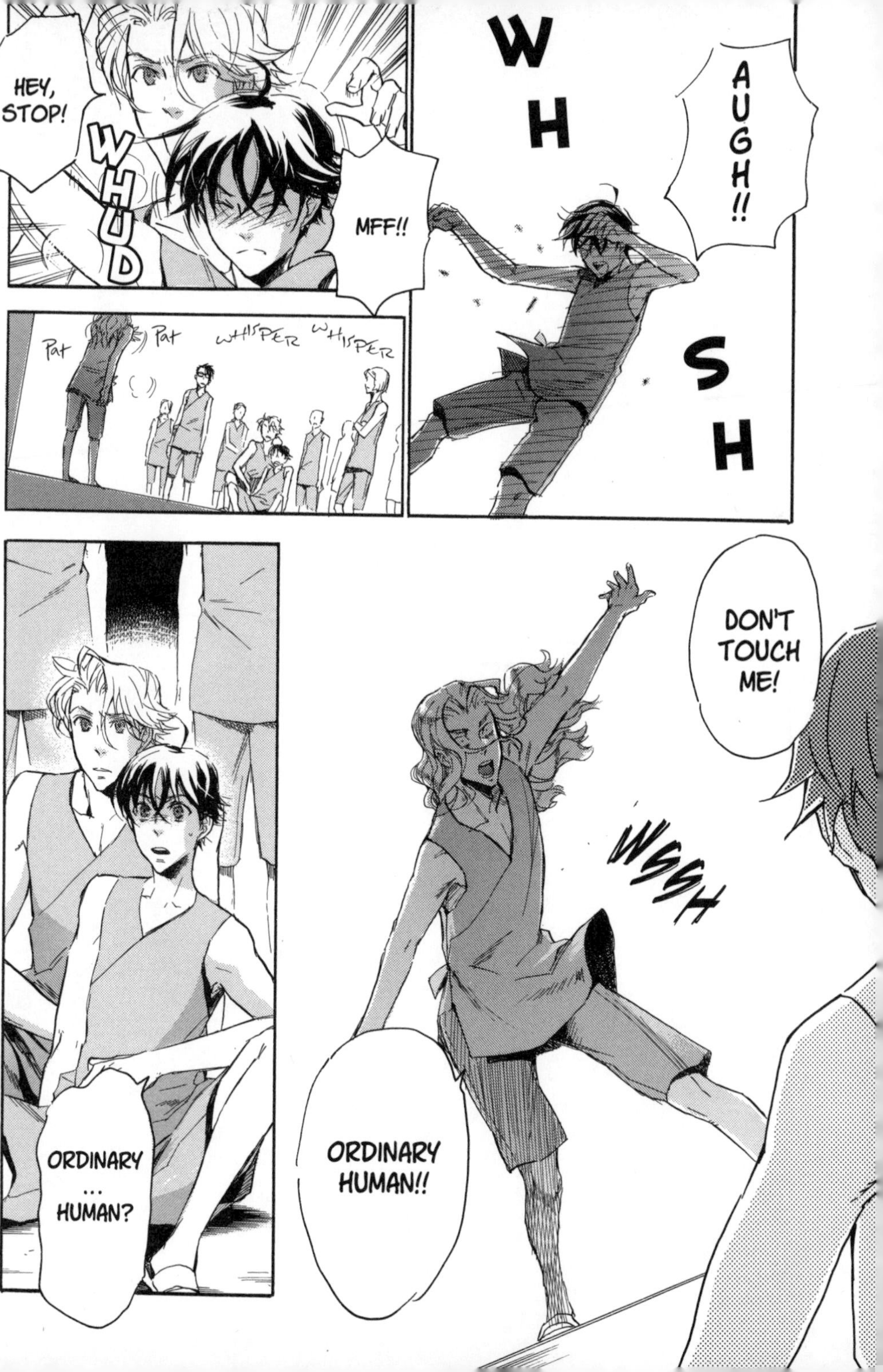
AUGH!!
WHSH
MFF!!
HEY, STOP!
WHUD
Pat Pat
WHISPER WHISPER
DON'T TOUCH ME!
WSSH
ORDINARY HUMAN!!
ORDINARY ... HUMAN?

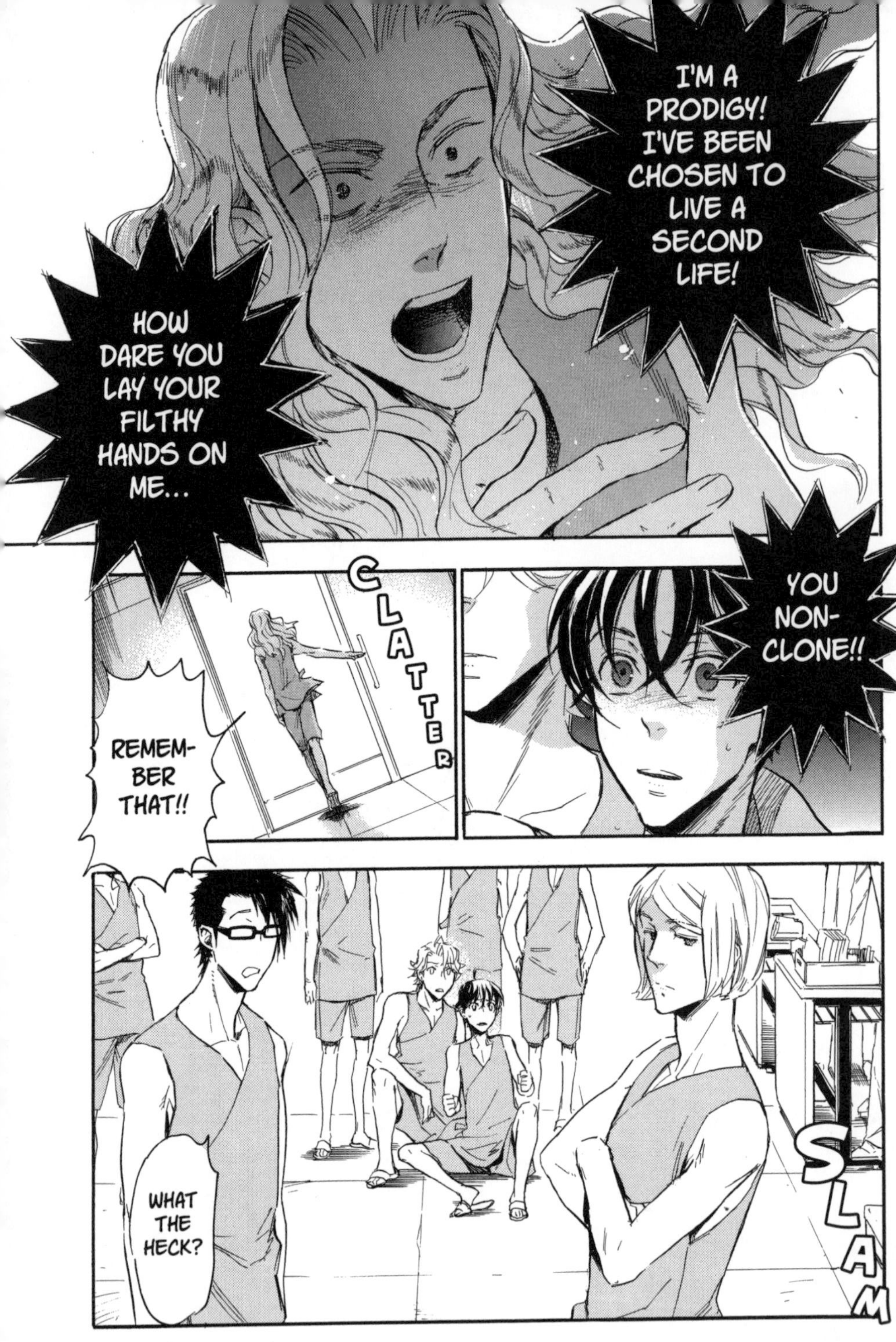
I'M A PRODIGY! I'VE BEEN CHOSEN TO LIVE A SECOND LIFE!
HOW DARE YOU LAY YOUR FILTHY HANDS ON ME...
YOU NON-CLONE!!
CLATTER
REMEMBER THAT!!
SLAM
WHAT THE HECK?

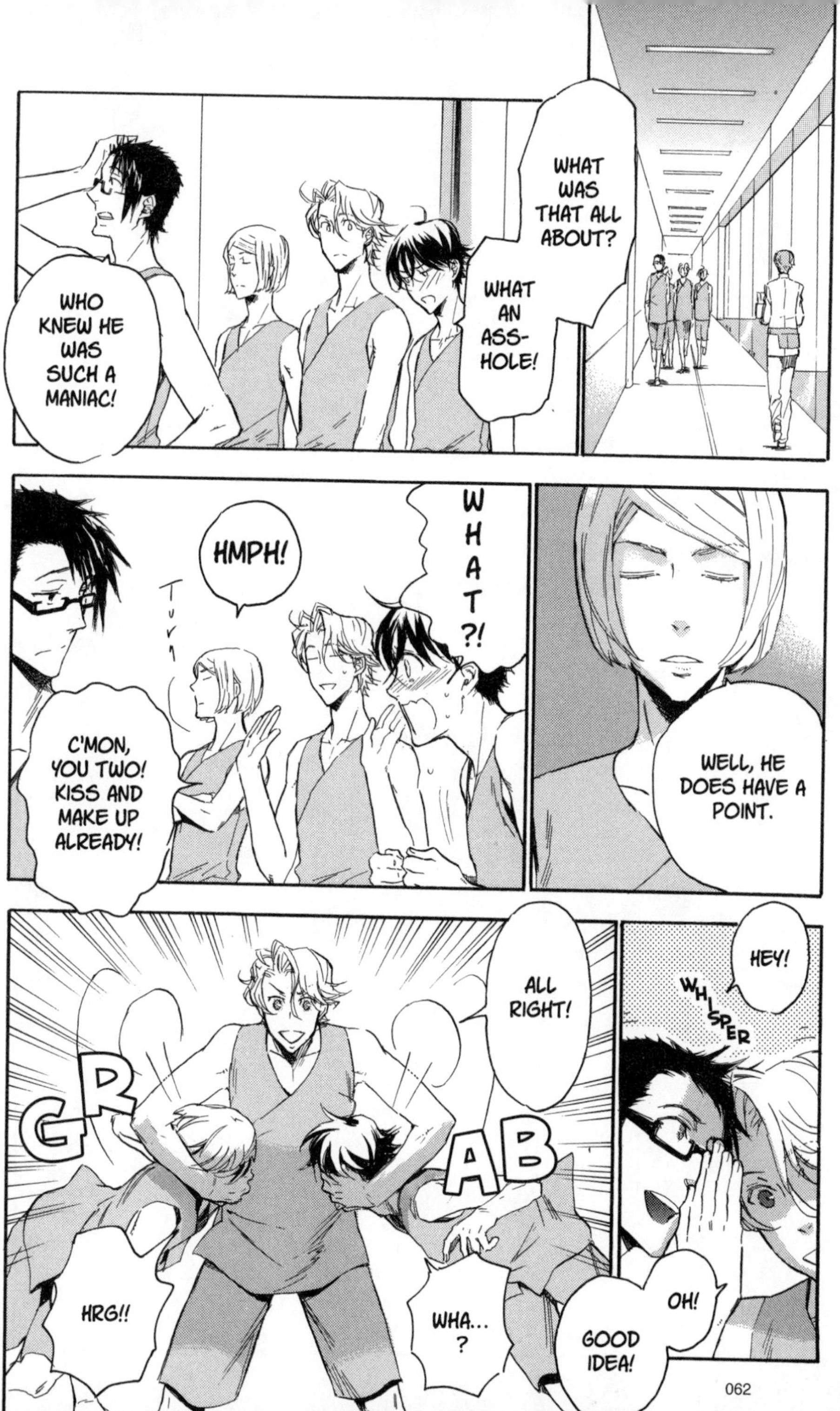
WHAT WAS THAT ALL ABOUT?
WHAT AN ASS-HOLE!
WHO KNEW HE WAS SUCH A MANIAC!
WELL, HE DOES HAVE A POINT.
WHAT?!
HMPH!
Turn
C'MON, YOU TWO! KISS AND MAKE UP ALREADY!
HEY!
WHISPER
OH! GOOD IDEA!
ALL RIGHT!
GRAB
WHA... ?
HRG!!

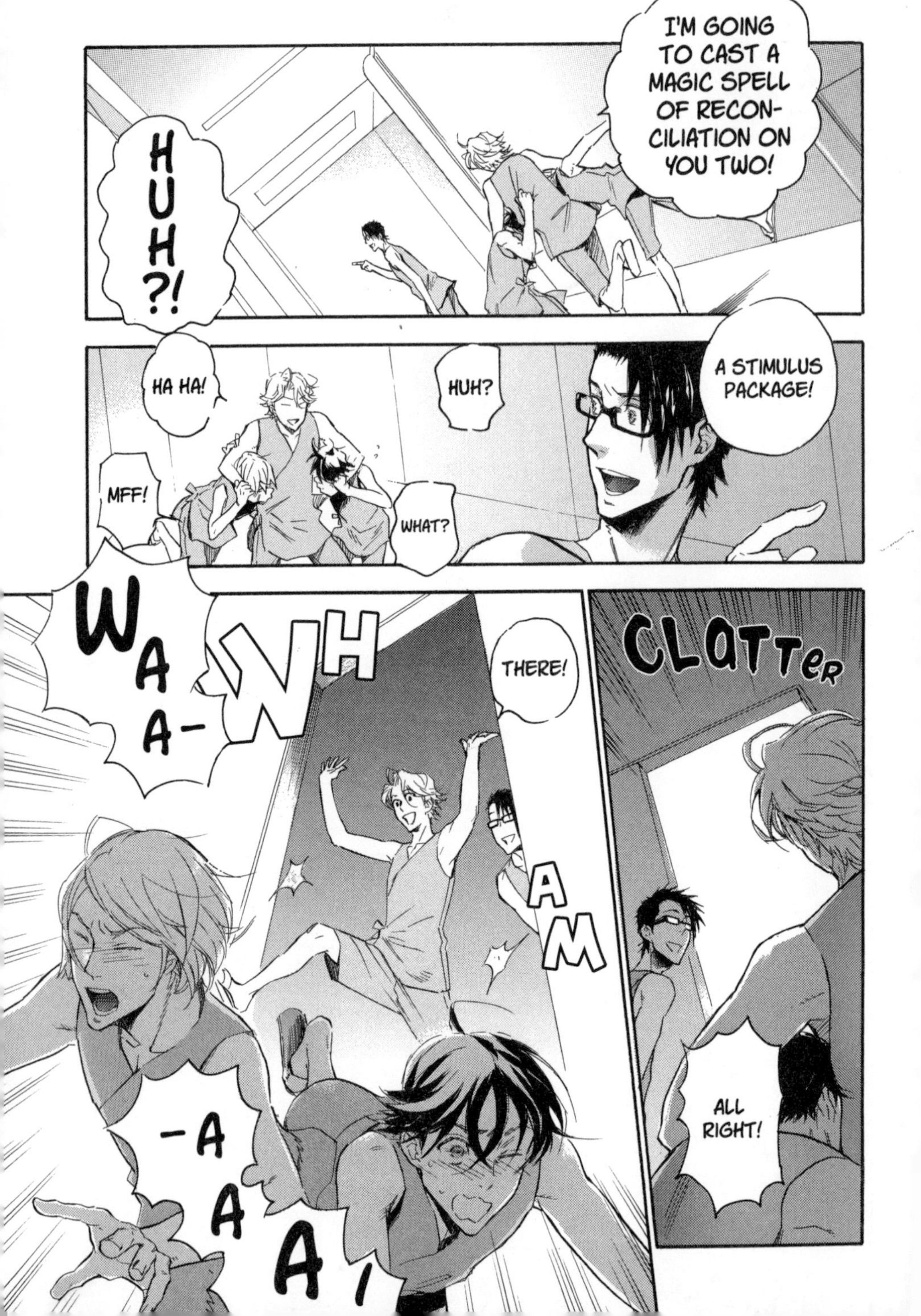
I'M GOING TO CAST A MAGIC SPELL OF RECON-CILIATION ON YOU TWO!
HUH?!
A STIMULUS PACKAGE!
HUH?
WHAT?
HA HA!
MFF!
CLATTER
ALL RIGHT!
THERE!
WAAA-
WHAM
-AAAAI

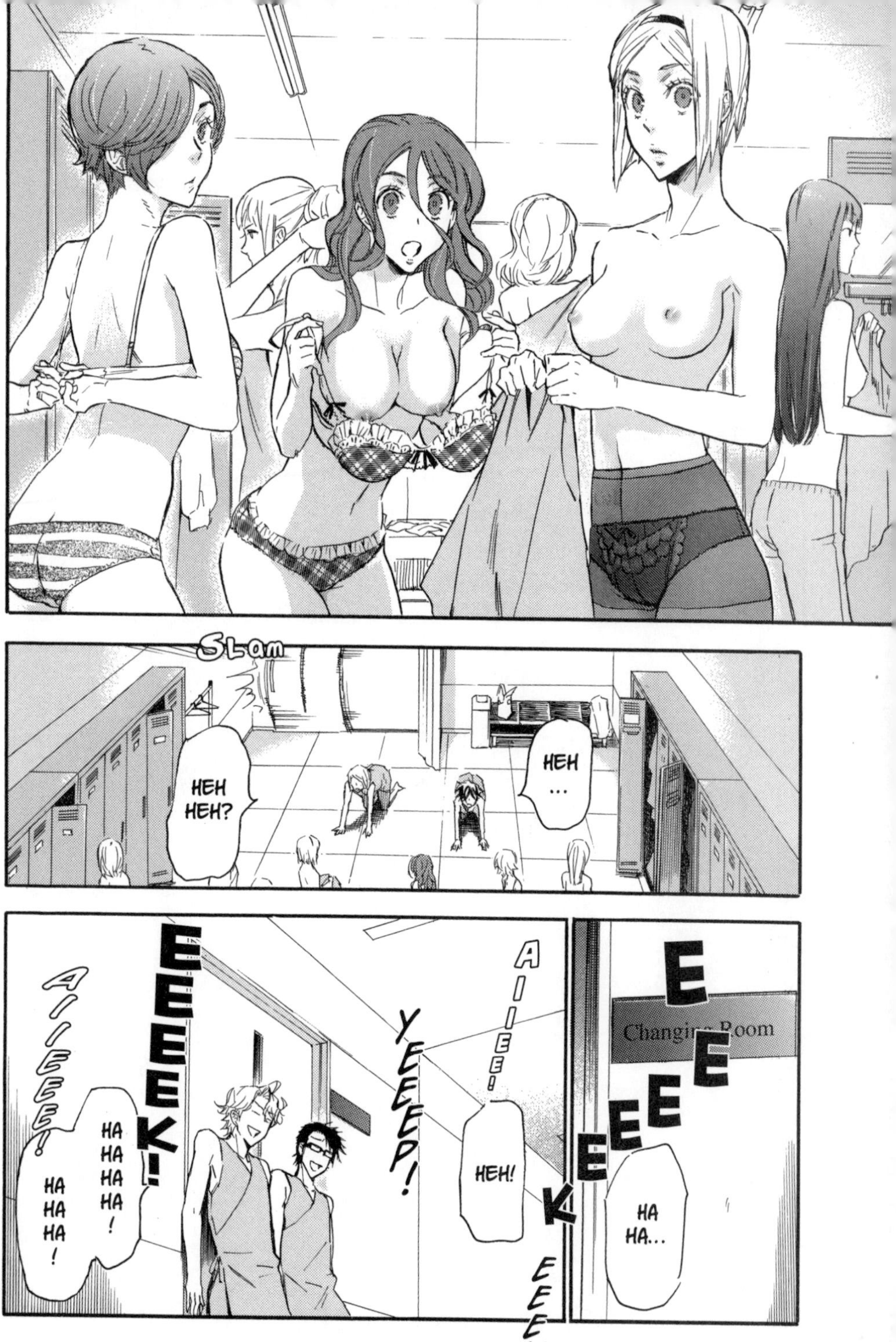

SLam
HEH ...
HEH HEH?
EEEEEEK
HA HA...
EEEK
AIIEE!
HEH!
YEEEP!
EEEEK!
HA HA HA HA!
AIIEEE!
HA HA HA!
Changing Room

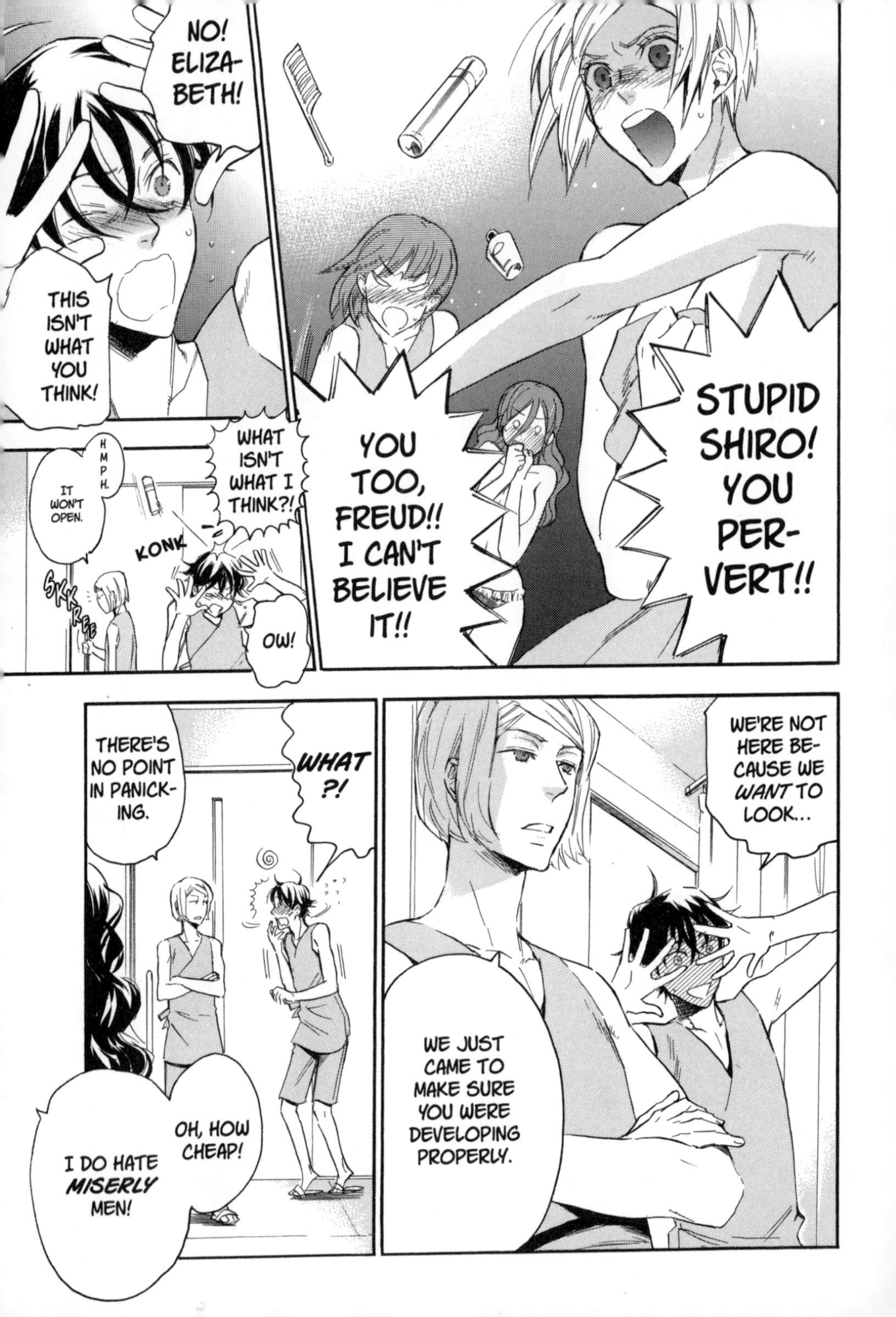
STUPID SHIRO! YOU PER-VERT!!
YOU TOO, FREUD!! I CAN'T BELIEVE IT!!
NO! ELIZA-BETH!
THIS ISN'T WHAT YOU THINK!
WHAT ISN'T WHAT I THINK?!
HMPH.
IT WON'T OPEN.
KONK
SKKREE
OW!
WE'RE NOT HERE BE-CAUSE WE WANT TO LOOK...
WE JUST CAME TO MAKE SURE YOU WERE DEVELOPING PROPERLY.
WHAT ?!
THERE'S NO POINT IN PANICK-ING.
OH, HOW CHEAP!
I DO HATE MISERLY MEN!

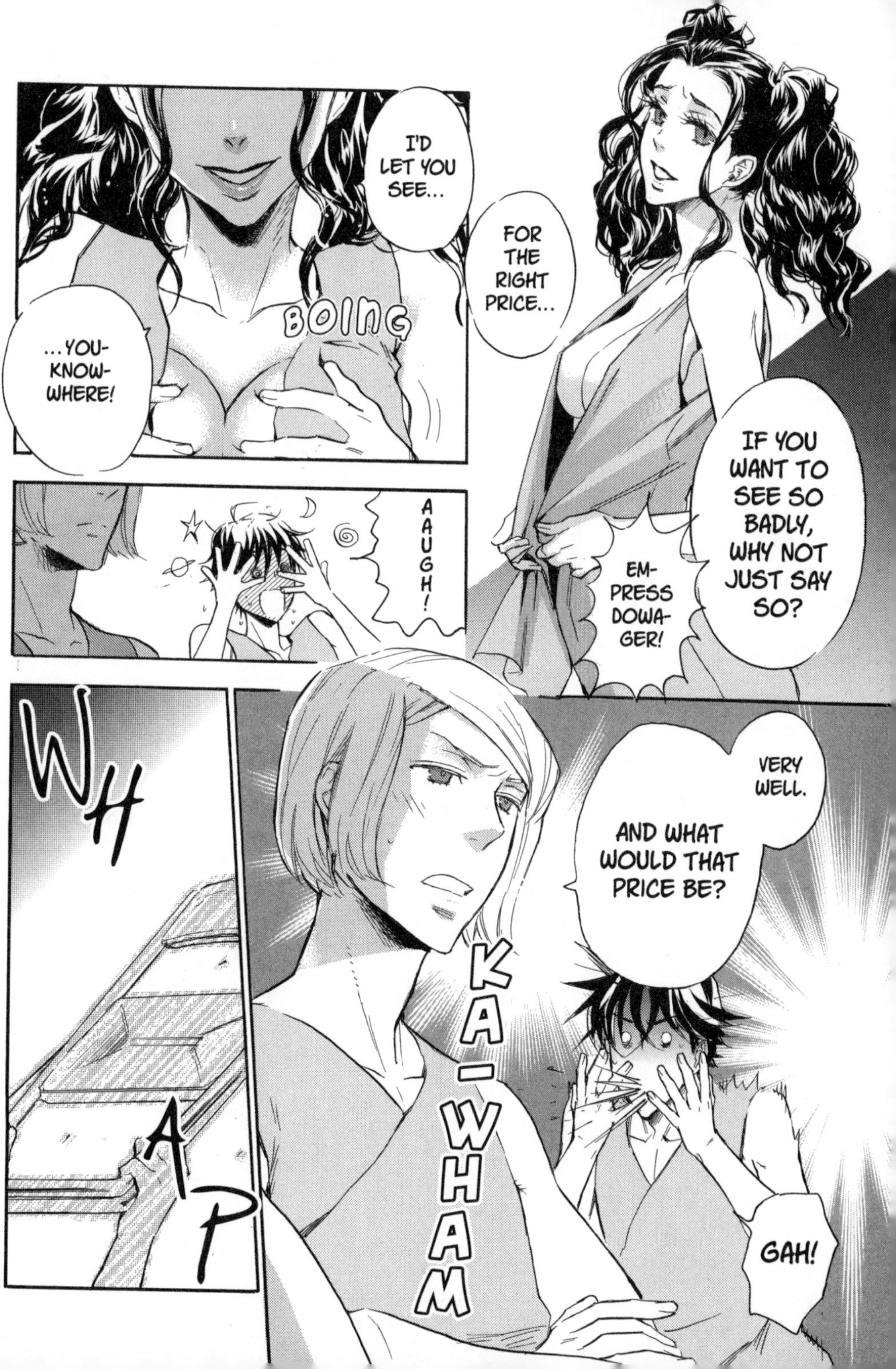
IF YOU WANT TO SEE SO BADLY, WHY NOT JUST SAY SO?
EM-PRESS DOWA-GER!
I'D LET YOU SEE...
FOR THE RIGHT PRICE...
BOING
...YOU-KNOW-WHERE!
AAUGH!
VERY WELL.
AND WHAT WOULD THAT PRICE BE?
KA-WHAM
GAH!
WHAP

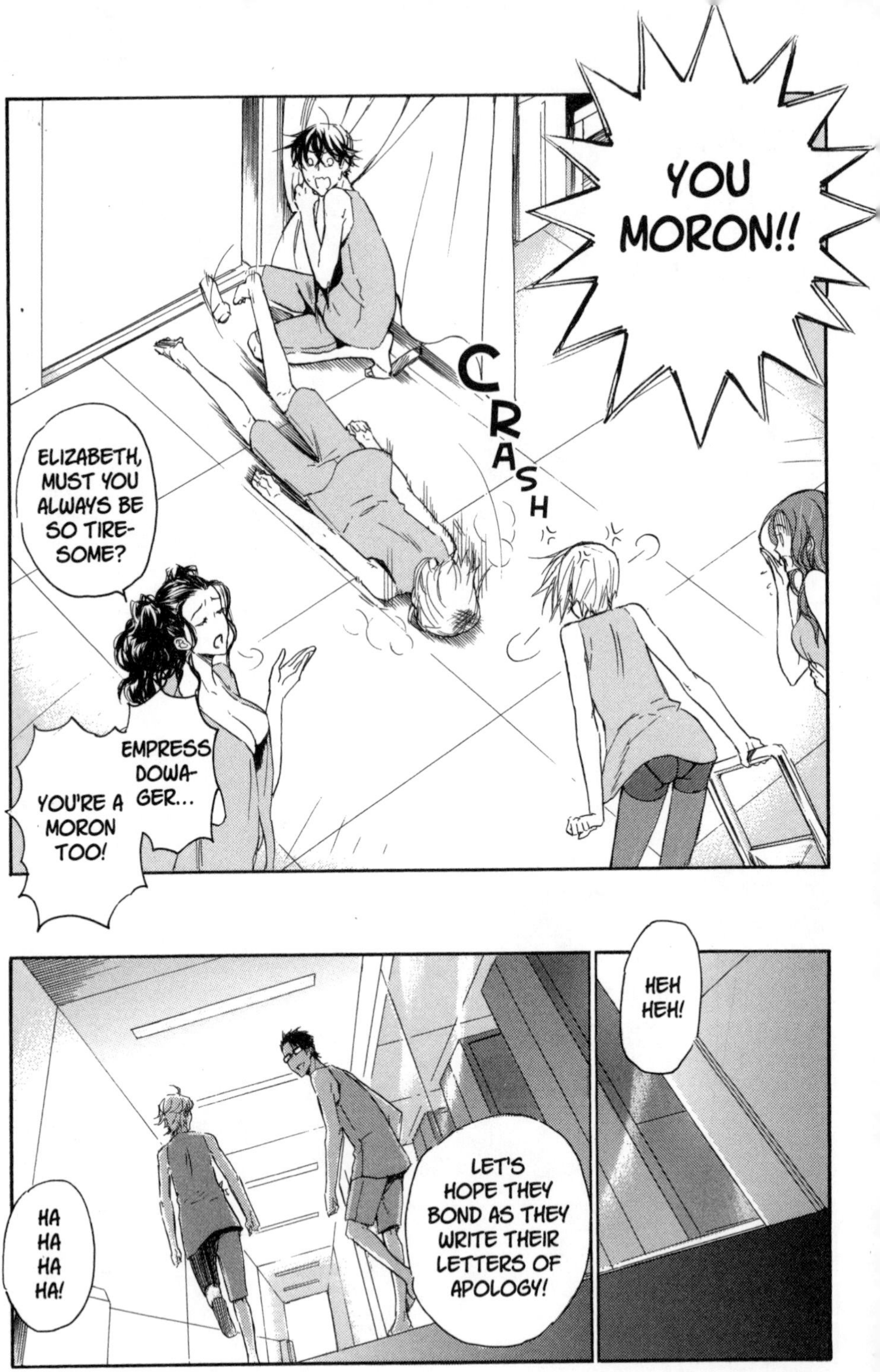
YOU MORON!!
CRASH
ELIZABETH, MUST YOU ALWAYS BE SO TIRE-SOME?
EMPRESS DOWA-GER...
YOU'RE A MORON TOO!
HEH HEH!
LET'S HOPE THEY BOND AS THEY WRITE THEIR LETTERS OF APOLOGY!
HA HA HA HA!

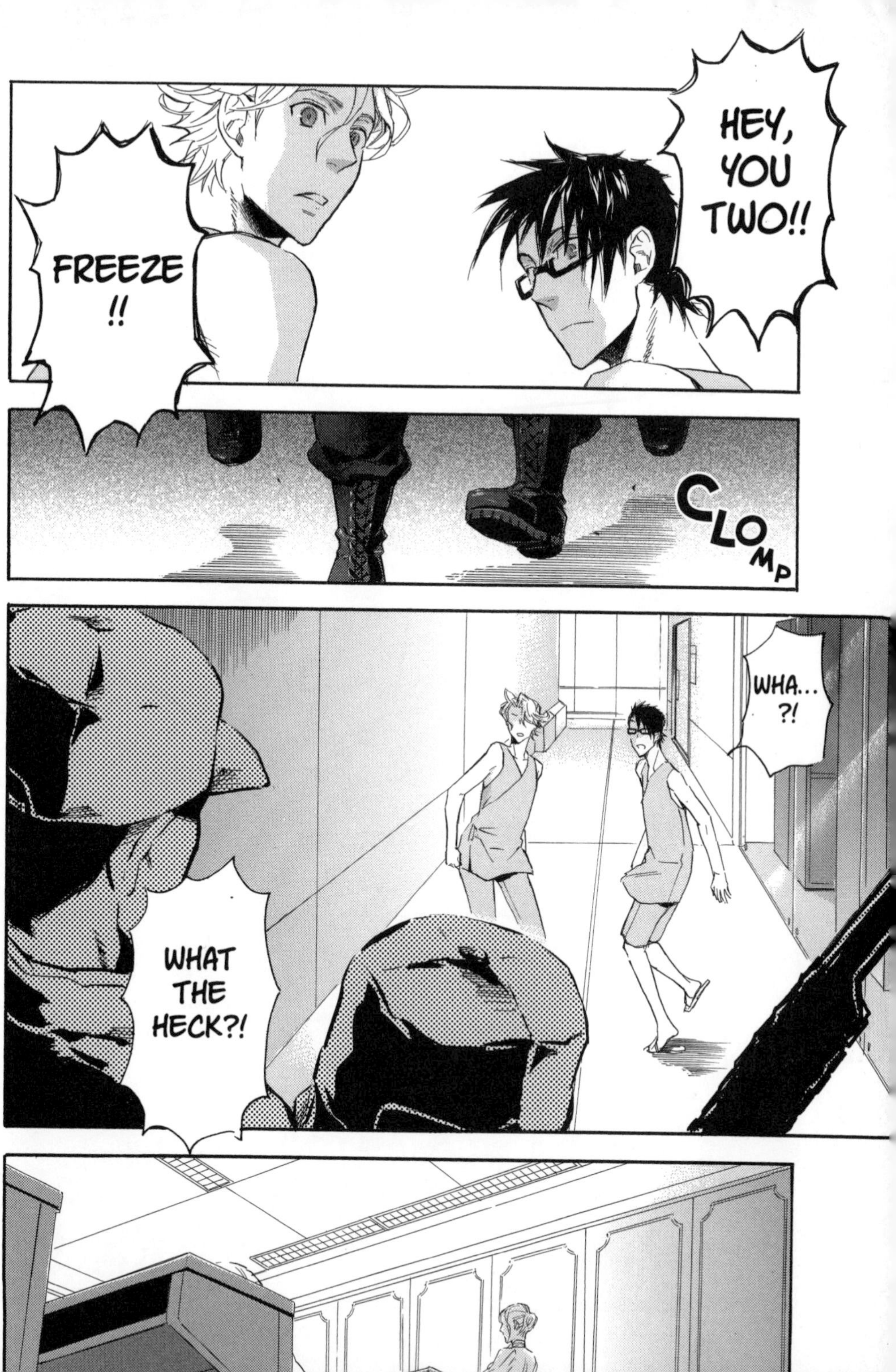
HEY, YOU TWO!!
FREEZE!!
CLOMP
WHA...?!
WHAT THE HECK?!

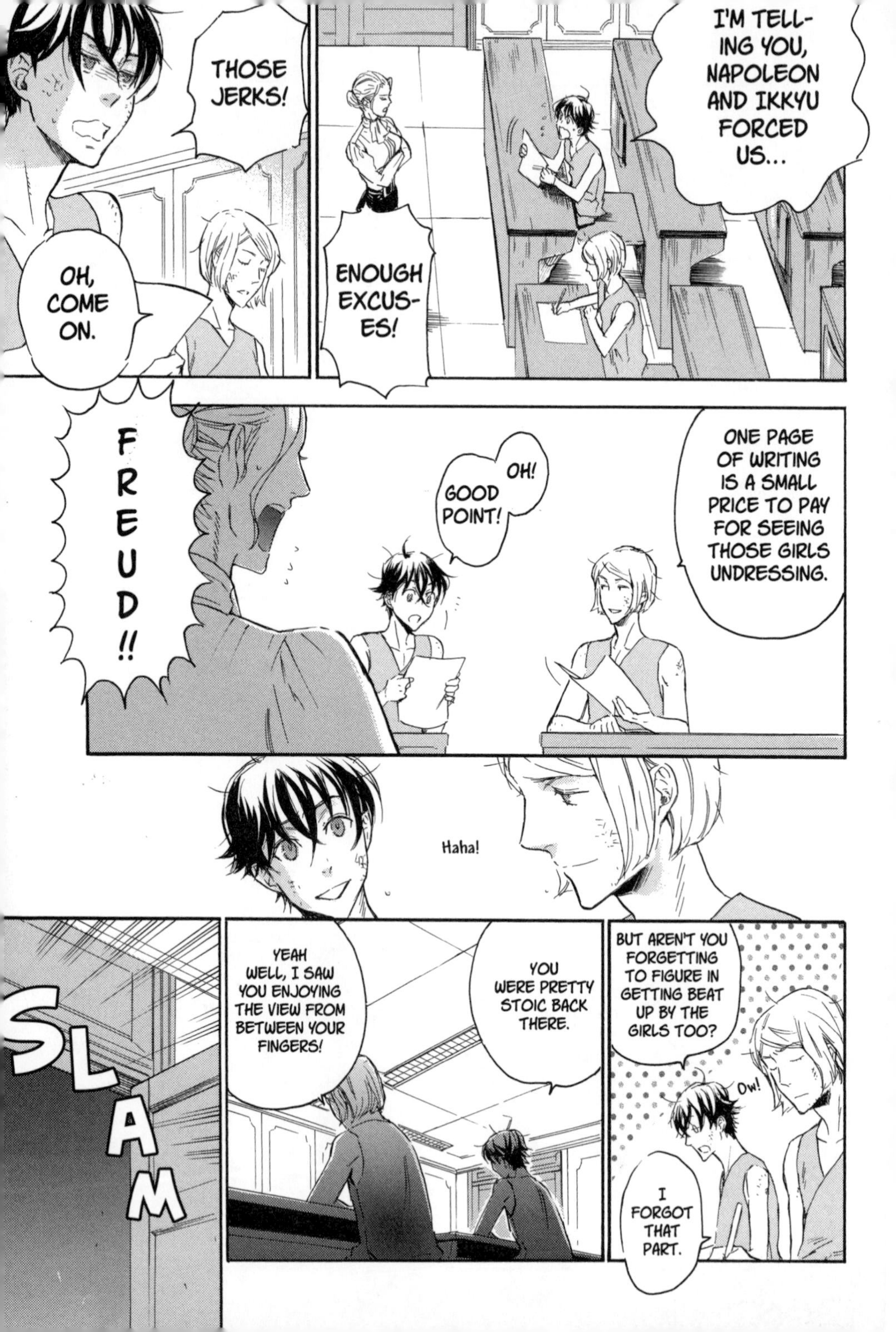
I'M TELLING YOU, NAPOLEON AND IKKYU FORCED US...
ENOUGH EXCUSES!
THOSE JERKS!
OH, COME ON.
ONE PAGE OF WRITING IS A SMALL PRICE TO PAY FOR SEEING THOSE GIRLS UNDRESSING.
OH! GOOD POINT!
FREUD!!
Haha!
BUT AREN'T YOU FORGETTING TO FIGURE IN GETTING BEAT UP BY THE GIRLS TOO?
Ow!
I FORGOT THAT PART.
YOU WERE PRETTY STOIC BACK THERE.
YEAH WELL, I SAW YOU ENJOYING THE VIEW FROM BETWEEN YOUR FINGERS!
SLAM

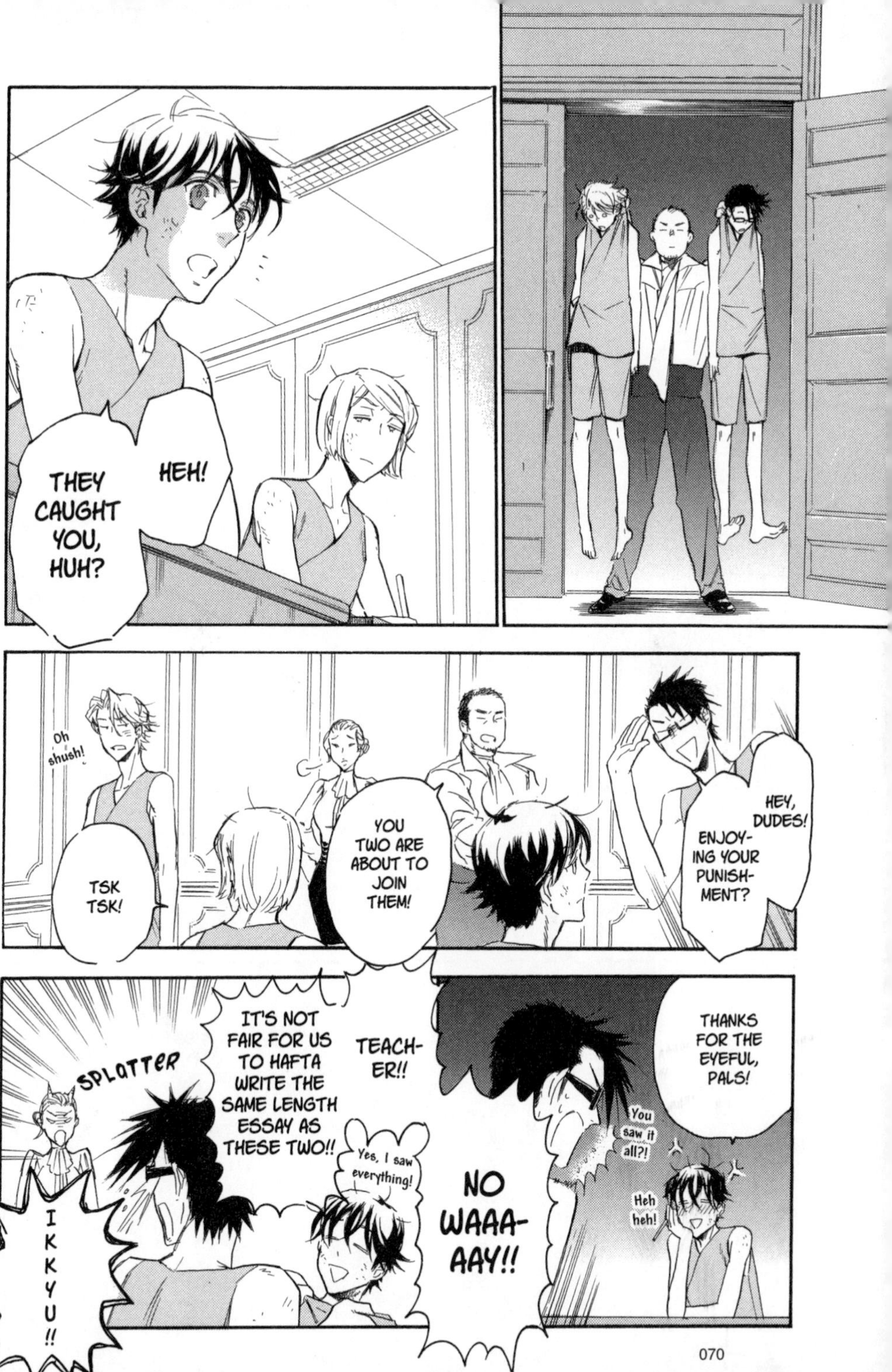
HEH!
THEY CAUGHT YOU, HUH?
HEY, DUDES! ENJOYING YOUR PUNISHMENT?
YOU TWO ARE ABOUT TO JOIN THEM!
TSK TSK!
Oh shush!
THANKS FOR THE EYEFUL, PALS!
You saw it all?!
Heh heh!
NO WAAAAAY!!
TEACHER!!
Yes, I saw everything!
IT'S NOT FAIR FOR US TO HAFTA WRITE THE SAME LENGTH ESSAY AS THESE TWO!!
SPLATTER
IKKYU!!

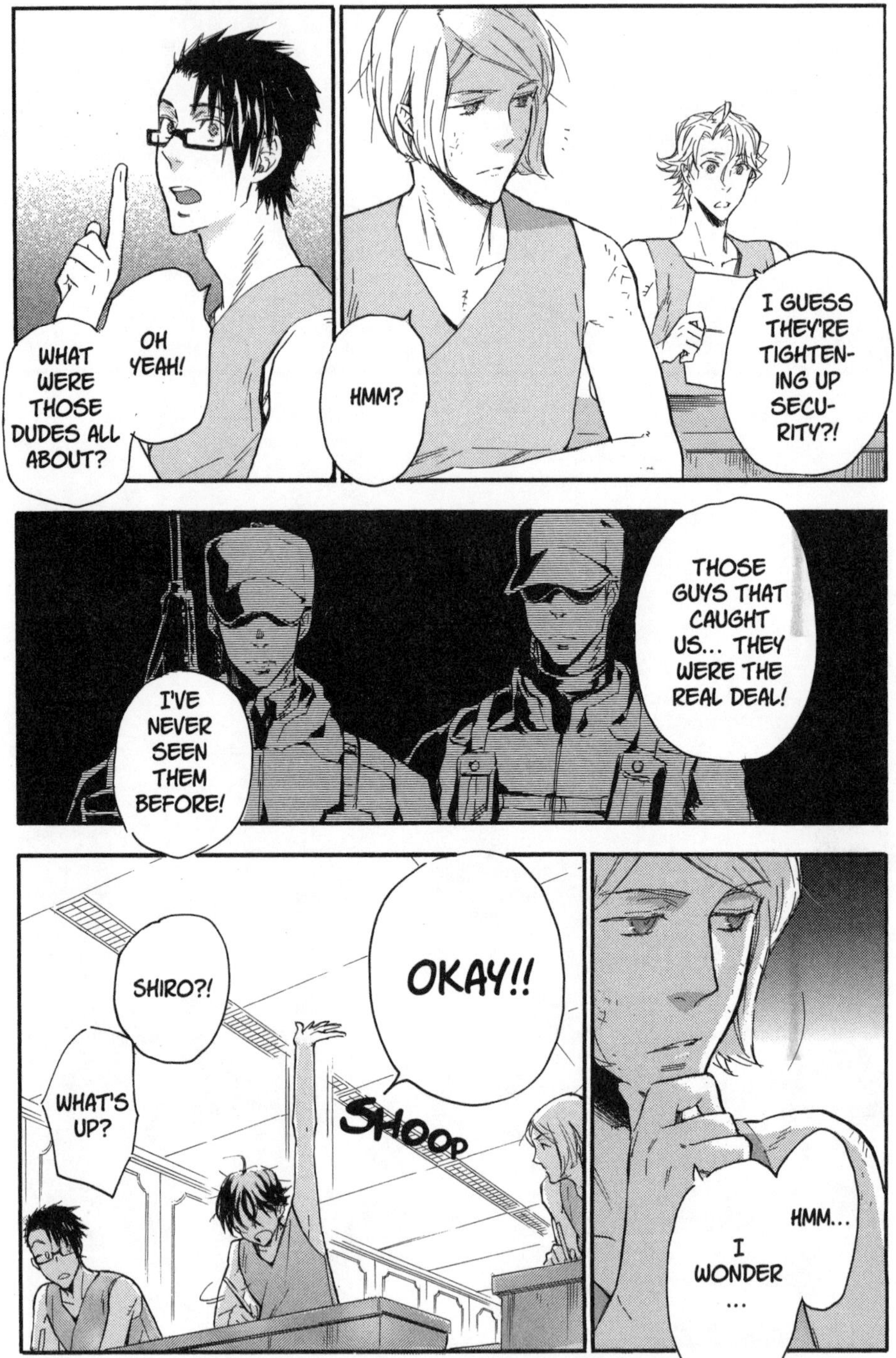
I GUESS THEY'RE TIGHTEN-ING UP SECU-RITY?!
HMM?
OH YEAH!
WHAT WERE THOSE DUDES ALL ABOUT?
THOSE GUYS THAT CAUGHT US... THEY WERE THE REAL DEAL!
I'VE NEVER SEEN THEM BEFORE!
HMM...
I WONDER ...
OKAY!!
SHIRO?!
SHOOP
WHAT'S UP?

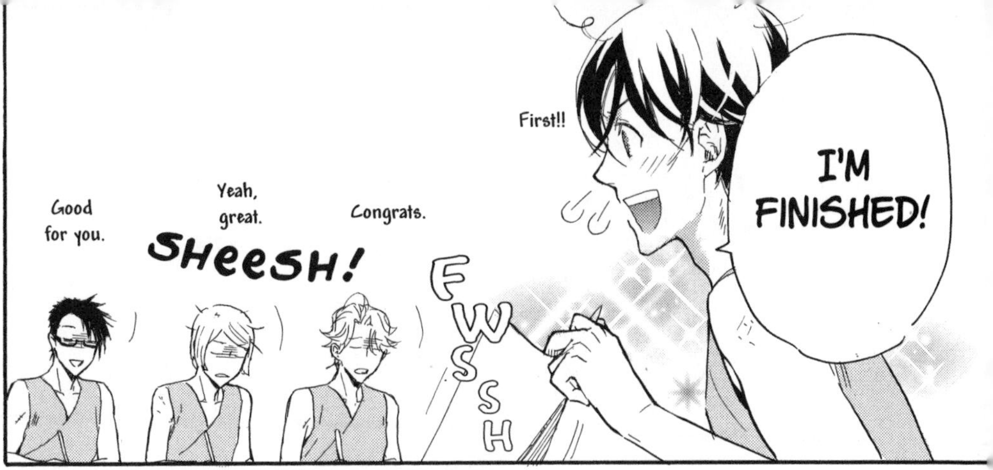
I'M FINISHED!
First!!
FWSSH
Congrats.
SHEESH!
Yeah, great.
Good for you.

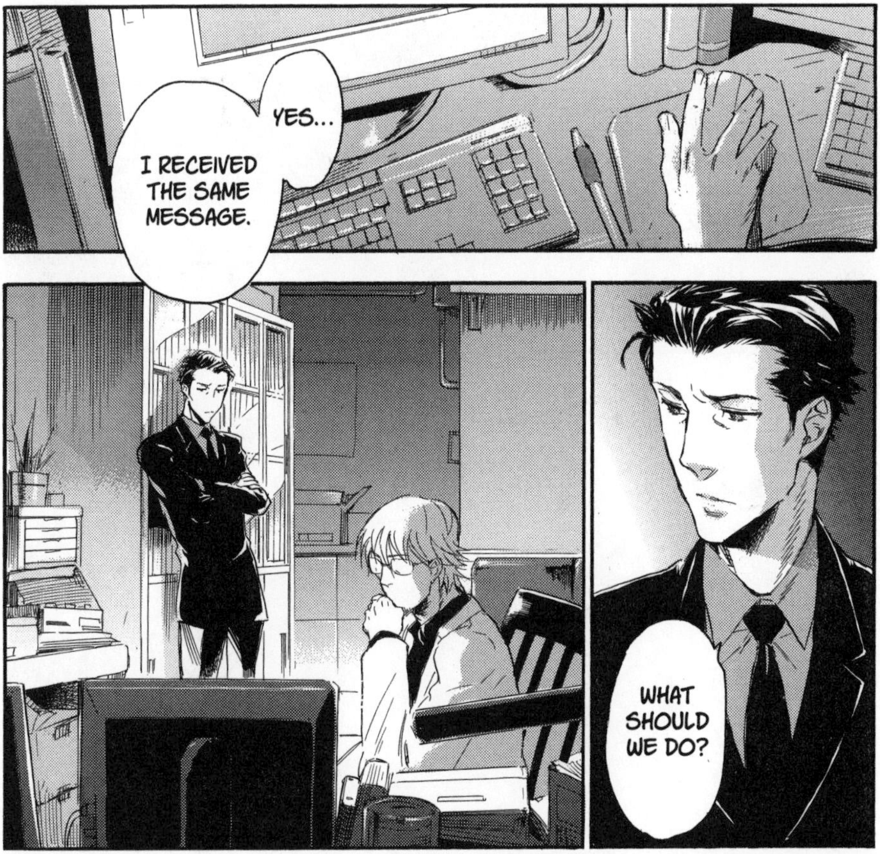
YES...
I RECEIVED THE SAME MESSAGE.
WHAT SHOULD WE DO?

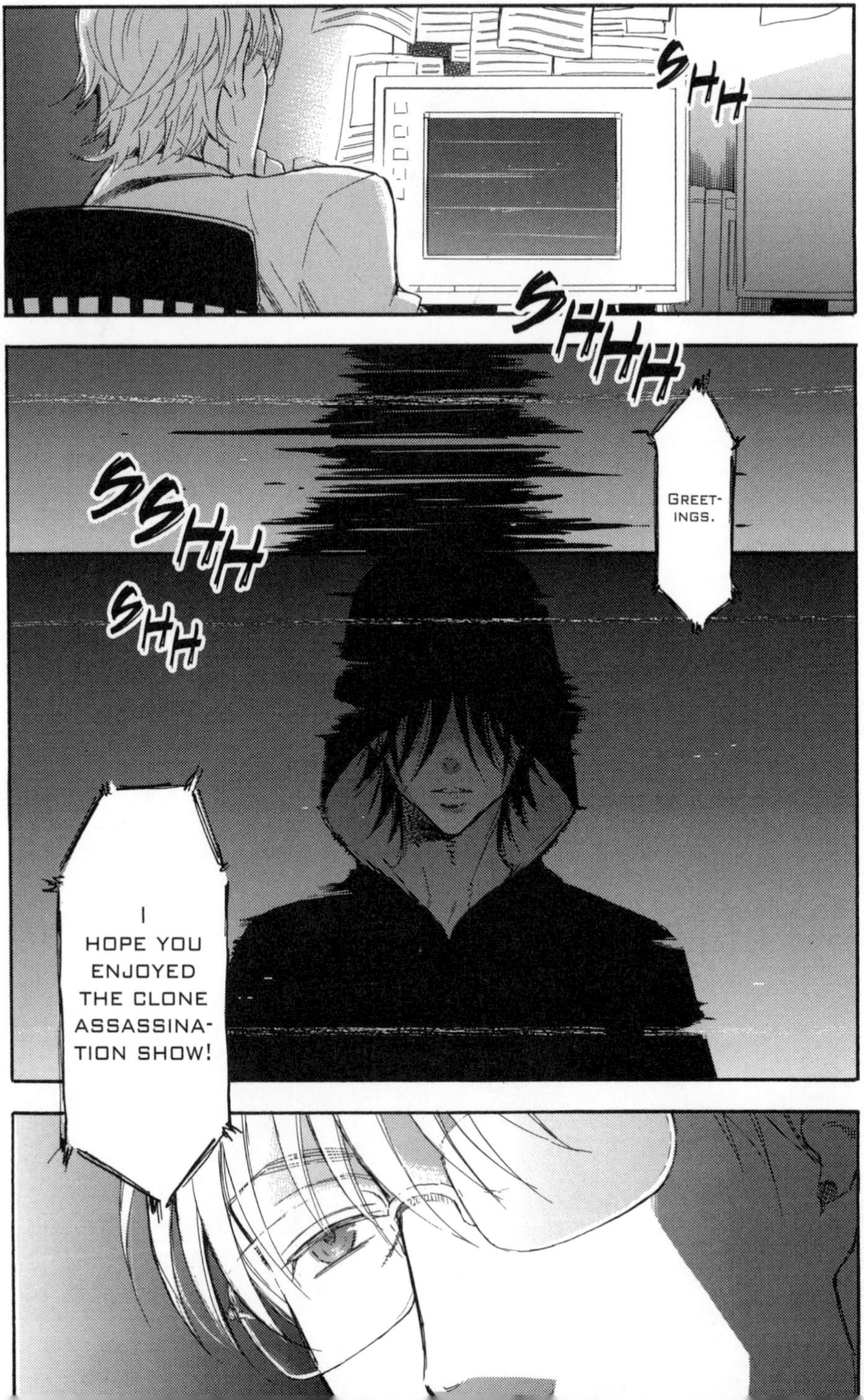
SHH
SHHHH
GREETINGS.
SSHHH
SHH
I HOPE YOU ENJOYED THE CLONE ASSASSINATION SHOW!

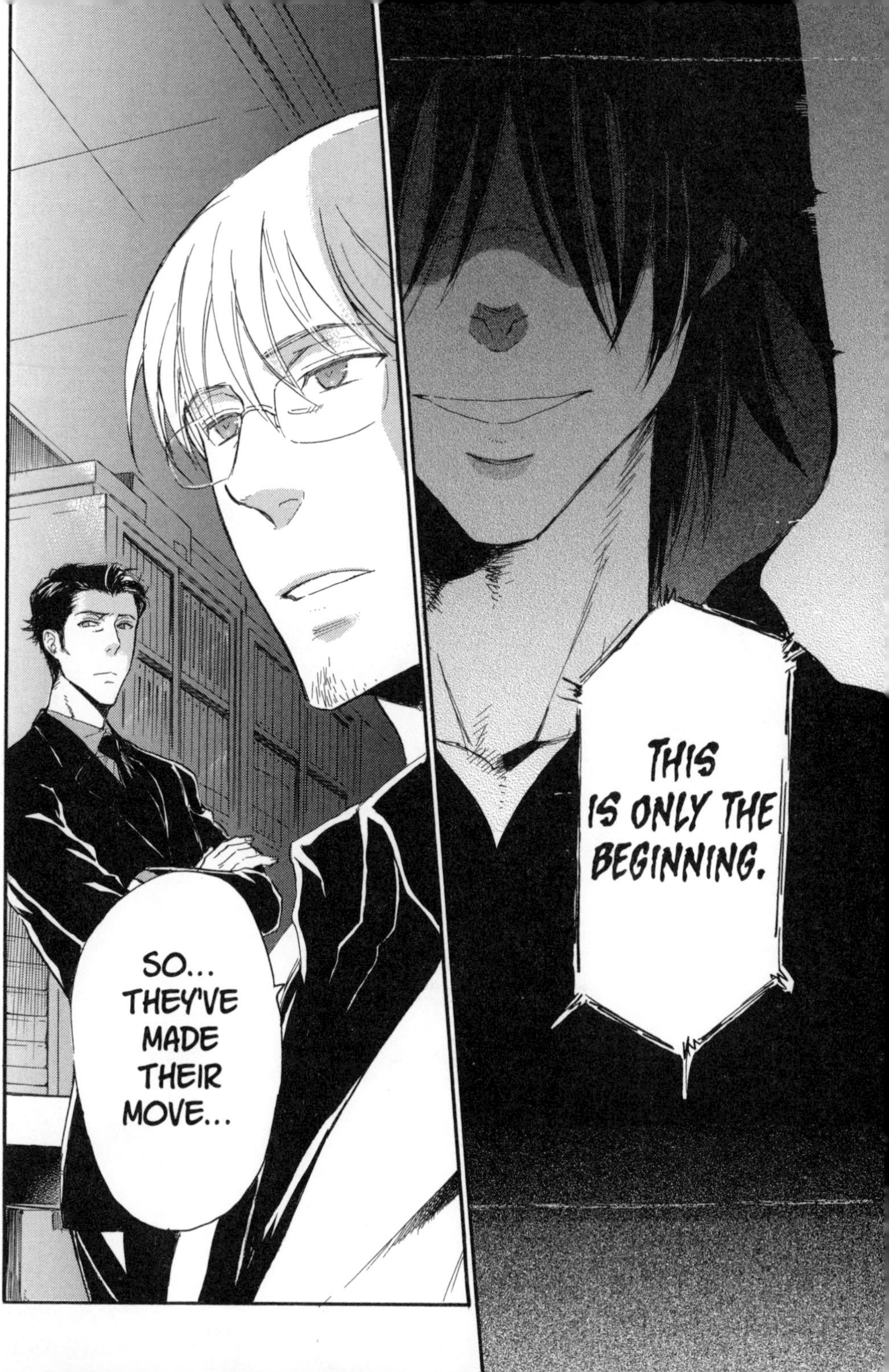
THIS IS ONLY THE BEGINNING.
SO... THEY'VE MADE THEIR MOVE...

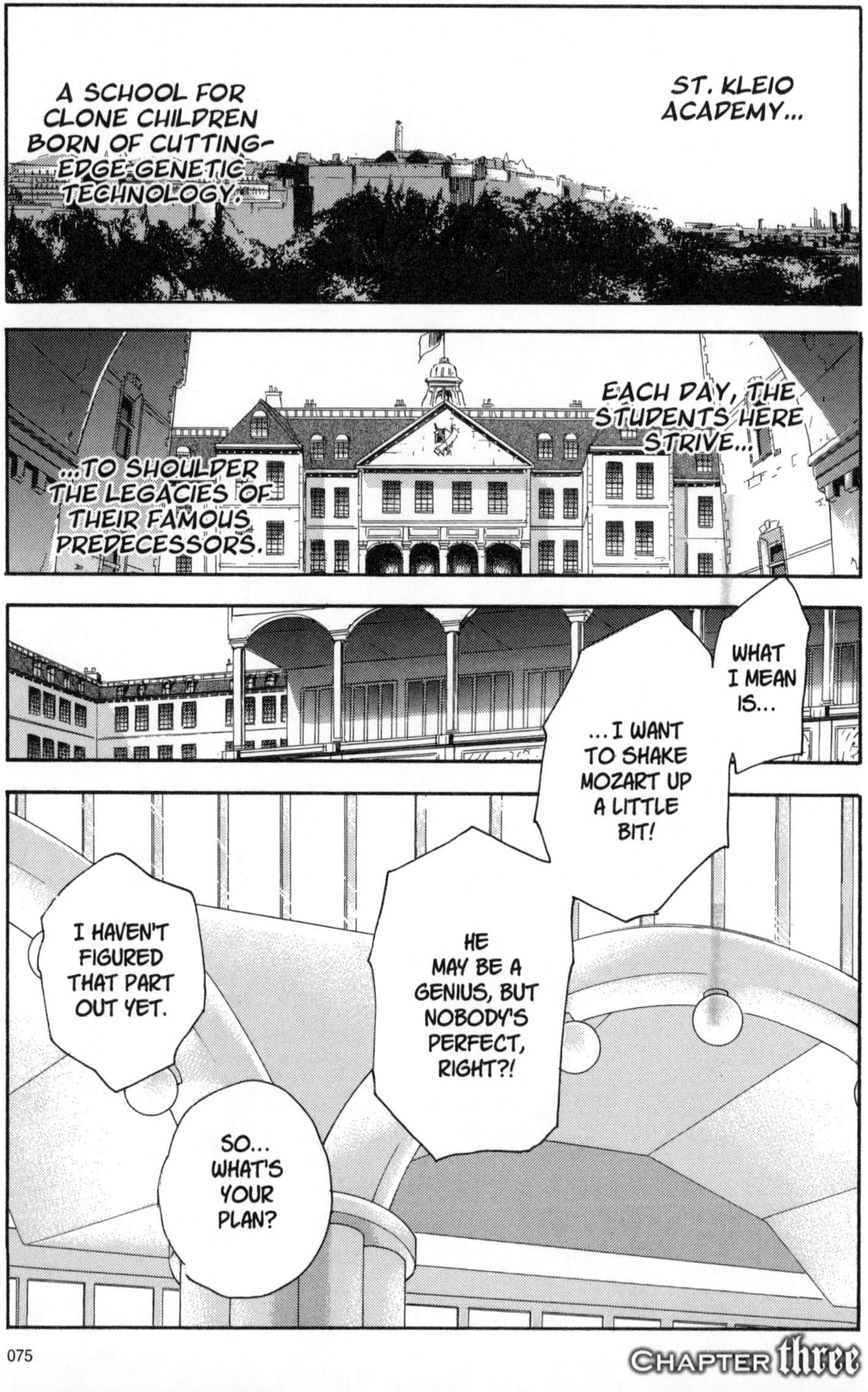
ST. KLEIO ACADEMY...
A SCHOOL FOR CLONE CHILDREN BORN OF CUTTING-EDGE GENETIC TECHNOLOGY.
EACH DAY, THE STUDENTS HERE STRIVE...
...TO SHOULDER THE LEGACIES OF THEIR FAMOUS PREDECESSORS.
WHAT I MEAN IS...
...I WANT TO SHAKE MOZART UP A LITTLE BIT!
HE MAY BE A GENIUS, BUT NOBODY'S PERFECT, RIGHT?!
SO... WHAT'S YOUR PLAN?
I HAVEN'T FIGURED THAT PART OUT YET.

CHAPTER three

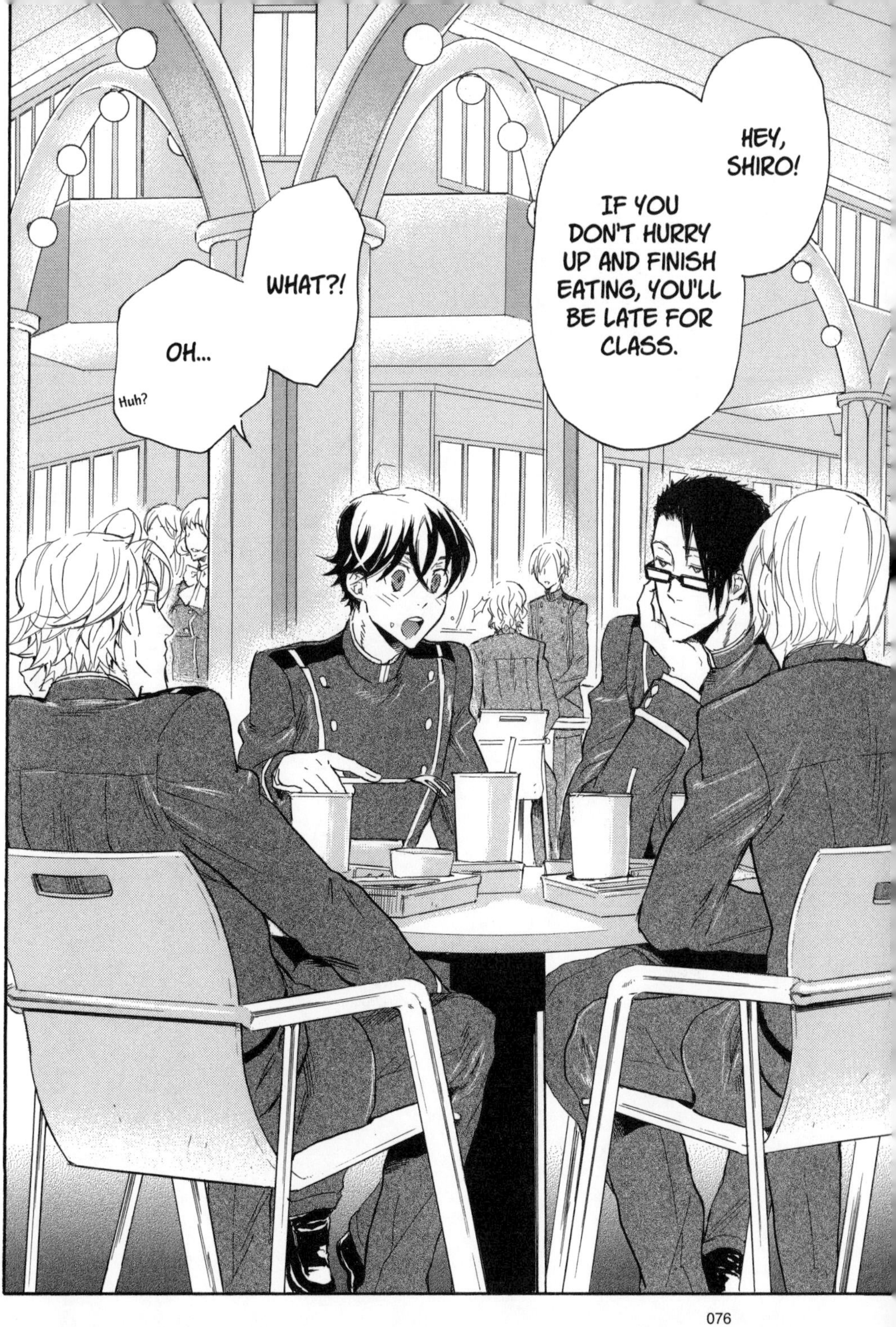
HEY, SHIRO!
IF YOU DON'T HURRY UP AND FINISH EATING, YOU'LL BE LATE FOR CLASS.
WHAT?!
OH...
Huh?

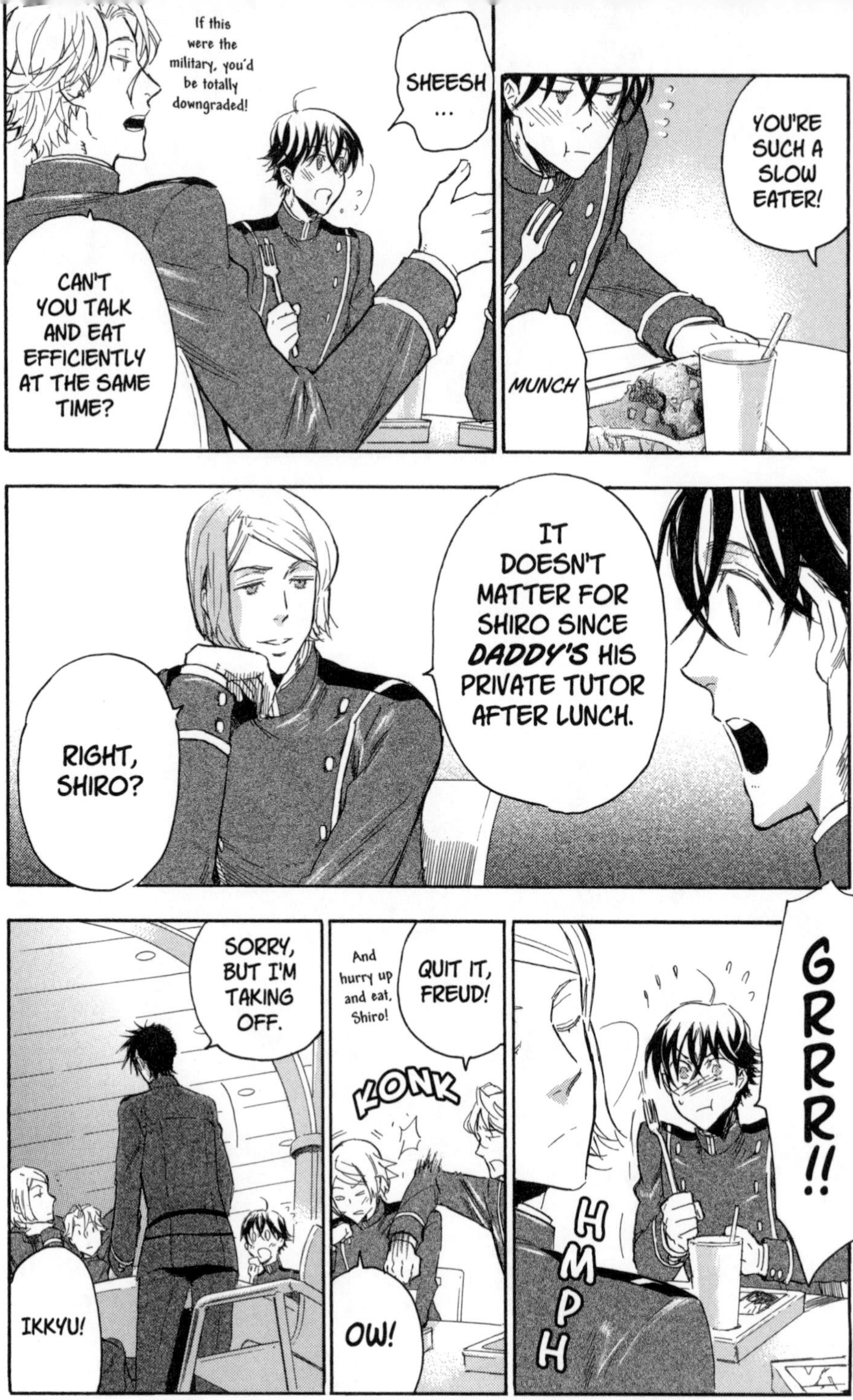
YOU'RE SUCH A SLOW EATER!
MUNCH
SHEESH ...
If this were the military, you'd be totally downgraded!
CAN'T YOU TALK AND EAT EFFICIENTLY AT THE SAME TIME?
IT DOESN'T MATTER FOR SHIRO SINCE DADDY'S HIS PRIVATE TUTOR AFTER LUNCH.
RIGHT, SHIRO?
GRRRR!!
HMPH
QUIT IT, FREUD!
And hurry up and eat, Shiro!
KONK
OW!
SORRY, BUT I'M TAKING OFF.
IKKYU!

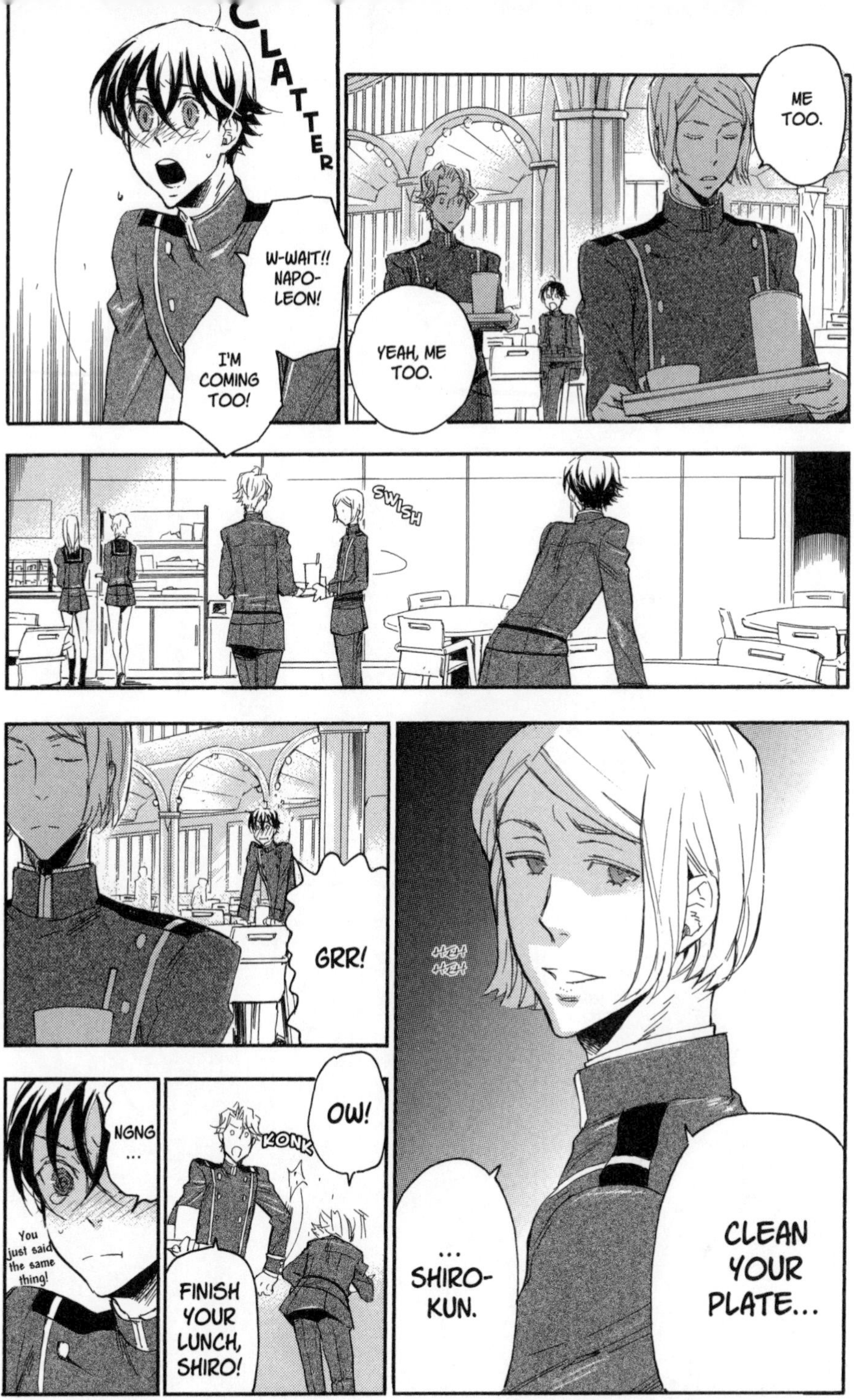
ME TOO.
YEAH, ME TOO.
CLATTER
W-WAIT!! NAPO-LEON!
I'M COMING TOO!
SWISH
CLEAN YOUR PLATE...
... SHIRO-KUN.
GRR!
OW!
KONK
FINISH YOUR LUNCH, SHIRO!
NGNG...
You just said the same thing!

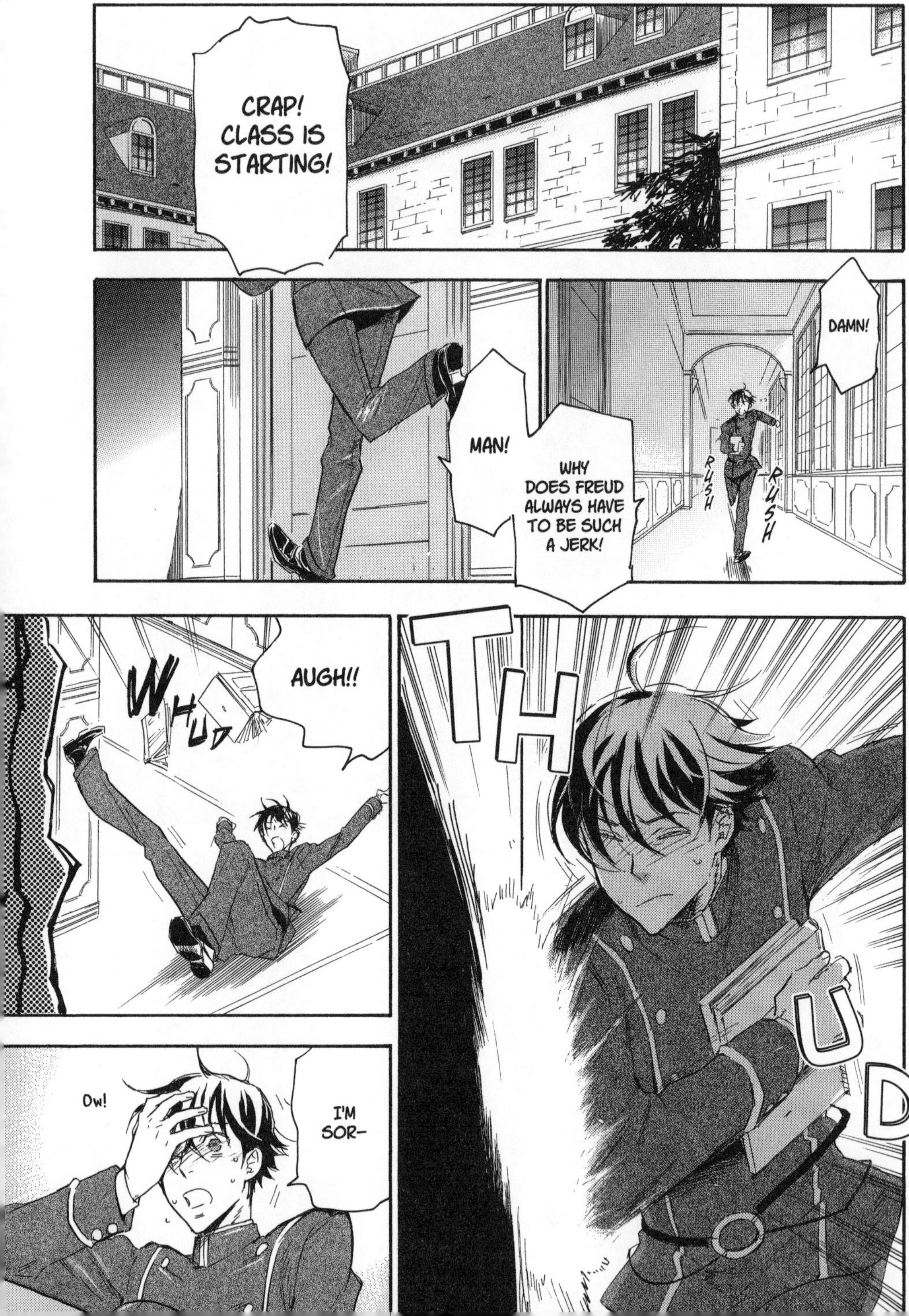
CRAP! CLASS IS STARTING!
DAMN!
RUSH RUSH
MAN!
WHY DOES FREUD ALWAYS HAVE TO BE SUCH A JERK!
THUD
WHUD
AUGH!!
OW!
I'M SOR-

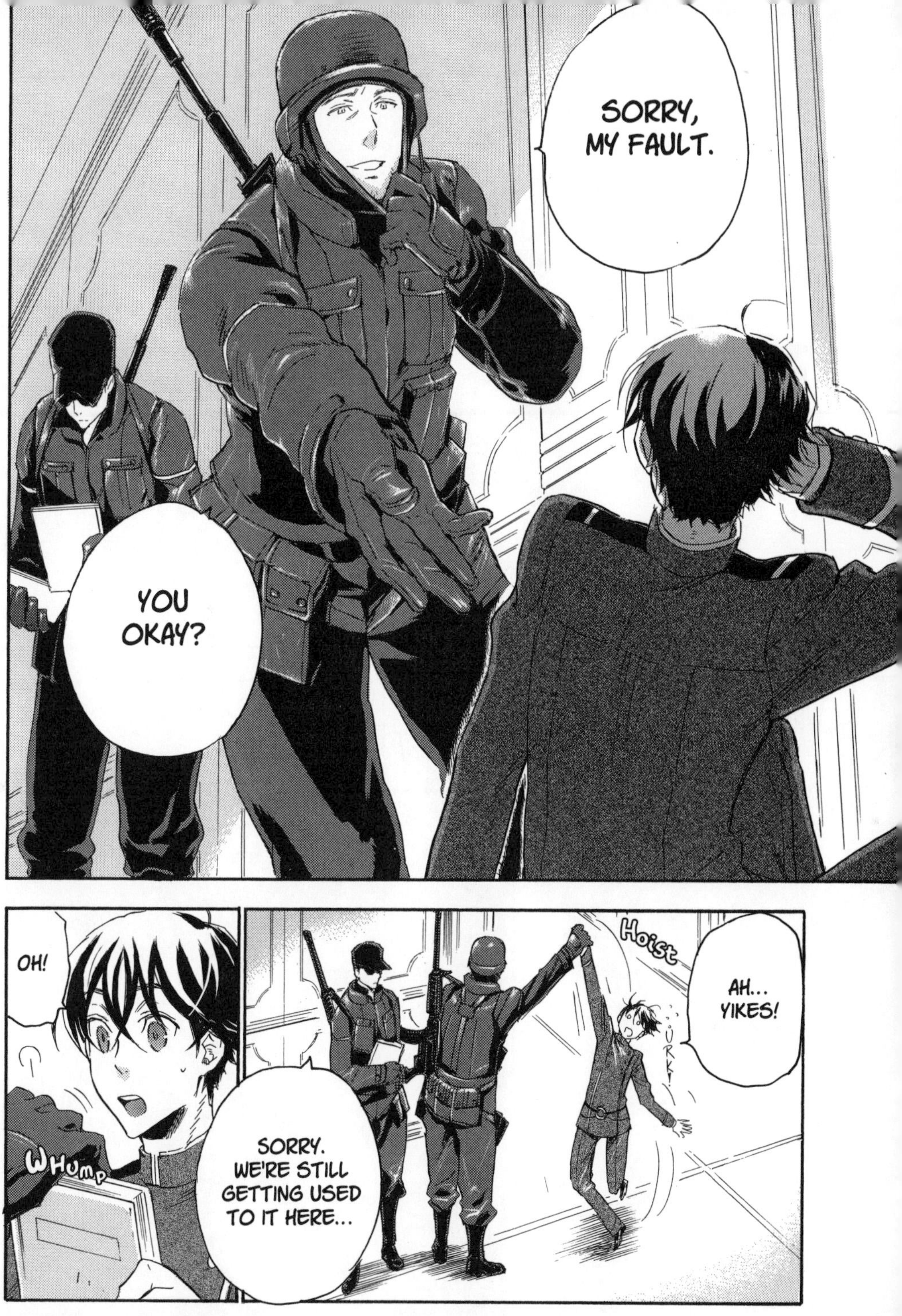
SORRY, MY FAULT.
YOU OKAY?
Hoist
AH... YIKES!
URK!
SORRY. WE'RE STILL GETTING USED TO IT HERE...
OH!
WHUMP

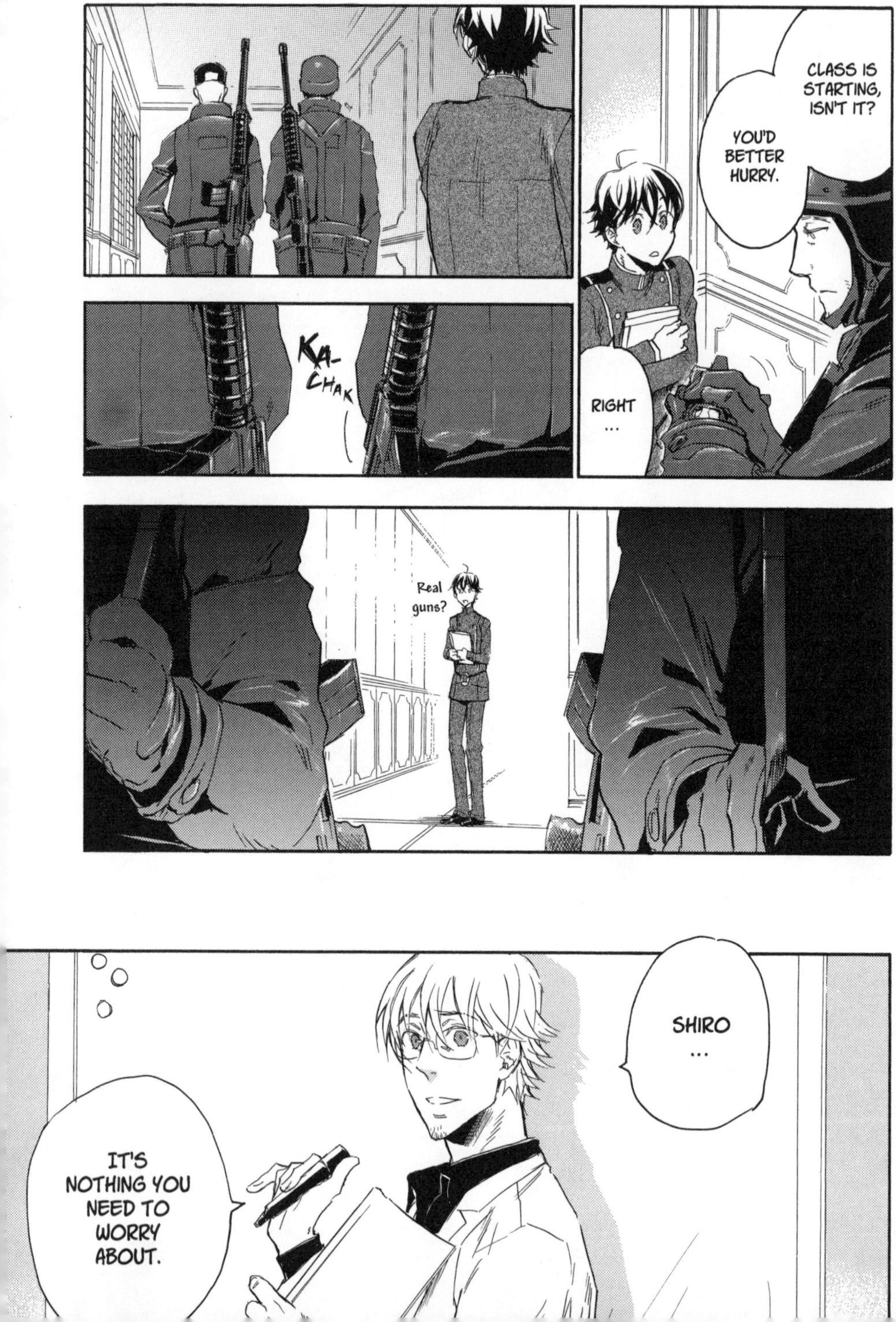
CLASS IS STARTING, ISN'T IT?
YOU'D BETTER HURRY.
RIGHT ...
KA-CHAK
Real guns?
SHIRO ...
IT'S NOTHING YOU NEED TO WORRY ABOUT.

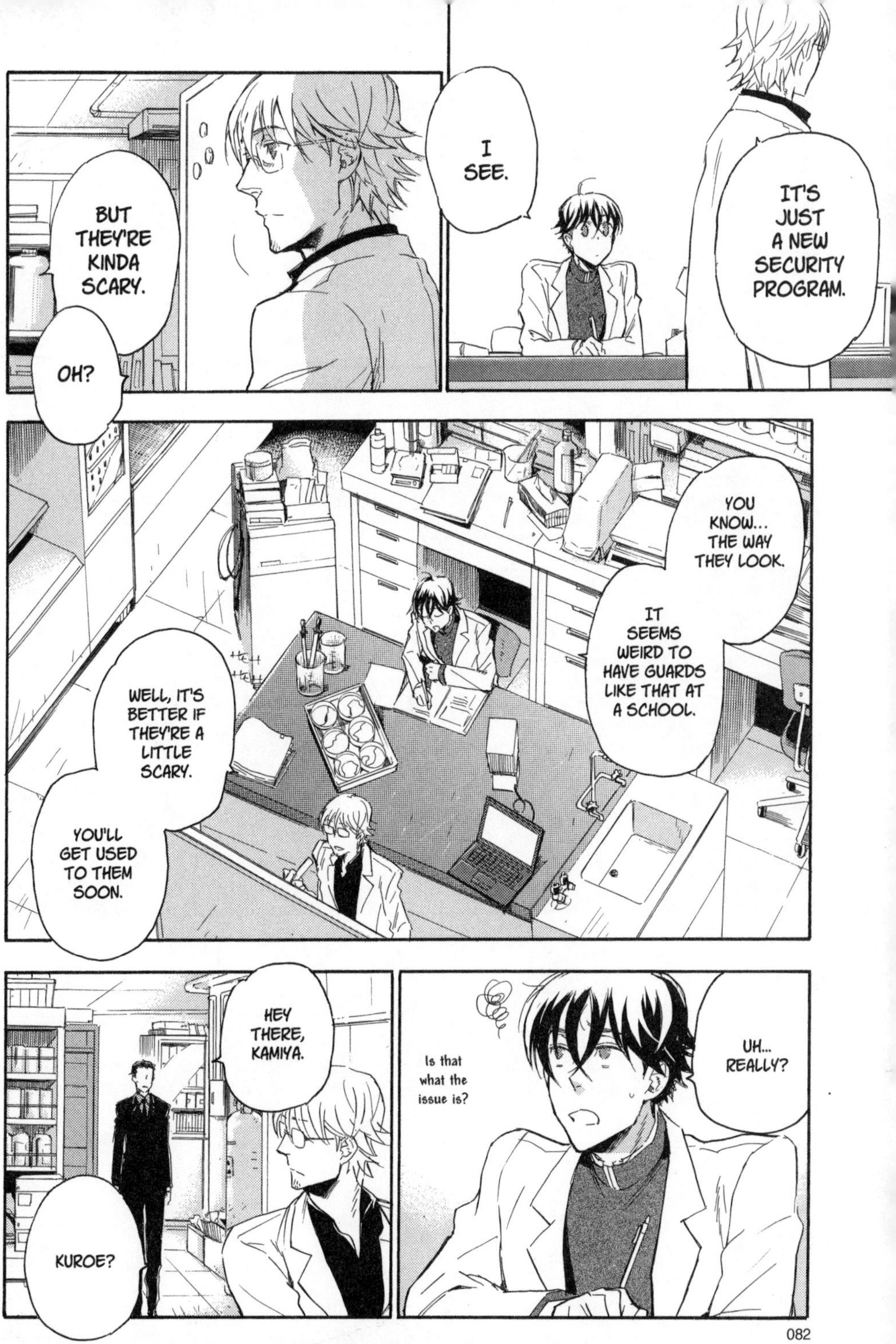
IT'S JUST A NEW SECURITY PROGRAM.
I SEE.
BUT THEY'RE KINDA SCARY.
OH?
YOU KNOW... THE WAY THEY LOOK.
IT SEEMS WEIRD TO HAVE GUARDS LIKE THAT AT A SCHOOL.
WELL, IT'S BETTER IF THEY'RE A LITTLE SCARY.
YOU'LL GET USED TO THEM SOON.
UH... REALLY?
Is that what the issue is?
HEY THERE, KAMIYA.
KUROE?

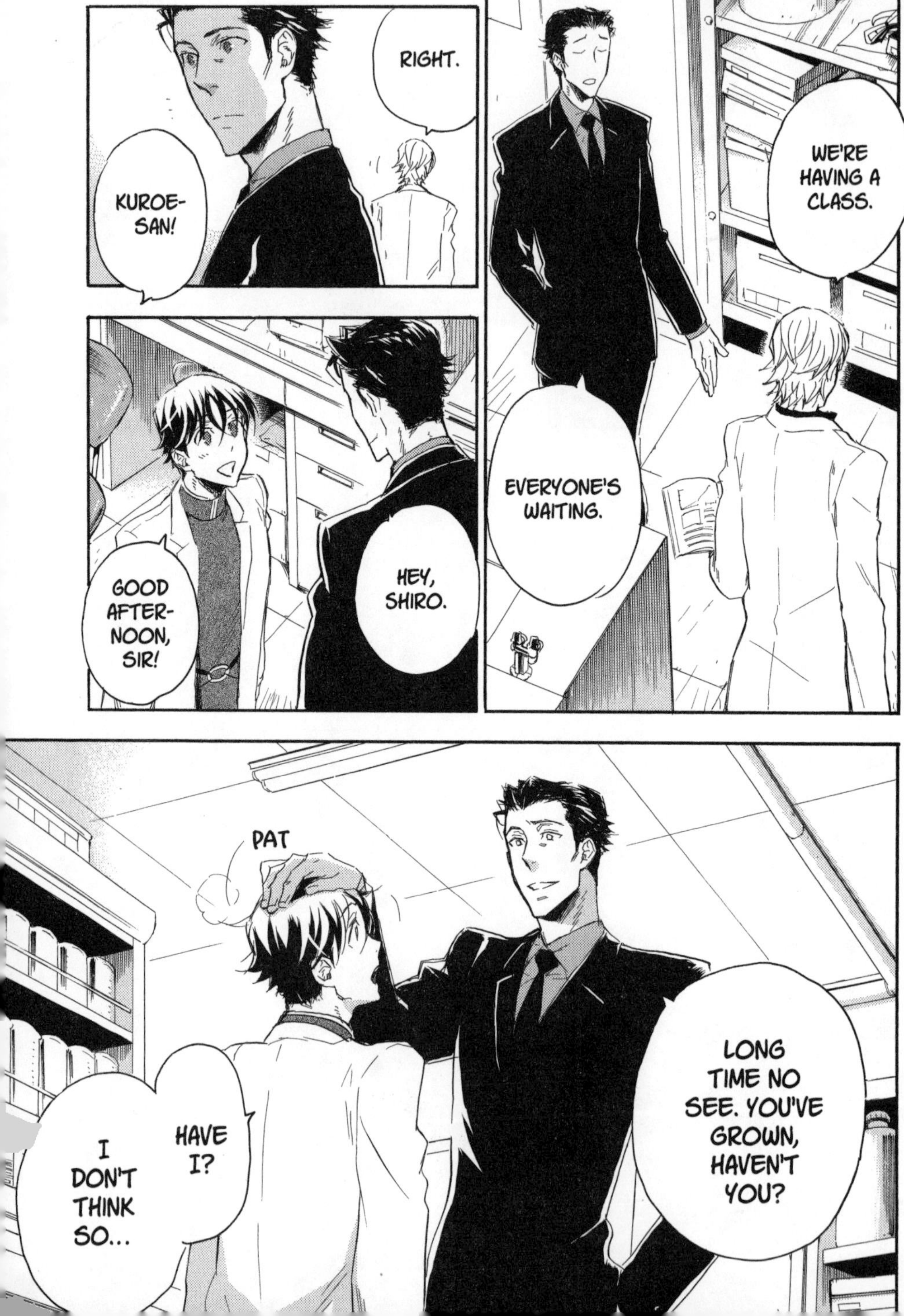
WE'RE HAVING A CLASS.
EVERYONE'S WAITING.
RIGHT.
KUROE-SAN!
HEY, SHIRO.
GOOD AFTERNOON, SIR!
PAT
LONG TIME NO SEE. YOU'VE GROWN, HAVEN'T YOU?
HAVE I?
I DON'T THINK SO...

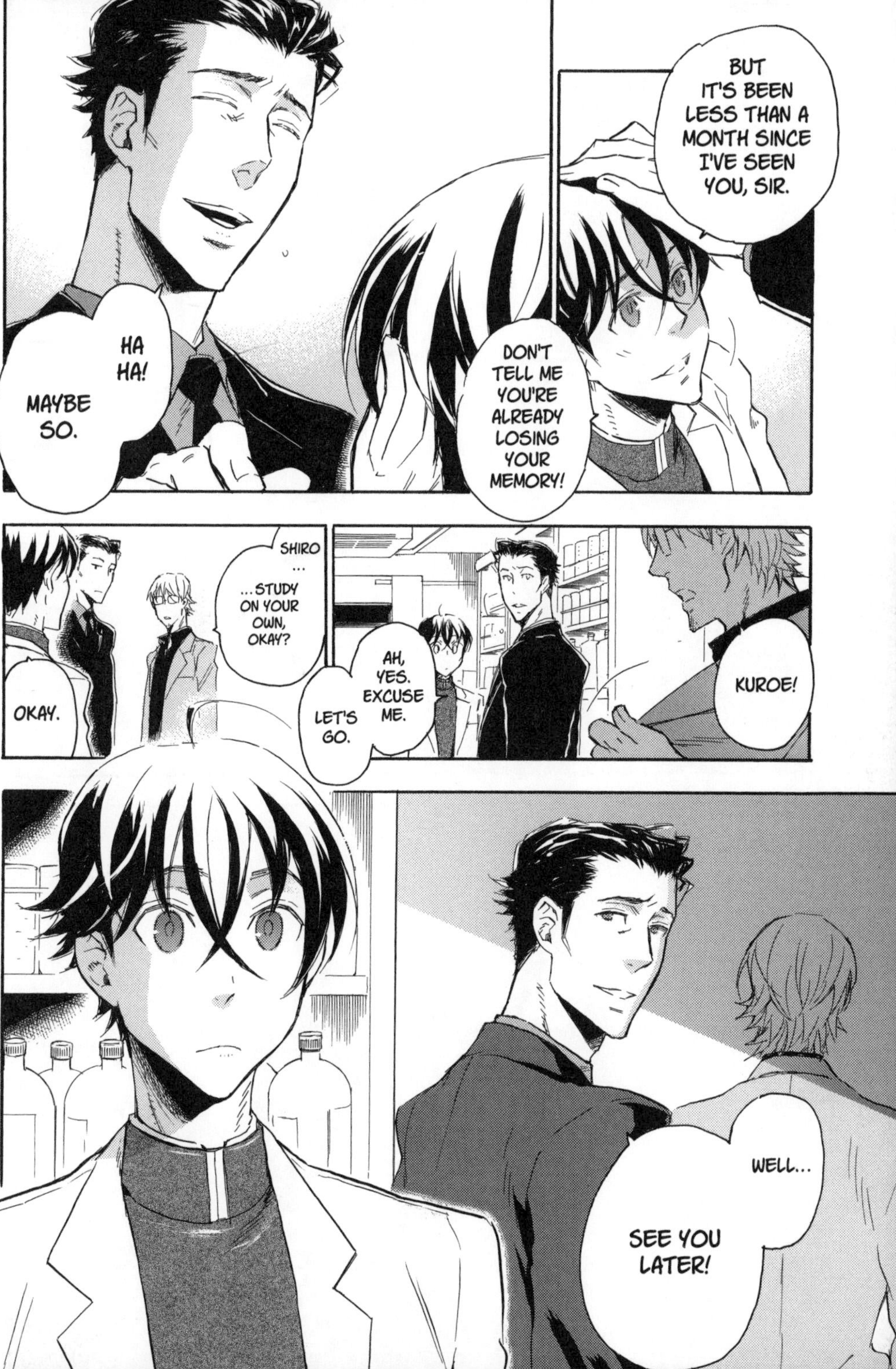
BUT IT'S BEEN LESS THAN A MONTH SINCE I'VE SEEN YOU, SIR.
DON'T TELL ME YOU'RE ALREADY LOSING YOUR MEMORY!
HA HA!
MAYBE SO.
KUROE!
AH, YES. EXCUSE ME.
LET'S GO.
SHIRO ...
...STUDY ON YOUR OWN, OKAY?
OKAY.
WELL...
SEE YOU LATER!

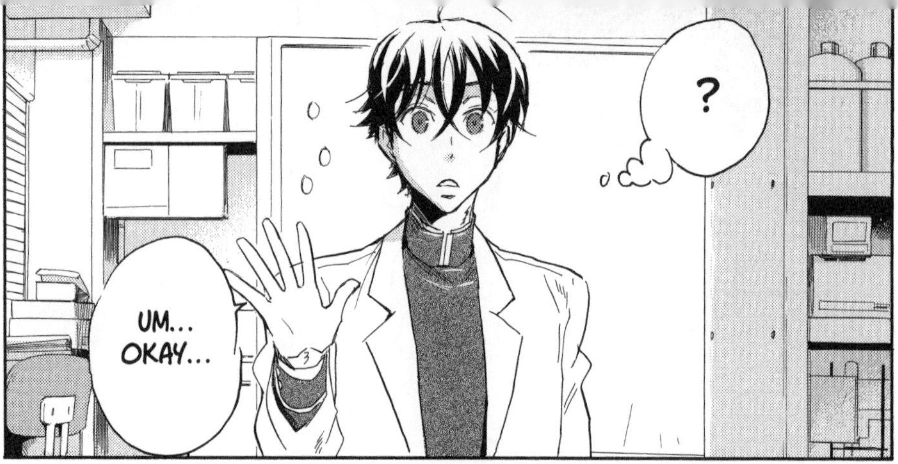
?
UM... OKAY...
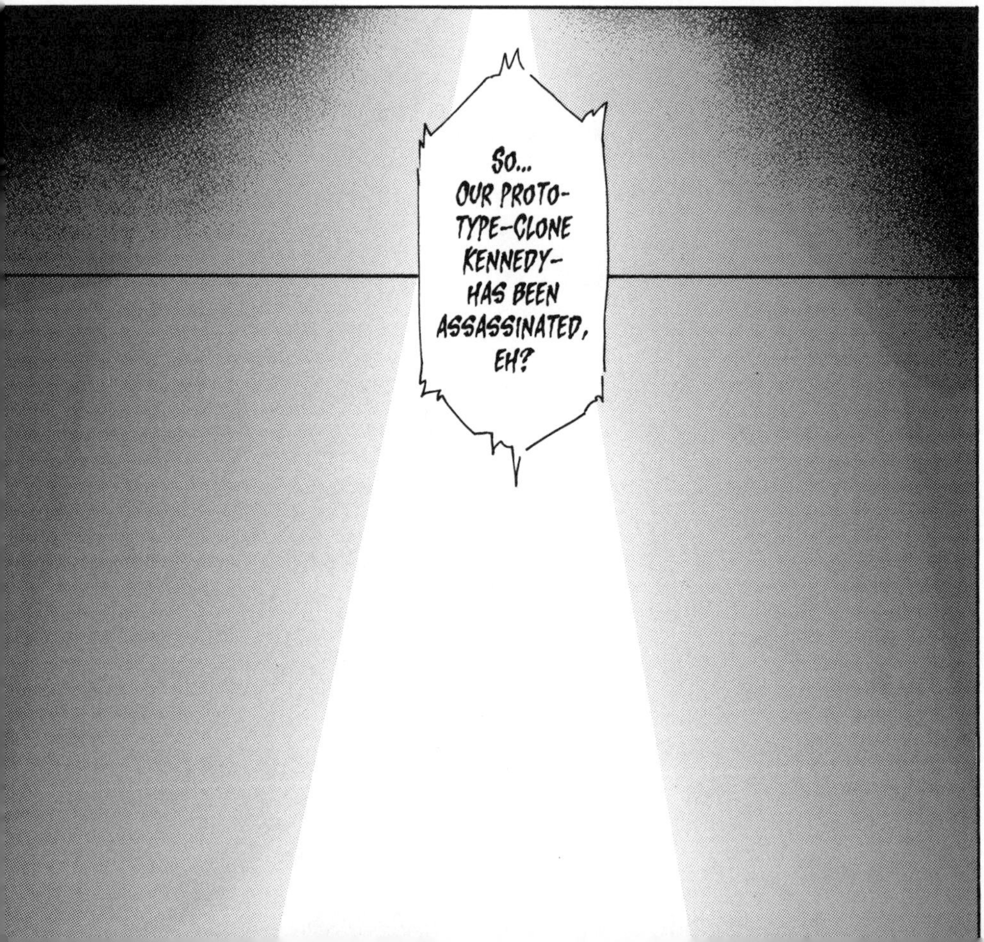
SO... OUR PROTO-TYPE-CLONE KENNEDY-HAS BEEN ASSASSINATED, EH?

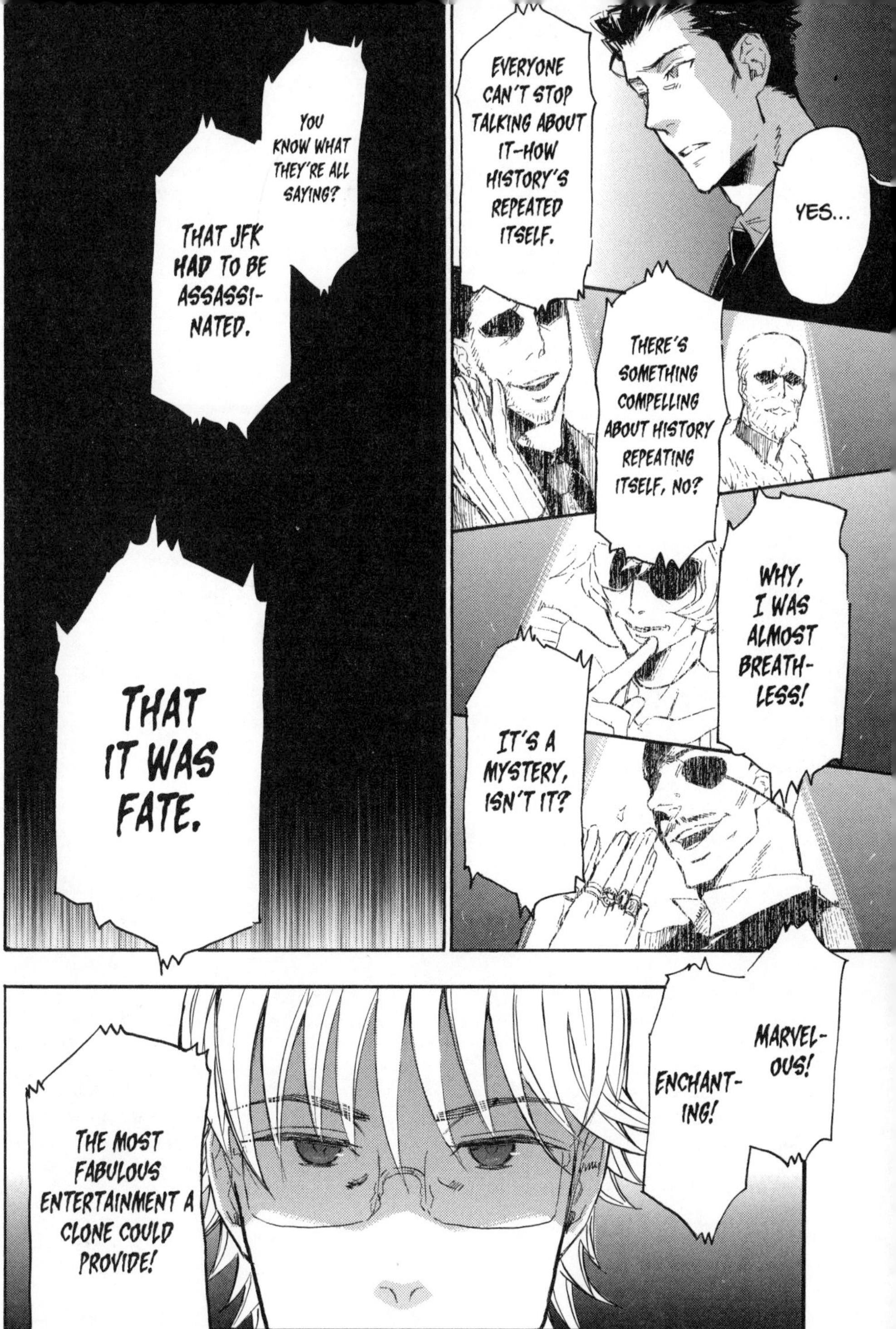
EVERYONE CAN'T STOP TALKING ABOUT IT–HOW HISTORY'S REPEATED ITSELF.
YES...
THERE'S SOMETHING COMPELLING ABOUT HISTORY REPEATING ITSELF, NO?
WHY, I WAS ALMOST BREATHLESS!
IT'S A MYSTERY, ISN'T IT?
YOU KNOW WHAT THEY'RE ALL SAYING?
THAT JFK HAD TO BE ASSASSINATED.
THAT IT WAS FATE.
MARVELOUS!
ENCHANTING!
THE MOST FABULOUS ENTERTAINMENT A CLONE COULD PROVIDE!

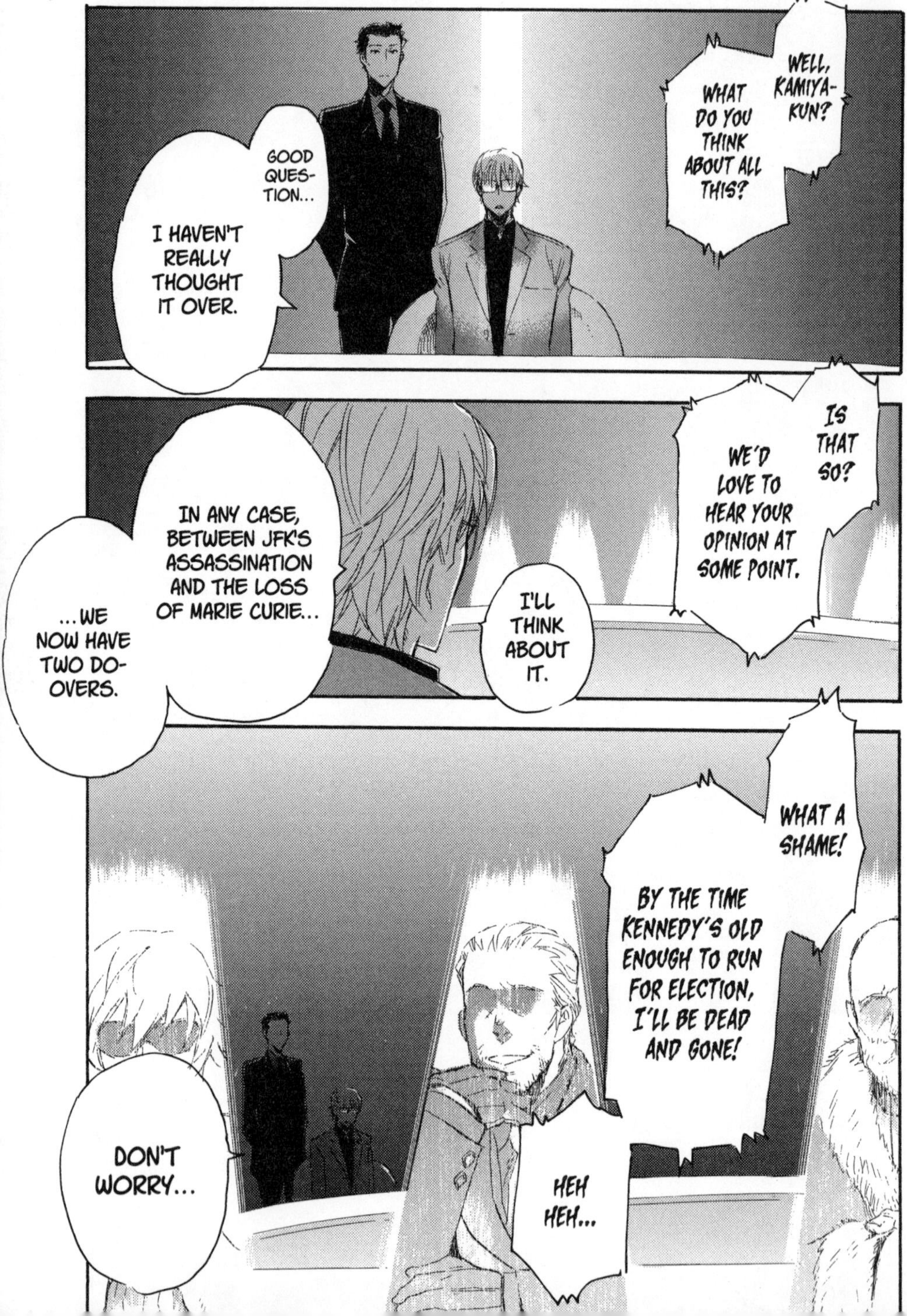
WELL, KAMIYA-KUN?
WHAT DO YOU THINK ABOUT ALL THIS?
GOOD QUES-TION...
I HAVEN'T REALLY THOUGHT IT OVER.
IS THAT SO?
WE'D LOVE TO HEAR YOUR OPINION AT SOME POINT.
I'LL THINK ABOUT IT.
IN ANY CASE, BETWEEN JFK'S ASSASSINATION AND THE LOSS OF MARIE CURIE...
...WE NOW HAVE TWO DO-OVERS.
WHAT A SHAME!
BY THE TIME KENNEDY'S OLD ENOUGH TO RUN FOR ELECTION, I'LL BE DEAD AND GONE!
HEH HEH...
DON'T WORRY...

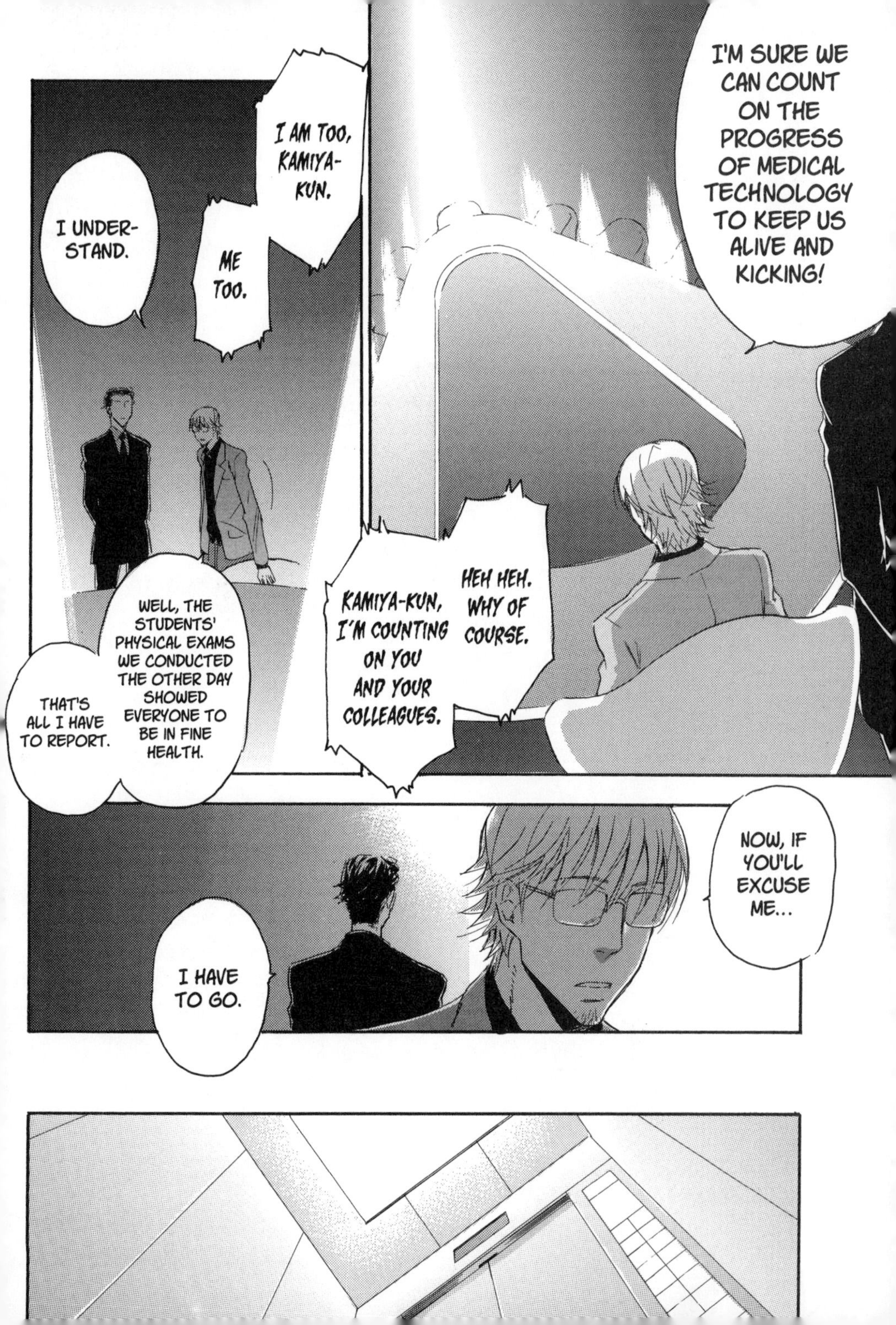
I'M SURE WE CAN COUNT ON THE PROGRESS OF MEDICAL TECHNOLOGY TO KEEP US ALIVE AND KICKING!
HEH HEH. WHY OF COURSE.
KAMIYA-KUN, I'M COUNTING ON YOU AND YOUR COLLEAGUES.
I AM TOO, KAMIYA-KUN.
ME TOO.
I UNDER-STAND.
WELL, THE STUDENTS' PHYSICAL EXAMS WE CONDUCTED THE OTHER DAY SHOWED EVERYONE TO BE IN FINE HEALTH.
THAT'S ALL I HAVE TO REPORT.
NOW, IF YOU'LL EXCUSE ME...
I HAVE TO GO.

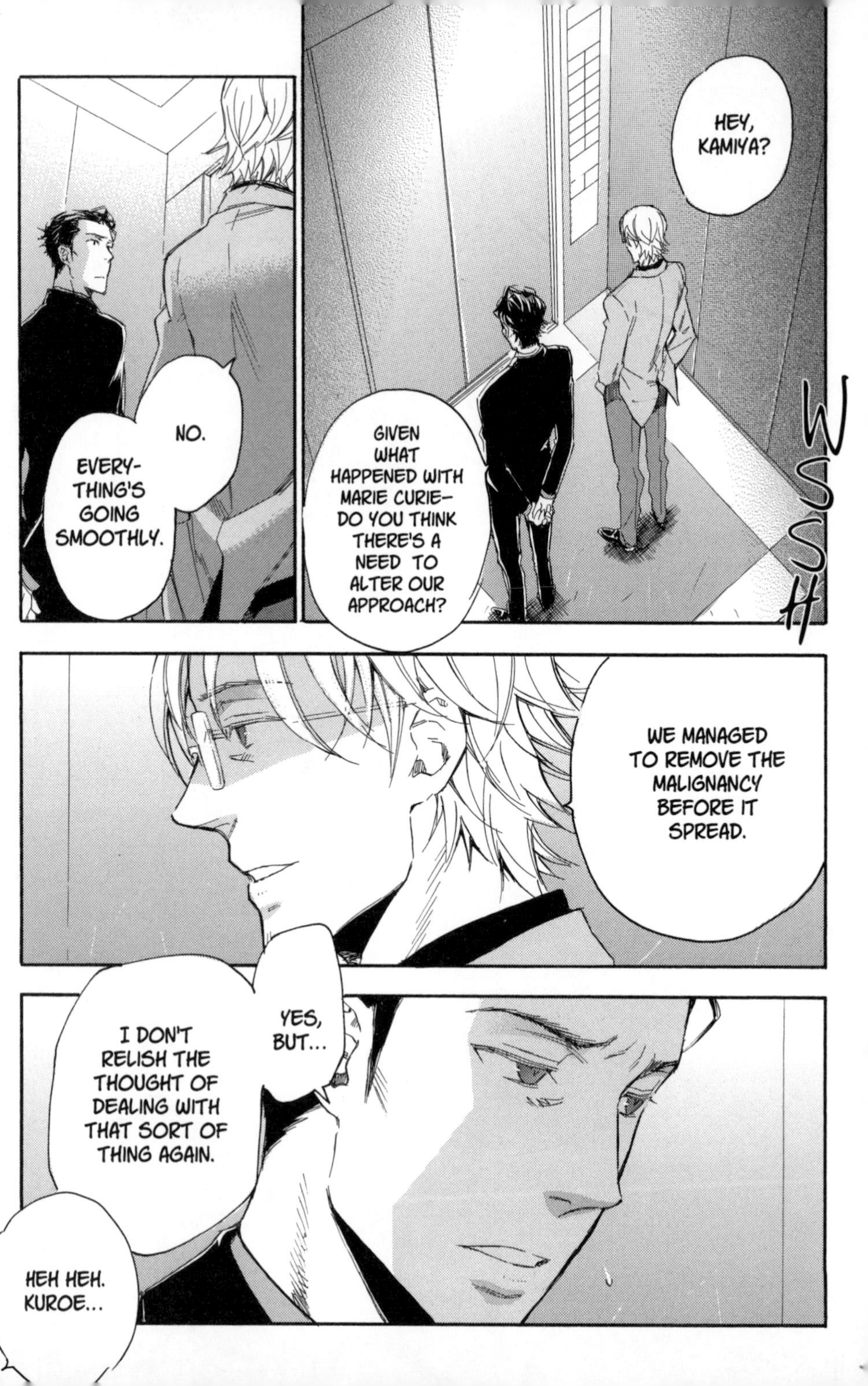
HEY, KAMIYA?
GIVEN WHAT HAPPENED WITH MARIE CURIE– DO YOU THINK THERE'S A NEED TO ALTER OUR APPROACH?
WSSH
NO.
EVERY-THING'S GOING SMOOTHLY.
WE MANAGED TO REMOVE THE MALIGNANCY BEFORE IT SPREAD.
YES, BUT...
I DON'T RELISH THE THOUGHT OF DEALING WITH THAT SORT OF THING AGAIN.
HEH HEH. KUROE...

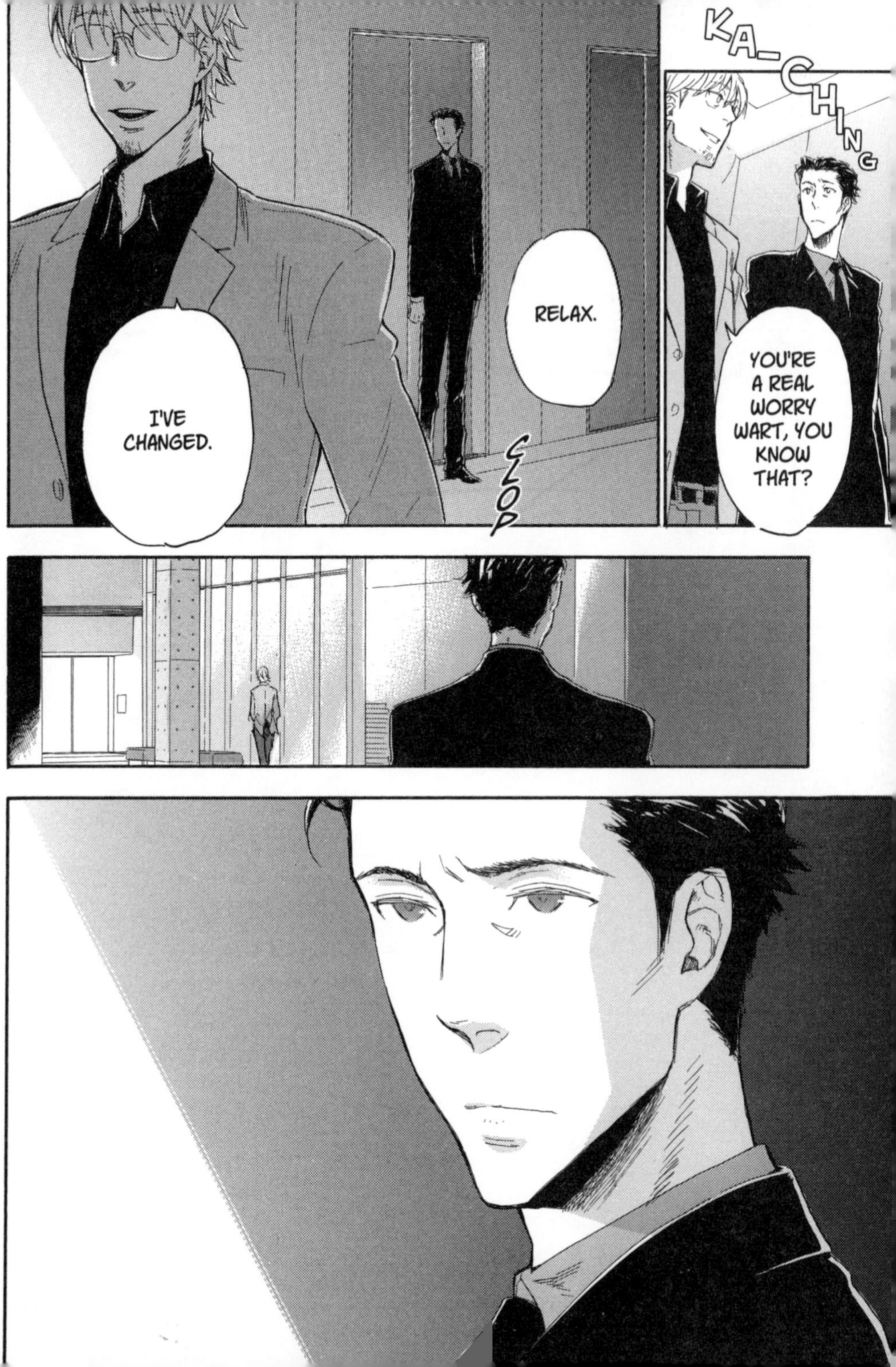
KA-CHING
YOU'RE A REAL WORRY WART, YOU KNOW THAT?
RELAX.
I'VE CHANGED.
CLOP

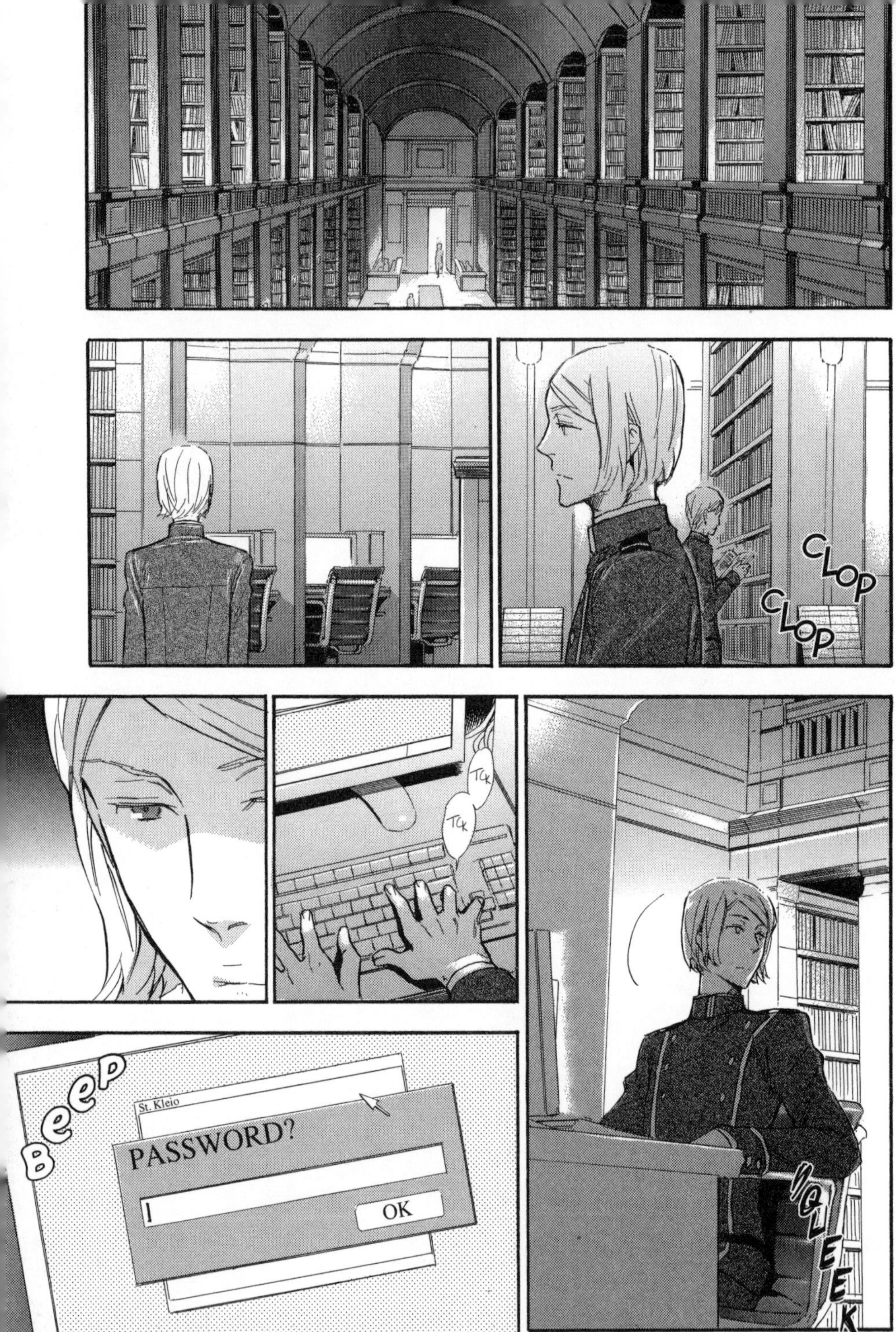
CLOP
CLOP
SQUEEK
TCK
TCK
BEEP
St. Kleio
PASSWORD?
I
OK

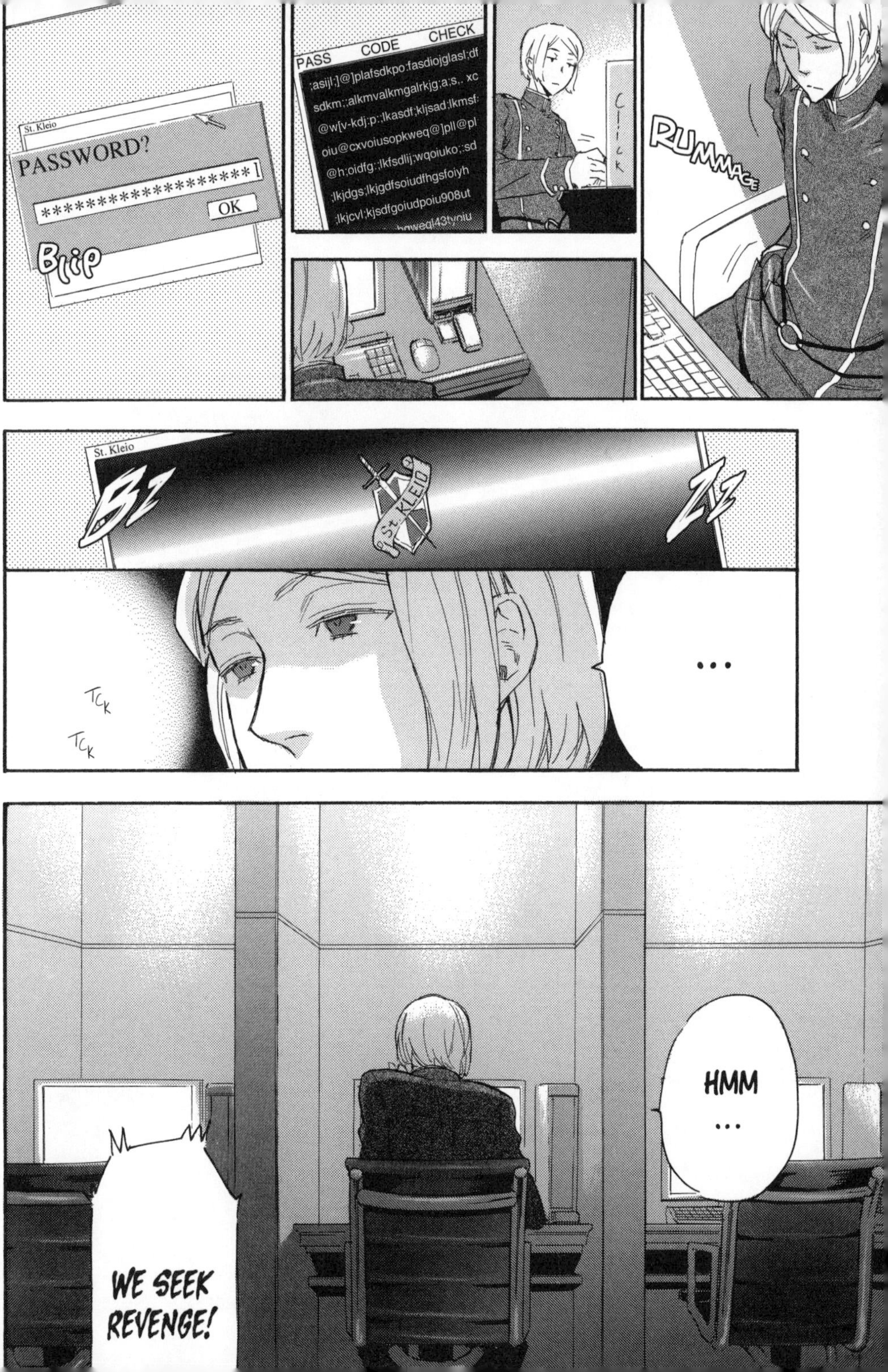

RUMMAGE
Click
PASS CODE CHECK
;asijl:]@]plafsdkpo:fasdiojglasl;df
sdkm:;alkmvalkmgalrkjg;a;s,. xc
@w[v-kdj:p:;lkasdf;kljsad:lkmsf:
oiu@cxvoiusopkweq@]pll@pl
@h;oidfg::lkfsdlij;wqoiuko;:sd
:lkjdgs;lkjgdfsoiudfhgsfoiyh
;lkjcvl;kjsdfgoiudpoiu908ut
St. Kleio
PASSWORD?
****
OK
Blip
St. Kleio
BZ
ZZ
ST. KLEIO
...
TCK
TCK
HMM ...
WE SEEK REVENGE!

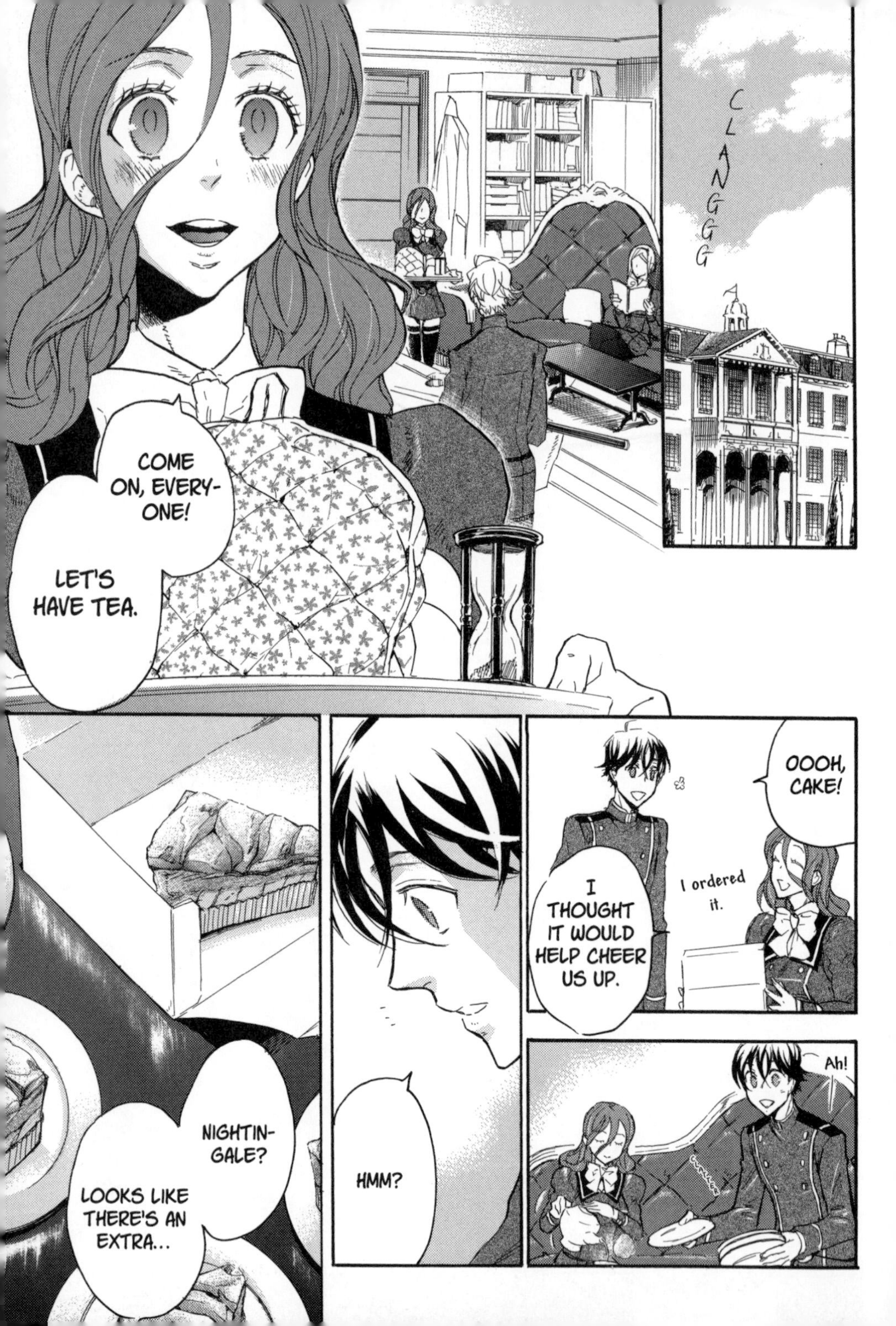
CLANGGG
COME ON, EVERY-ONE!
LET'S HAVE TEA.
OOOH, CAKE!
I ordered it.
I THOUGHT IT WOULD HELP CHEER US UP.
Ah!
HMM?
NIGHTIN-GALE?
LOOKS LIKE THERE'S AN EXTRA...

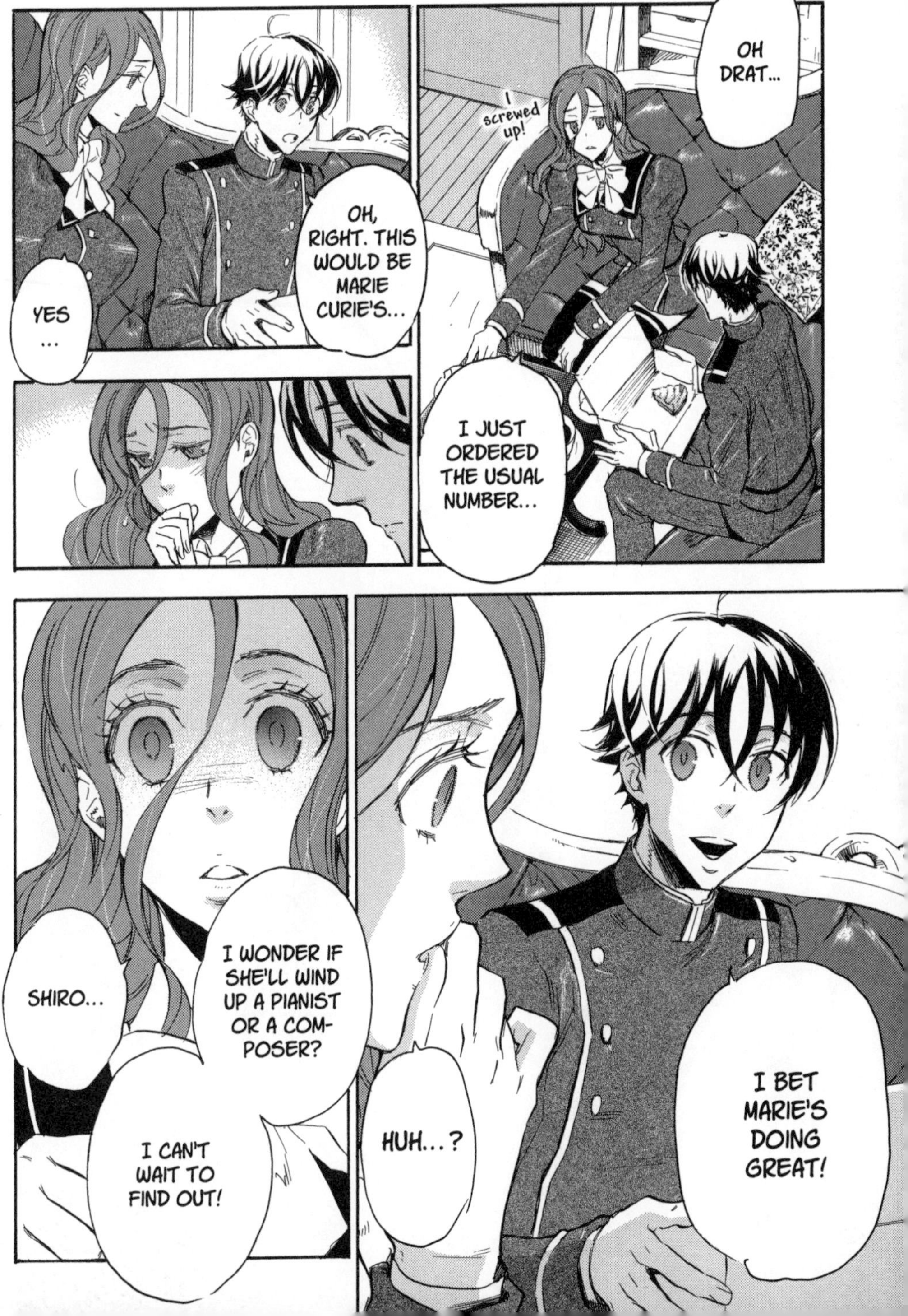
OH DRAT...
I screwed up!
I JUST ORDERED THE USUAL NUMBER...
OH, RIGHT. THIS WOULD BE MARIE CURIE'S...
YES ...
I BET MARIE'S DOING GREAT!
HUH...?
I WONDER IF SHE'LL WIND UP A PIANIST OR A COM-POSER?
SHIRO...
I CAN'T WAIT TO FIND OUT!

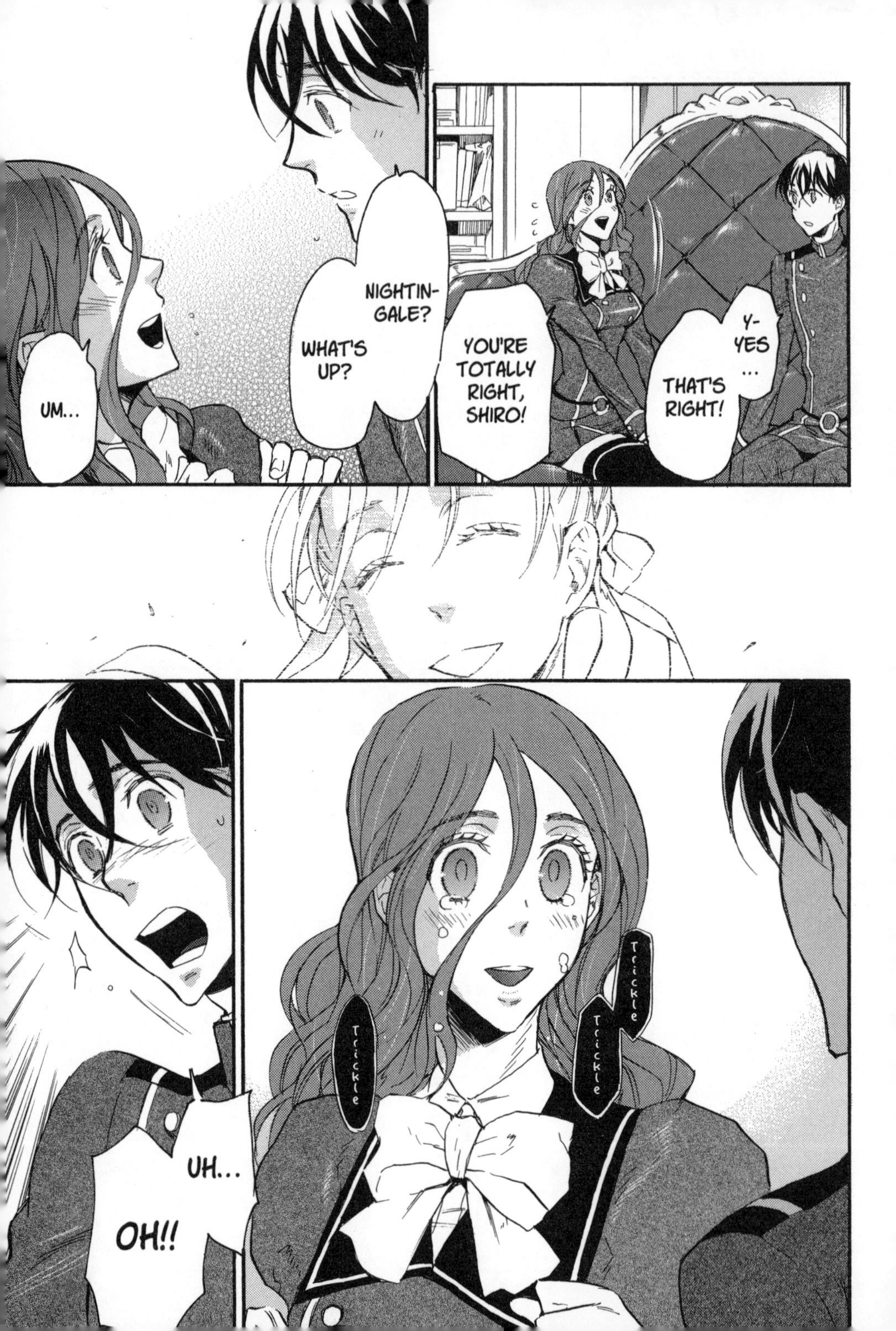
Y-YES...
THAT'S RIGHT!
YOU'RE TOTALLY RIGHT, SHIRO!
NIGHTIN-GALE?
WHAT'S UP?
UM...
Trickle
Trickle
Trickle
UH...
OH!!

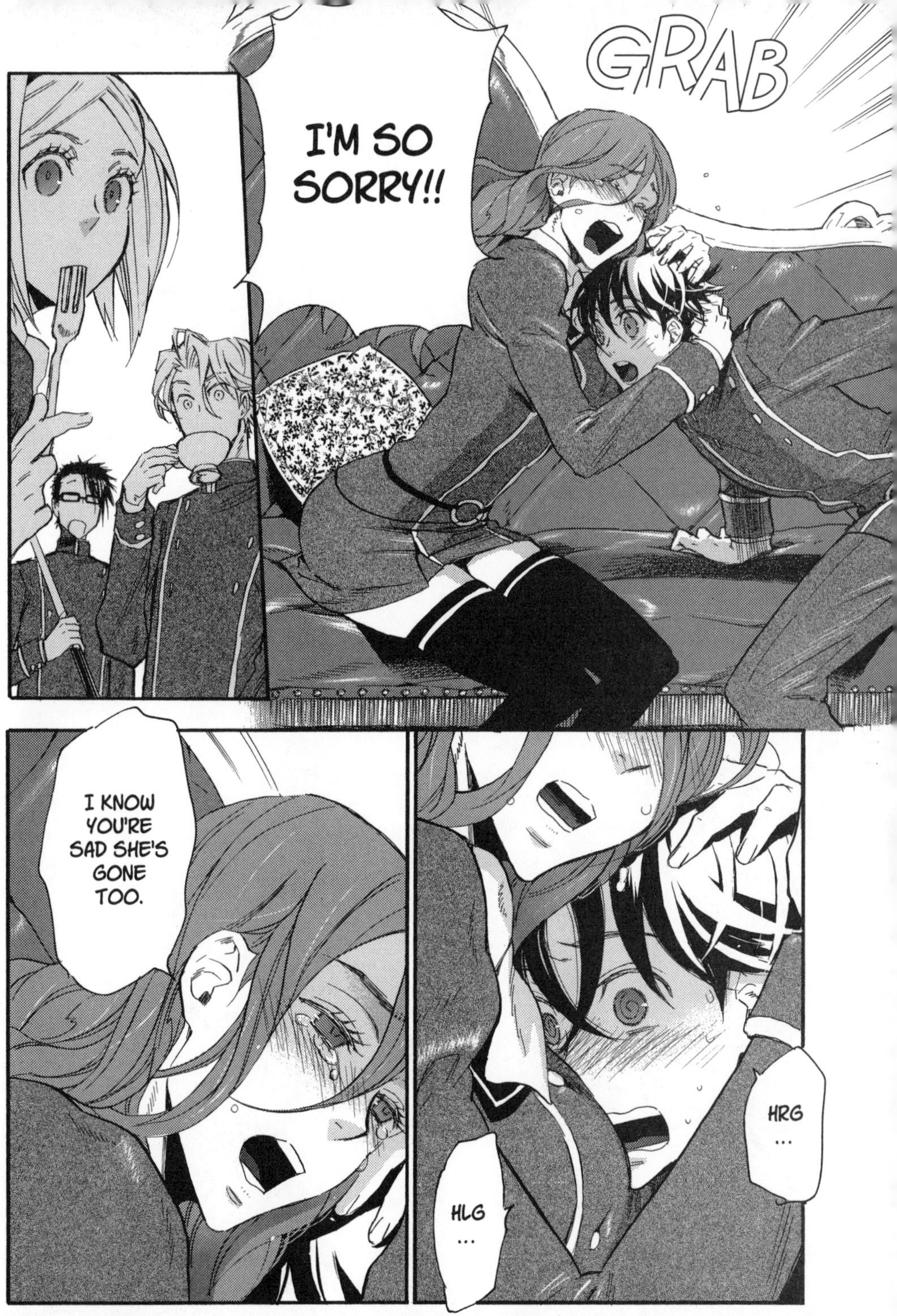
GRAB
I'M SO SORRY!!
HRG ...
HLG ...
I KNOW YOU'RE SAD SHE'S GONE TOO.

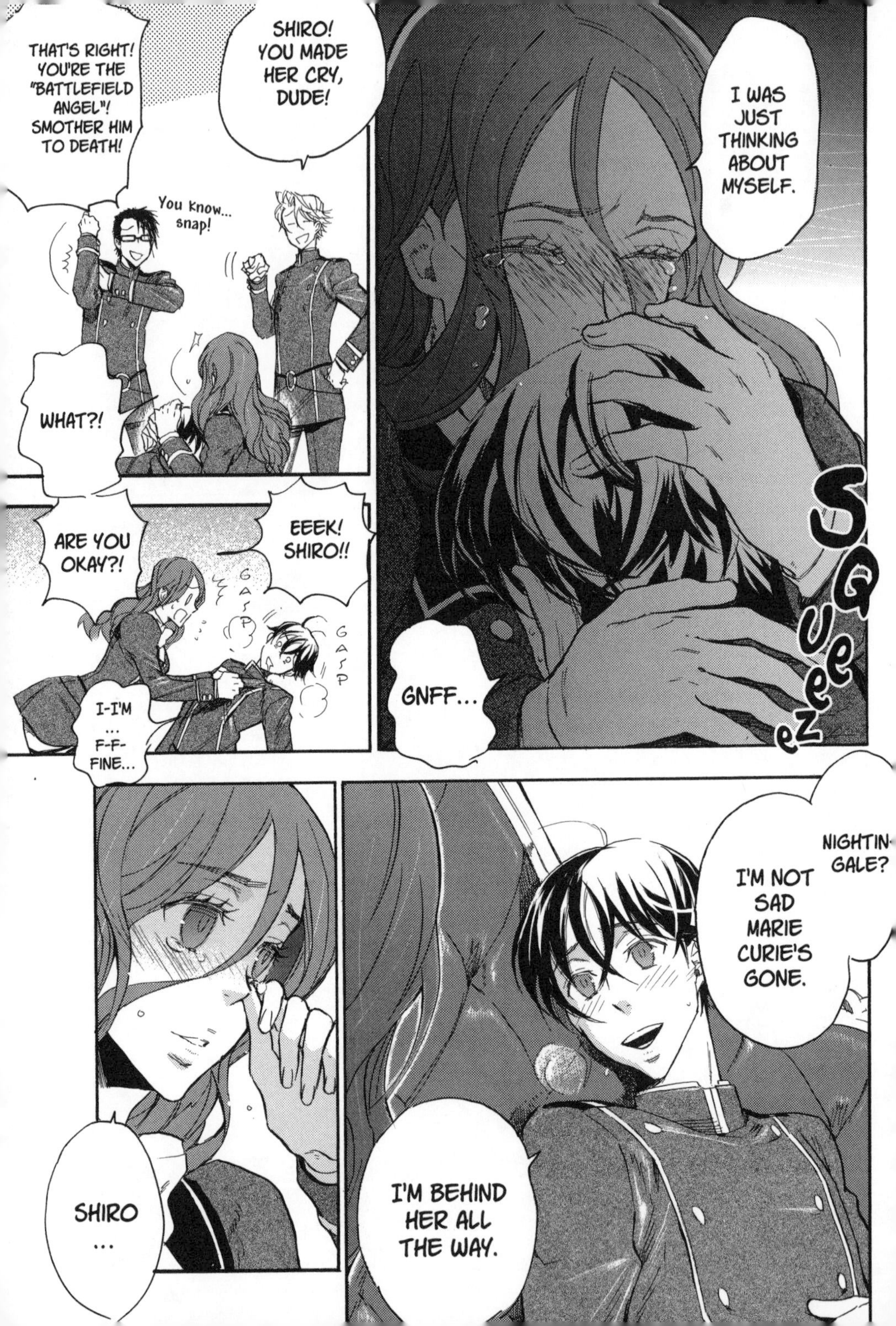
I WAS JUST THINKING ABOUT MYSELF.
GNFF...
SQUEEZE
SHIRO! YOU MADE HER CRY, DUDE!
THAT'S RIGHT! YOU'RE THE "BATTLEFIELD ANGEL"! SMOTHER HIM TO DEATH!
You know... snap!
WHAT?!
EEEK! SHIRO!!
ARE YOU OKAY?!
GASP
GASP
I-I'M ... F-F-FINE...
NIGHTINGALE?
I'M NOT SAD MARIE CURIE'S GONE.
I'M BEHIND HER ALL THE WAY.
SHIRO ...

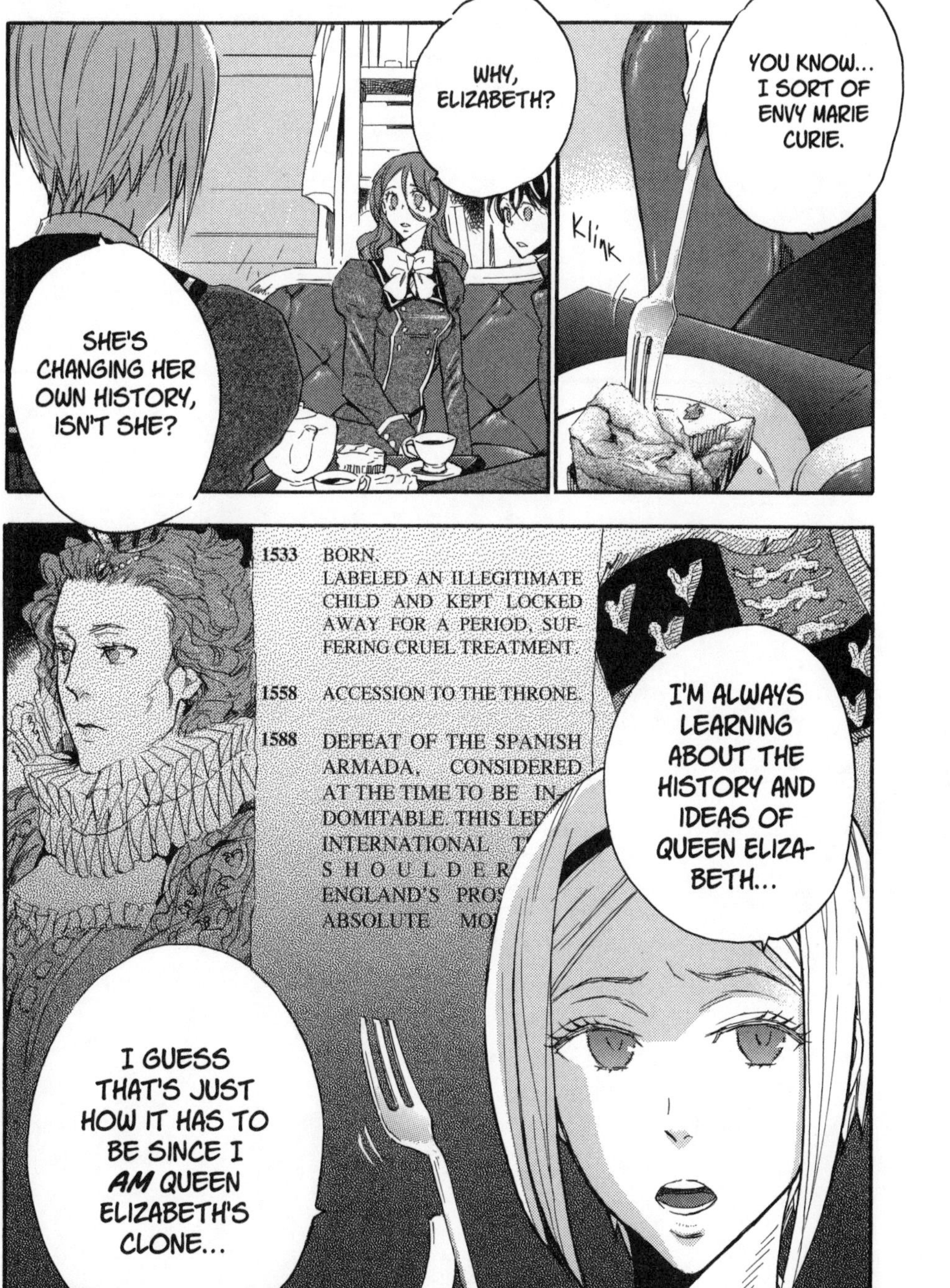
YOU KNOW... I SORT OF ENVY MARIE CURIE.
Klink
WHY, ELIZABETH?
SHE'S CHANGING HER OWN HISTORY, ISN'T SHE?
1533 BORN.
LABELED AN ILLEGITIMATE CHILD AND KEPT LOCKED AWAY FOR A PERIOD, SUFFERING CRUEL TREATMENT.
1558 ACCESSION TO THE THRONE.
1588 DEFEAT OF THE SPANISH ARMADA, CONSIDERED AT THE TIME TO BE INDOMITABLE. THIS LED
INTERNATIONAL
SHOULDER
ENGLAND'S PROS
ABSOLUTE MO
I'M ALWAYS LEARNING ABOUT THE HISTORY AND IDEAS OF QUEEN ELIZABETH...
I GUESS THAT'S JUST HOW IT HAS TO BE SINCE I *AM* QUEEN ELIZABETH'S CLONE...

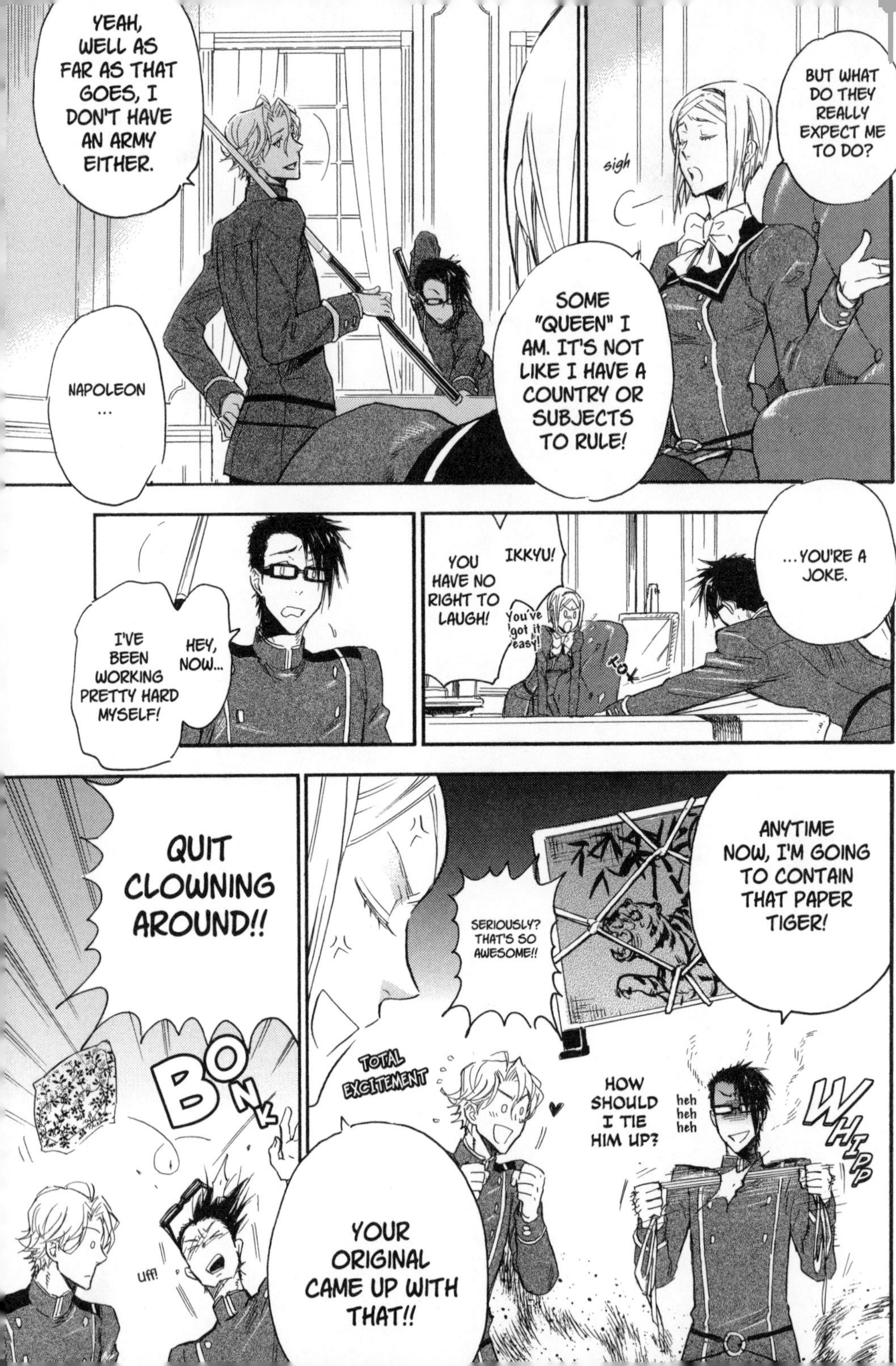
BUT WHAT DO THEY REALLY EXPECT ME TO DO?
sigh
SOME "QUEEN" I AM. IT'S NOT LIKE I HAVE A COUNTRY OR SUBJECTS TO RULE!
YEAH, WELL AS FAR AS THAT GOES, I DON'T HAVE AN ARMY EITHER.
NAPOLEON ...
...YOU'RE A JOKE.
IKKYU!
YOU HAVE NO RIGHT TO LAUGH!
You've got it easy!
HEY, NOW...
I'VE BEEN WORKING PRETTY HARD MYSELF!
ANYTIME NOW, I'M GOING TO CONTAIN THAT PAPER TIGER!
SERIOUSLY? THAT'S SO AWESOME!!
WHIP
heh heh heh
HOW SHOULD I TIE HIM UP?
TOTAL EXCITEMENT
YOUR ORIGINAL CAME UP WITH THAT!!
QUIT CLOWNING AROUND!!
BONK
Uff!

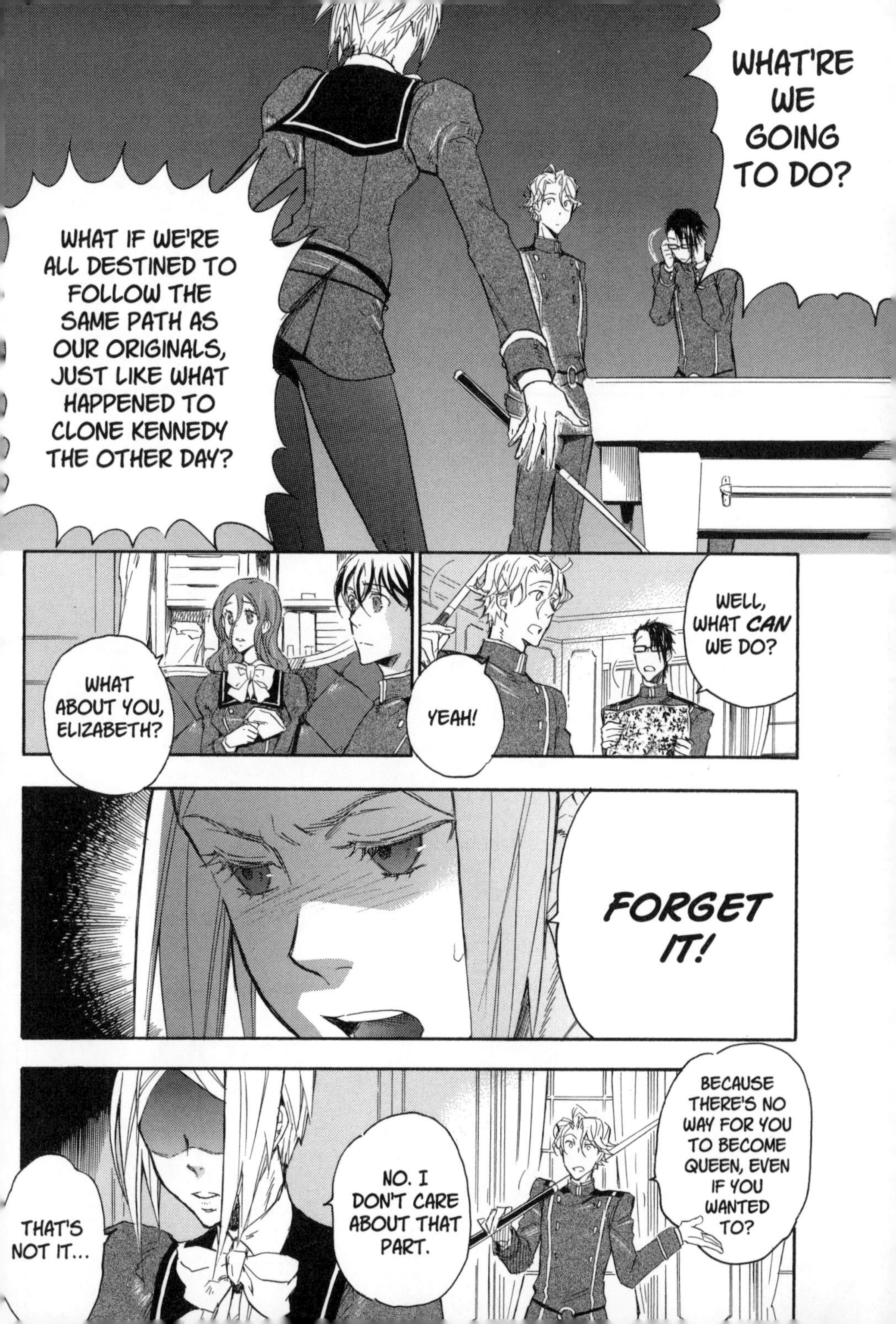
WHAT'RE WE GOING TO DO?
WHAT IF WE'RE ALL DESTINED TO FOLLOW THE SAME PATH AS OUR ORIGINALS, JUST LIKE WHAT HAPPENED TO CLONE KENNEDY THE OTHER DAY?
WELL, WHAT *CAN* WE DO?
YEAH!
WHAT ABOUT YOU, ELIZABETH?
FORGET IT!
BECAUSE THERE'S NO WAY FOR YOU TO BECOME QUEEN, EVEN IF YOU WANTED TO?
NO. I DON'T CARE ABOUT THAT PART.
THAT'S NOT IT...

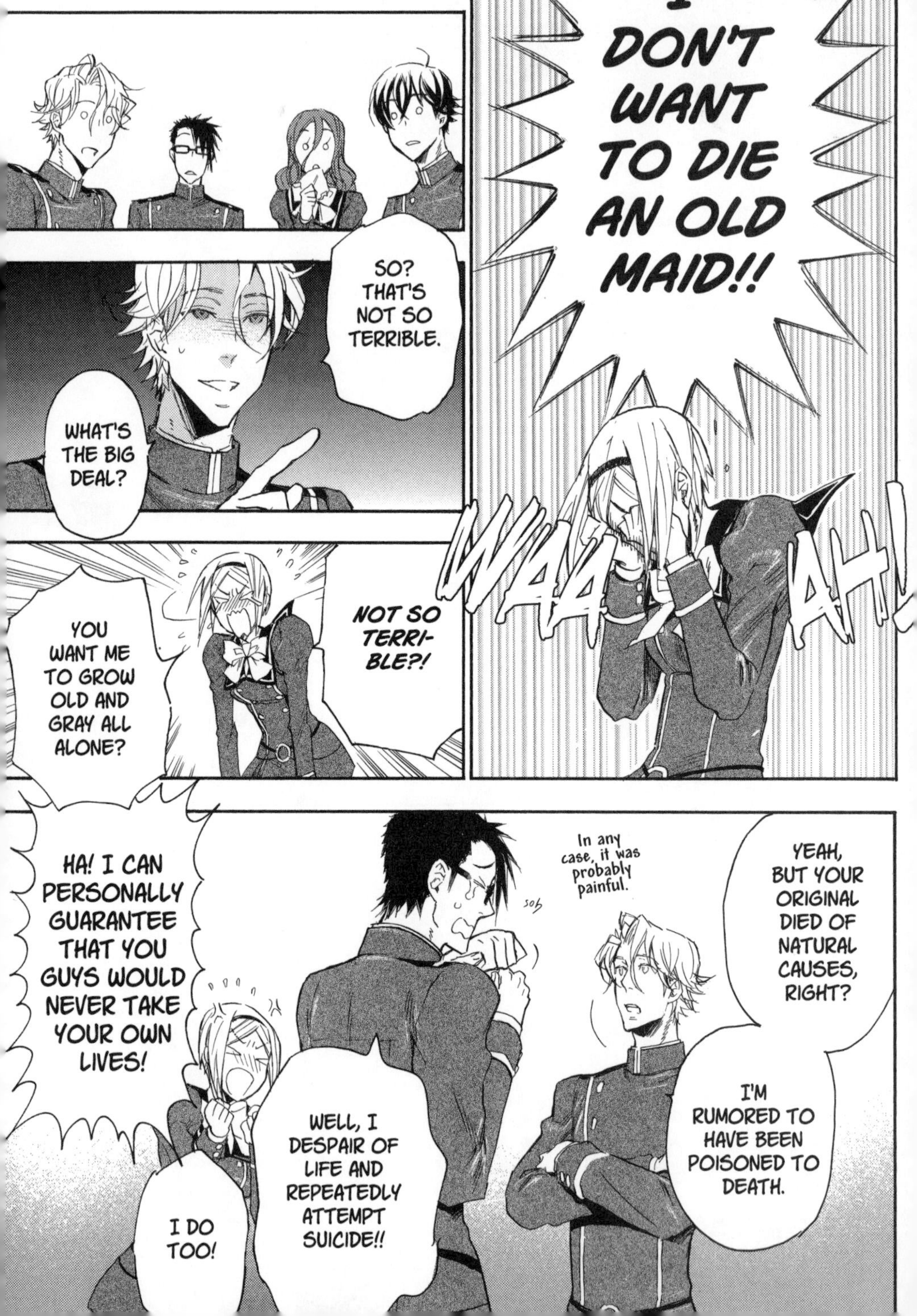
I DON'T WANT TO DIE AN OLD MAID!!
WAAAH!
SO? THAT'S NOT SO TERRIBLE.
WHAT'S THE BIG DEAL?
NOT SO TERRIBLE?!
YOU WANT ME TO GROW OLD AND GRAY ALL ALONE?
YEAH, BUT YOUR ORIGINAL DIED OF NATURAL CAUSES, RIGHT?
In any case, it was probably painful.
I'M RUMORED TO HAVE BEEN POISONED TO DEATH.
sob
WELL, I DESPAIR OF LIFE AND REPEATEDLY ATTEMPT SUICIDE!!
HA! I CAN PERSONALLY GUARANTEE THAT YOU GUYS WOULD NEVER TAKE YOUR OWN LIVES!
I DO TOO!

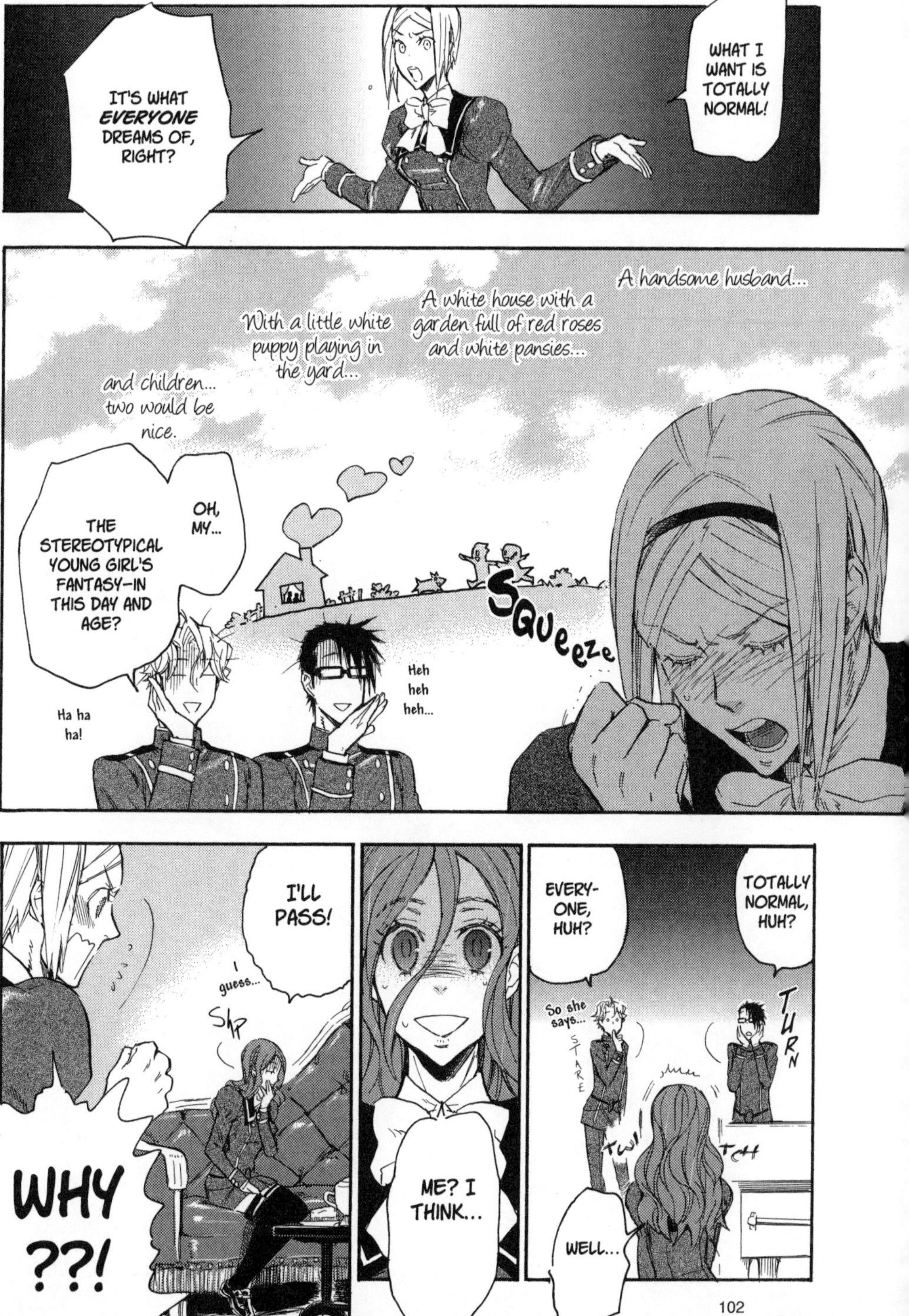
WHAT I WANT IS TOTALLY NORMAL!
IT'S WHAT *EVERYONE* DREAMS OF, RIGHT?
A handsome husband...
A white house with a garden full of red roses and white pansies...
With a little white puppy playing in the yard...
and children... two would be nice.
SQUEEZE
Heh heh heh...
OH, MY...
THE STEREOTYPICAL YOUNG GIRL'S FANTASY—IN THIS DAY AND AGE?
Ha ha ha!
TOTALLY NORMAL, HUH?
TURN
EVERY-ONE, HUH?
So she says...
STARE
TCH
TWI
WELL...
ME? I THINK...
I'LL PASS!
I guess...
Slp
WHY ??!

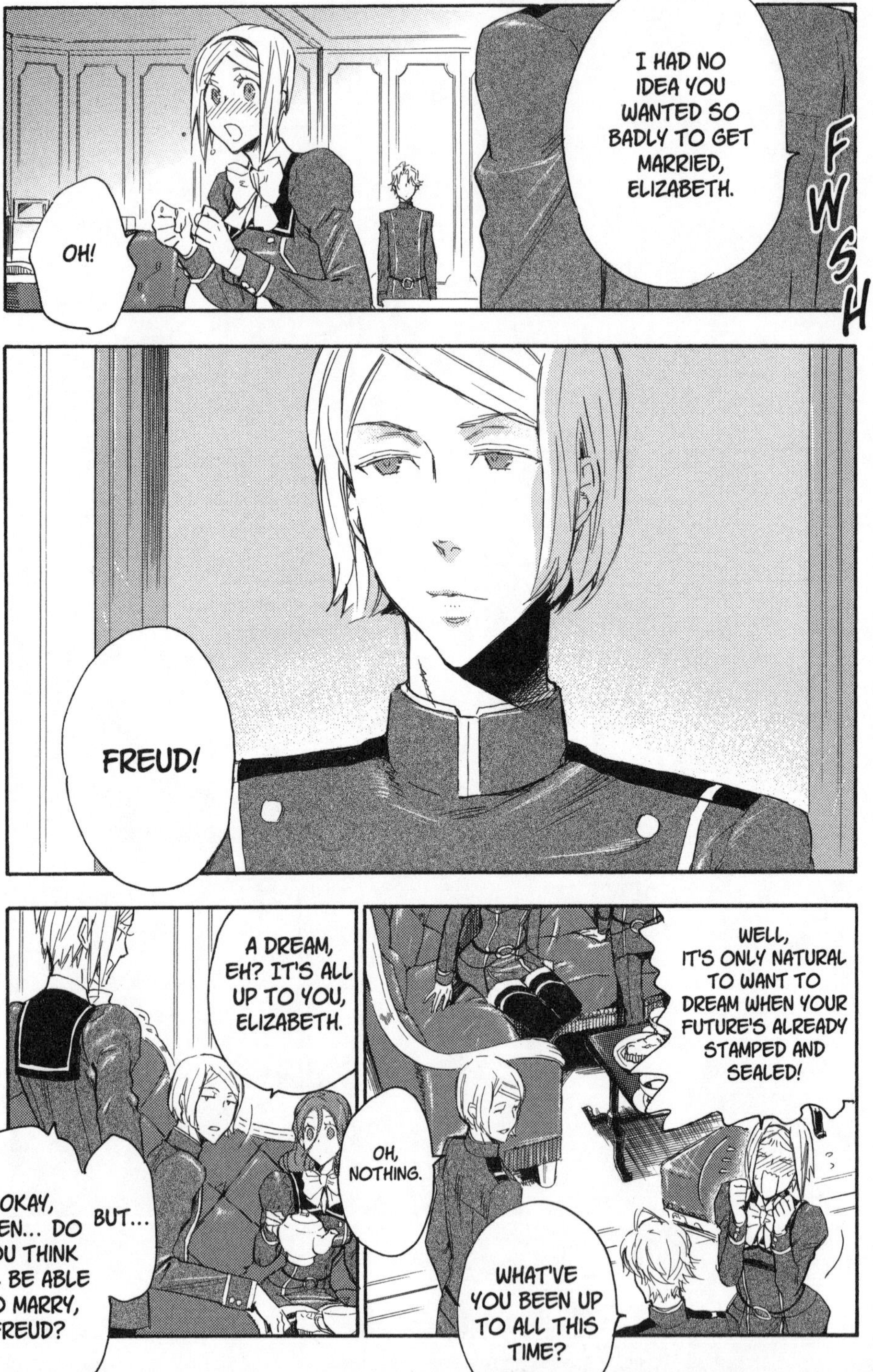
I HAD NO IDEA YOU WANTED SO BADLY TO GET MARRIED, ELIZABETH.
FWSH
OH!
FREUD!
WELL, IT'S ONLY NATURAL TO WANT TO DREAM WHEN YOUR FUTURE'S ALREADY STAMPED AND SEALED!
WHAT'VE YOU BEEN UP TO ALL THIS TIME?
OH, NOTHING.
A DREAM, EH? IT'S ALL UP TO YOU, ELIZABETH.
BUT...
OKAY, THEN... DO YOU THINK I'LL BE ABLE TO MARRY, FREUD?

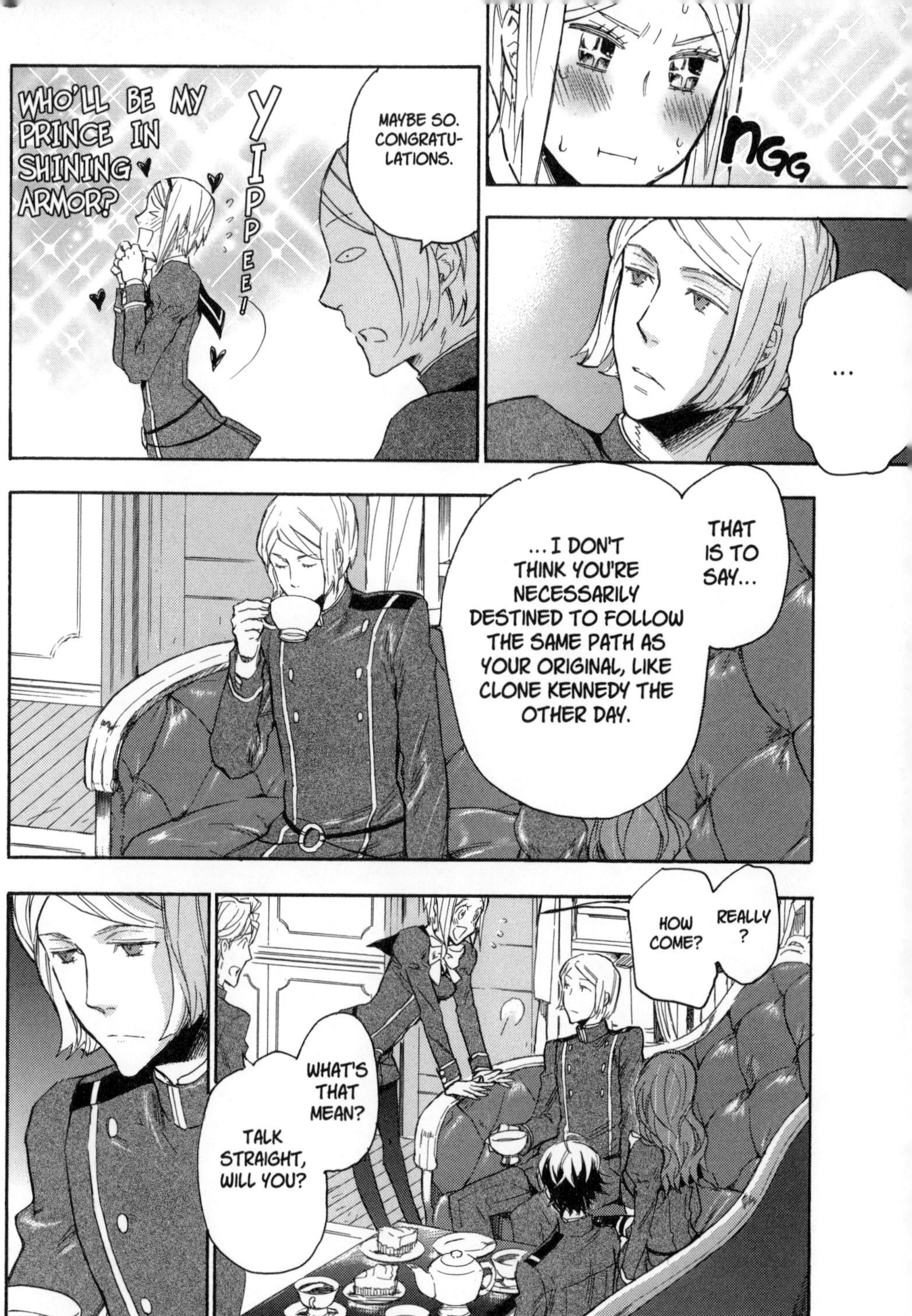
nGG
...
MAYBE SO. CONGRATU-LATIONS.
YIPPEE!
WHO'LL BE MY PRINCE IN SHINING ARMOR?
THAT IS TO SAY...
...I DON'T THINK YOU'RE NECESSARILY DESTINED TO FOLLOW THE SAME PATH AS YOUR ORIGINAL, LIKE CLONE KENNEDY THE OTHER DAY.
REALLY?
HOW COME?
WHAT'S THAT MEAN?
TALK STRAIGHT, WILL YOU?

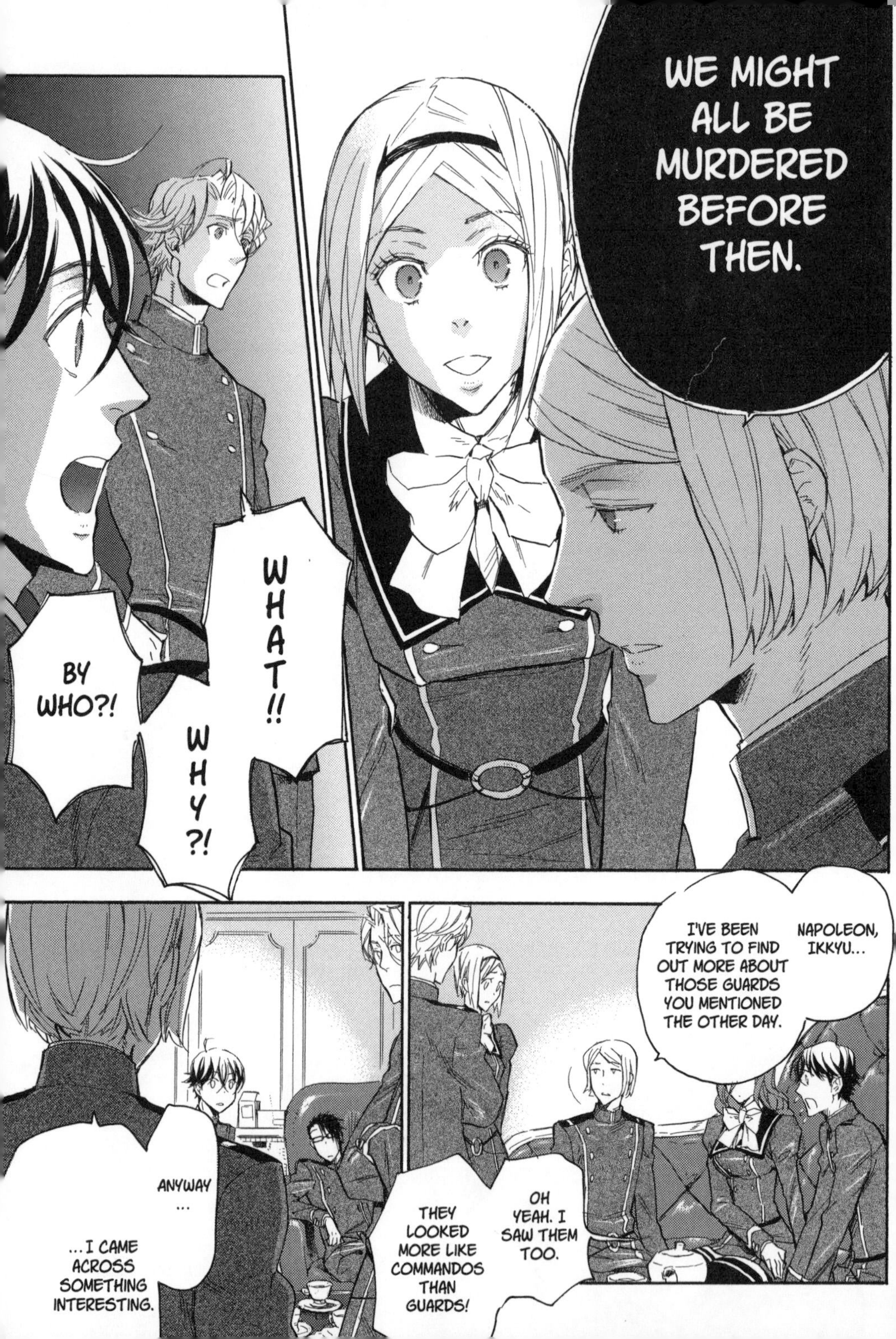
WE MIGHT ALL BE MURDERED BEFORE THEN.
WHAT!!
WHY?!
BY WHO?!
NAPOLEON, IKKYU...
I'VE BEEN TRYING TO FIND OUT MORE ABOUT THOSE GUARDS YOU MENTIONED THE OTHER DAY.
OH YEAH. I SAW THEM TOO.
THEY LOOKED MORE LIKE COMMANDOS THAN GUARDS!
ANYWAY...
...I CAME ACROSS SOMETHING INTERESTING.

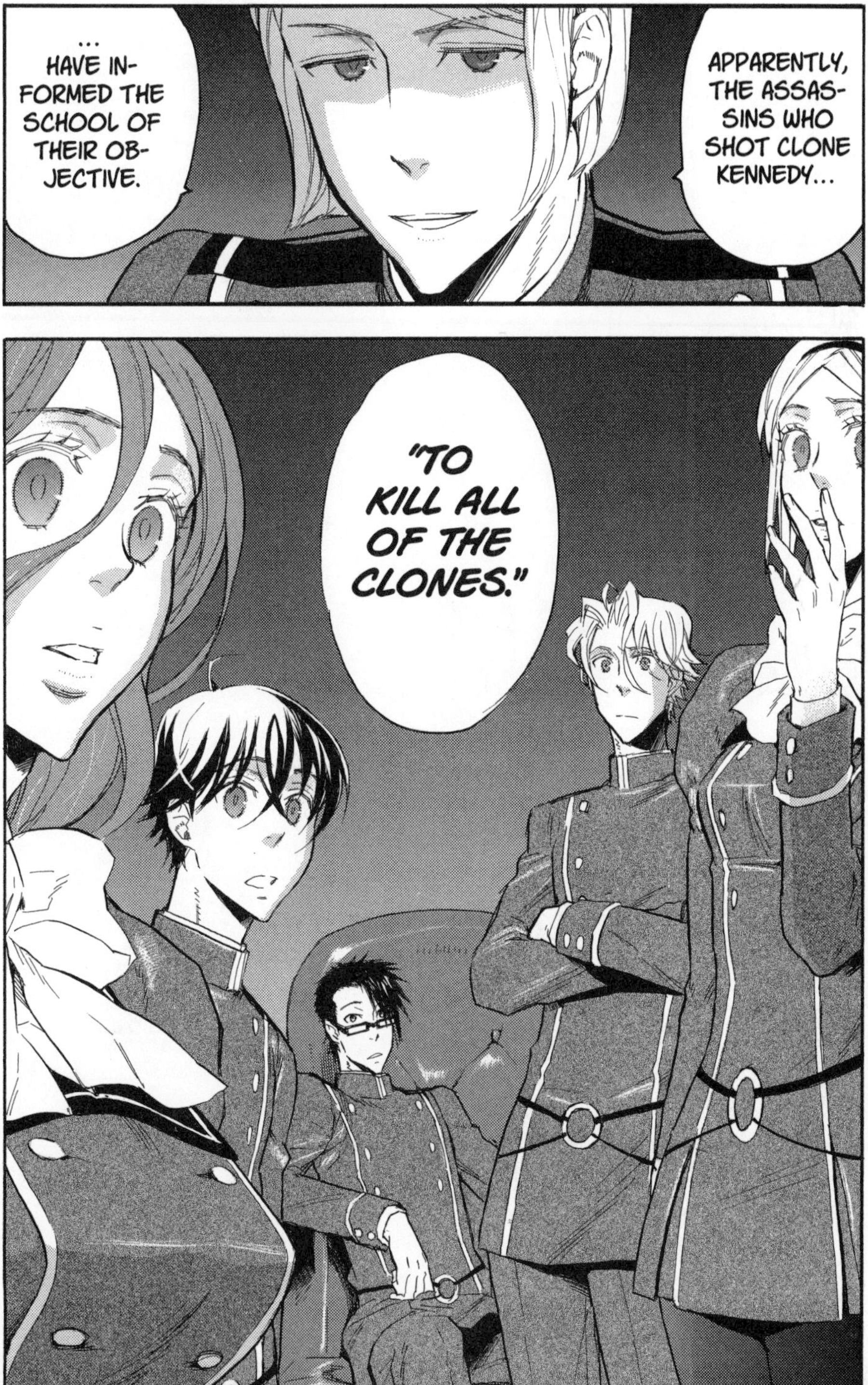
APPARENTLY, THE ASSASSINS WHO SHOT CLONE KENNEDY...
... HAVE INFORMED THE SCHOOL OF THEIR OBJECTIVE.
"TO KILL ALL OF THE CLONES."

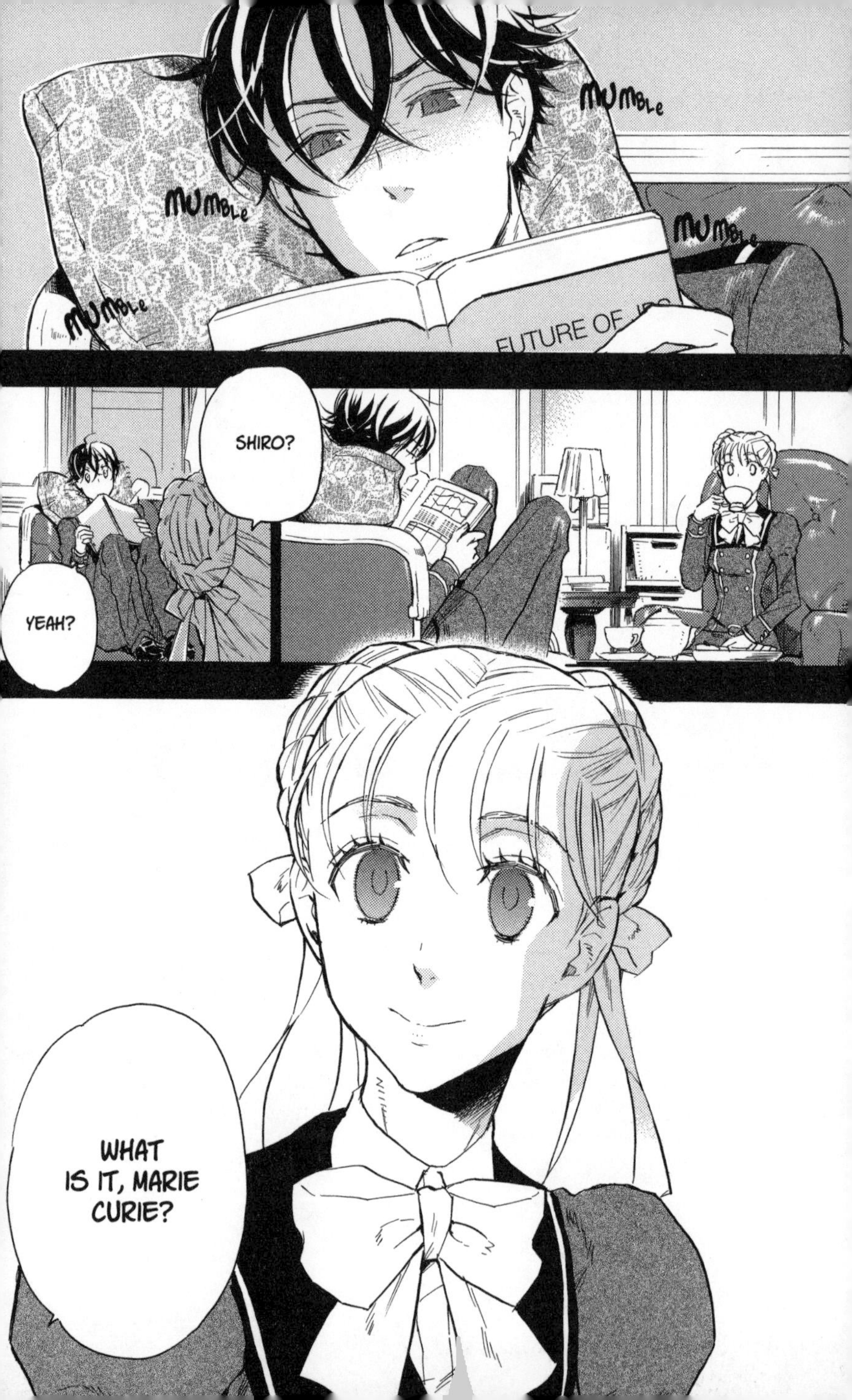
MUMBLE
MUMBLE
MUMBLE
MUMBLE
FUTURE OF
SHIRO?
YEAH?
WHAT IS IT, MARIE CURIE?

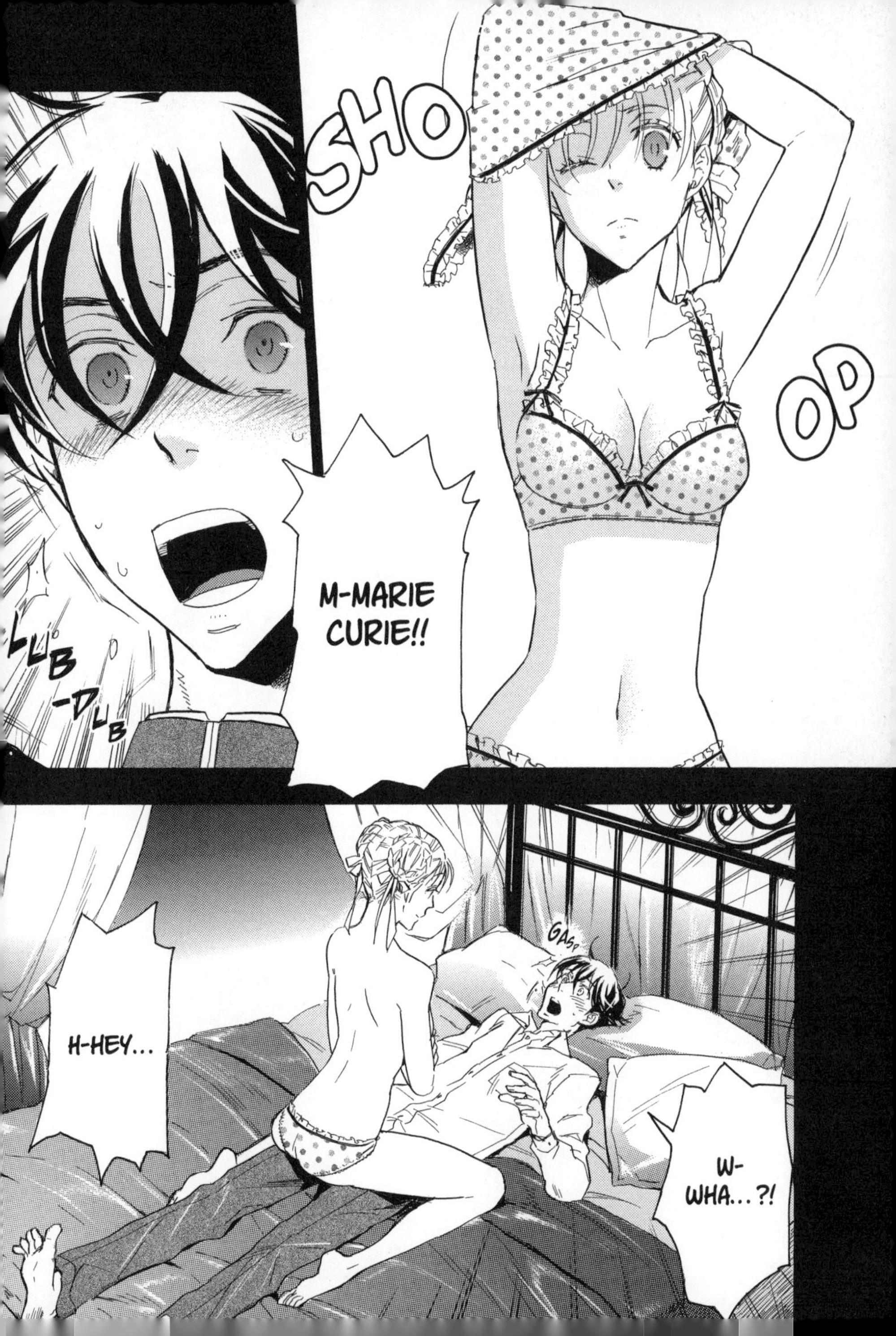
SHO
OP
M-MARIE CURIE!!
LUB-DUB
GASP
W-WHA...?!
H-HEY...

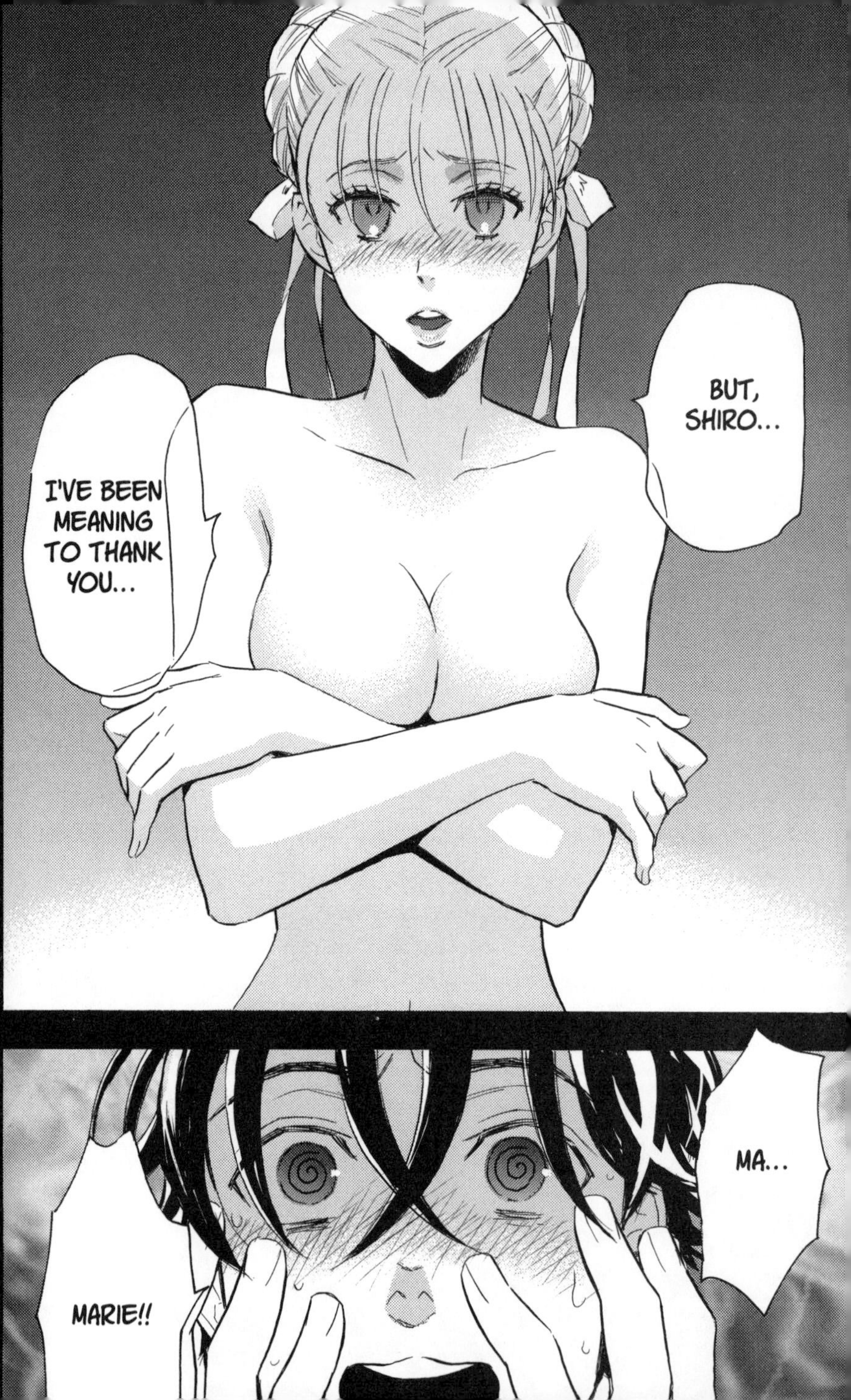
BUT, SHIRO...
I'VE BEEN MEANING TO THANK YOU...
MA...
MARIE!!

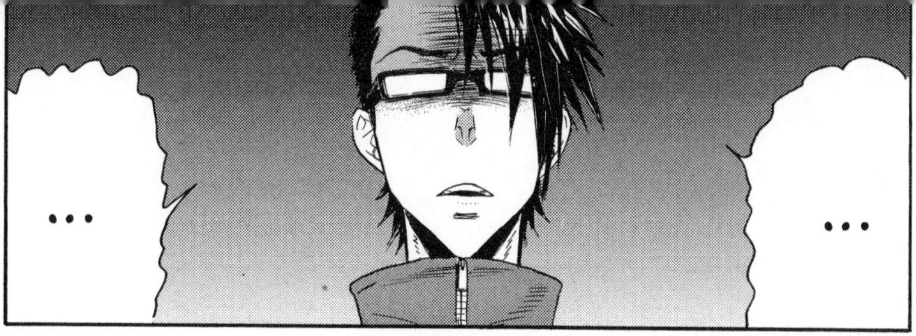
...
...

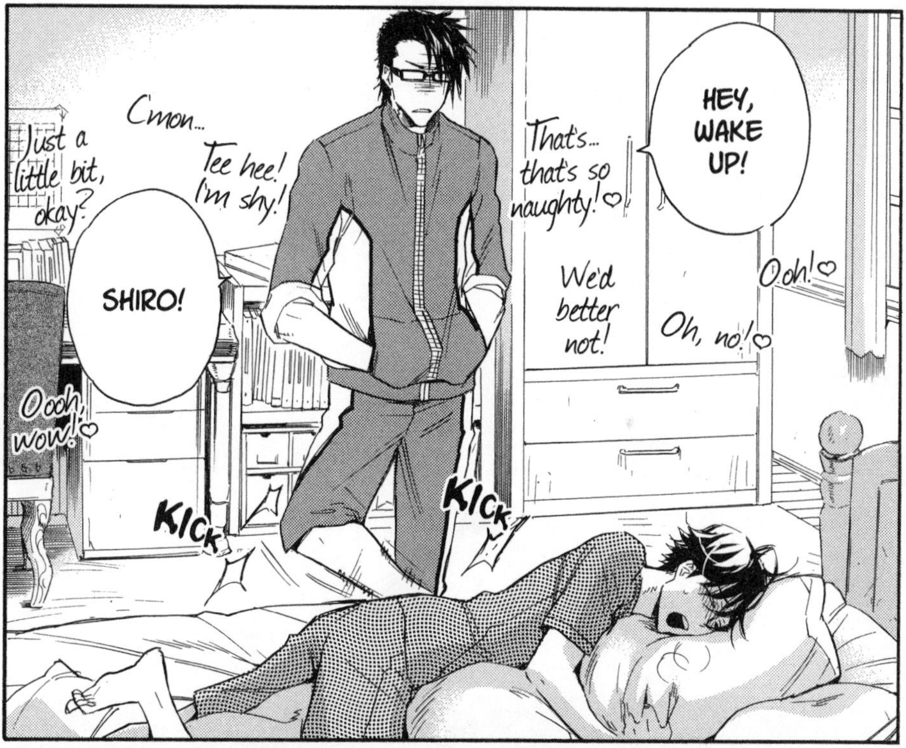
HEY, WAKE UP!
That's... that's so naughty!♡
Ooh!♡
Oh, no!♡
We'd better not!
KICK
Tee hee! I'm shy!
C'mon...
Just a little bit, okay?
SHIRO!
Oooh, wow!♡
KICK

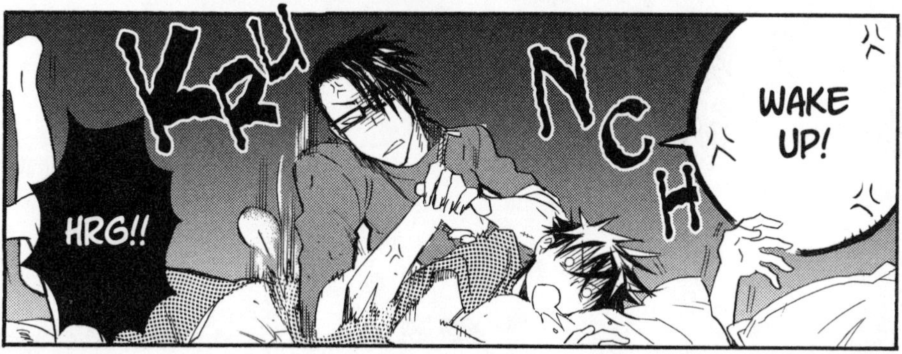
WAKE UP!
KRUNCH
HRG!!

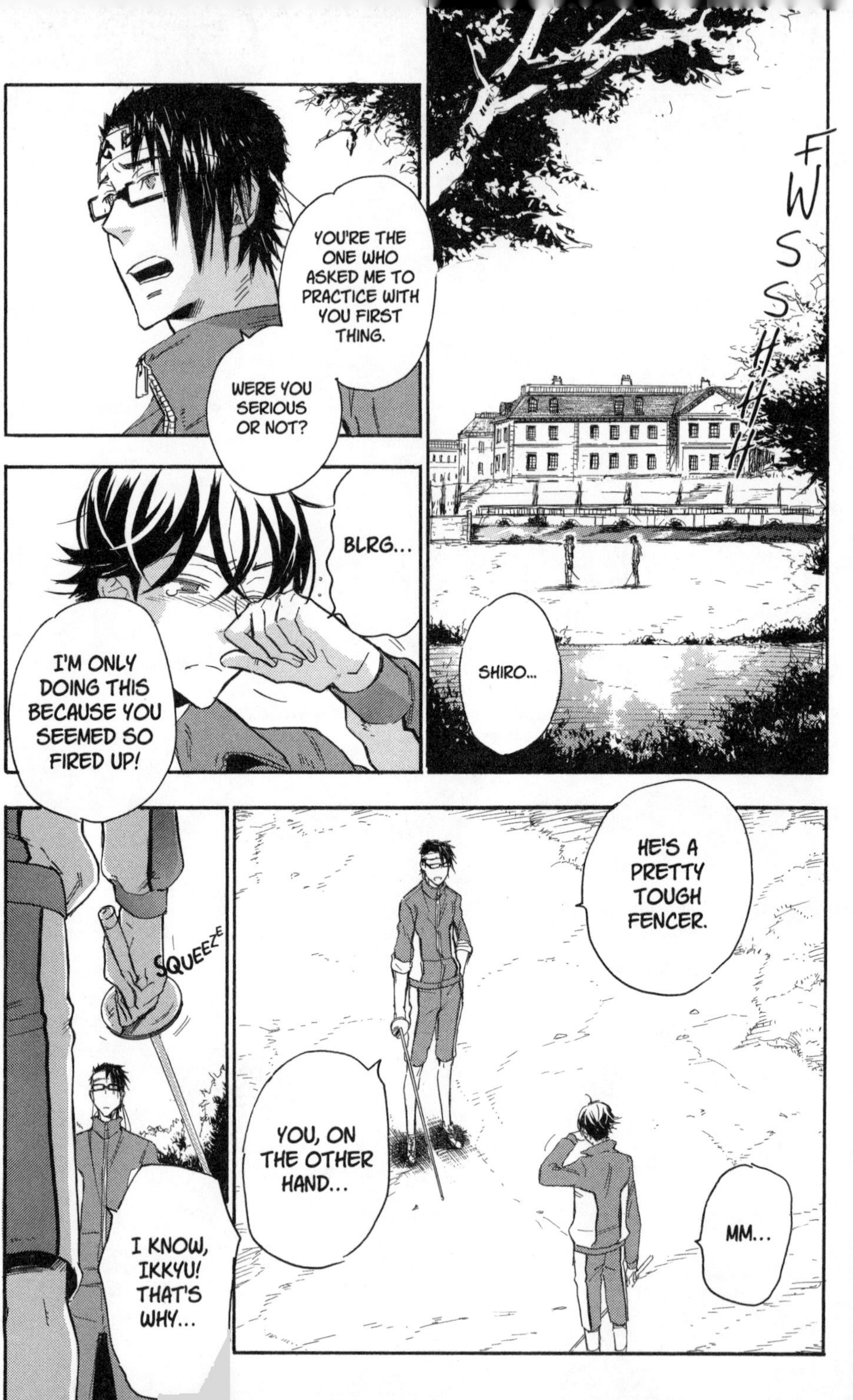
FWSSHHHH
SHIRO...
YOU'RE THE ONE WHO ASKED ME TO PRACTICE WITH YOU FIRST THING.
WERE YOU SERIOUS OR NOT?
BLRG...
I'M ONLY DOING THIS BECAUSE YOU SEEMED SO FIRED UP!
HE'S A PRETTY TOUGH FENCER.
YOU, ON THE OTHER HAND...
MM...
SQUEEZE
I KNOW, IKKYU! THAT'S WHY...

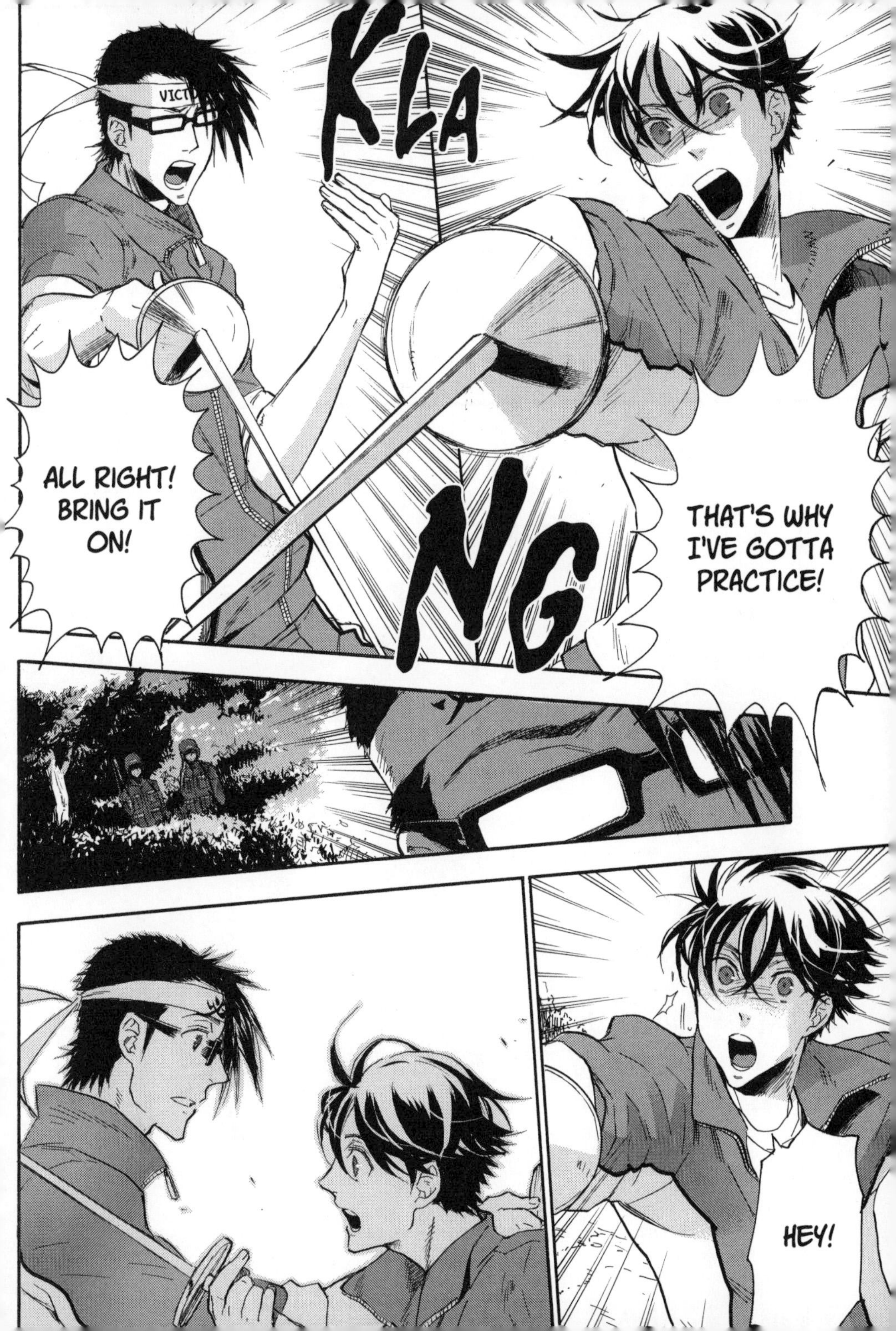
THAT'S WHY I'VE GOTTA PRACTICE!
KLANG
ALL RIGHT! BRING IT ON!
HEY!

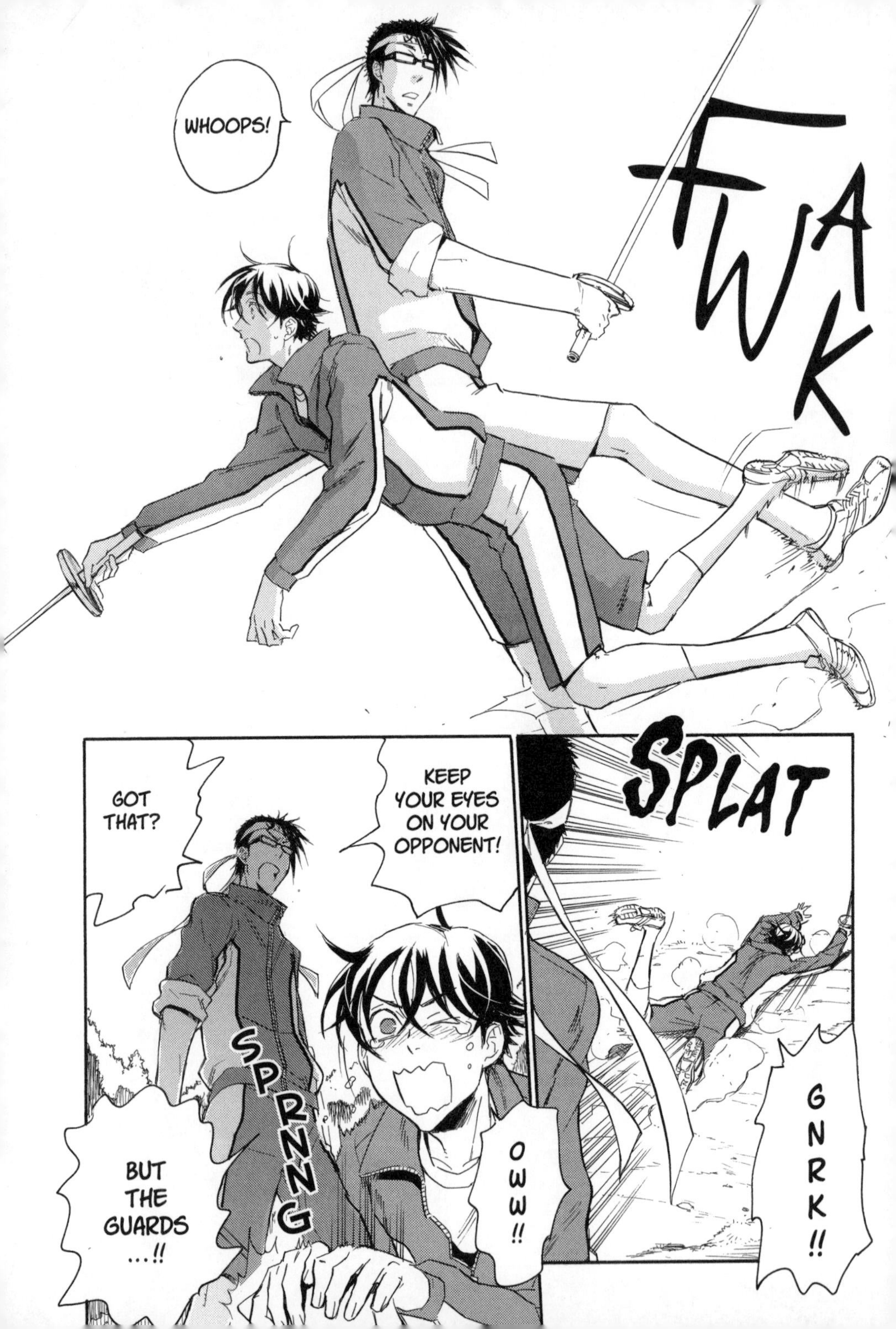
WHOOPS!
FWAK
SPLAT
GNRK!!
KEEP YOUR EYES ON YOUR OPPONENT!
GOT THAT?
OWW!!
SPRNNG
BUT THE GUARDS ...!!

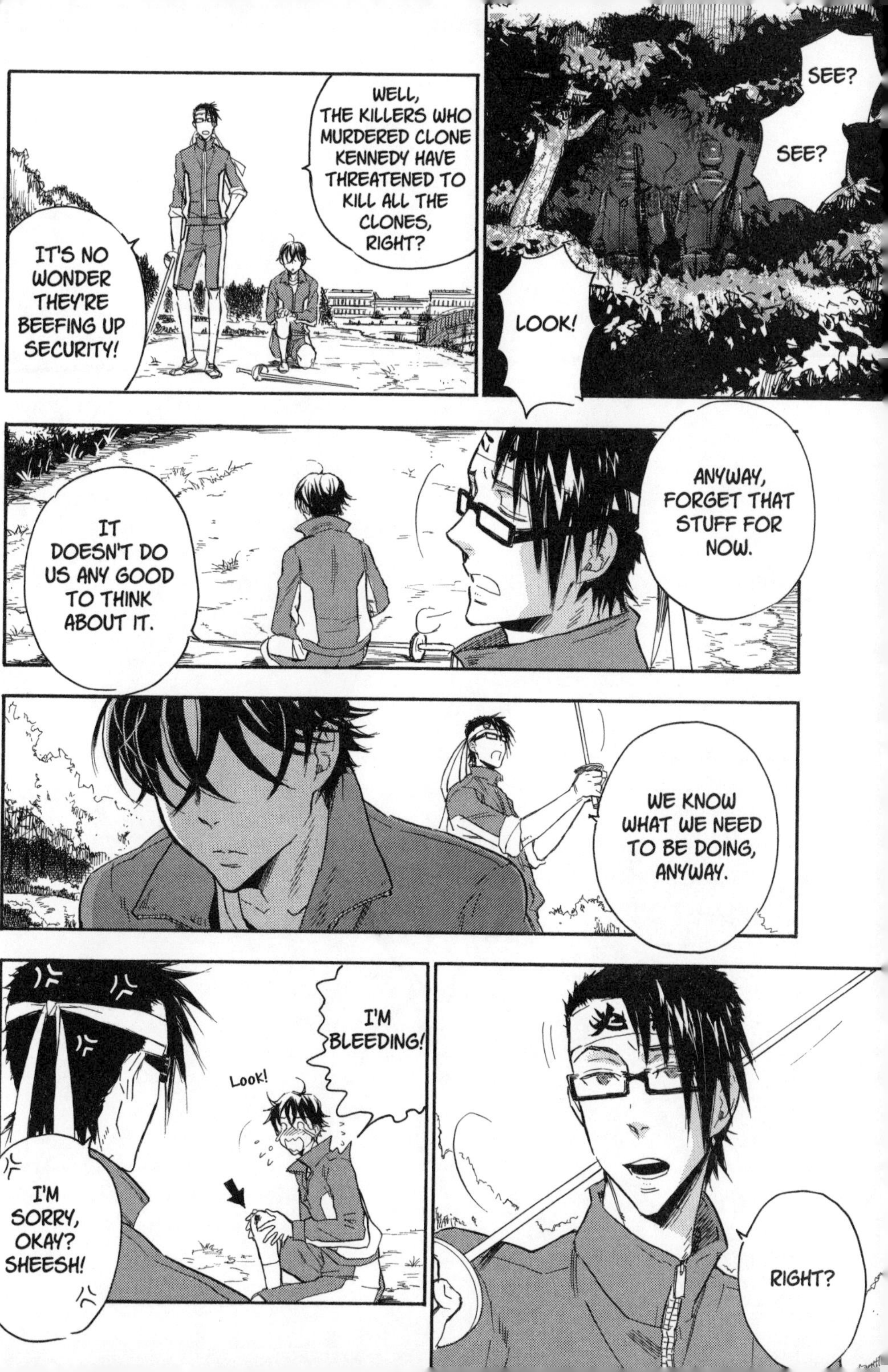
SEE?
SEE?
LOOK!
WELL, THE KILLERS WHO MURDERED CLONE KENNEDY HAVE THREATENED TO KILL ALL THE CLONES, RIGHT?
IT'S NO WONDER THEY'RE BEEFING UP SECURITY!
ANYWAY, FORGET THAT STUFF FOR NOW.
IT DOESN'T DO US ANY GOOD TO THINK ABOUT IT.
WE KNOW WHAT WE NEED TO BE DOING, ANYWAY.
RIGHT?
I'M BLEEDING!
Look!
I'M SORRY, OKAY? SHEESH!

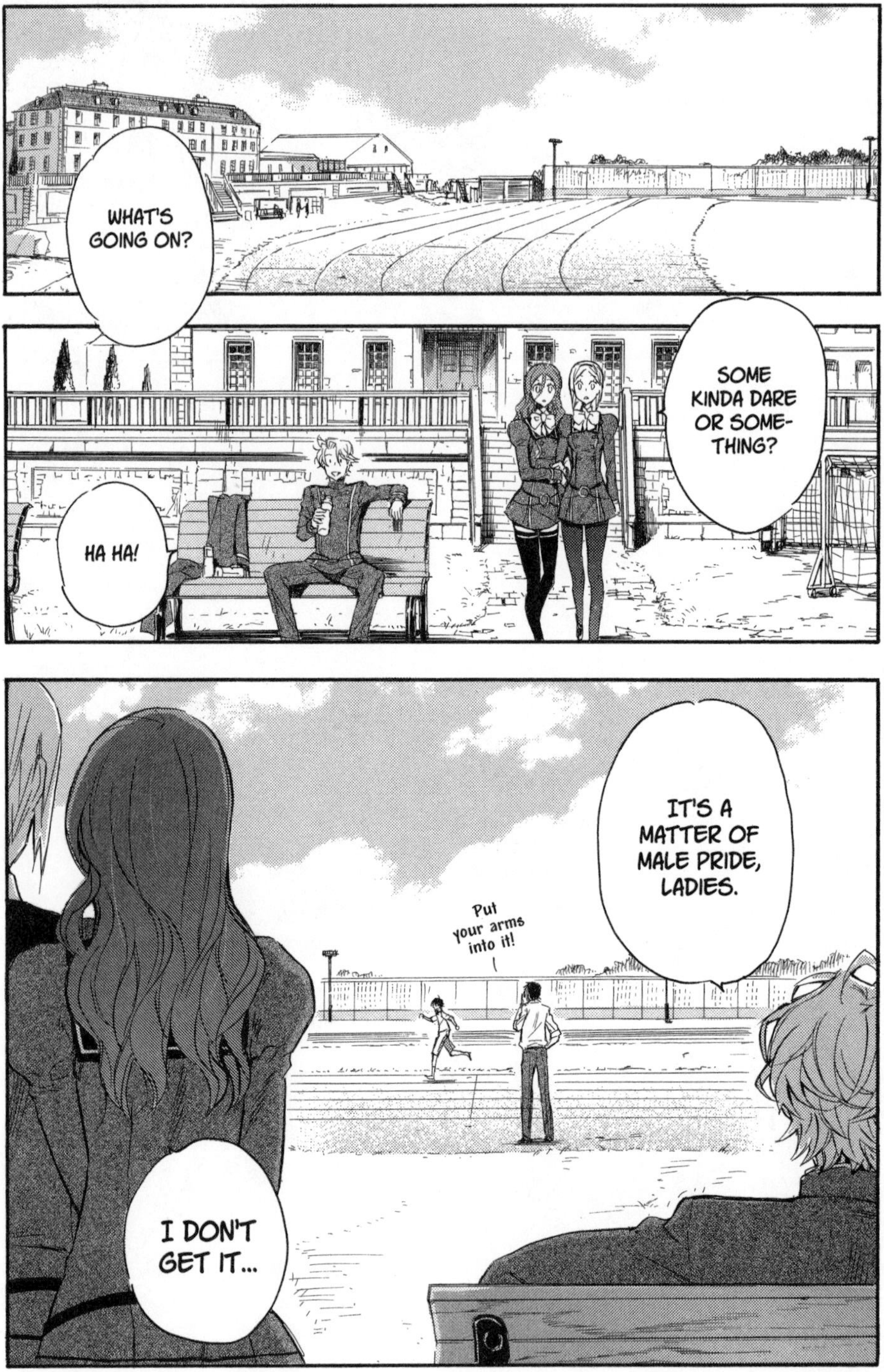
WHAT'S GOING ON?
SOME KINDA DARE OR SOME-THING?
HA HA!
IT'S A MATTER OF MALE PRIDE, LADIES.
Put your arms into it!
I DON'T GET IT...

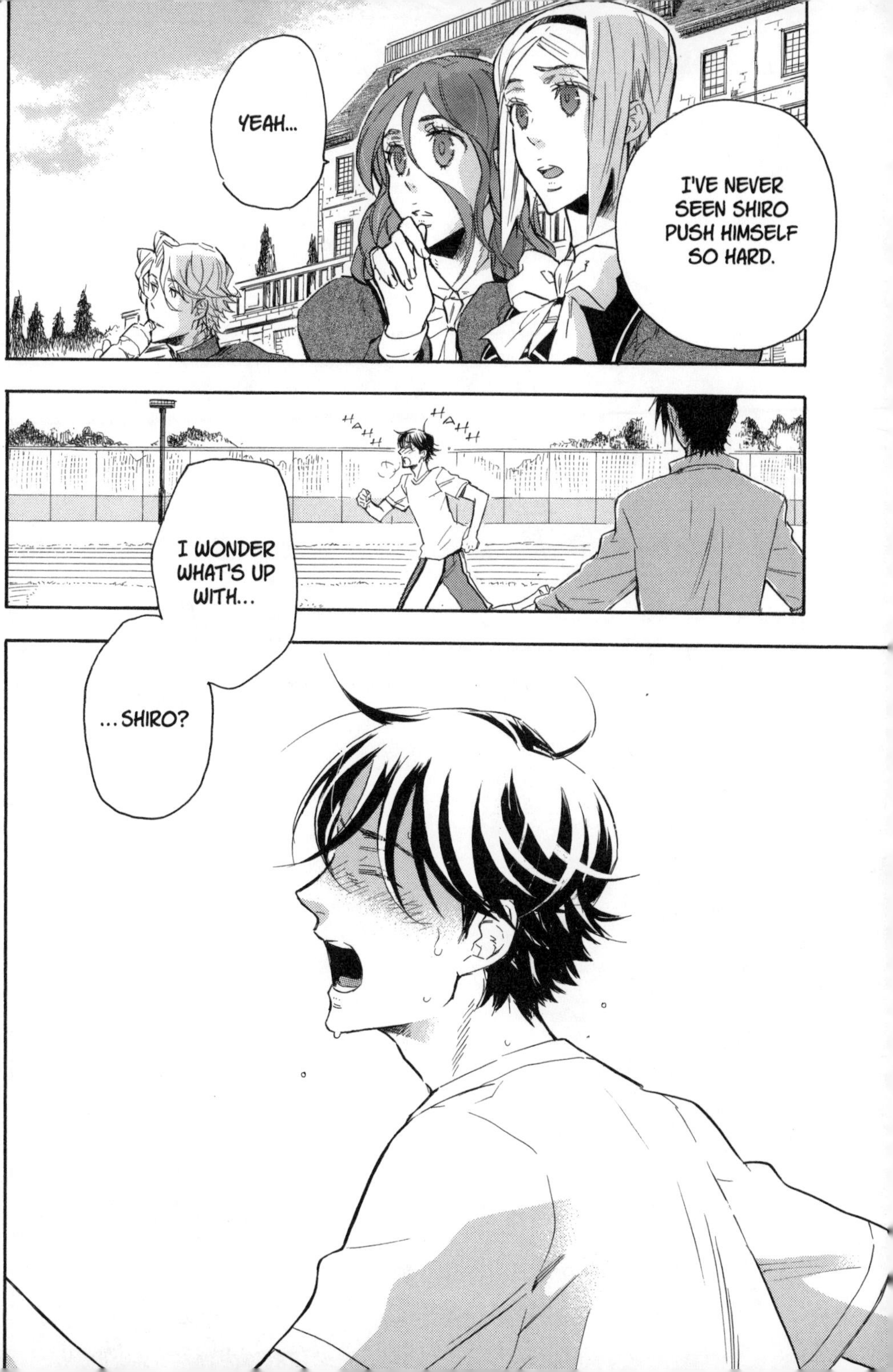
I'VE NEVER SEEN SHIRO PUSH HIMSELF SO HARD.
YEAH...
HAHH
HAHH
I WONDER WHAT'S UP WITH...
...SHIRO?

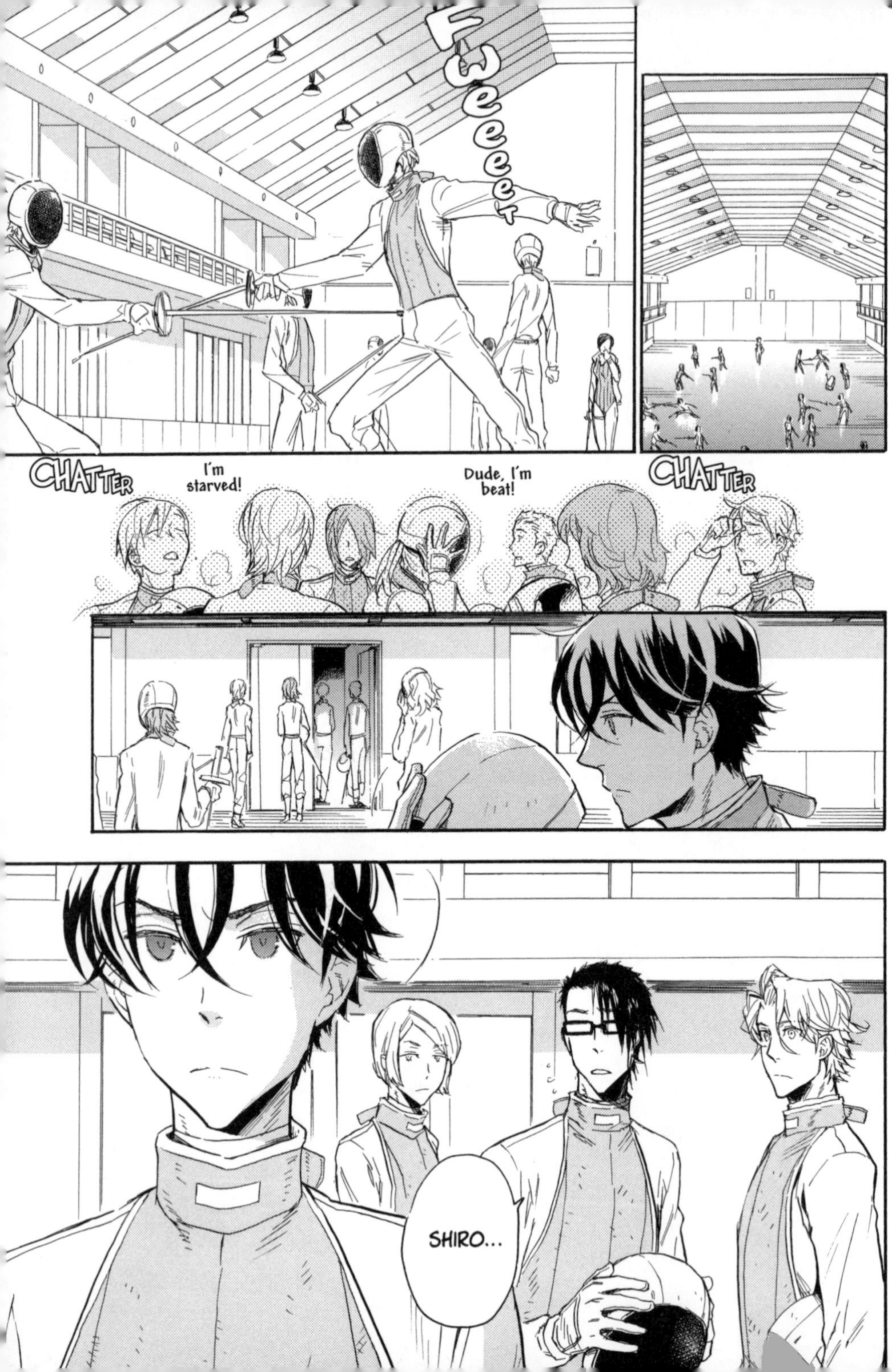
Fweeeet
CHATTER
Dude, I'm beat!
I'm starved!
CHATTER
SHIRO...

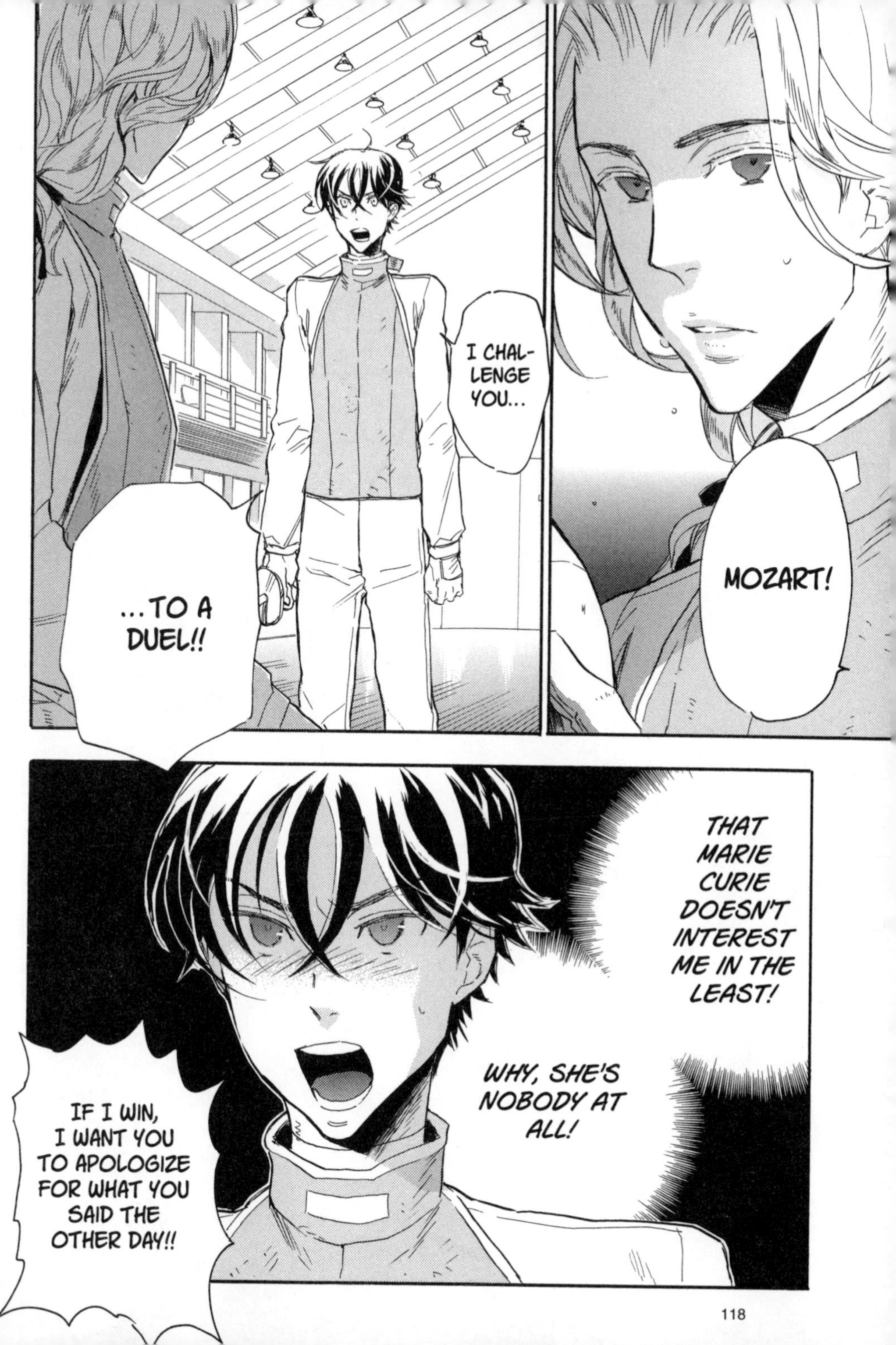
MOZART!
I CHAL-LENGE YOU...
...TO A DUEL!!
THAT MARIE CURIE DOESN'T INTEREST ME IN THE LEAST!
WHY, SHE'S NOBODY AT ALL!
IF I WIN, I WANT YOU TO APOLOGIZE FOR WHAT YOU SAID THE OTHER DAY!!

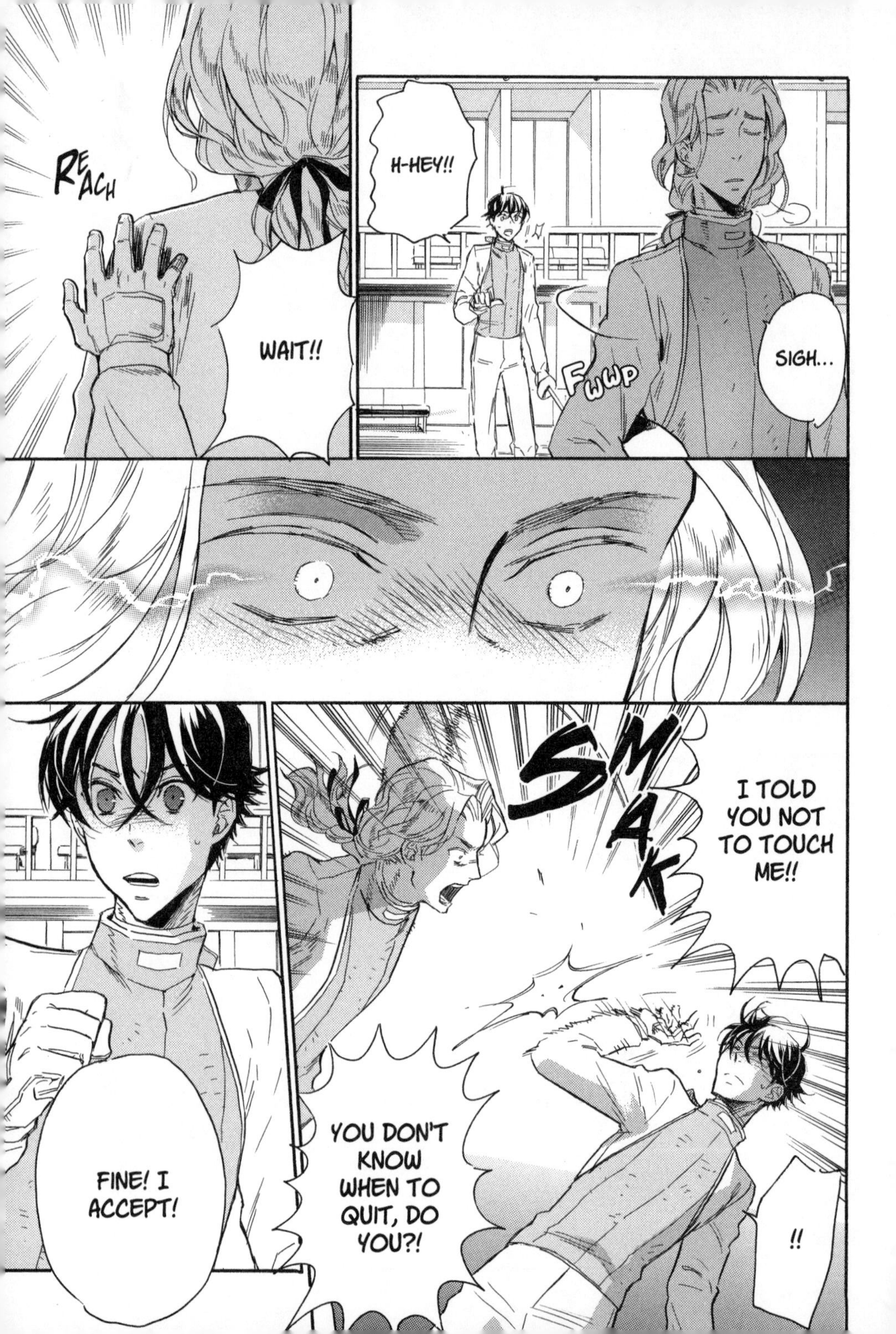
H-HEY!!
SIGH...
FWWP
REACH
WAIT!!
I TOLD YOU NOT TO TOUCH ME!!
SMAK
YOU DON'T KNOW WHEN TO QUIT, DO YOU?!
!!
FINE! I ACCEPT!

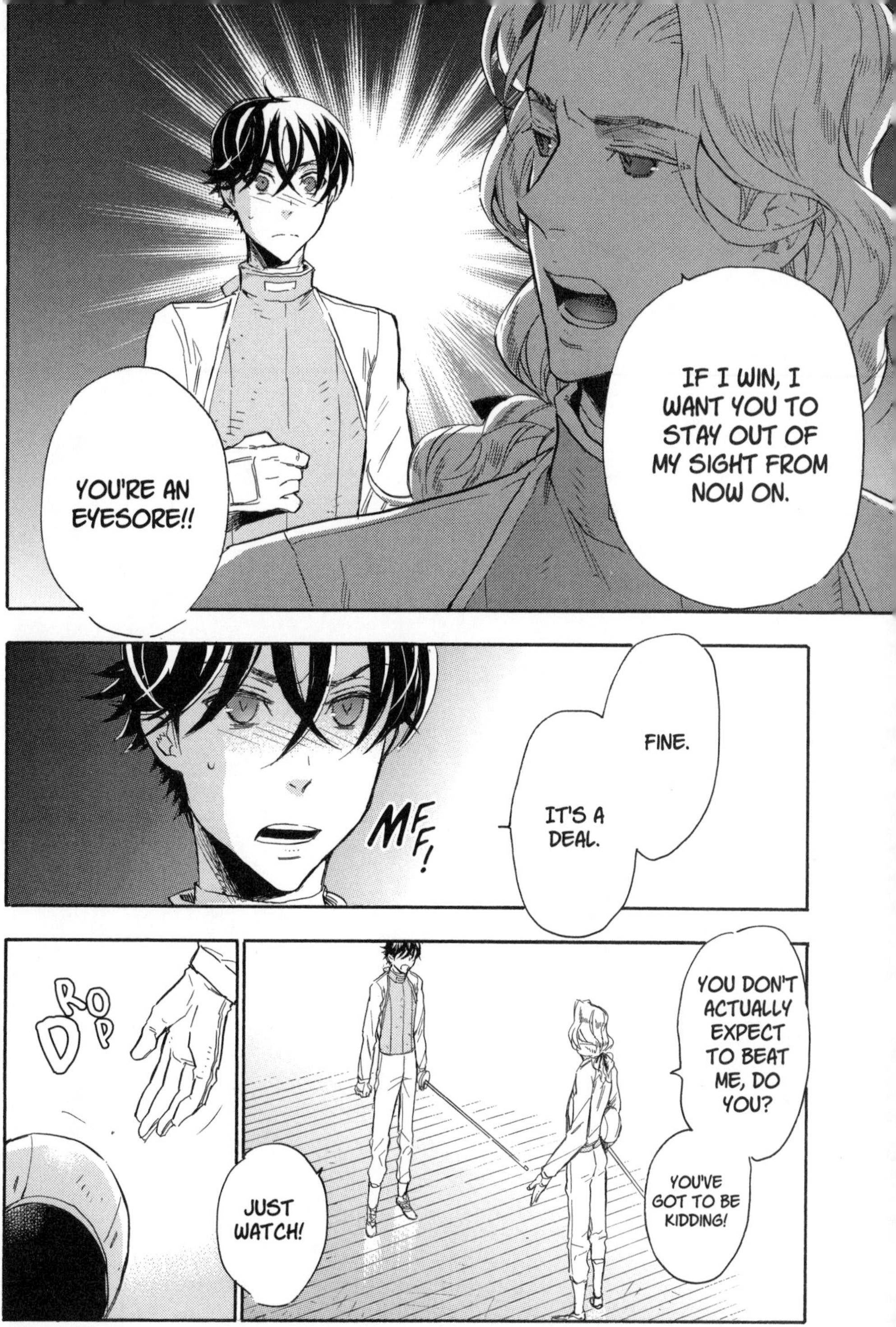
IF I WIN, I WANT YOU TO STAY OUT OF MY SIGHT FROM NOW ON.
YOU'RE AN EYESORE!!
FINE.
IT'S A DEAL.
MFF!
YOU DON'T ACTUALLY EXPECT TO BEAT ME, DO YOU?
YOU'VE GOT TO BE KIDDING!
JUST WATCH!
DROP

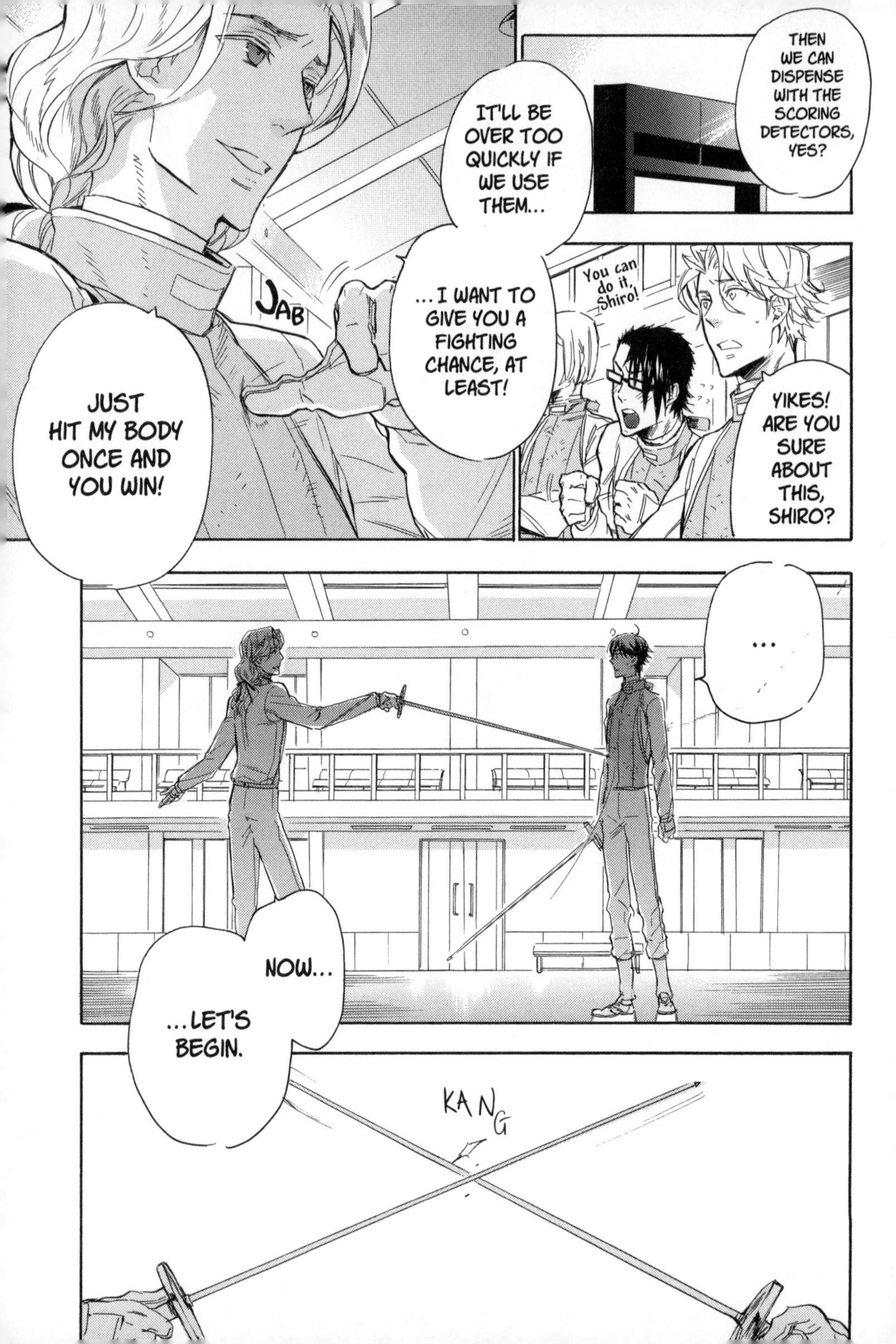
THEN WE CAN DISPENSE WITH THE SCORING DETECTORS, YES?
You can do it, Shiro!
YIKES! ARE YOU SURE ABOUT THIS, SHIRO?
IT'LL BE OVER TOO QUICKLY IF WE USE THEM...
...I WANT TO GIVE YOU A FIGHTING CHANCE, AT LEAST!
JAB
JUST HIT MY BODY ONCE AND YOU WIN!
...
NOW...
...LET'S BEGIN.
KANG

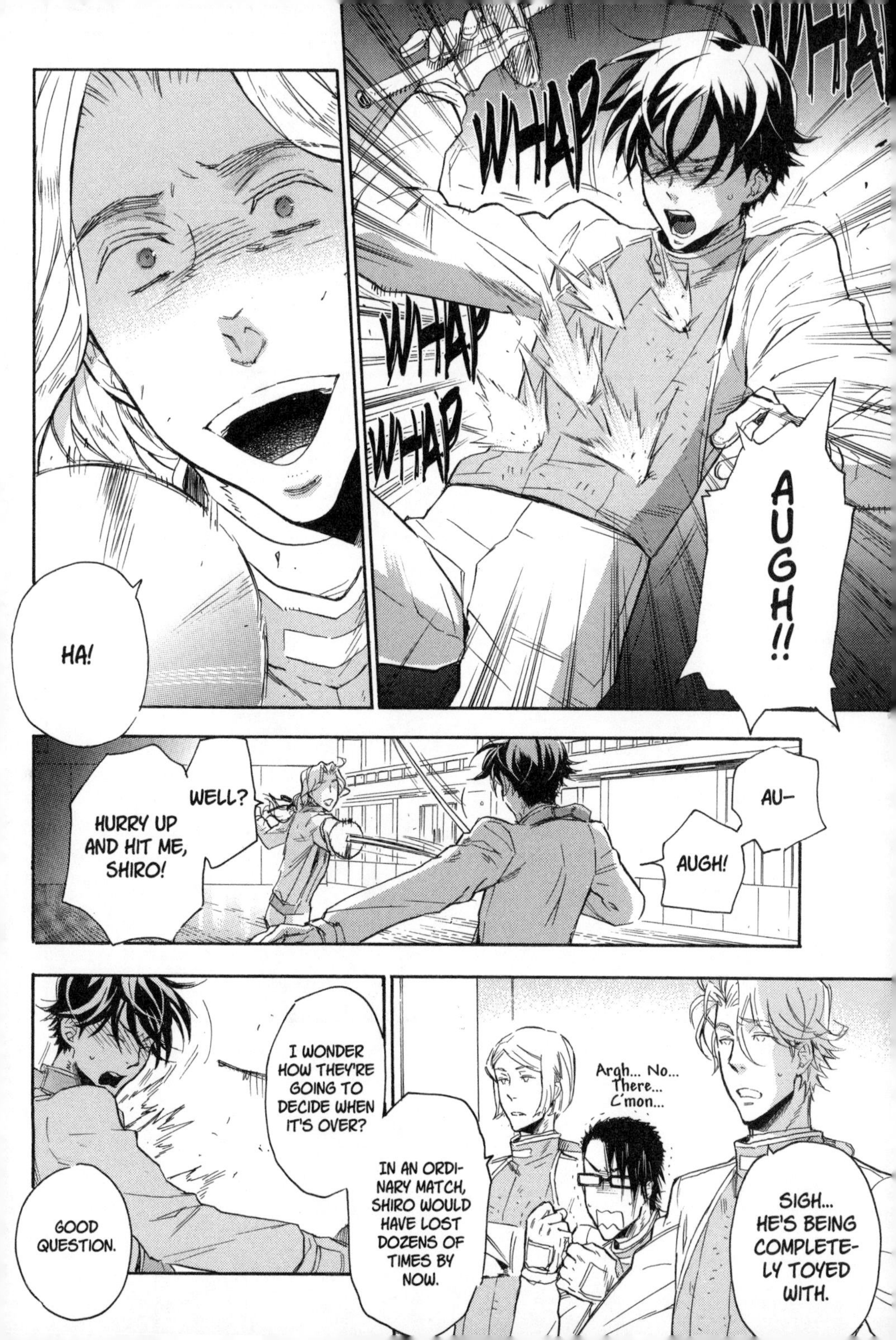
WHAP
WHAP
WHAP
WHAP
AUGH!!
HA!
AU-
AUGH!
WELL?
HURRY UP AND HIT ME, SHIRO!
SIGH... HE'S BEING COMPLETE-LY TOYED WITH.
Argh... No... There... C'mon...
IN AN ORDI-NARY MATCH, SHIRO WOULD HAVE LOST DOZENS OF TIMES BY NOW.
I WONDER HOW THEY'RE GOING TO DECIDE WHEN IT'S OVER?
GOOD QUESTION.

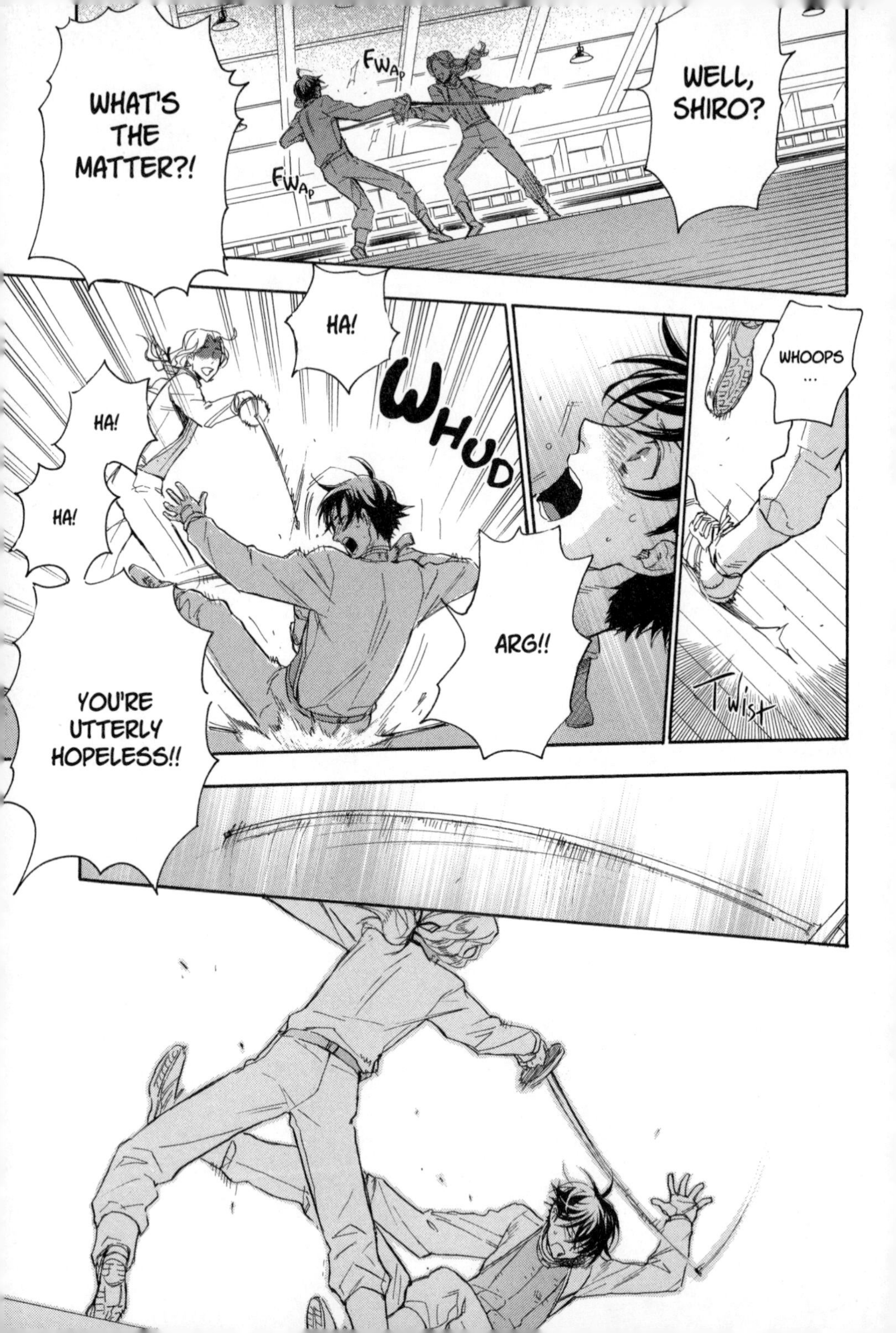
WELL, SHIRO?
FWAP
FWAP
WHAT'S THE MATTER?!
WHOOPS...
TWIST
ARG!!
HA!
WHUD
HA!
HA!
YOU'RE UTTERLY HOPELESS!!

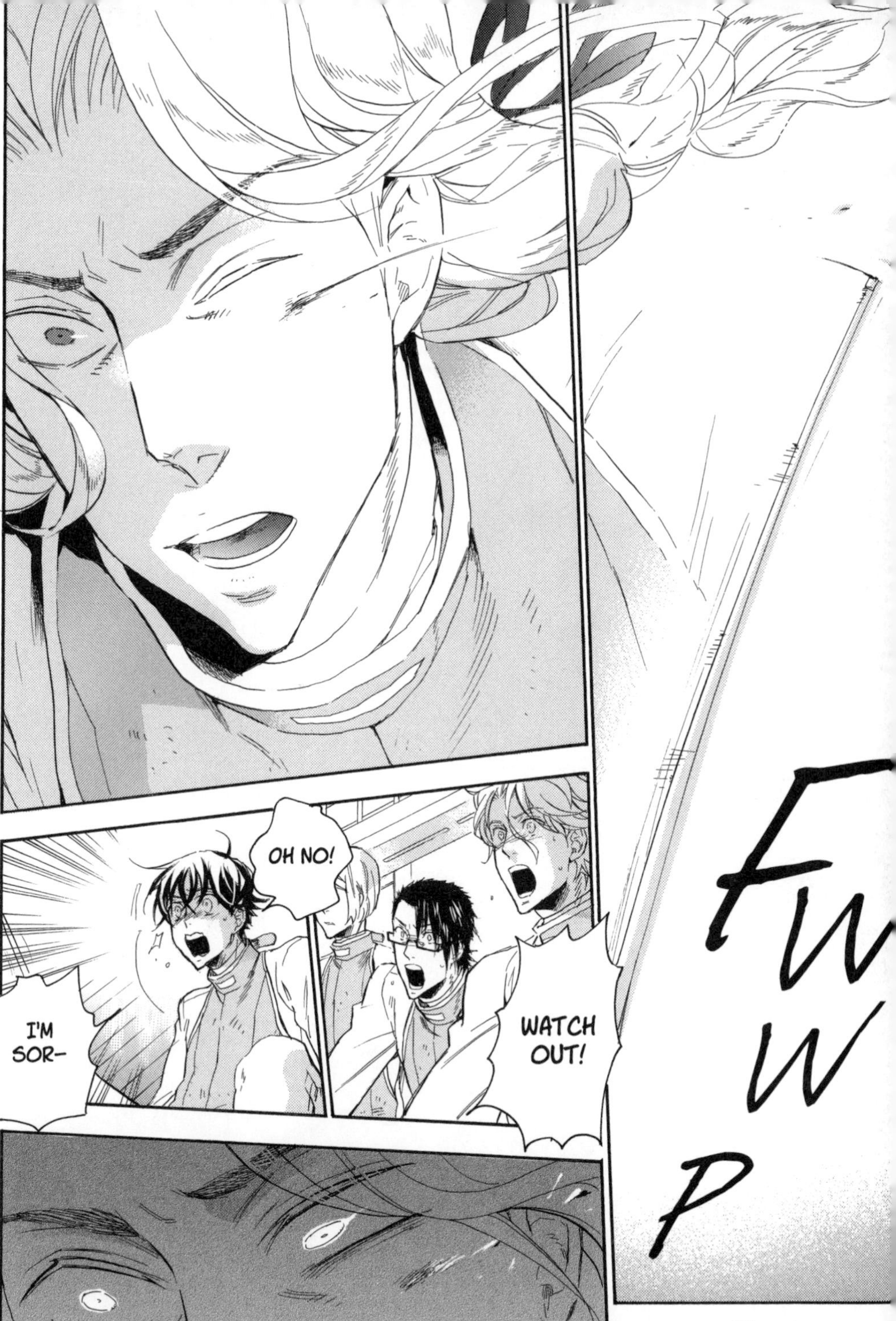
FWUP
WATCH OUT!
OH NO!
I'M SOR-

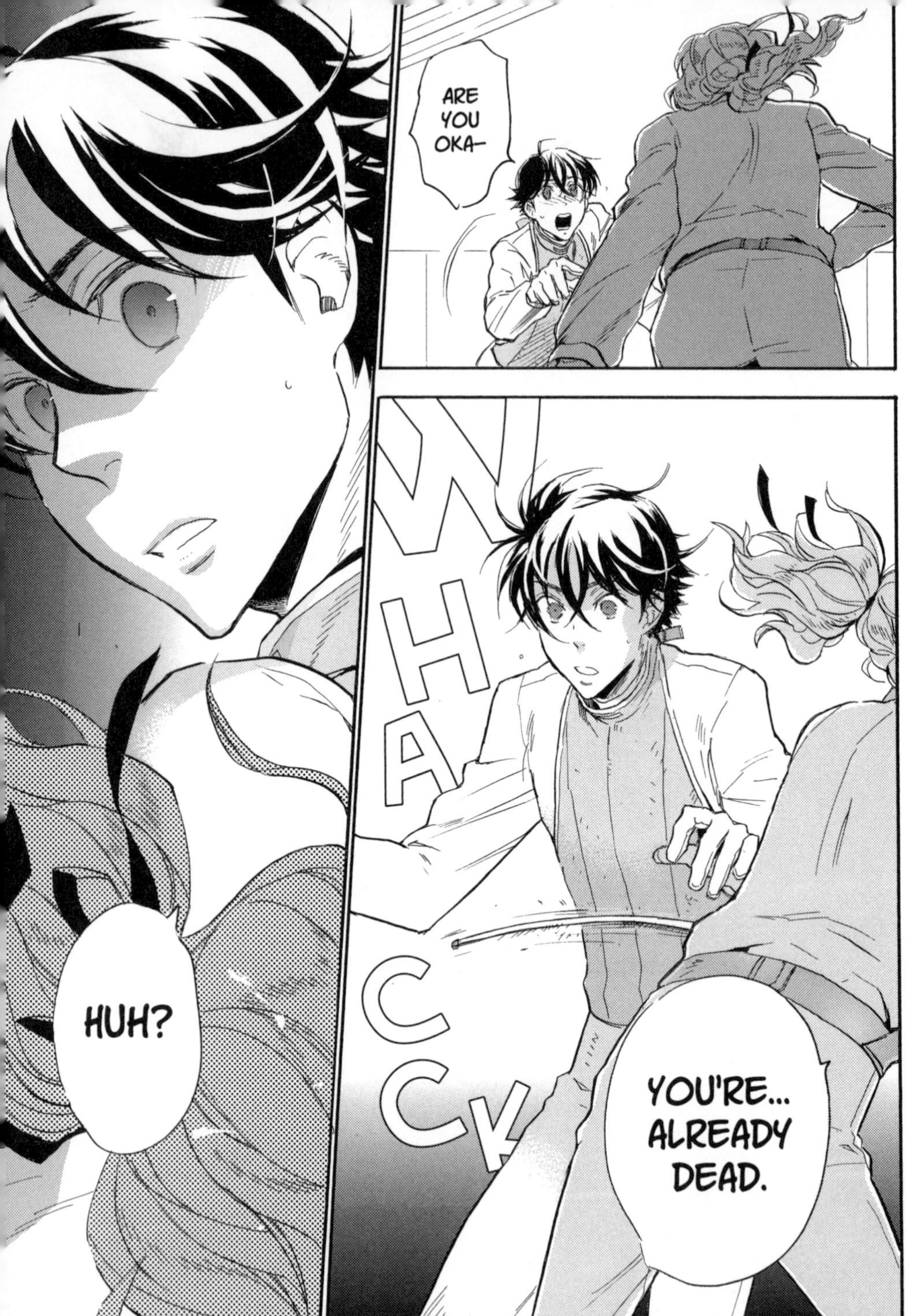
ARE YOU OKA—
WHACK
YOU'RE... ALREADY DEAD.
HUH?

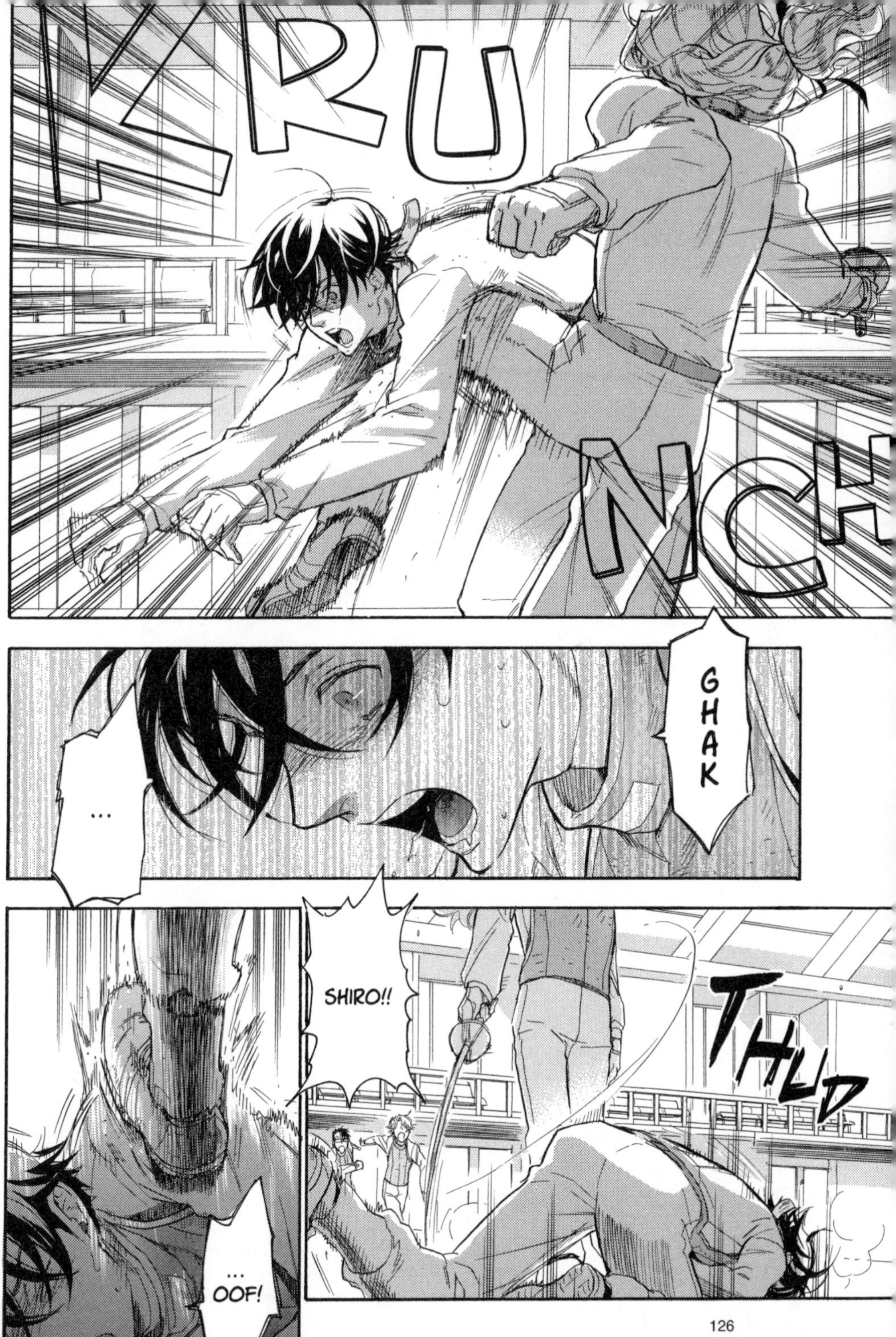
KRU
NCH
GHAK
...
SHIRO!!
THUD
...
OOF!

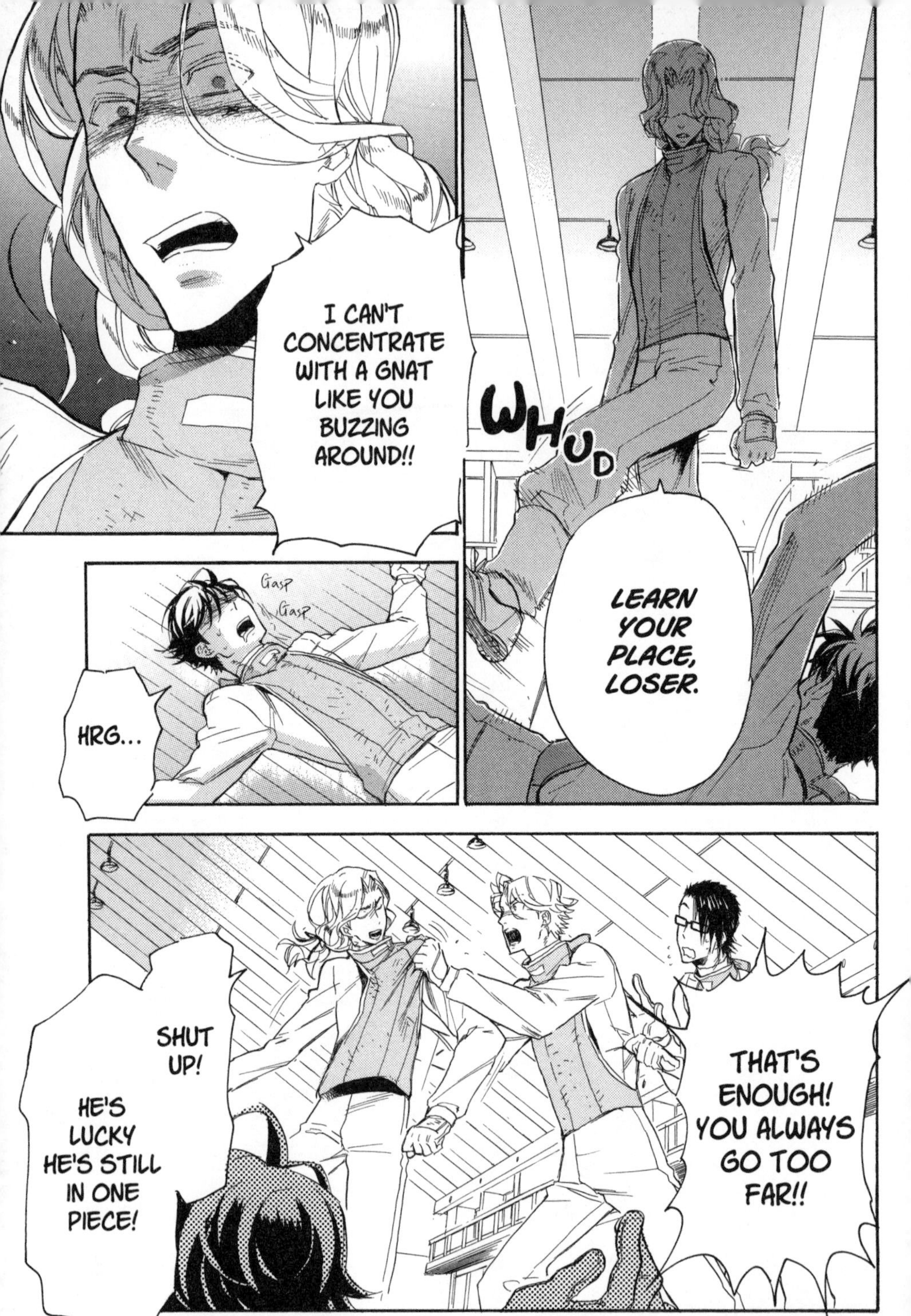
WHUD
LEARN YOUR PLACE, LOSER.
I CAN'T CONCENTRATE WITH A GNAT LIKE YOU BUZZING AROUND!!
Gasp
Gasp
HRG...
THAT'S ENOUGH! YOU ALWAYS GO TOO FAR!!
SHUT UP!
HE'S LUCKY HE'S STILL IN ONE PIECE!

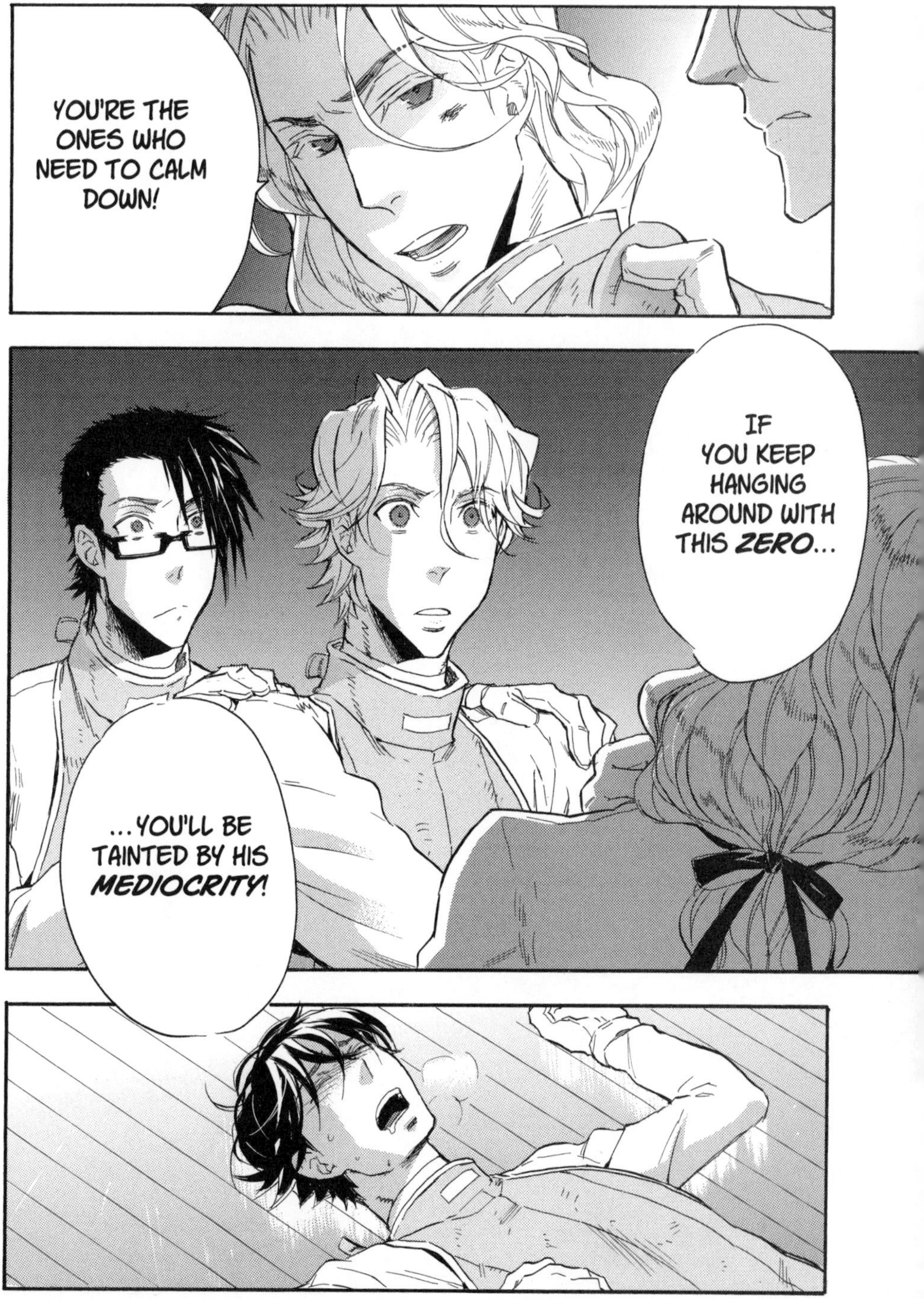
YOU'RE THE ONES WHO NEED TO CALM DOWN!
IF YOU KEEP HANGING AROUND WITH THIS ZERO...
...YOU'LL BE TAINTED BY HIS MEDIOCRITY!

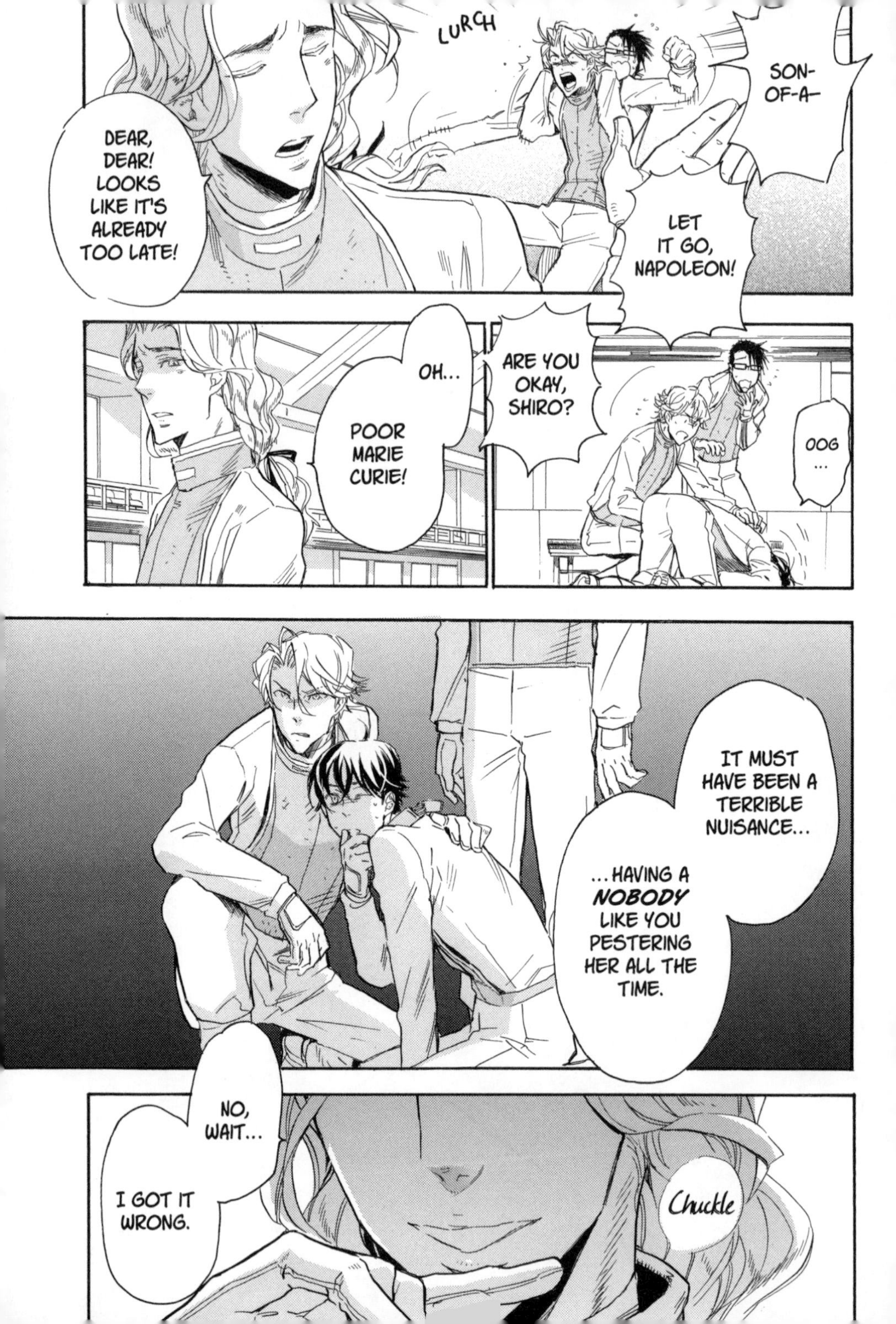
SON-OF-A-
LURCH
LET IT GO, NAPOLEON!
DEAR, DEAR! LOOKS LIKE IT'S ALREADY TOO LATE!
ARE YOU OKAY, SHIRO?
OOG ...
OH...
POOR MARIE CURIE!
IT MUST HAVE BEEN A TERRIBLE NUISANCE...
...HAVING A **NOBODY** LIKE YOU PESTERING HER ALL THE TIME.
Chuckle
NO, WAIT...
I GOT IT WRONG.

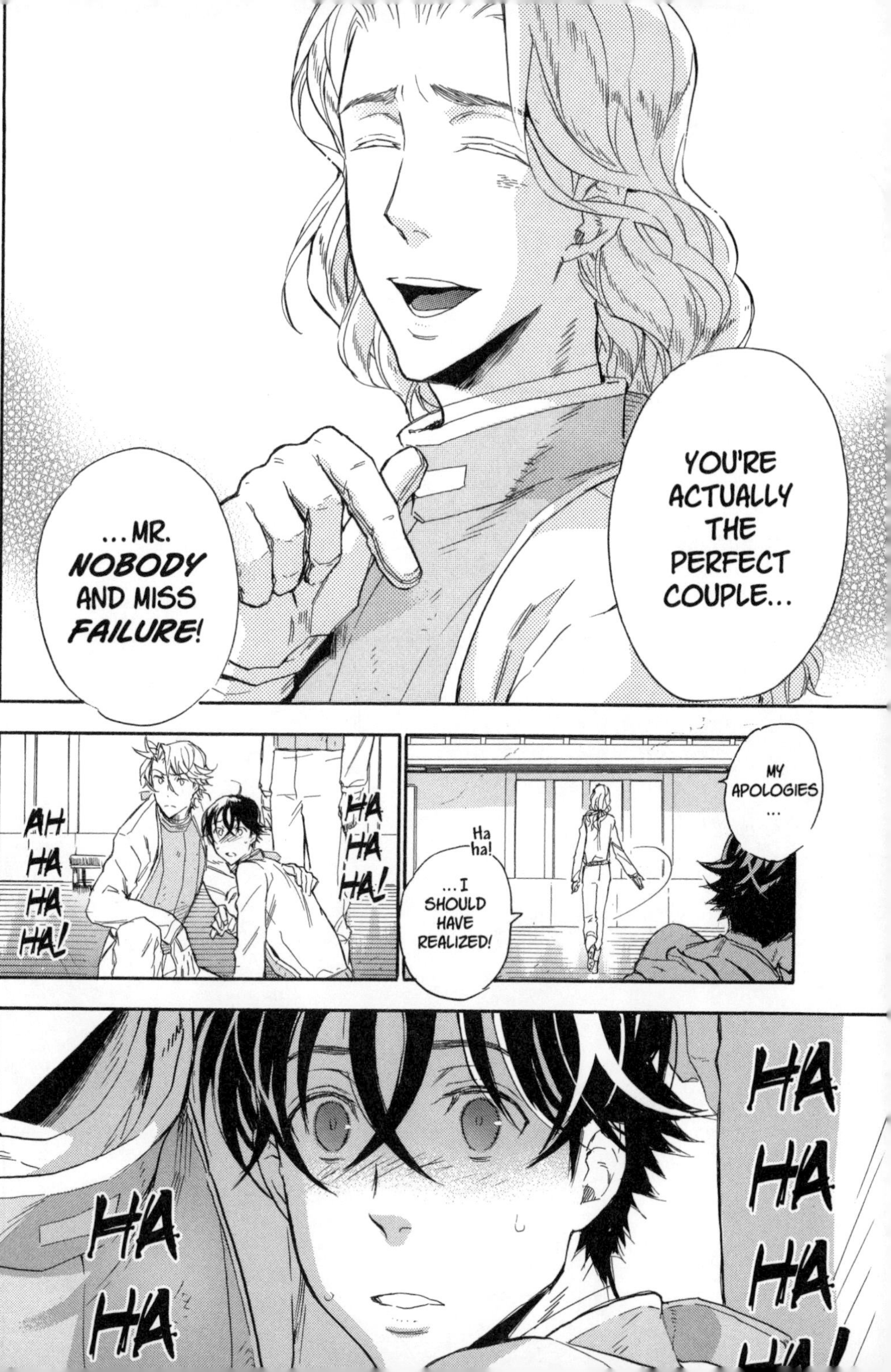
YOU'RE ACTUALLY THE PERFECT COUPLE...
...MR. NOBODY AND MISS FAILURE!
MY APOLOGIES ...
Ha ha!
...I SHOULD HAVE REALIZED!
HA HA HA!
AH HA HA HA!
HA HA HA HA HA!
HA HA HA

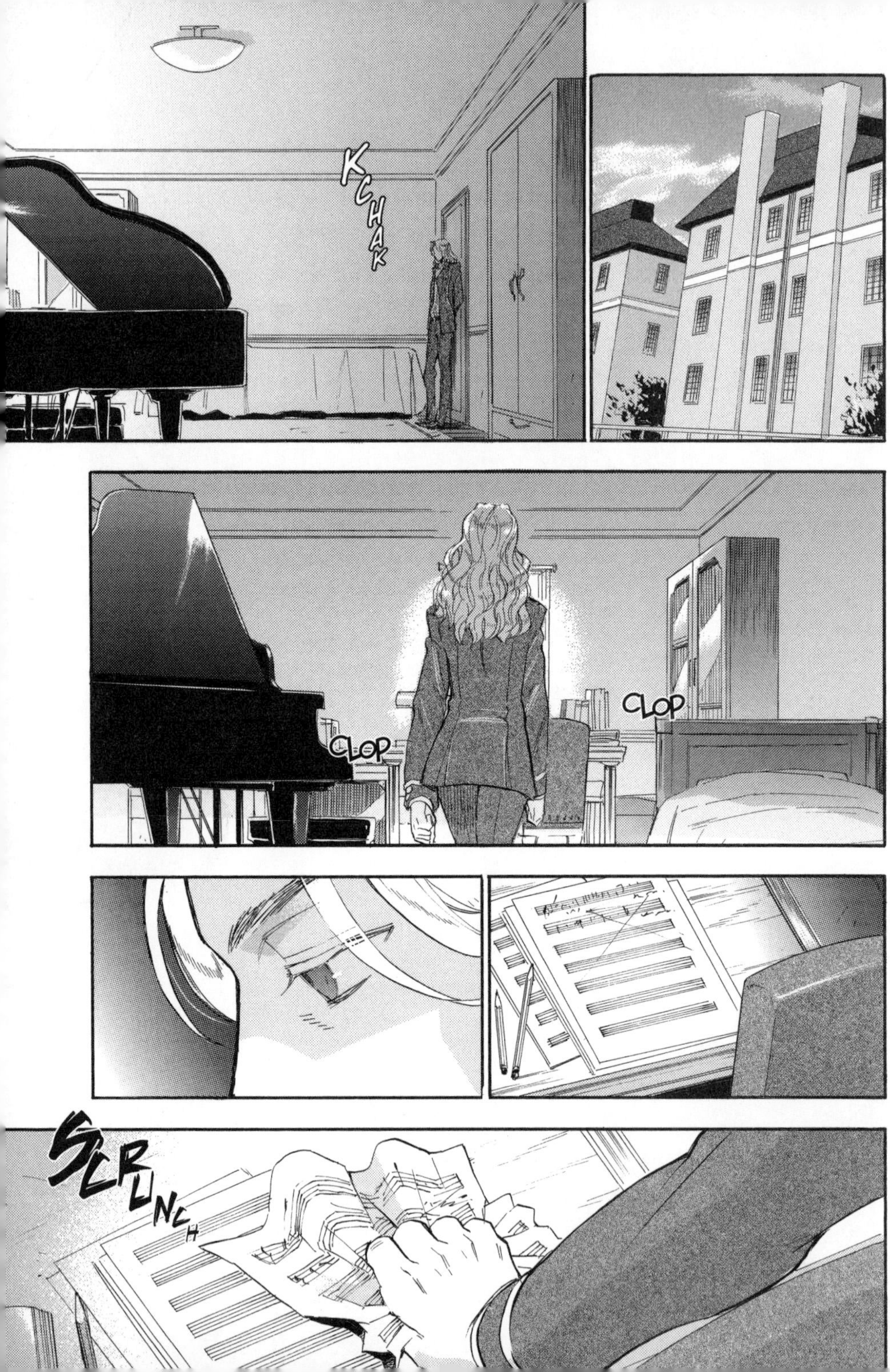
KCHAK
CLOP
CLOP
SCRUNCH

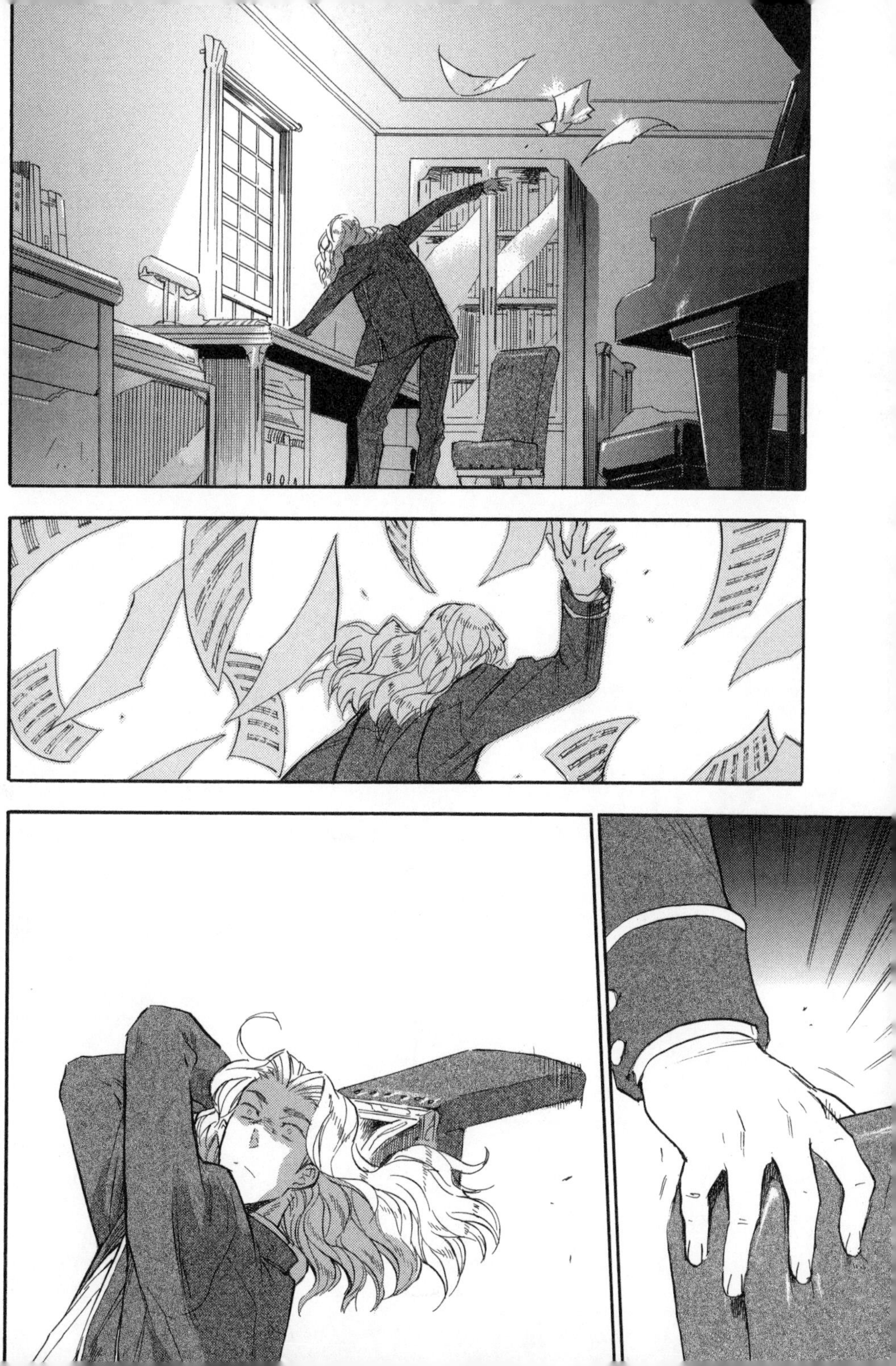

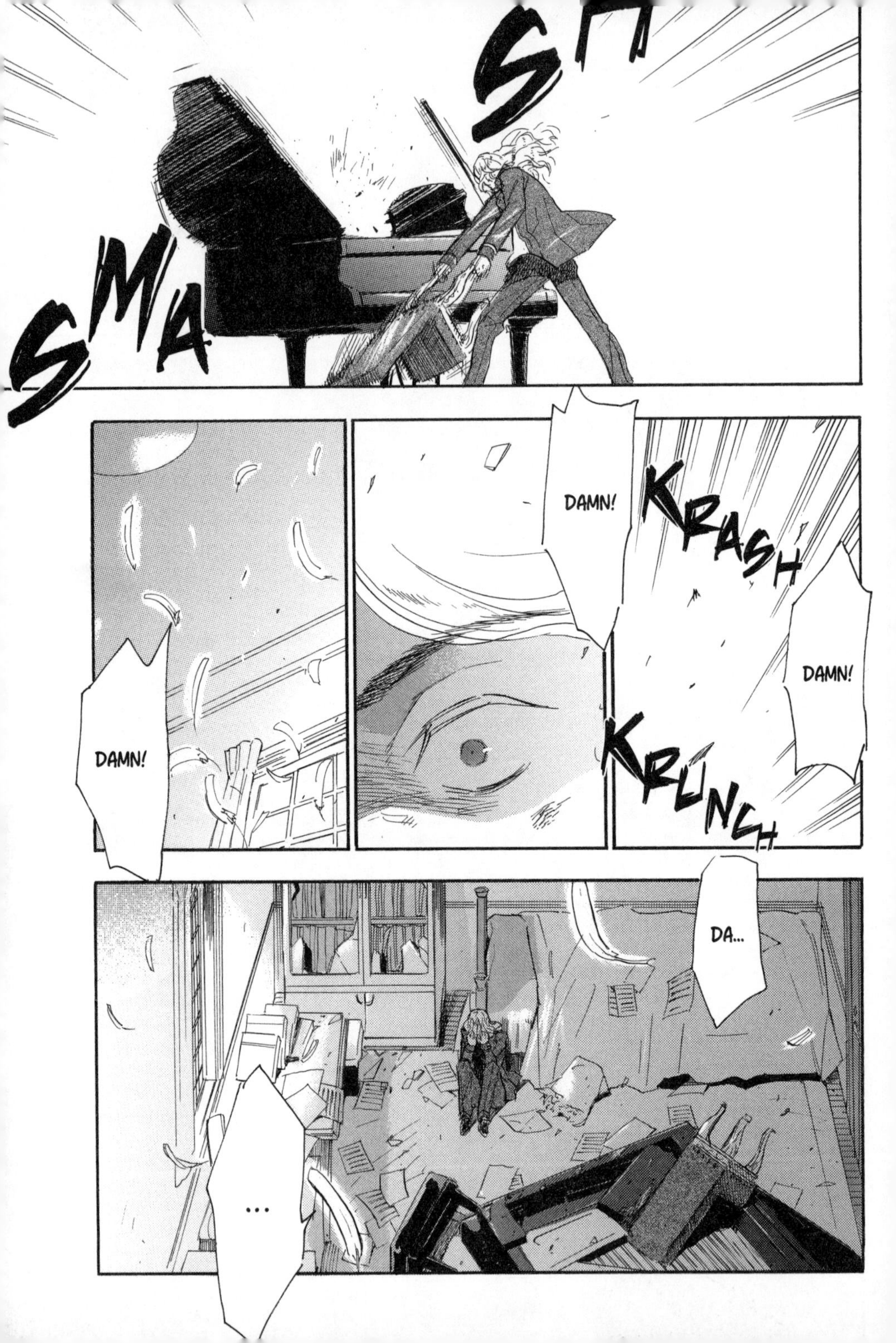
SMA
SH
KRASH
DAMN!
KRUNCH
DAMN!
DAMN!
DA...
...

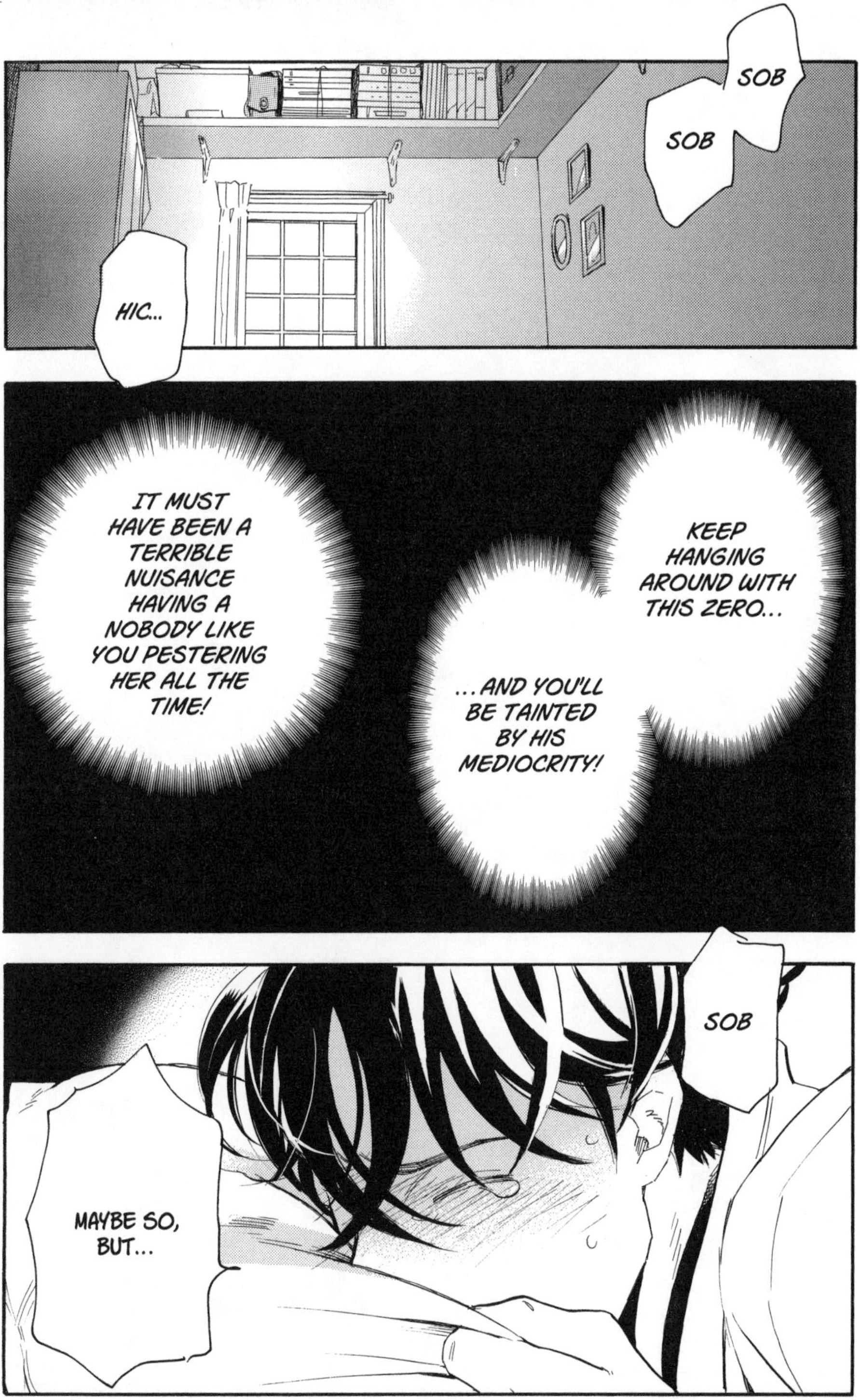
SOB
SOB
HIC...
KEEP HANGING AROUND WITH THIS ZERO...
...AND YOU'LL BE TAINTED BY HIS MEDIOCRITY!
IT MUST HAVE BEEN A TERRIBLE NUISANCE HAVING A NOBODY LIKE YOU PESTERING HER ALL THE TIME!
SOB
MAYBE SO, BUT...

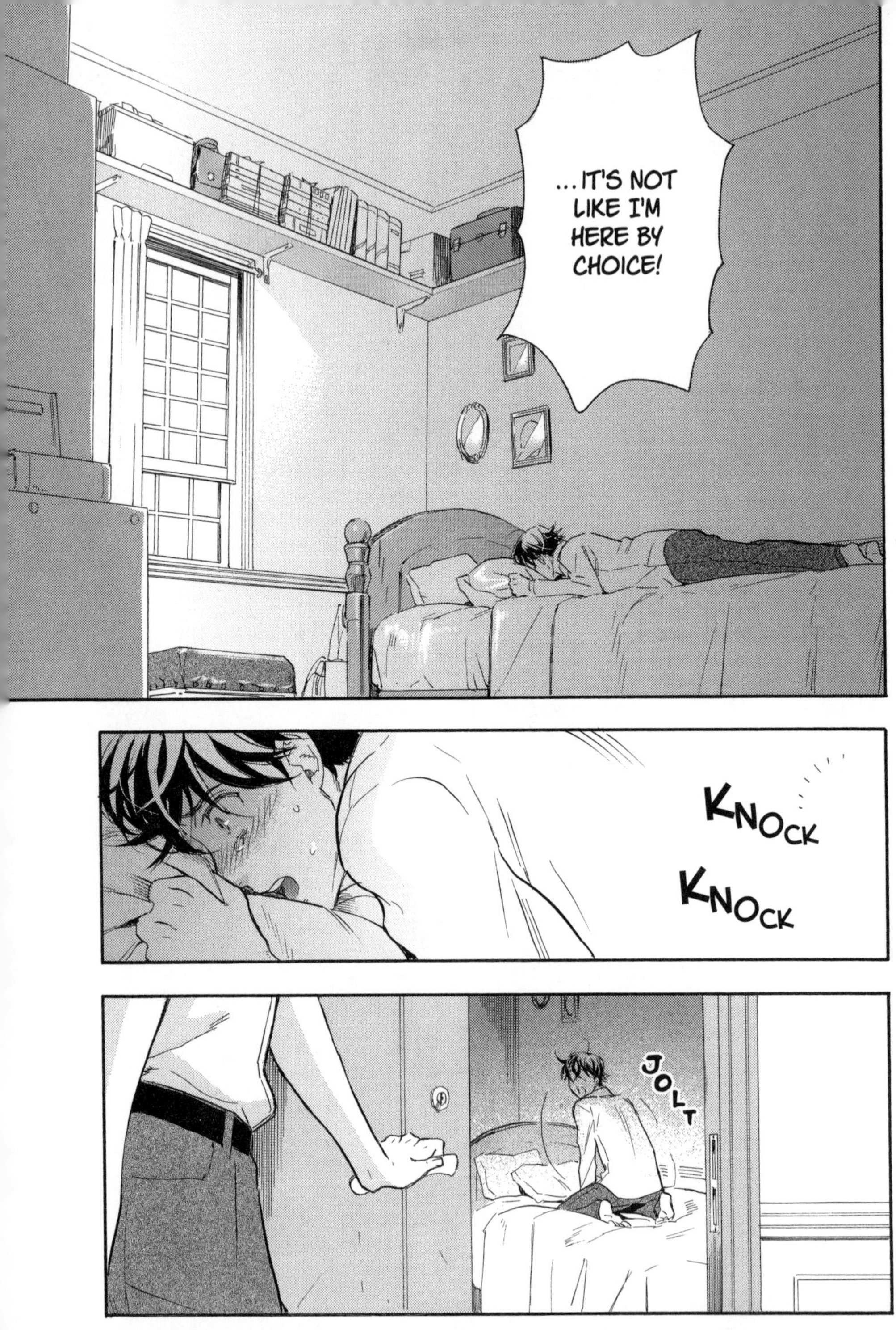
...IT'S NOT LIKE I'M HERE BY CHOICE!
KNOCK
KNOCK
JOLT

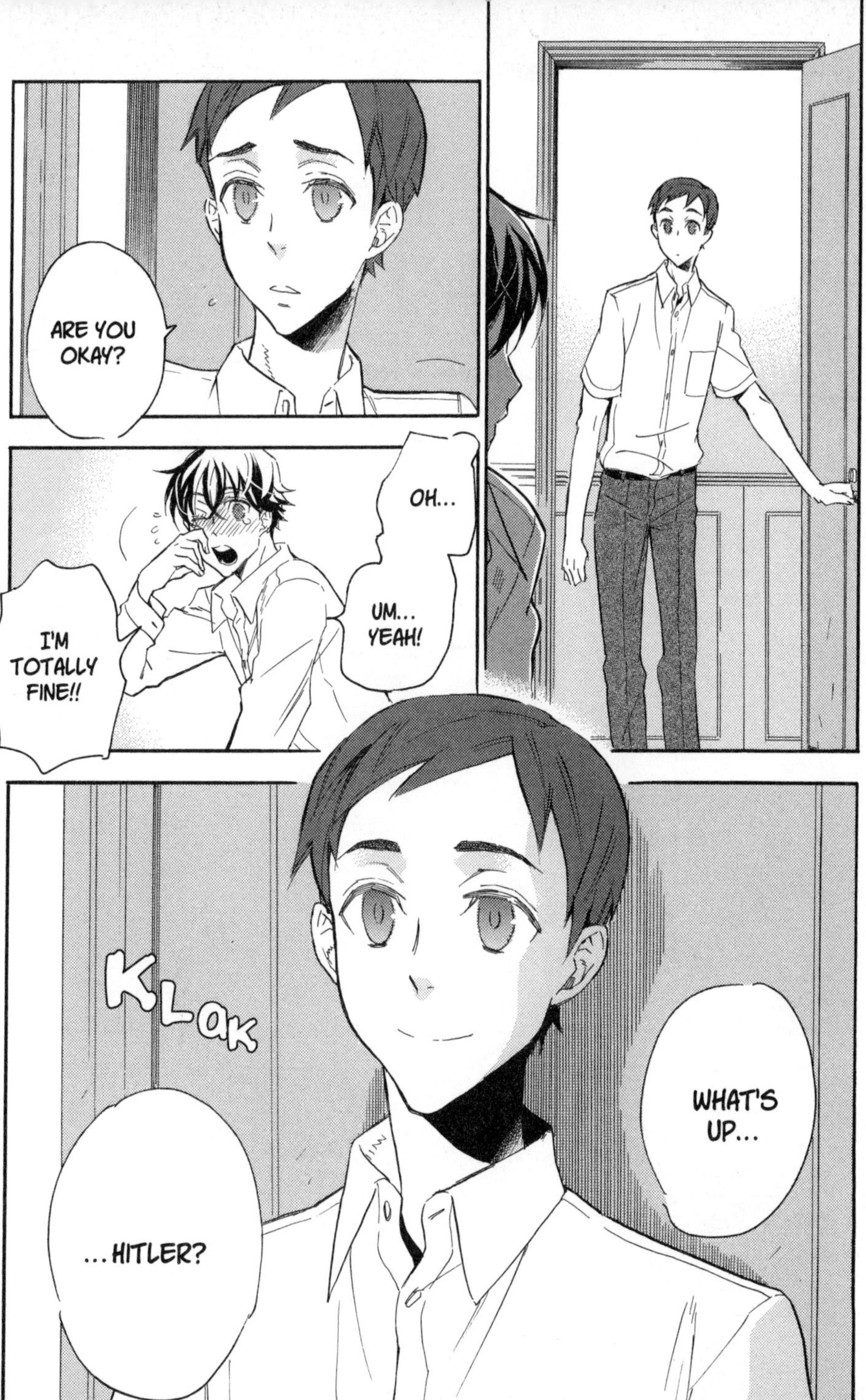
ARE YOU OKAY?
OH...
UM... YEAH!
I'M TOTALLY FINE!!
KLak
WHAT'S UP...
...HITLER?

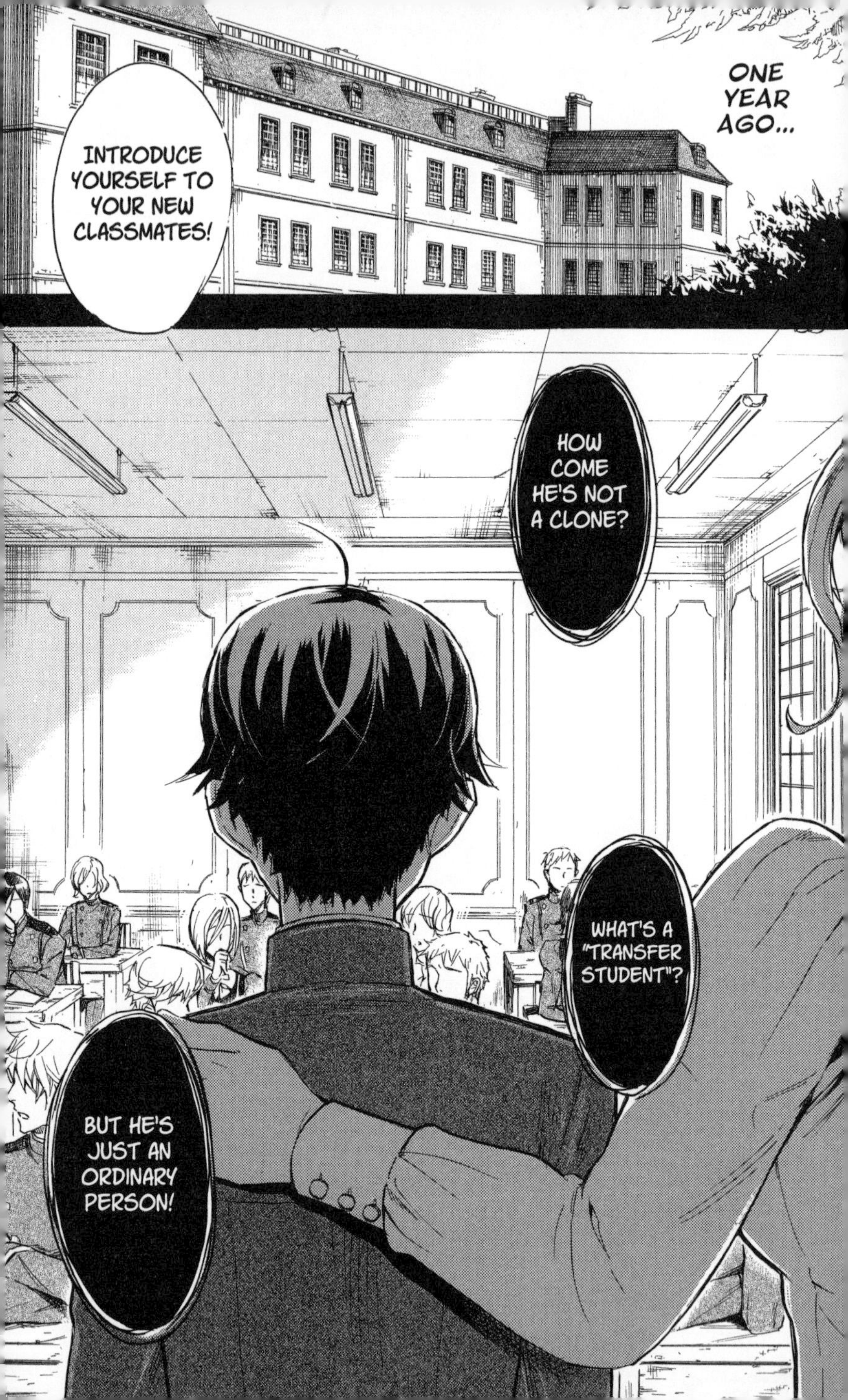
ONE YEAR AGO...
INTRODUCE YOURSELF TO YOUR NEW CLASSMATES!
HOW COME HE'S NOT A CLONE?
WHAT'S A "TRANSFER STUDENT"?
BUT HE'S JUST AN ORDINARY PERSON!

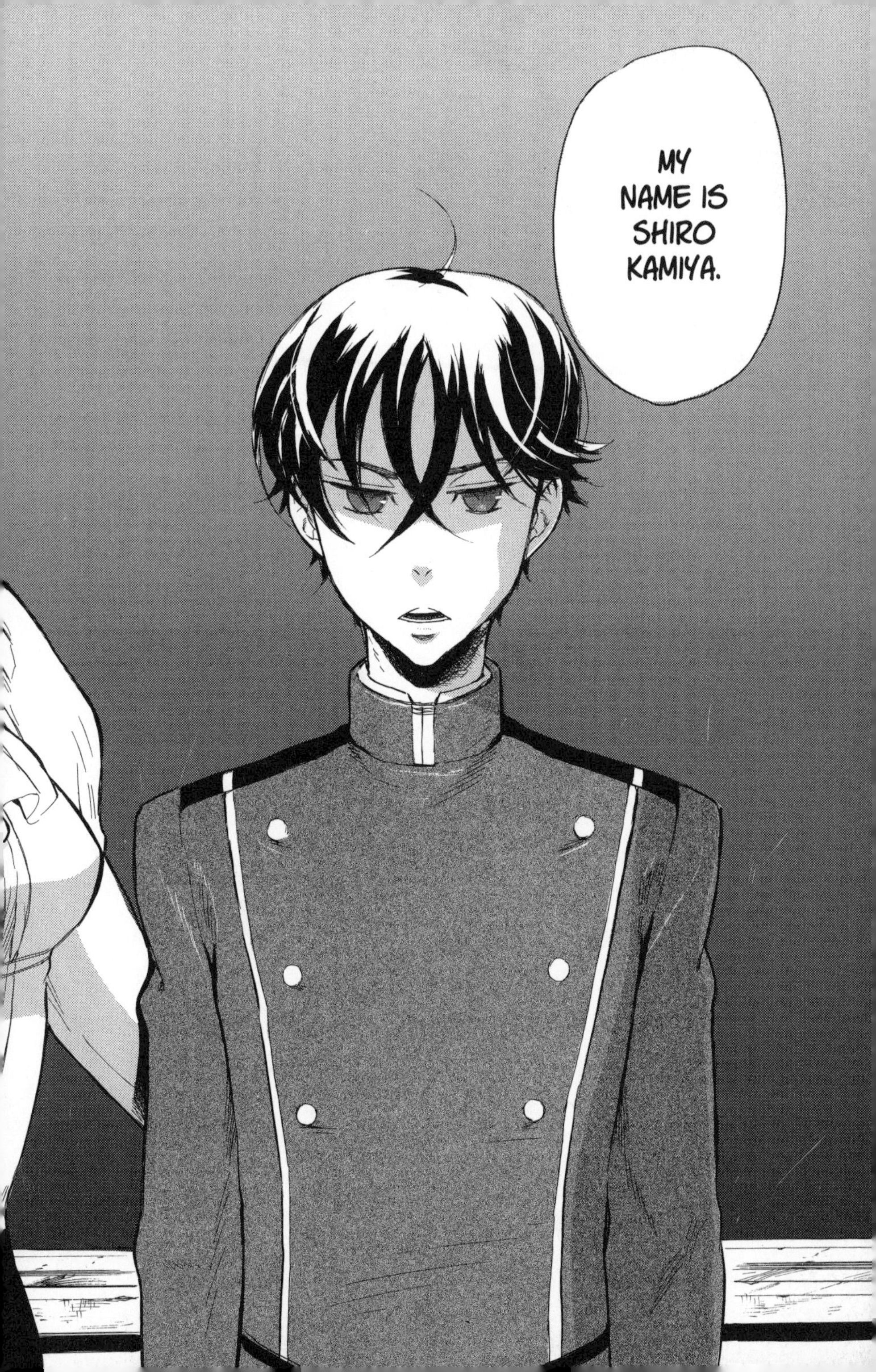
MY NAME IS SHIRO KAMIYA.

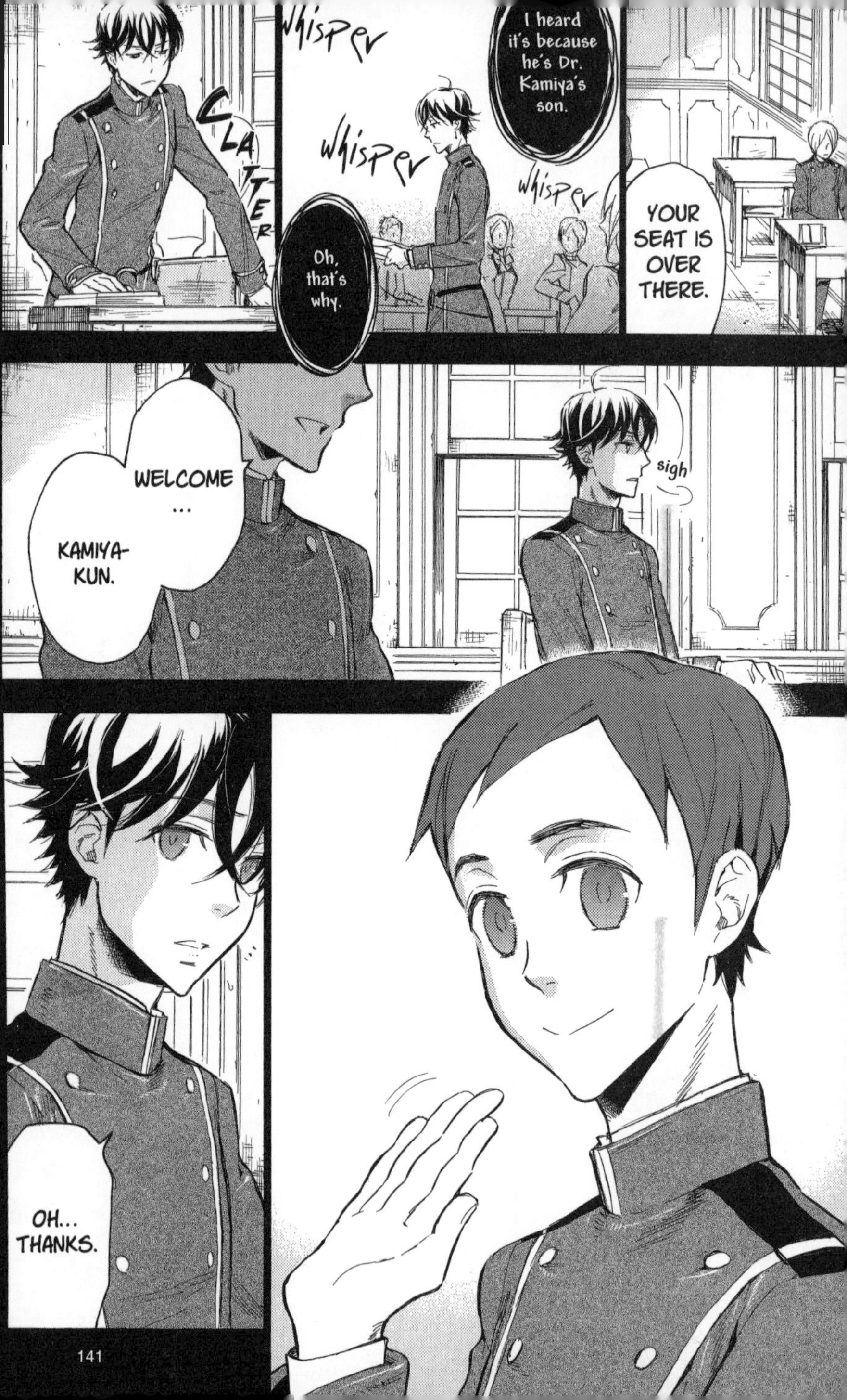
YOUR SEAT IS OVER THERE.
whisper
whisper
I heard it's because he's Dr. Kamiya's son.
whisper
Oh, that's why.
CLATTER
sigh
WELCOME ... KAMIYA-KUN.
OH... THANKS.

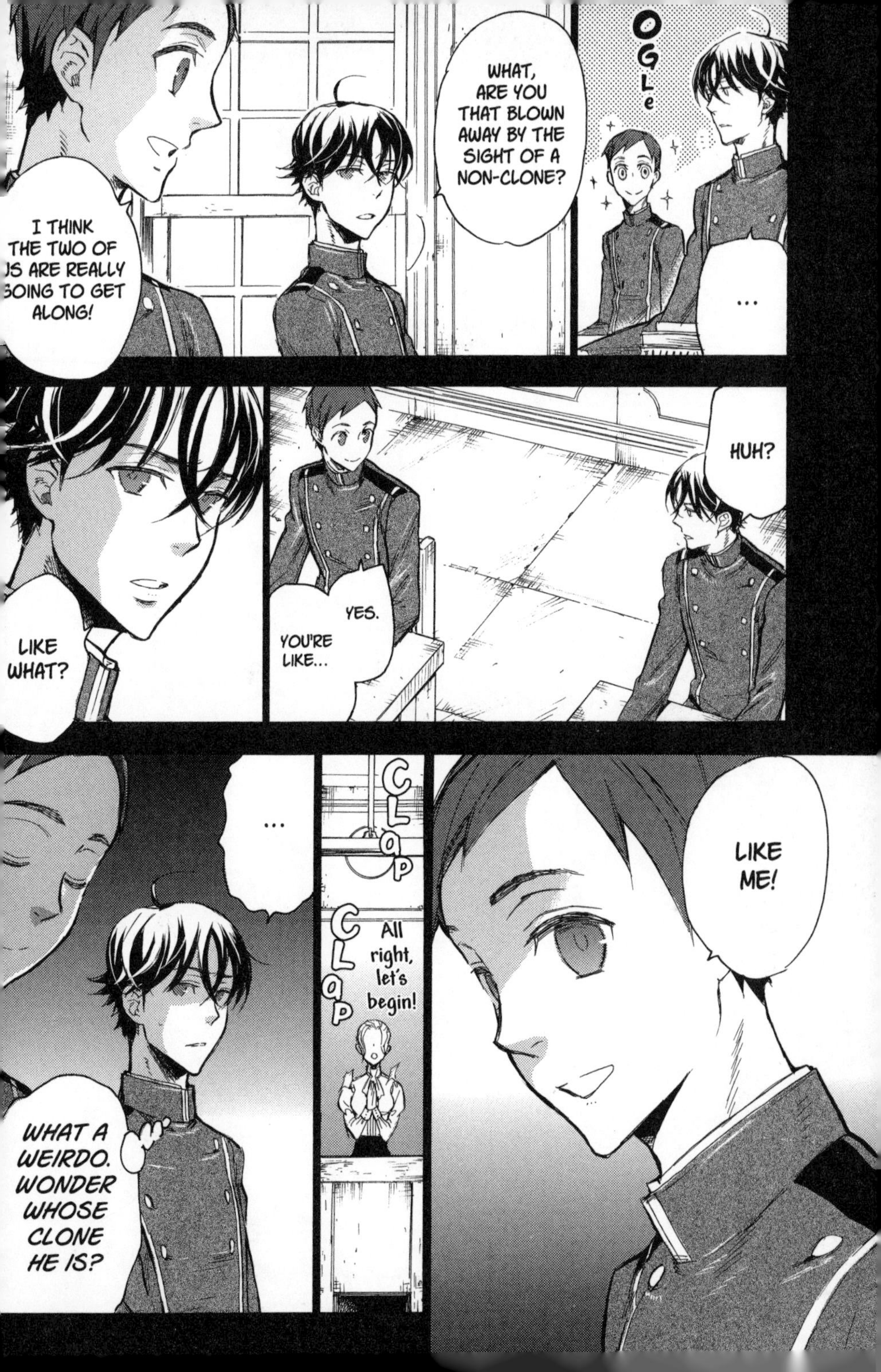
OGLe
...
WHAT, ARE YOU THAT BLOWN AWAY BY THE SIGHT OF A NON-CLONE?
I THINK THE TWO OF US ARE REALLY GOING TO GET ALONG!
HUH?
YES.
YOU'RE LIKE...
LIKE WHAT?
LIKE ME!
CLAP
CLAP
All right, let's begin!
...
WHAT A WEIRDO. WONDER WHOSE CLONE HE IS?

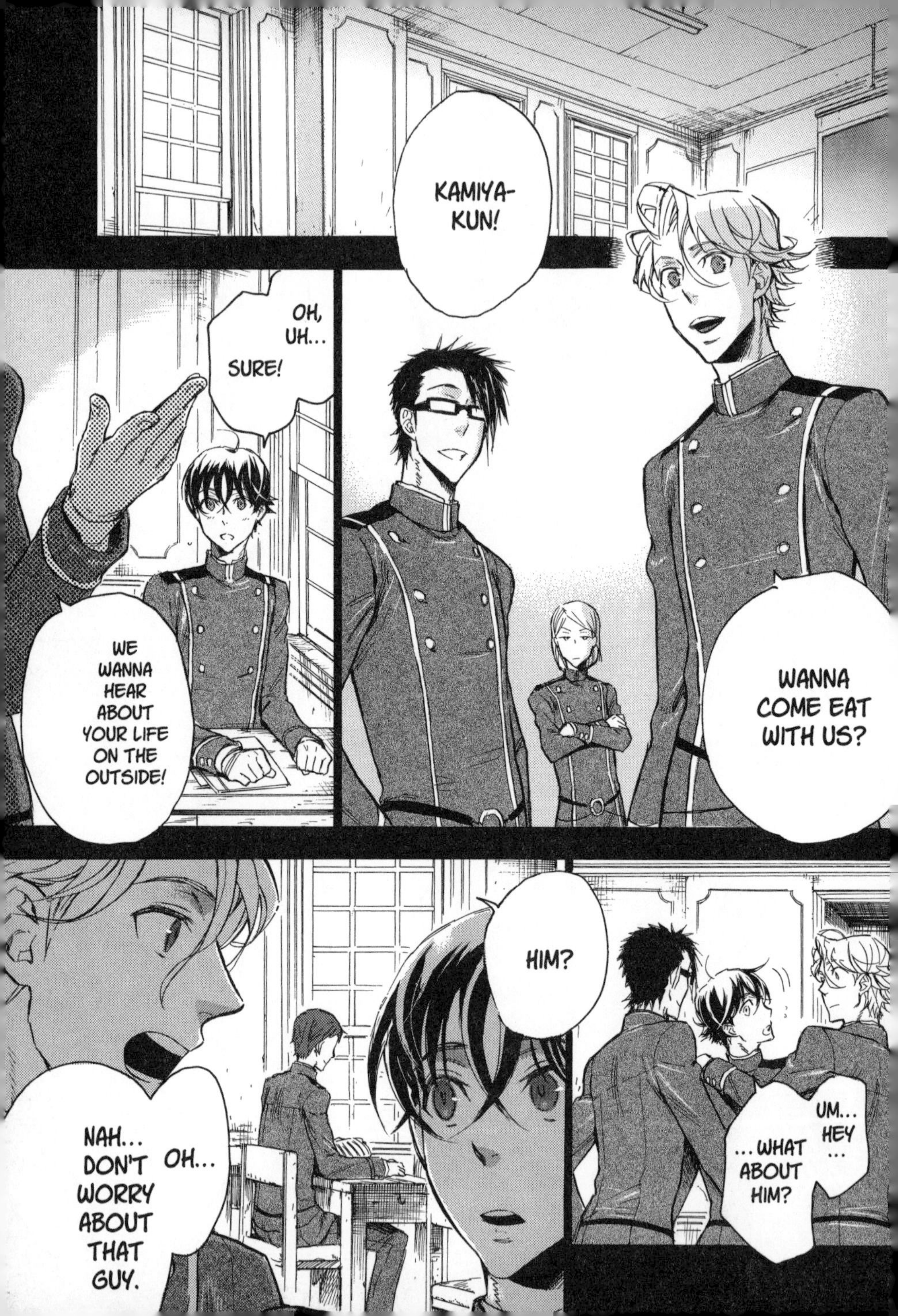
KAMIYA-KUN!
WANNA COME EAT WITH US?
OH, UH... SURE!
WE WANNA HEAR ABOUT YOUR LIFE ON THE OUTSIDE!
UM... HEY...
...WHAT ABOUT HIM?
HIM?
OH...
NAH... DON'T WORRY ABOUT THAT GUY.

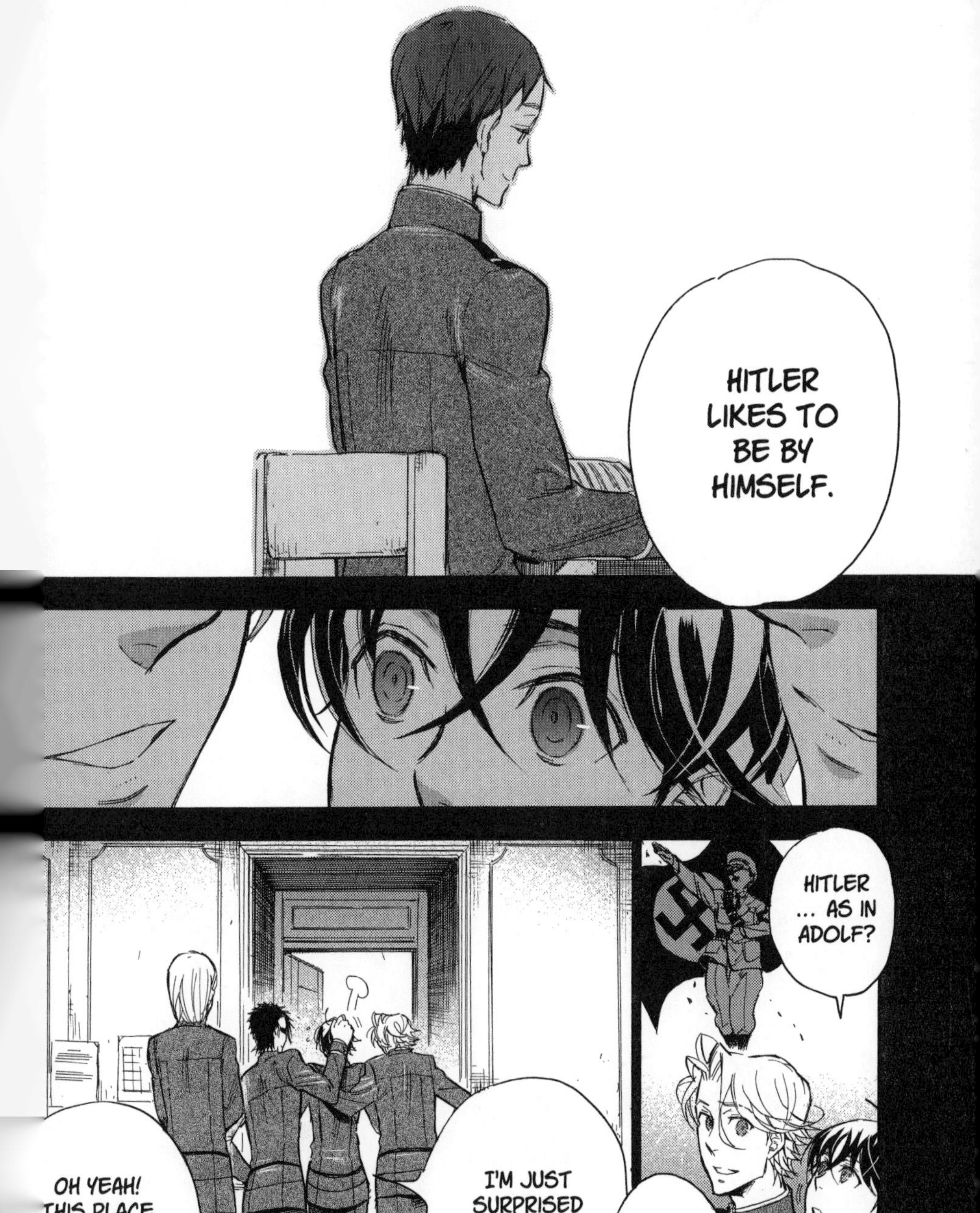
HITLER LIKES TO BE BY HIMSELF.
HITLER ... AS IN ADOLF?
YEAH. WHO ELSE?
I'M JUST SURPRISED THEY MADE A CLONE OF HIM.
OH YEAH! THIS PLACE S CRAWLING ITH HEROES ND MANIACS!

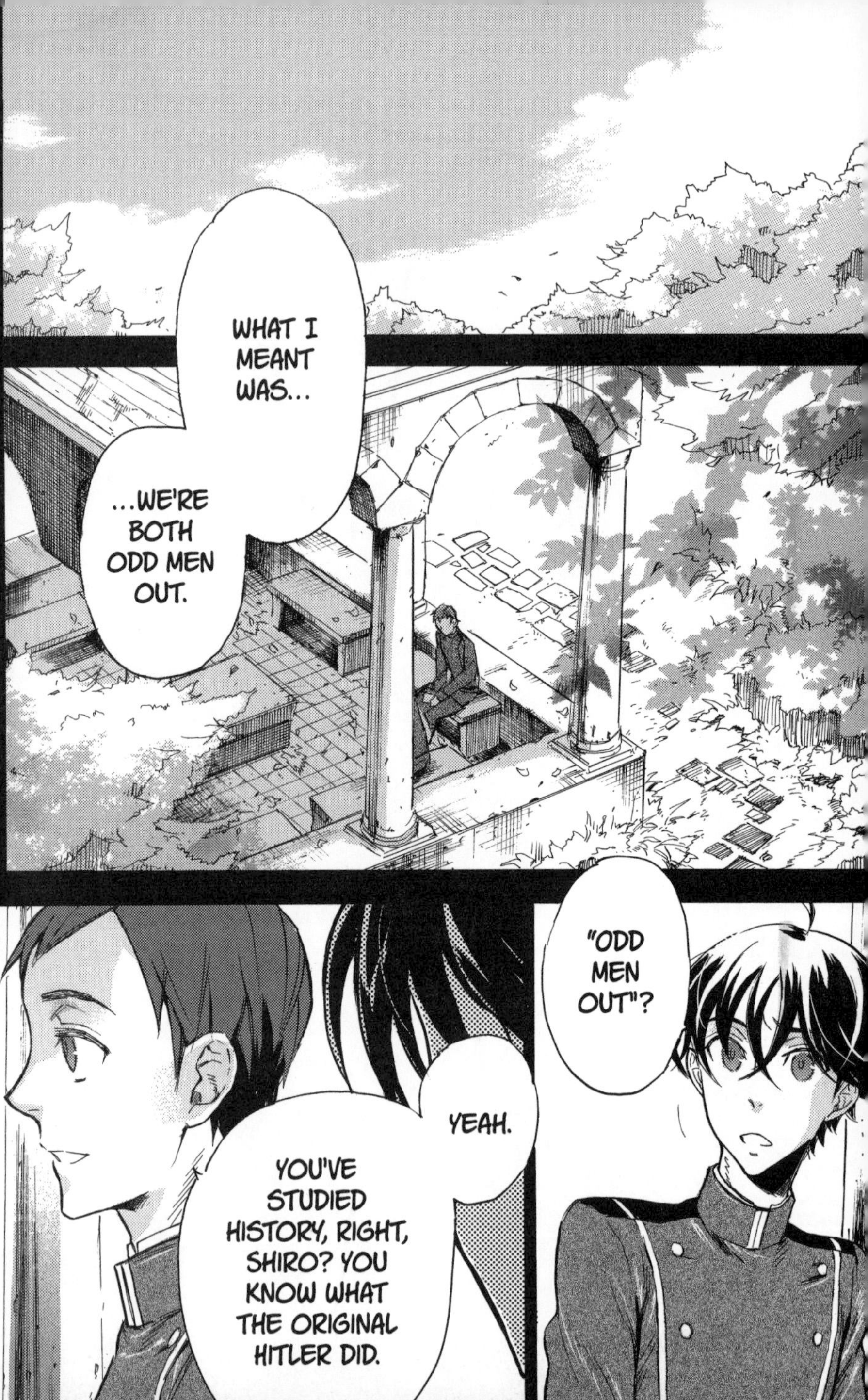
WHAT I MEANT WAS...
...WE'RE BOTH ODD MEN OUT.
"ODD MEN OUT"?
YEAH.
YOU'VE STUDIED HISTORY, RIGHT, SHIRO? YOU KNOW WHAT THE ORIGINAL HITLER DID.

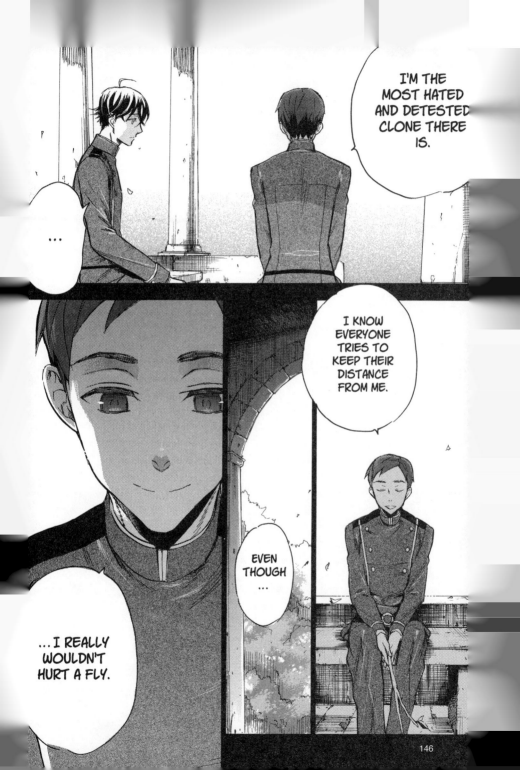

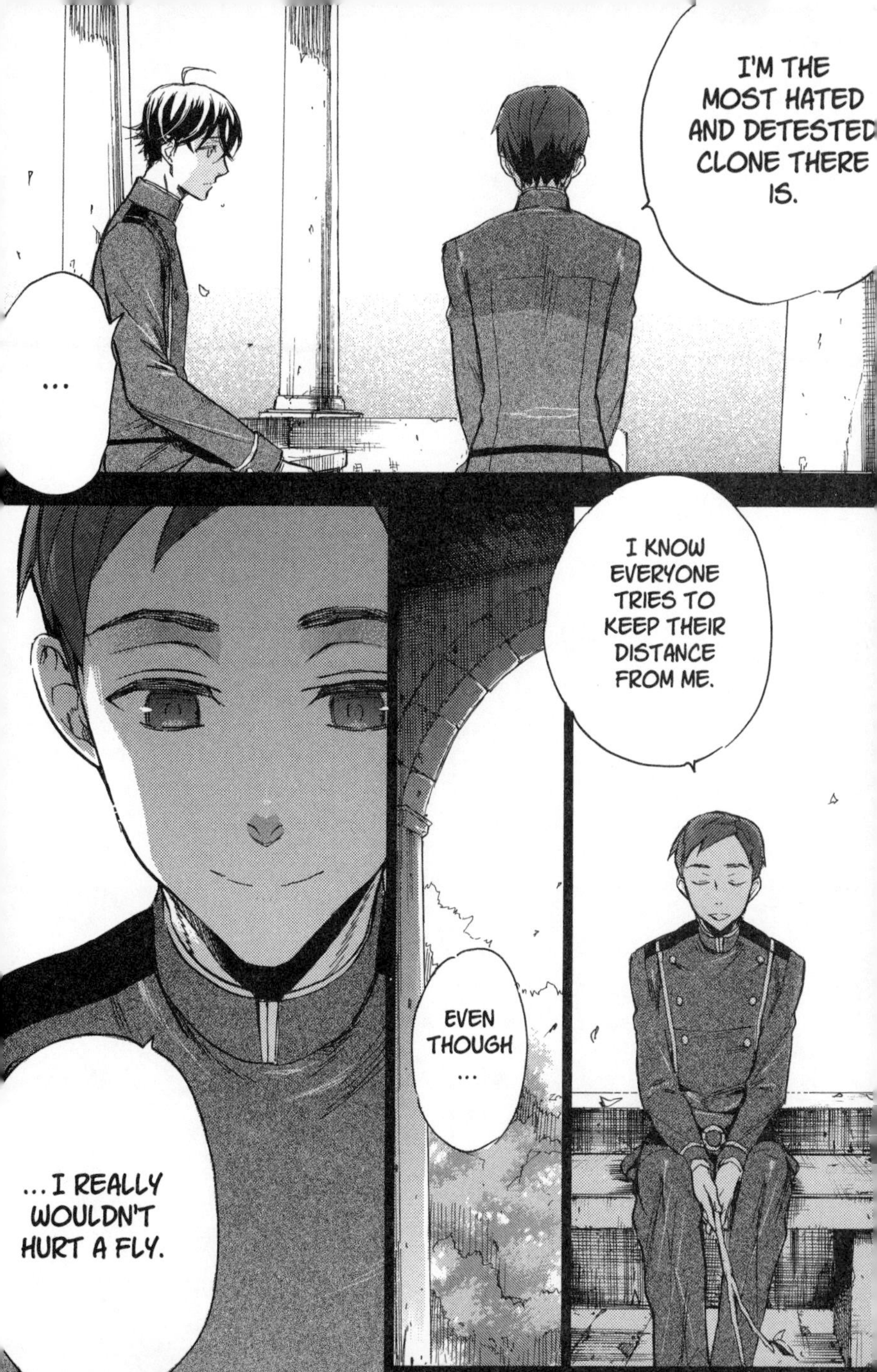
I'M THE MOST HATED AND DETESTED CLONE THERE IS.
...
I KNOW EVERYONE TRIES TO KEEP THEIR DISTANCE FROM ME.
EVEN THOUGH ...
...I REALLY WOULDN'T HURT A FLY.

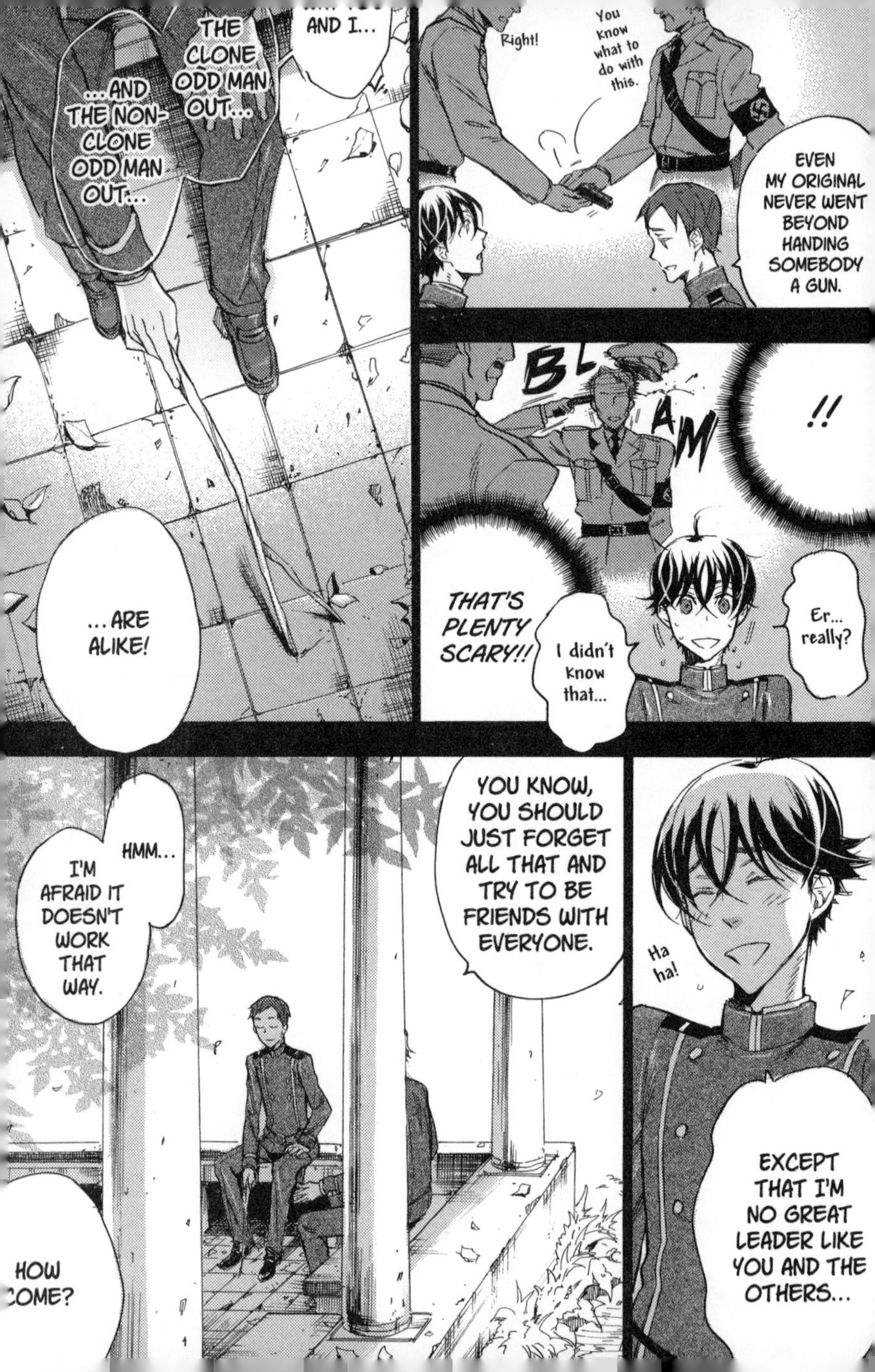
You know what to do with this.
Right!
EVEN MY ORIGINAL NEVER WENT BEYOND HANDING SOMEBODY A GUN.
BLAM
!!
Er... really?
I didn't know that...
THAT'S PLENTY SCARY!!
AND I...
THE CLONE ODD MAN OUT...
...AND THE NON-CLONE ODD MAN OUT...
...ARE ALIKE!
Ha ha!
EXCEPT THAT I'M NO GREAT LEADER LIKE YOU AND THE OTHERS...
YOU KNOW, YOU SHOULD JUST FORGET ALL THAT AND TRY TO BE FRIENDS WITH EVERYONE.
HMM... I'M AFRAID IT DOESN'T WORK THAT WAY.
HOW COME?

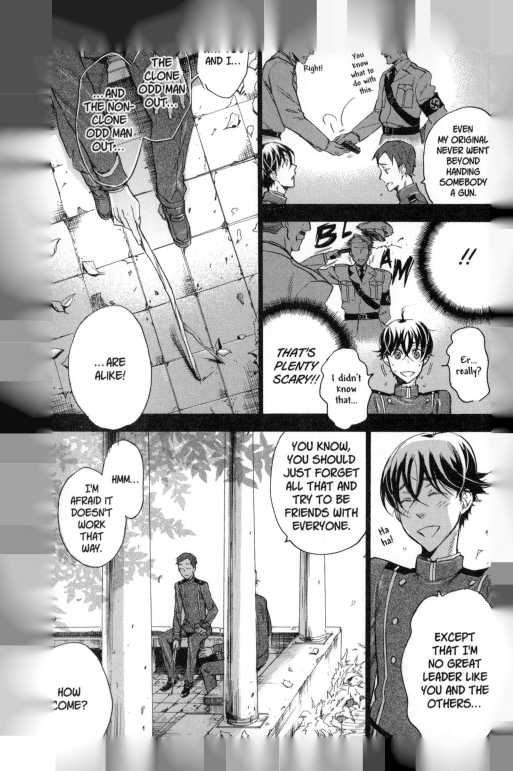

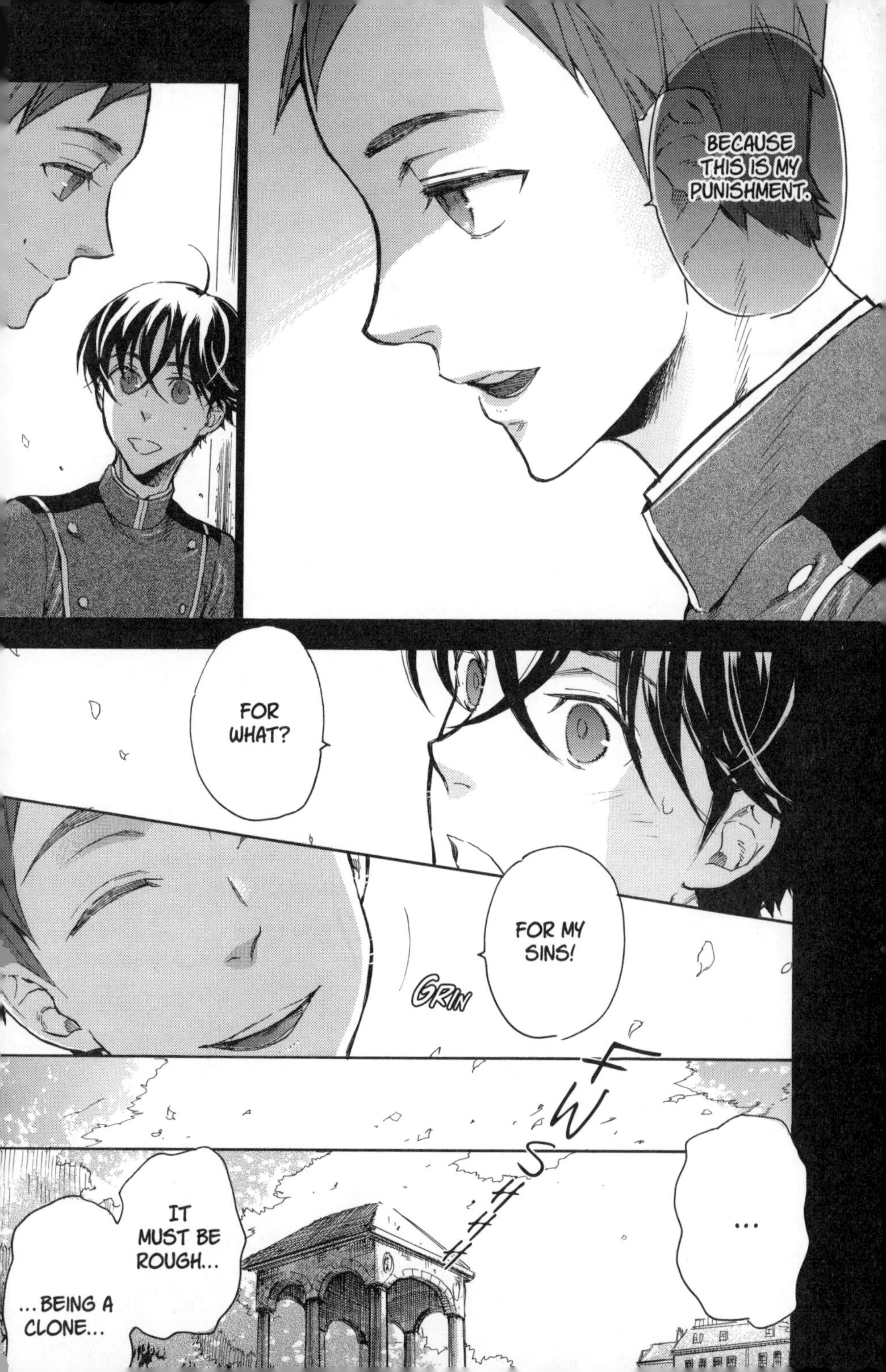
BECAUSE THIS IS MY PUNISHMENT.
FOR WHAT?
FOR MY SINS!
GRIN
FWSHHHH
...
IT MUST BE ROUGH...
...BEING A CLONE...

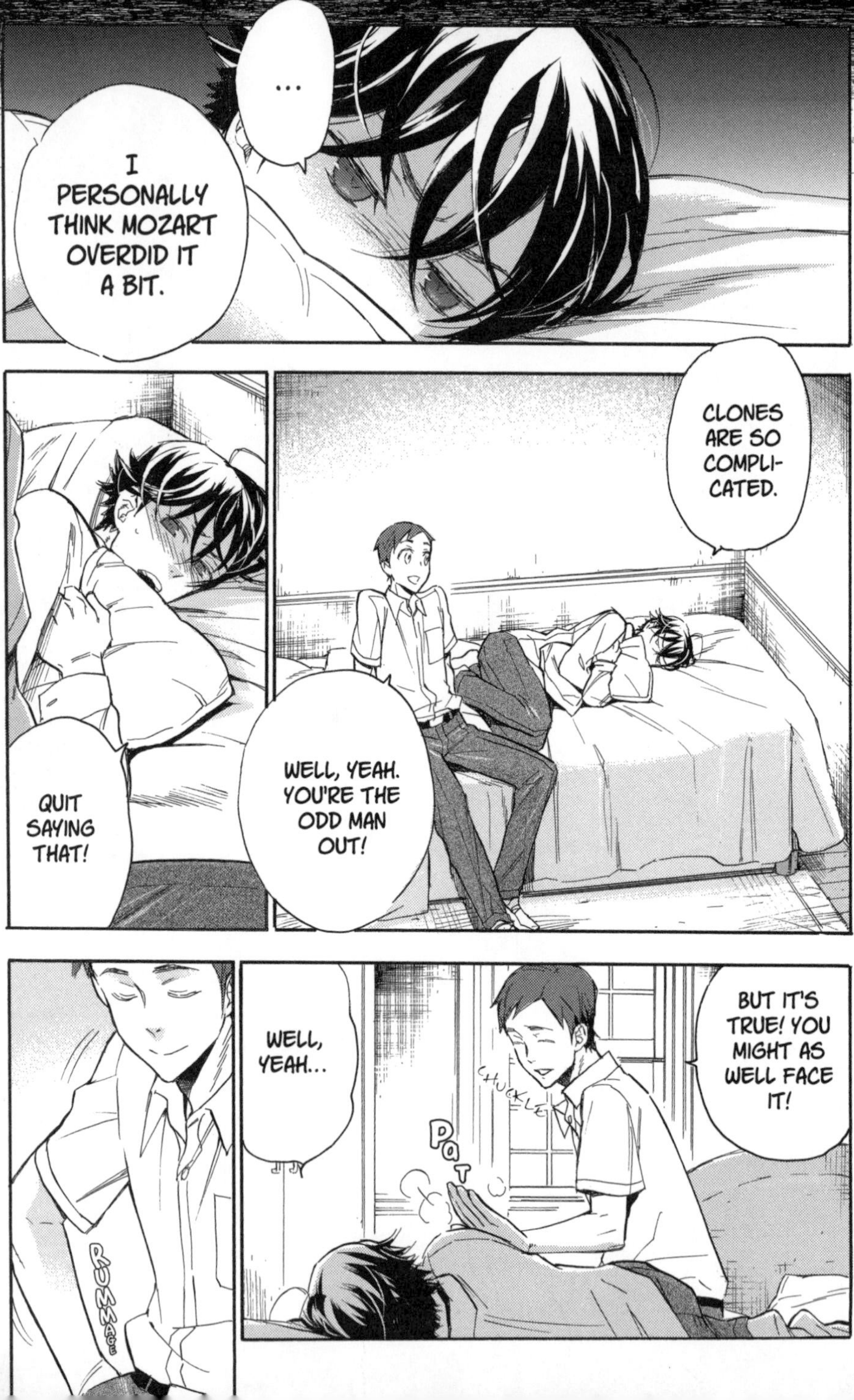
...
I PERSONALLY THINK MOZART OVERDID IT A BIT.
CLONES ARE SO COMPLICATED.
WELL, YEAH. YOU'RE THE ODD MAN OUT!
QUIT SAYING THAT!
BUT IT'S TRUE! YOU MIGHT AS WELL FACE IT!
CHUCKLE
PAT
WELL, YEAH...
RUMMAGE

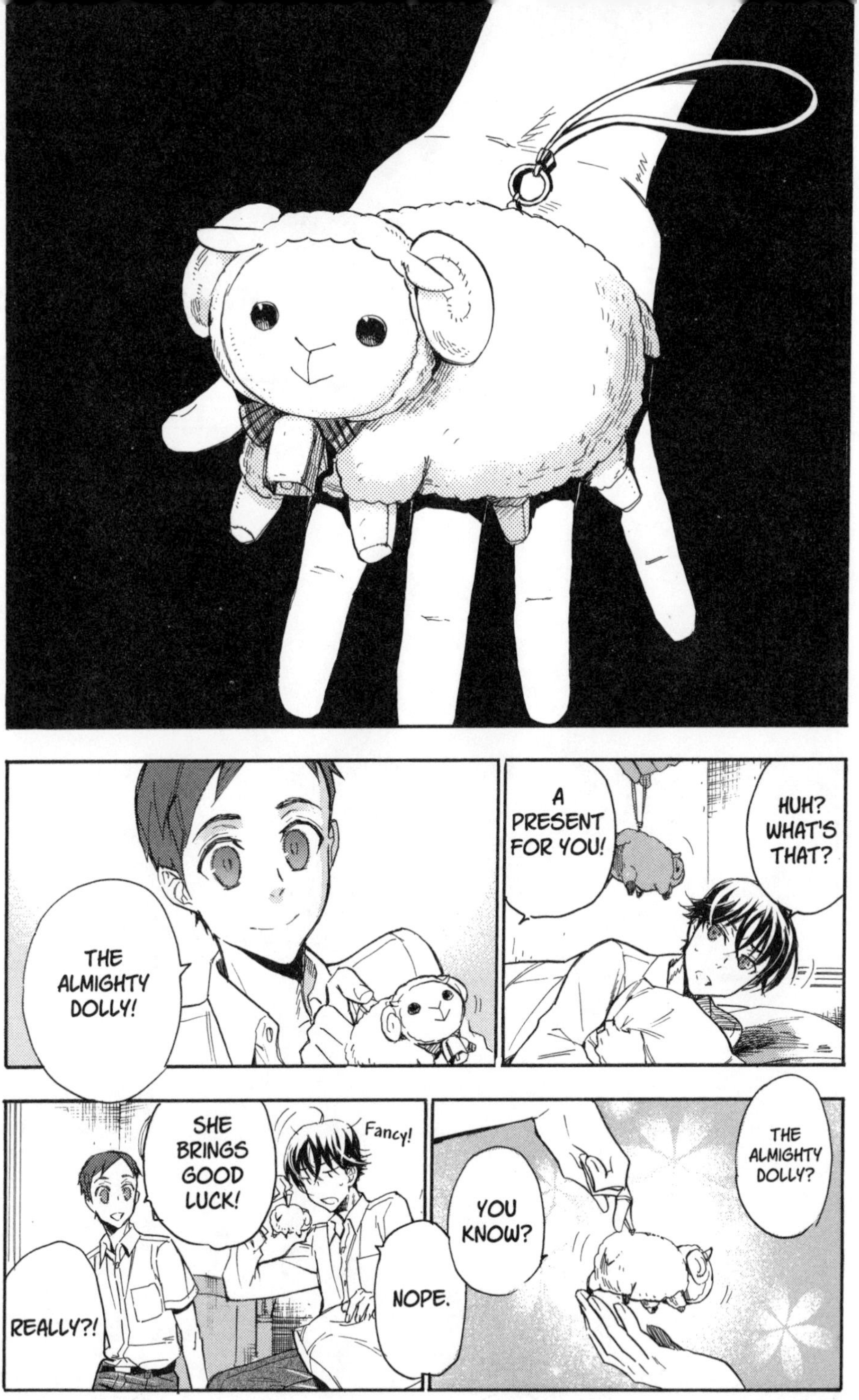
HUH? WHAT'S THAT?
A PRESENT FOR YOU!
THE ALMIGHTY DOLLY!
THE ALMIGHTY DOLLY?
YOU KNOW?
NOPE.
SHE BRINGS GOOD LUCK!
Fancy!
REALLY?!

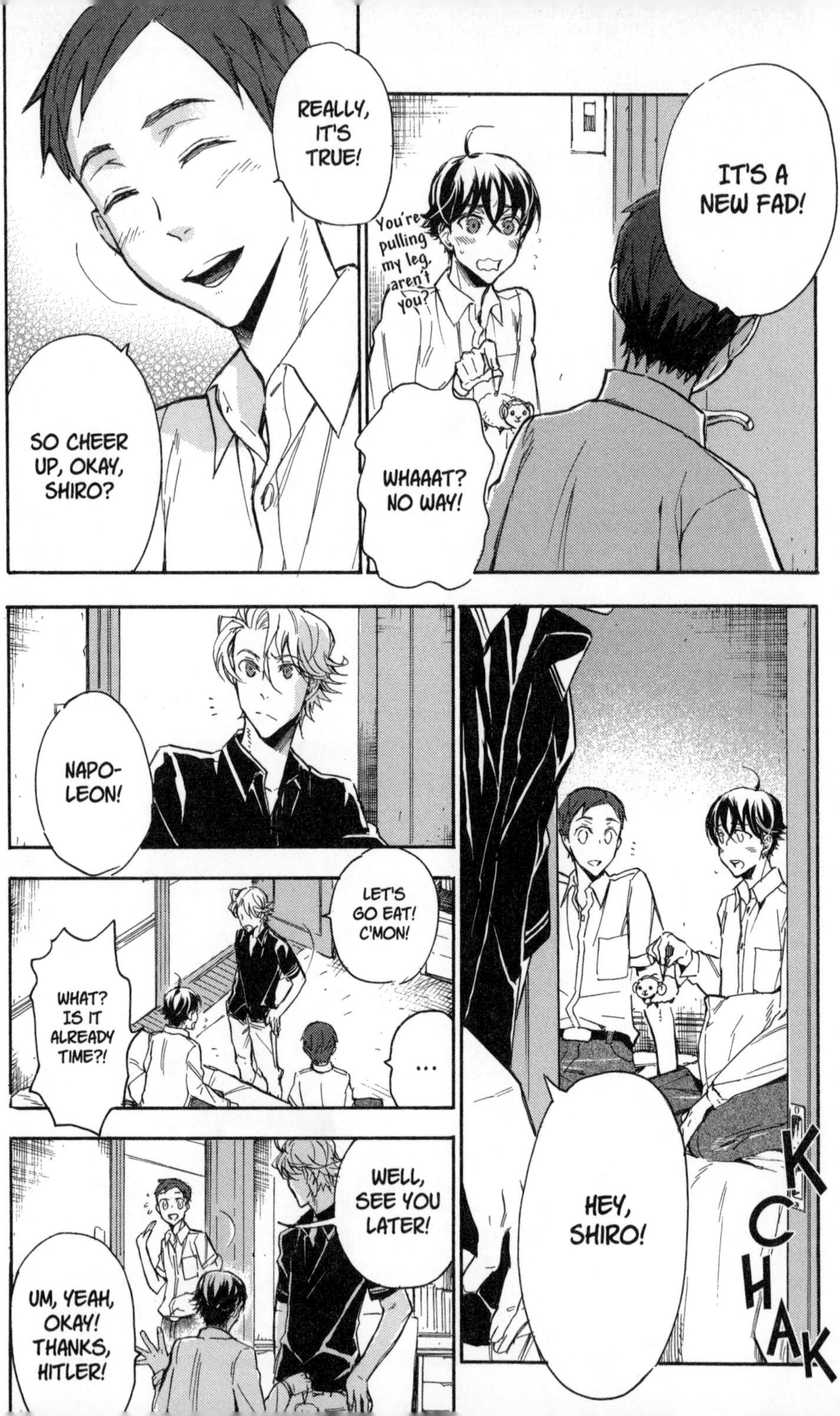
IT'S A NEW FAD!
You're pulling my leg, aren't you?
WHAAAT? NO WAY!
REALLY, IT'S TRUE!
SO CHEER UP, OKAY, SHIRO?
KCHAK
HEY, SHIRO!
NAPO-LEON!
LET'S GO EAT! C'MON!
...
WHAT? IS IT ALREADY TIME?!
WELL, SEE YOU LATER!
UM, YEAH, OKAY! THANKS, HITLER!

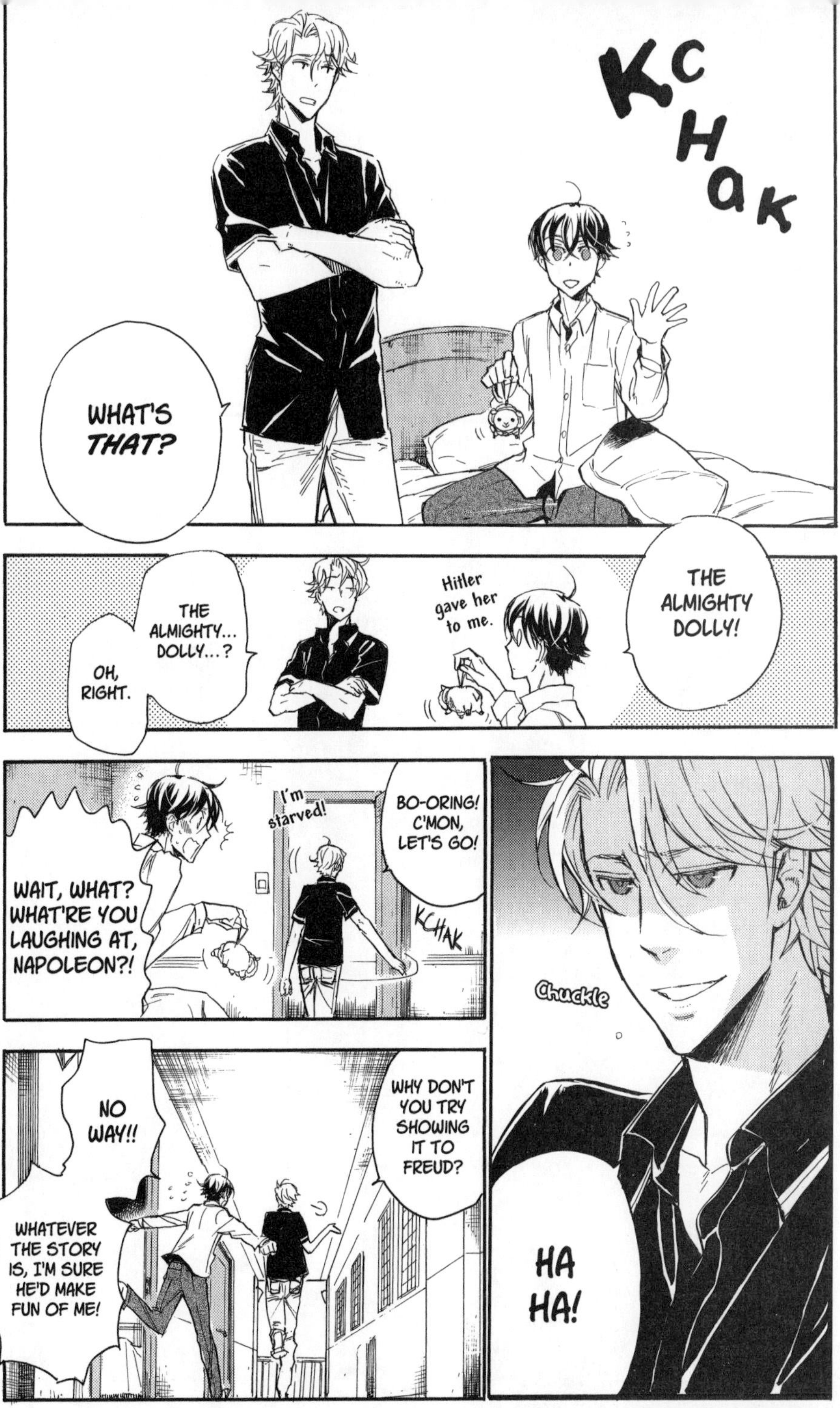
KCHAK
WHAT'S *THAT?*
THE ALMIGHTY DOLLY!
Hitler gave her to me.
THE ALMIGHTY... DOLLY...?
OH, RIGHT.
Chuckle
HA HA!
BO-ORING! C'MON, LET'S GO!
I'm starved!
KCHAK
WAIT, WHAT? WHAT'RE YOU LAUGHING AT, NAPOLEON?!
WHY DON'T YOU TRY SHOWING IT TO FREUD?
NO WAY!!
WHATEVER THE STORY IS, I'M SURE HE'D MAKE FUN OF ME!

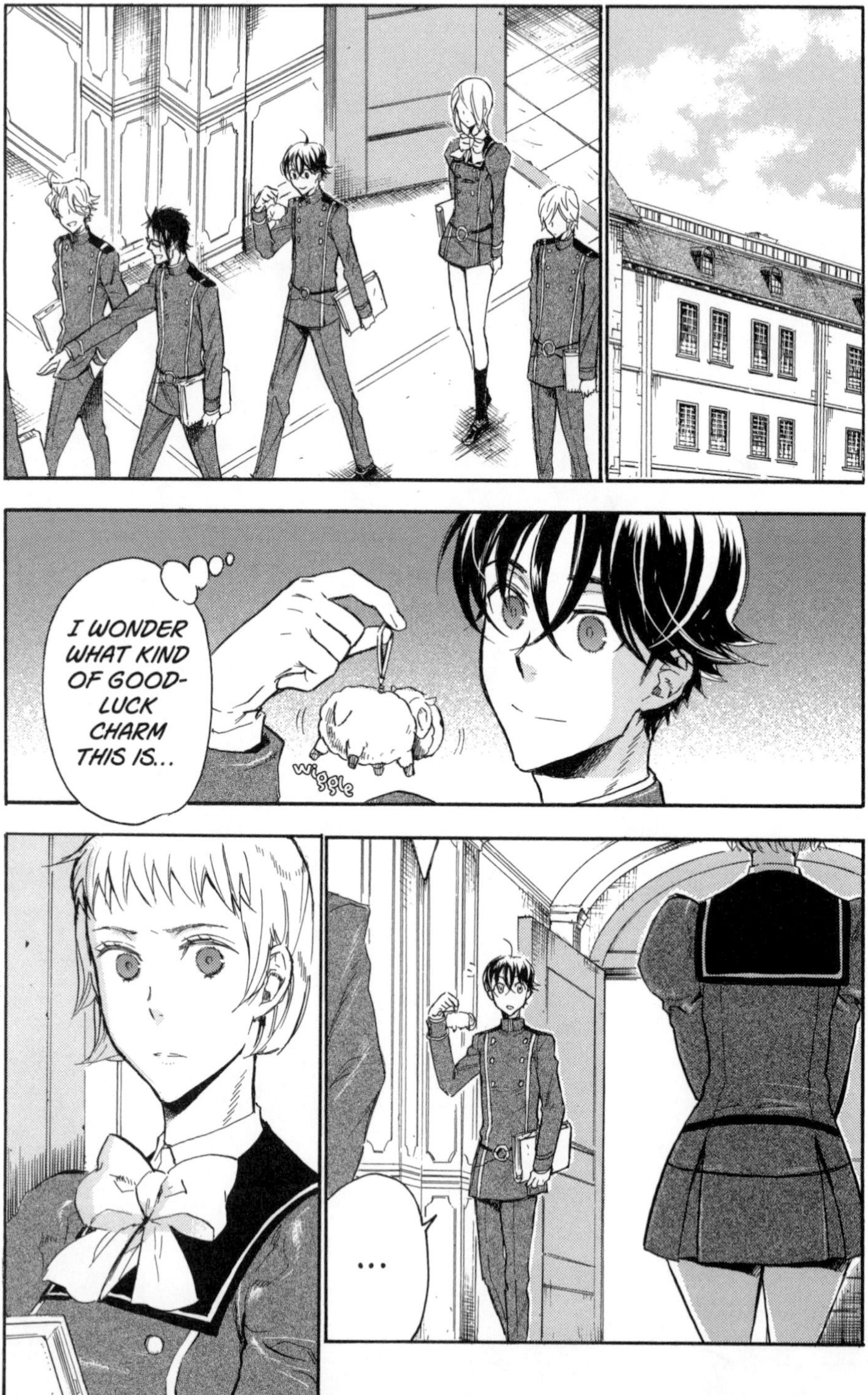
I WONDER WHAT KIND OF GOOD-LUCK CHARM THIS IS...
wiggle
...

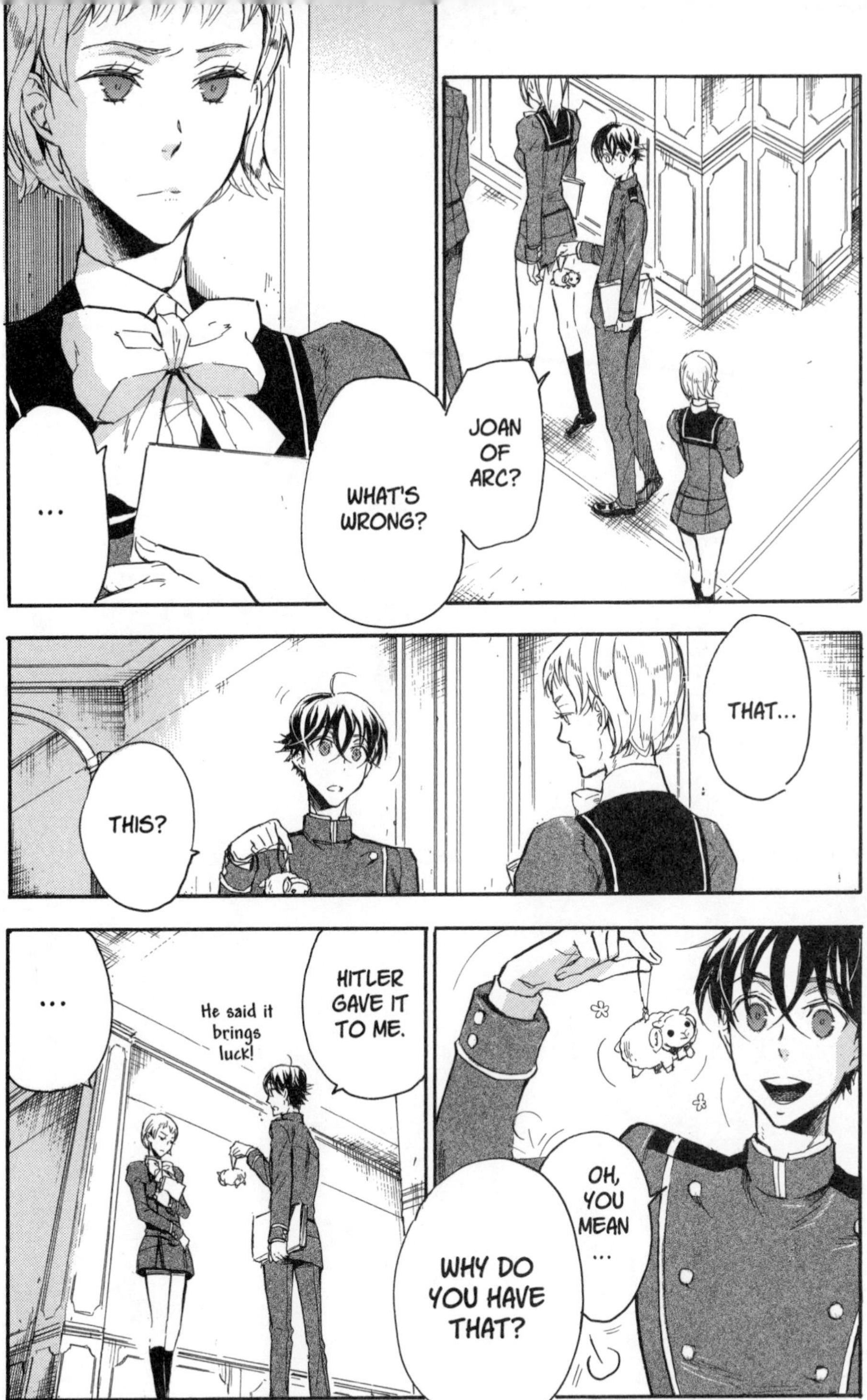
JOAN OF ARC?
WHAT'S WRONG?
...
THAT...
THIS?
WHY DO YOU HAVE THAT?
OH, YOU MEAN...
HITLER GAVE IT TO ME.
He said it brings luck!
...

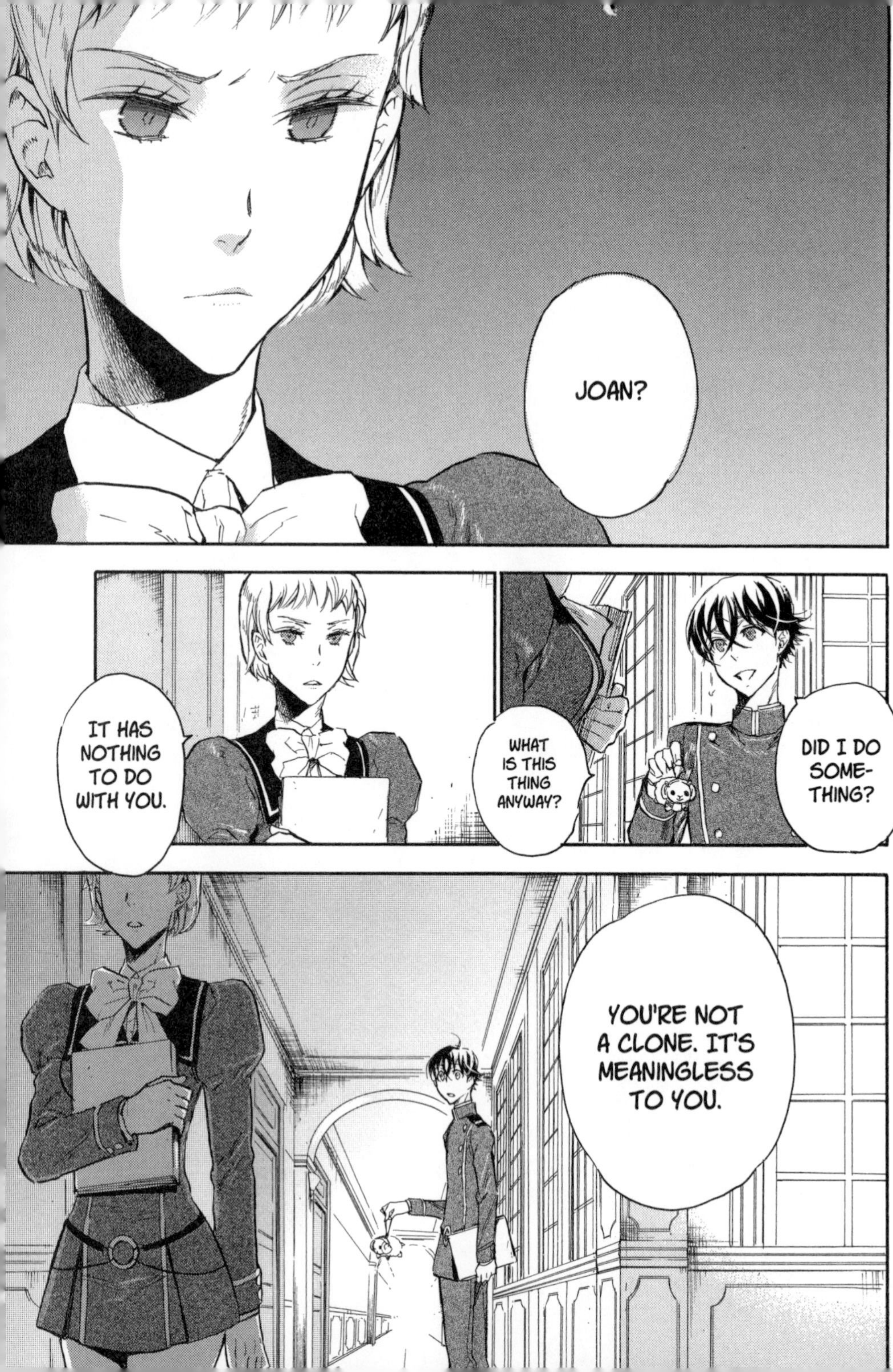
JOAN?
DID I DO SOME-THING?
WHAT IS THIS THING ANYWAY?
IT HAS NOTHING TO DO WITH YOU.
YOU'RE NOT A CLONE. IT'S MEANINGLESS TO YOU.

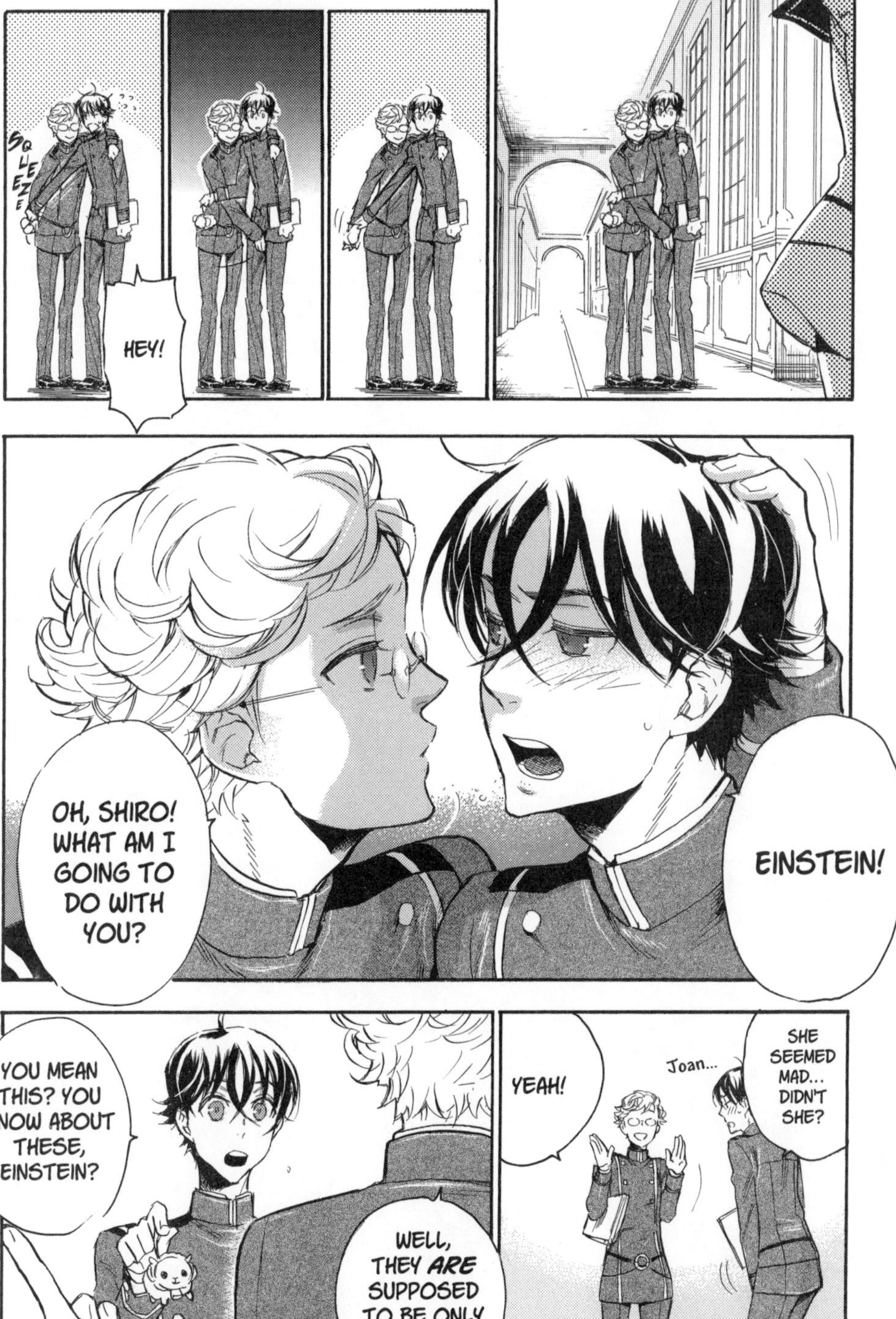

HEY!
SQUEEZE
EINSTEIN!
OH, SHIRO! WHAT AM I GOING TO DO WITH YOU?
SHE SEEMED MAD... DIDN'T SHE?
Joan...
YEAH!
YOU MEAN THIS? YOU KNOW ABOUT THESE, EINSTEIN?
WELL, THEY *ARE* SUPPOSED TO BE ONLY FOR CLONES!

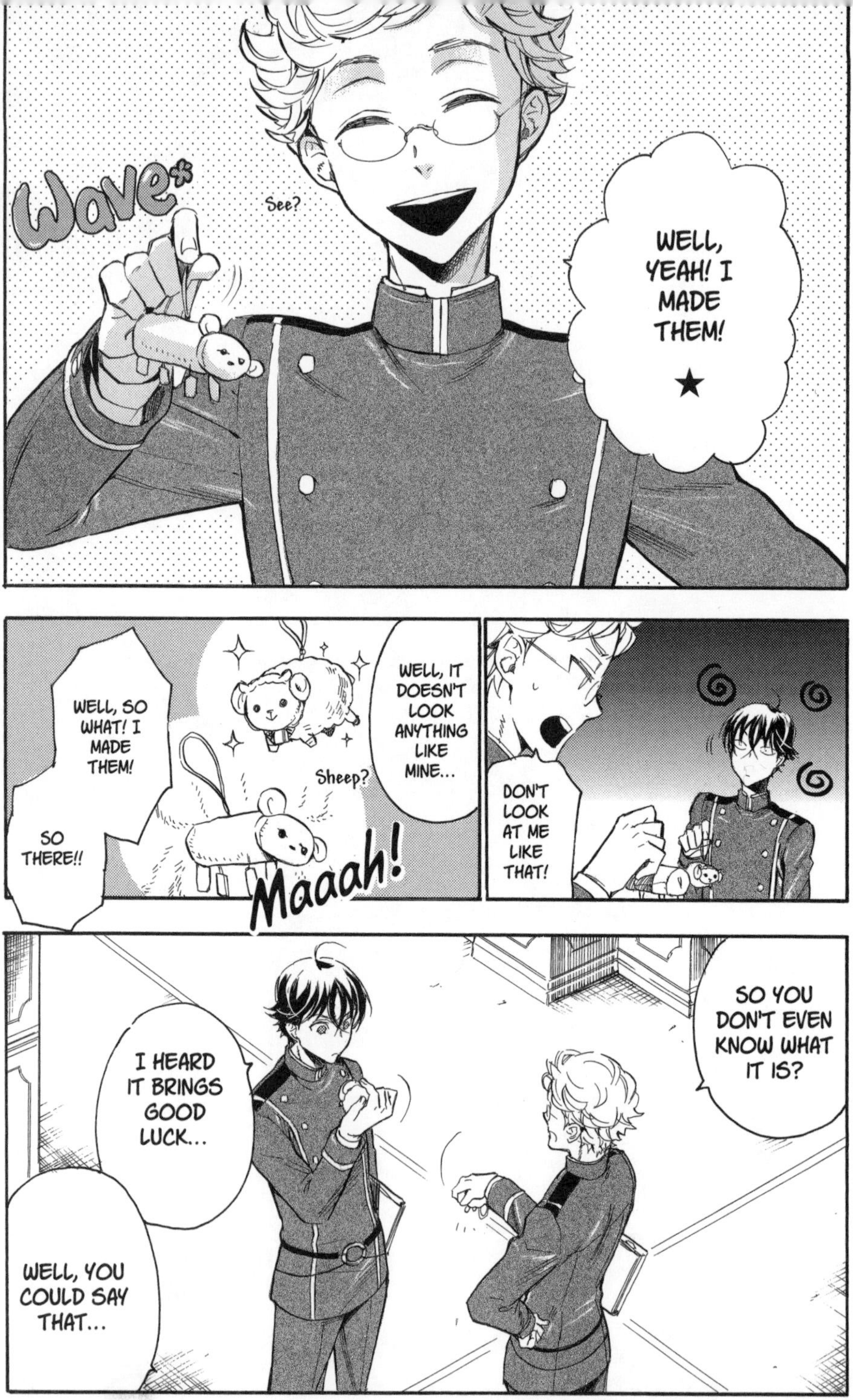
WELL, YEAH! I MADE THEM! ★
See?
Wave
DON'T LOOK AT ME LIKE THAT!
WELL, IT DOESN'T LOOK ANYTHING LIKE MINE...
Sheep?
WELL, SO WHAT! I MADE THEM!
SO THERE!!
Maaah!
SO YOU DON'T EVEN KNOW WHAT IT IS?
I HEARD IT BRINGS GOOD LUCK...
WELL, YOU COULD SAY THAT...

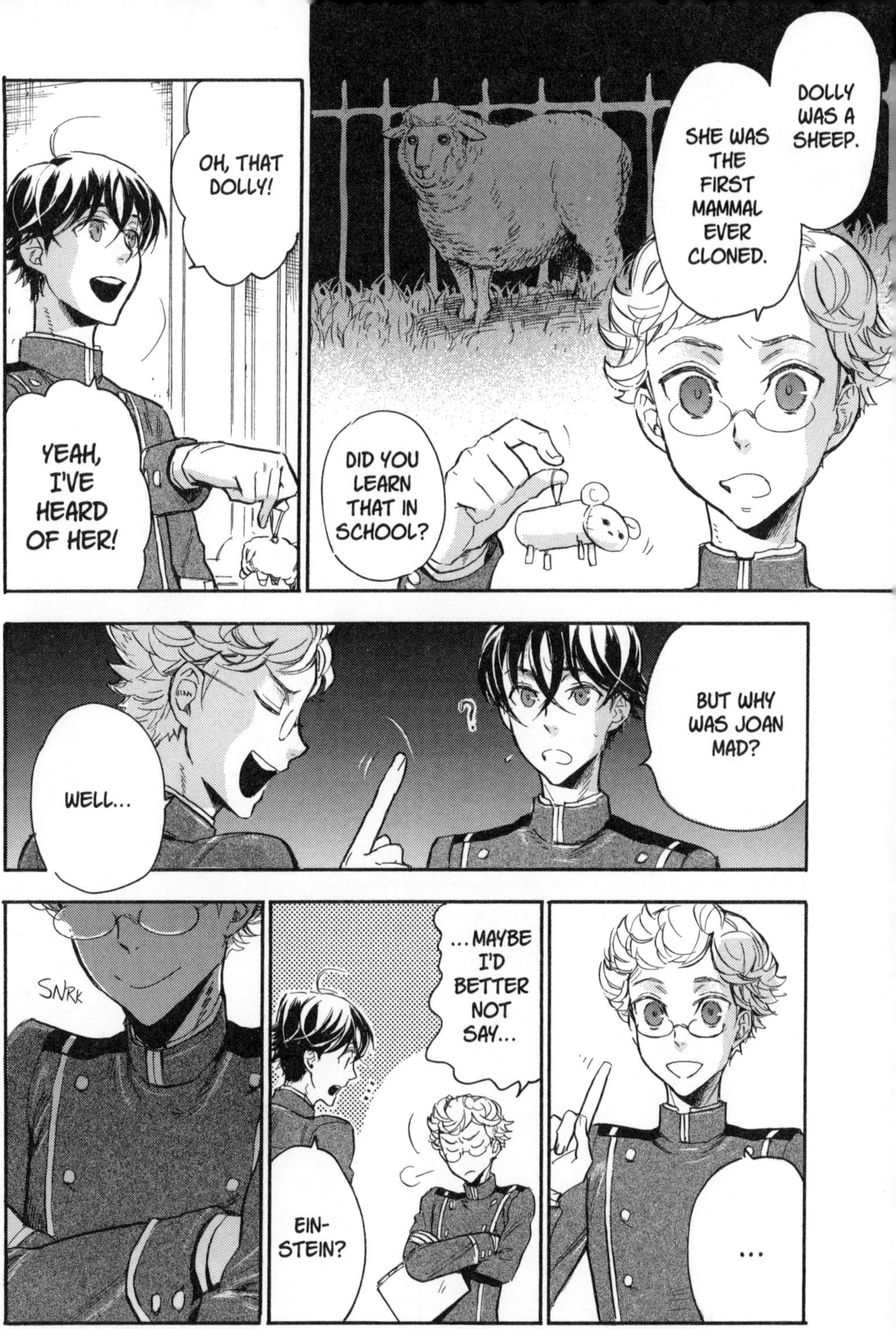
DOLLY WAS A SHEEP.
SHE WAS THE FIRST MAMMAL EVER CLONED.
DID YOU LEARN THAT IN SCHOOL?
OH, THAT DOLLY!
YEAH, I'VE HEARD OF HER!
BUT WHY WAS JOAN MAD?
?
WELL...
...
...MAYBE I'D BETTER NOT SAY...
EIN-STEIN?
SNRK

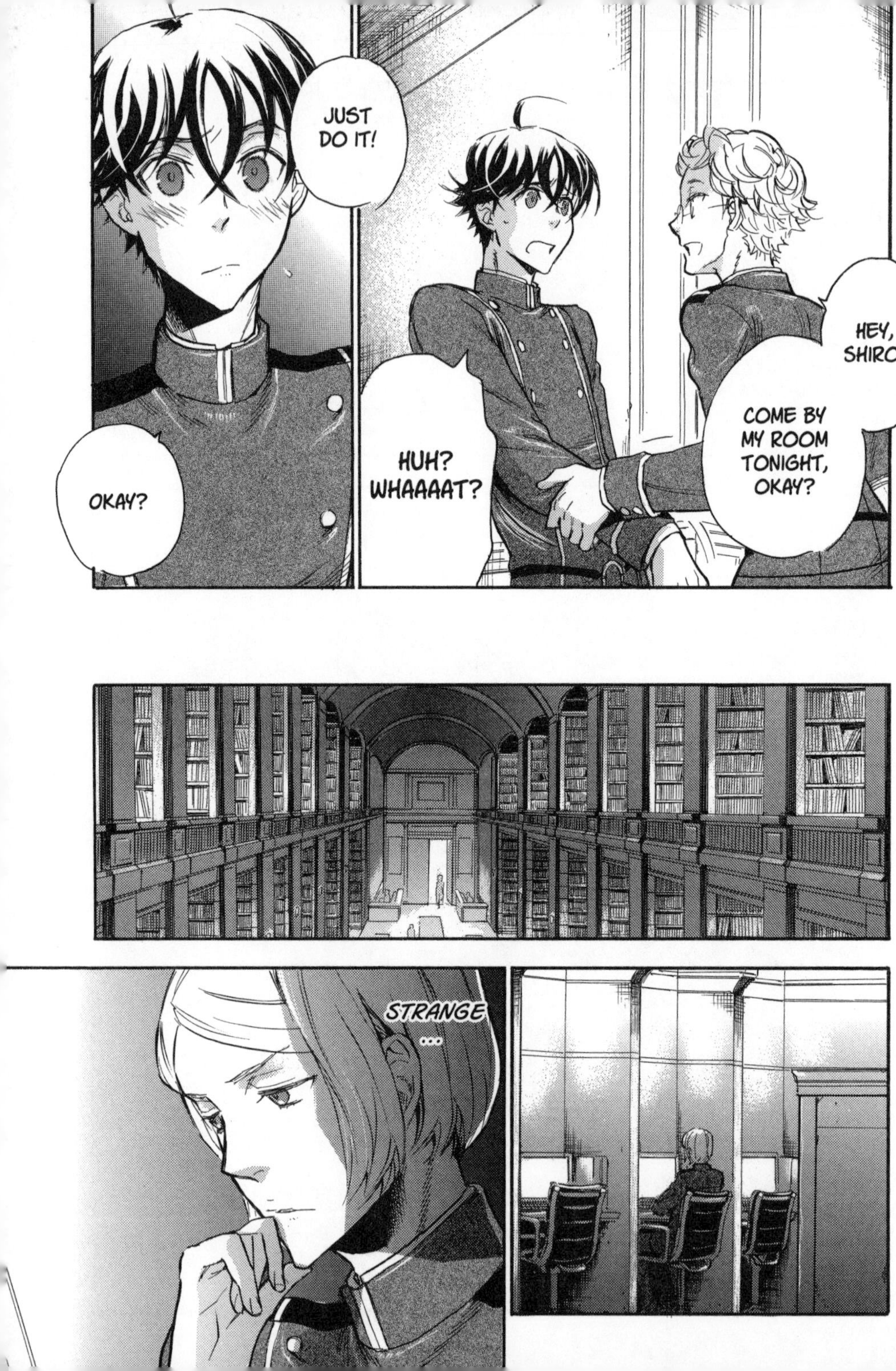
HEY, SHIRO!
COME BY MY ROOM TONIGHT, OKAY?
HUH? WHAAAAT?
JUST DO IT!
OKAY?
STRANGE ...

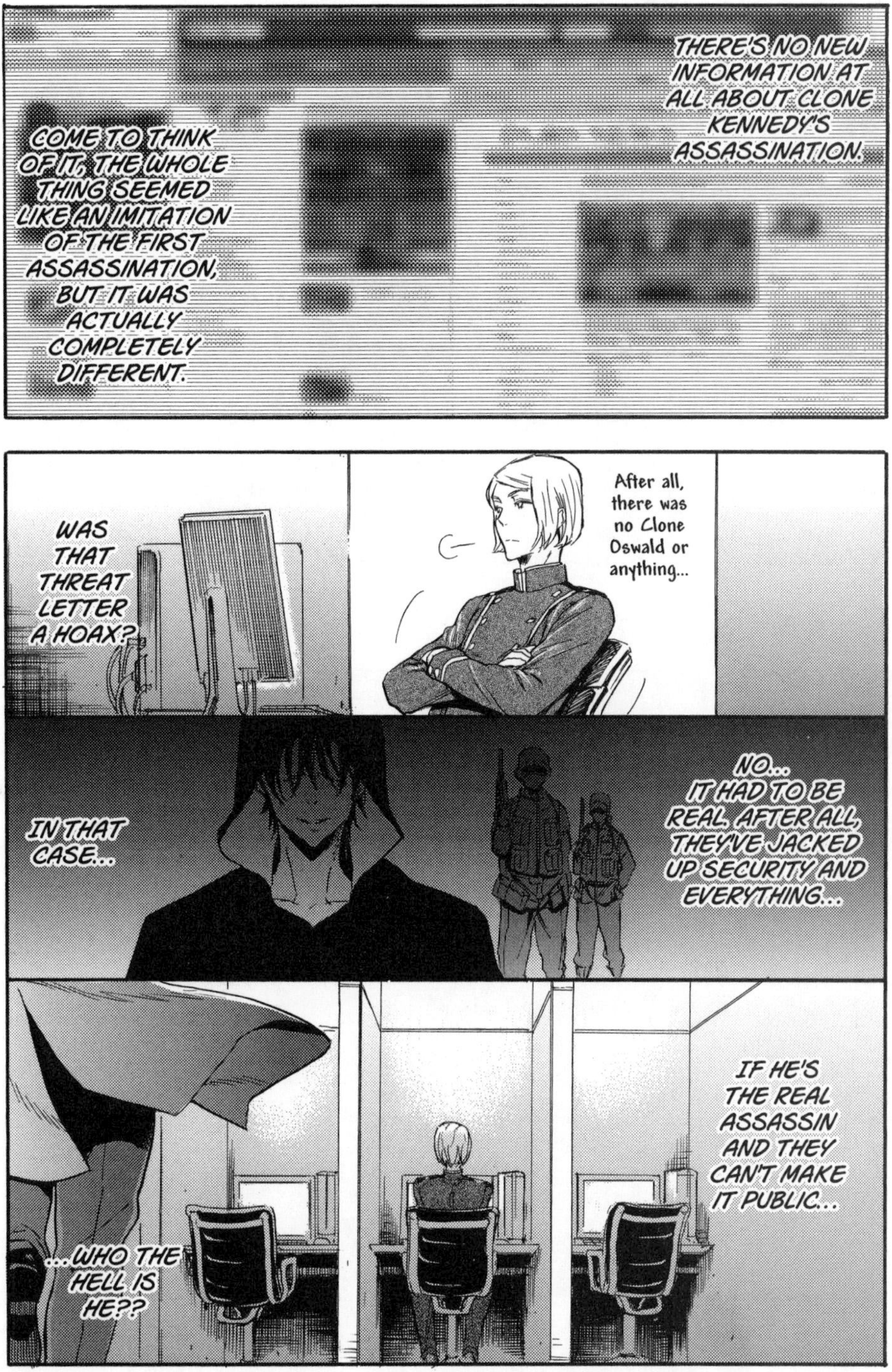
THERE'S NO NEW INFORMATION AT ALL ABOUT CLONE KENNEDY'S ASSASSINATION.
COME TO THINK OF IT, THE WHOLE THING SEEMED LIKE AN IMITATION OF THE FIRST ASSASSINATION, BUT IT WAS ACTUALLY COMPLETELY DIFFERENT.
After all, there was no Clone Oswald or anything...
WAS THAT THREAT LETTER A HOAX?
NO... IT HAD TO BE REAL. AFTER ALL, THEY'VE JACKED UP SECURITY AND EVERYTHING...
IN THAT CASE...
IF HE'S THE REAL ASSASSIN AND THEY CAN'T MAKE IT PUBLIC...
...WHO THE HELL IS HE??

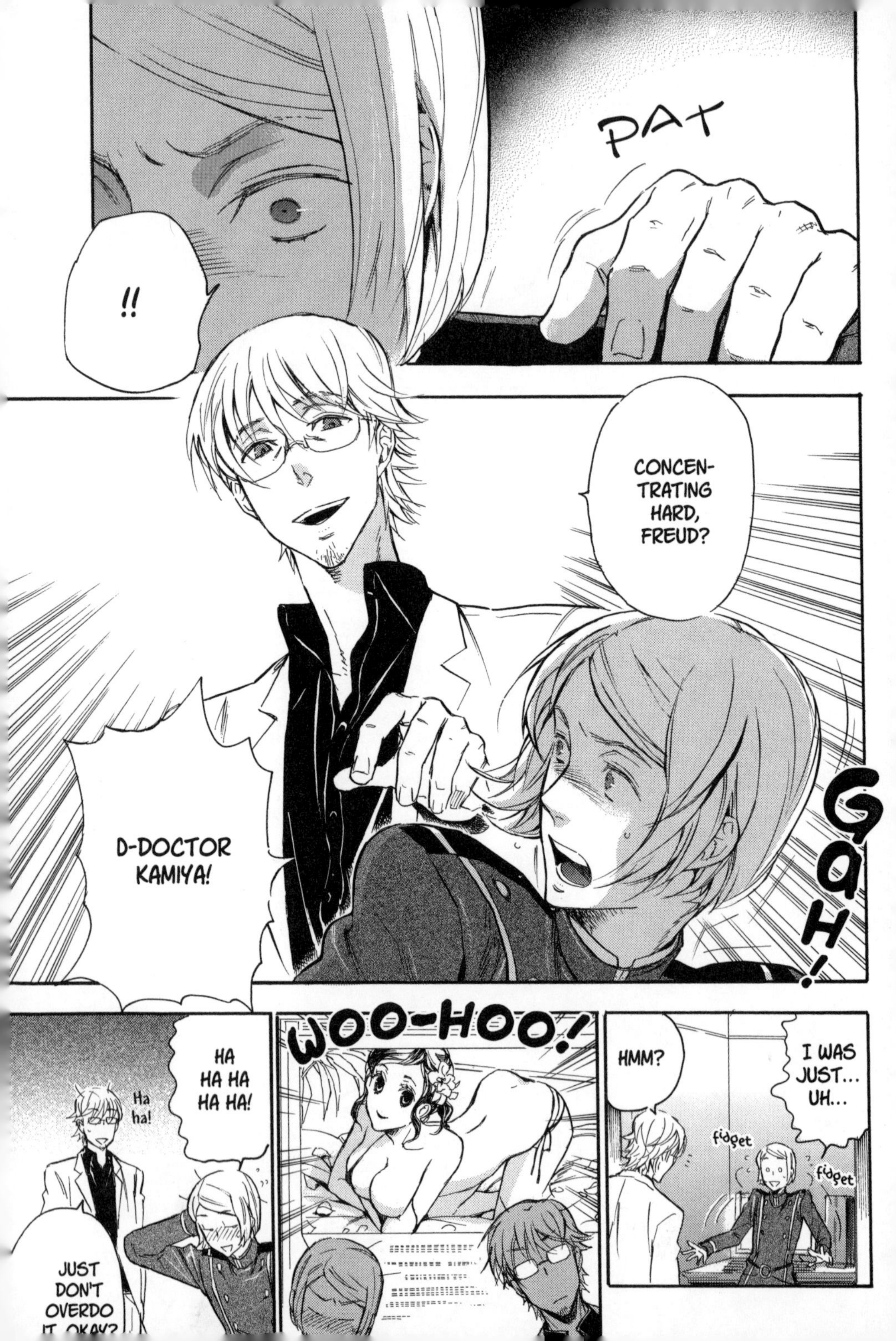
PAT
!!
CONCEN-TRATING HARD, FREUD?
GAH!
D-DOCTOR KAMIYA!
I WAS JUST... UH...
fidget
fidget
HMM?
WOO-HOO!
HA HA HA HA HA!
Ha ha!
JUST DON'T OVERDO IT, OKAY?

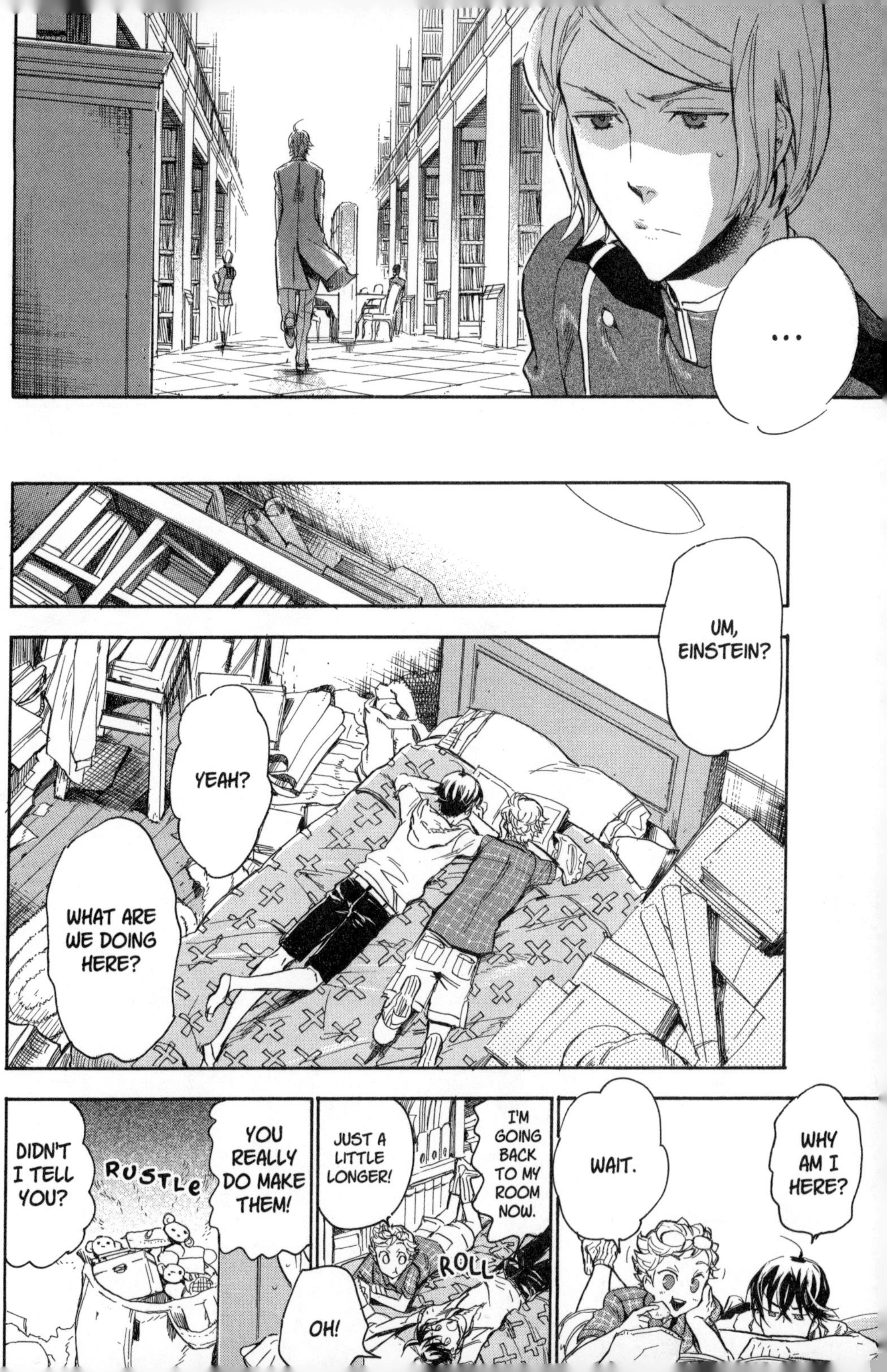
...
UM, EINSTEIN?
YEAH?
WHAT ARE WE DOING HERE?
WHY AM I HERE?
WAIT.
I'M GOING BACK TO MY ROOM NOW.
JUST A LITTLE LONGER!
ROLL
OH!
YOU REALLY DO MAKE THEM!
RUSTLE
DIDN'T I TELL YOU?

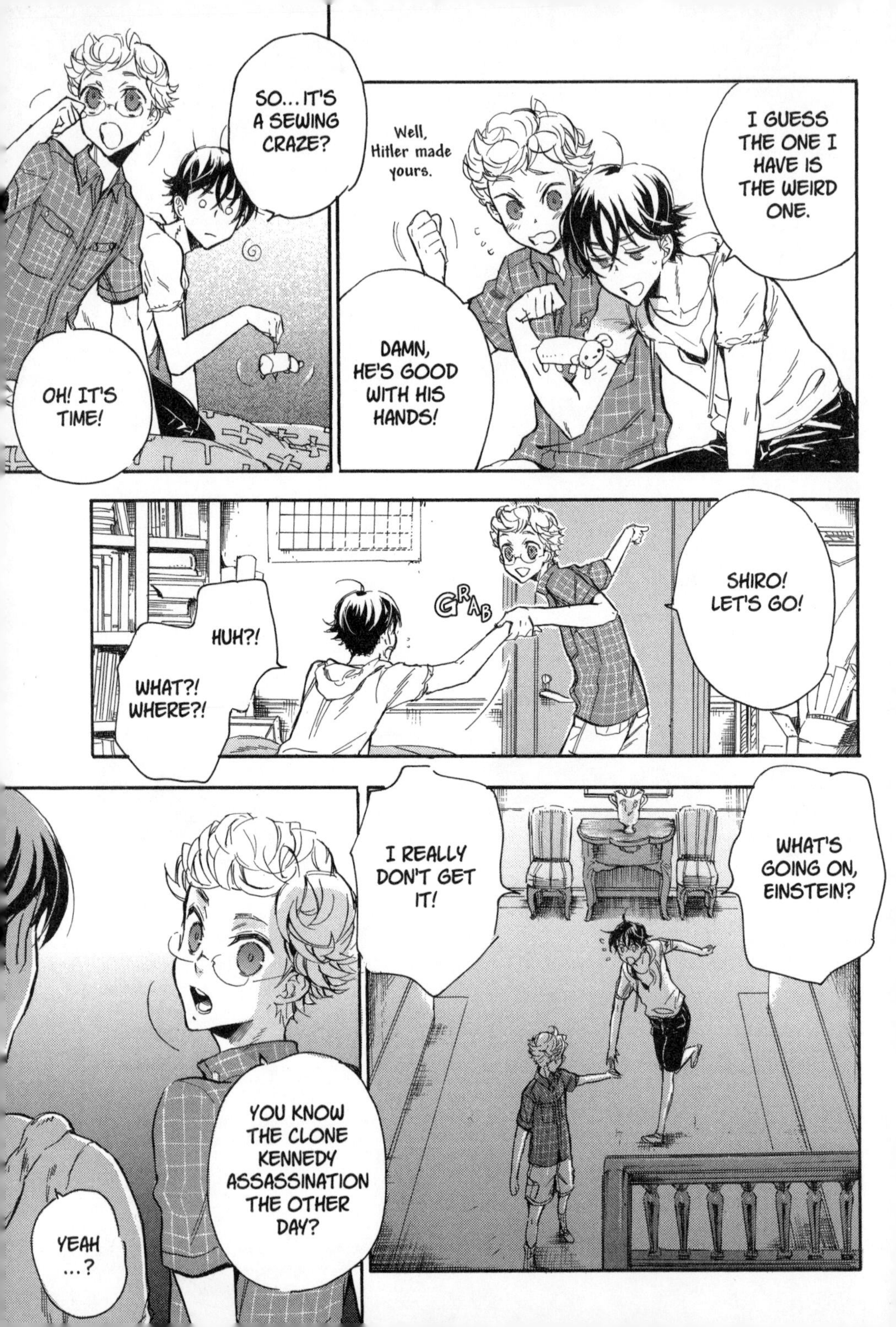
I GUESS THE ONE I HAVE IS THE WEIRD ONE.
Well, Hitler made yours.
DAMN, HE'S GOOD WITH HIS HANDS!
SO... IT'S A SEWING CRAZE?
OH! IT'S TIME!
SHIRO! LET'S GO!
GRAB
HUH?!
WHAT?! WHERE?!
WHAT'S GOING ON, EINSTEIN?
I REALLY DON'T GET IT!
YOU KNOW THE CLONE KENNEDY ASSASSINATION THE OTHER DAY?
YEAH ...?

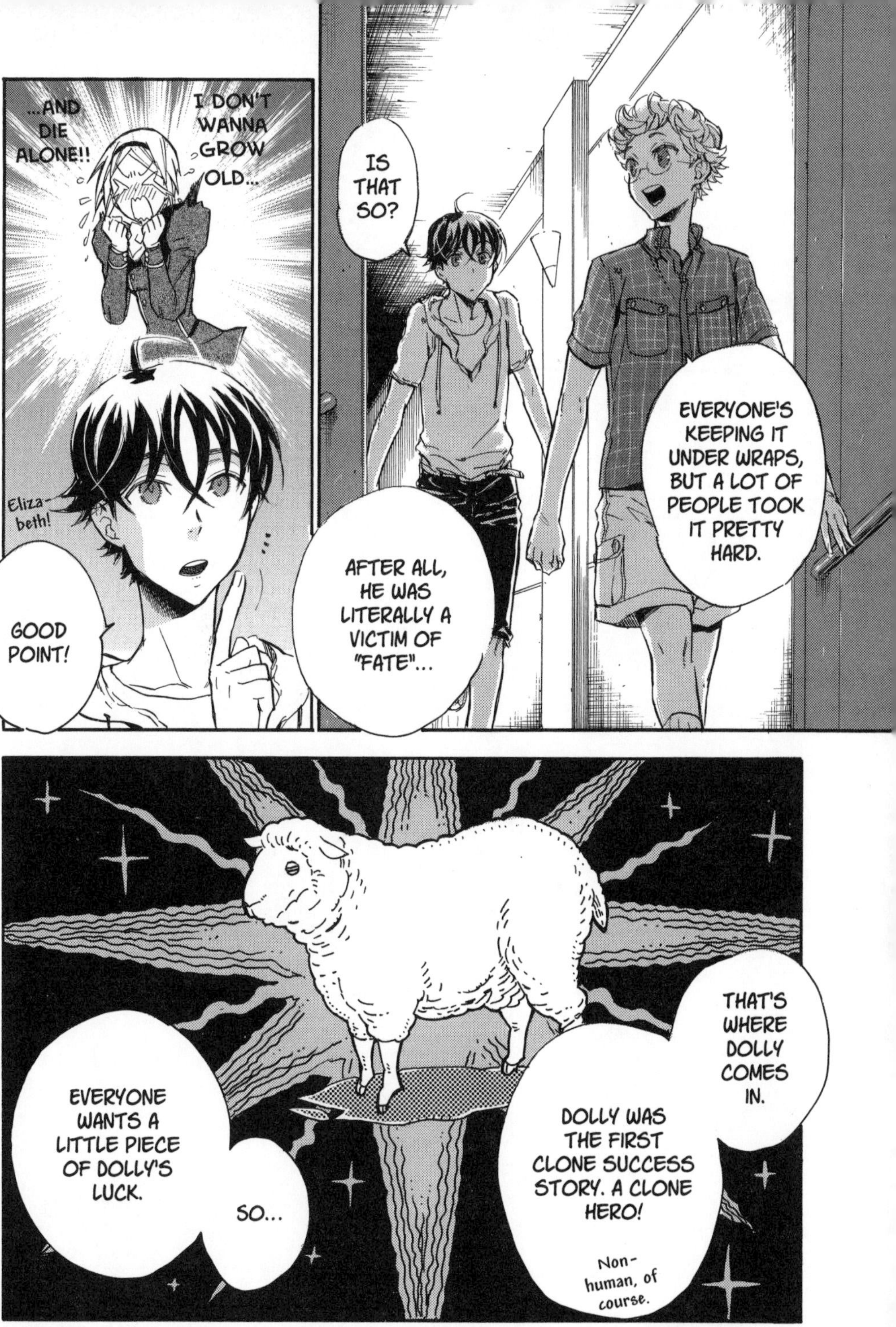
IS THAT SO?
EVERYONE'S KEEPING IT UNDER WRAPS, BUT A LOT OF PEOPLE TOOK IT PRETTY HARD.
AFTER ALL, HE WAS LITERALLY A VICTIM OF "FATE"...
I DON'T WANNA GROW OLD...
...AND DIE ALONE!!
Eliza-beth!
GOOD POINT!
THAT'S WHERE DOLLY COMES IN.
DOLLY WAS THE FIRST CLONE SUCCESS STORY. A CLONE HERO!
Non-human, of course.
SO...
EVERYONE WANTS A LITTLE PIECE OF DOLLY'S LUCK.

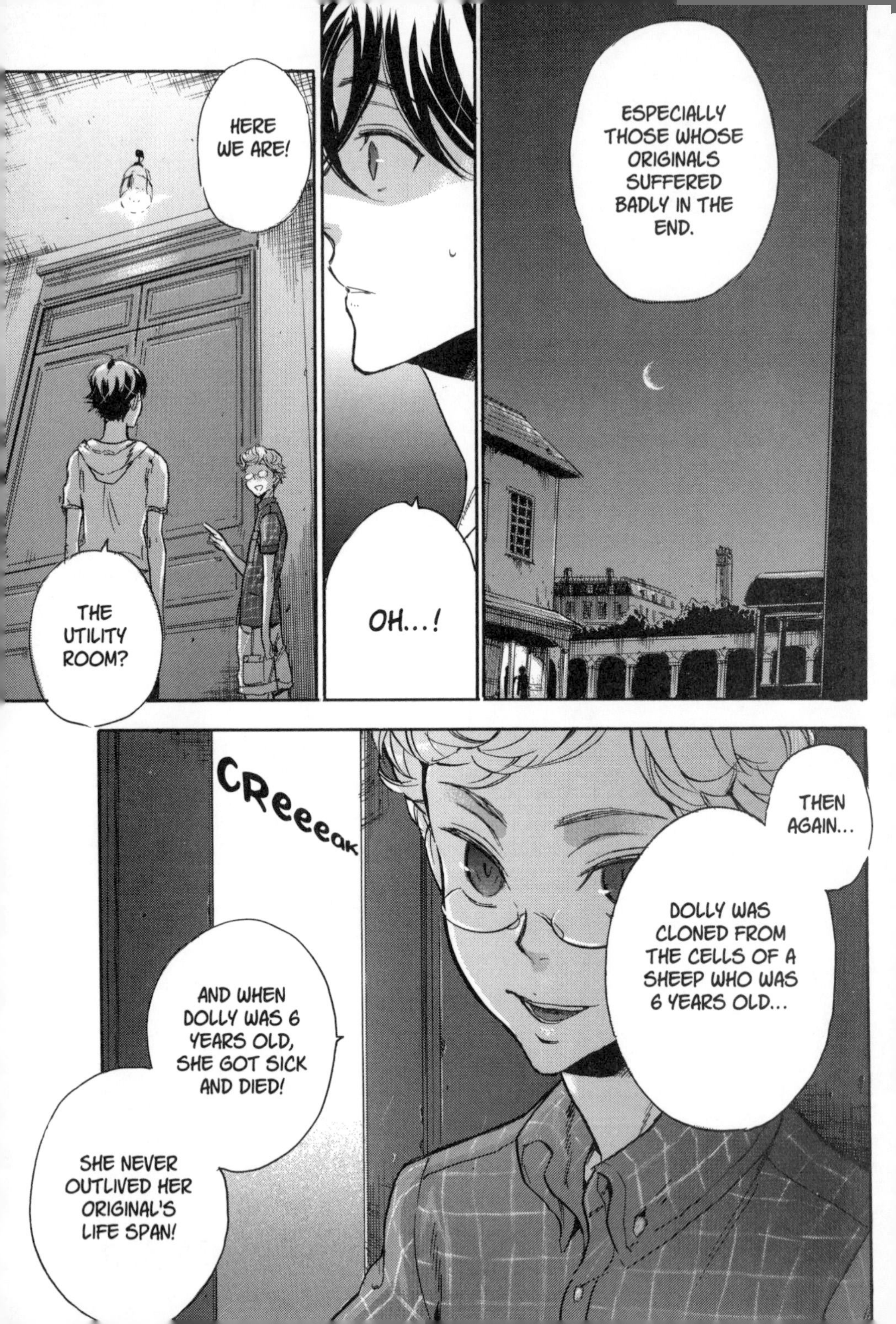
ESPECIALLY THOSE WHOSE ORIGINALS SUFFERED BADLY IN THE END.
OH...!
HERE WE ARE!
THE UTILITY ROOM?
THEN AGAIN...
DOLLY WAS CLONED FROM THE CELLS OF A SHEEP WHO WAS 6 YEARS OLD...
CReeeeak
AND WHEN DOLLY WAS 6 YEARS OLD, SHE GOT SICK AND DIED!
SHE NEVER OUTLIVED HER ORIGINAL'S LIFE SPAN!

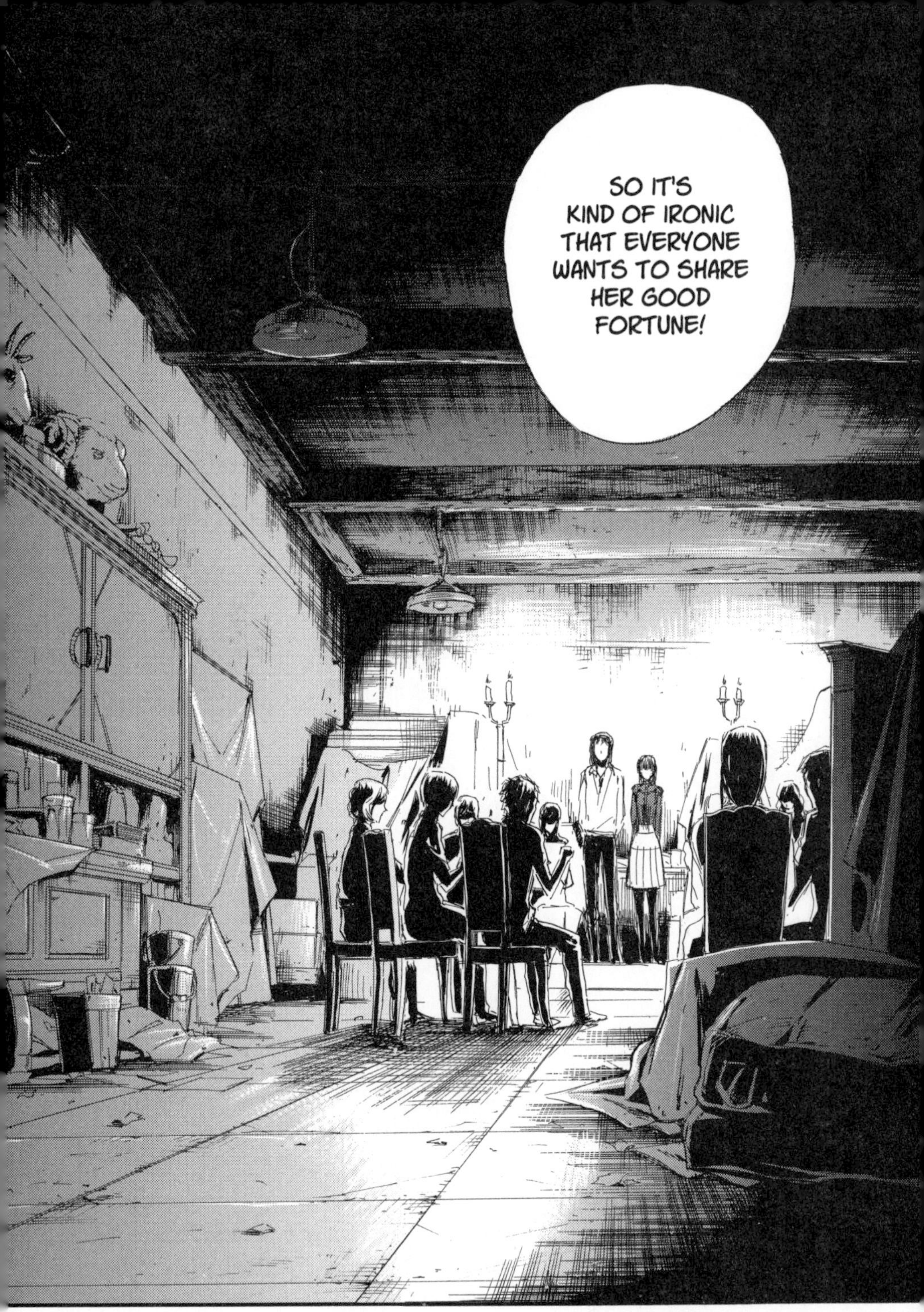
SO IT'S KIND OF IRONIC THAT EVERYONE WANTS TO SHARE HER GOOD FORTUNE!

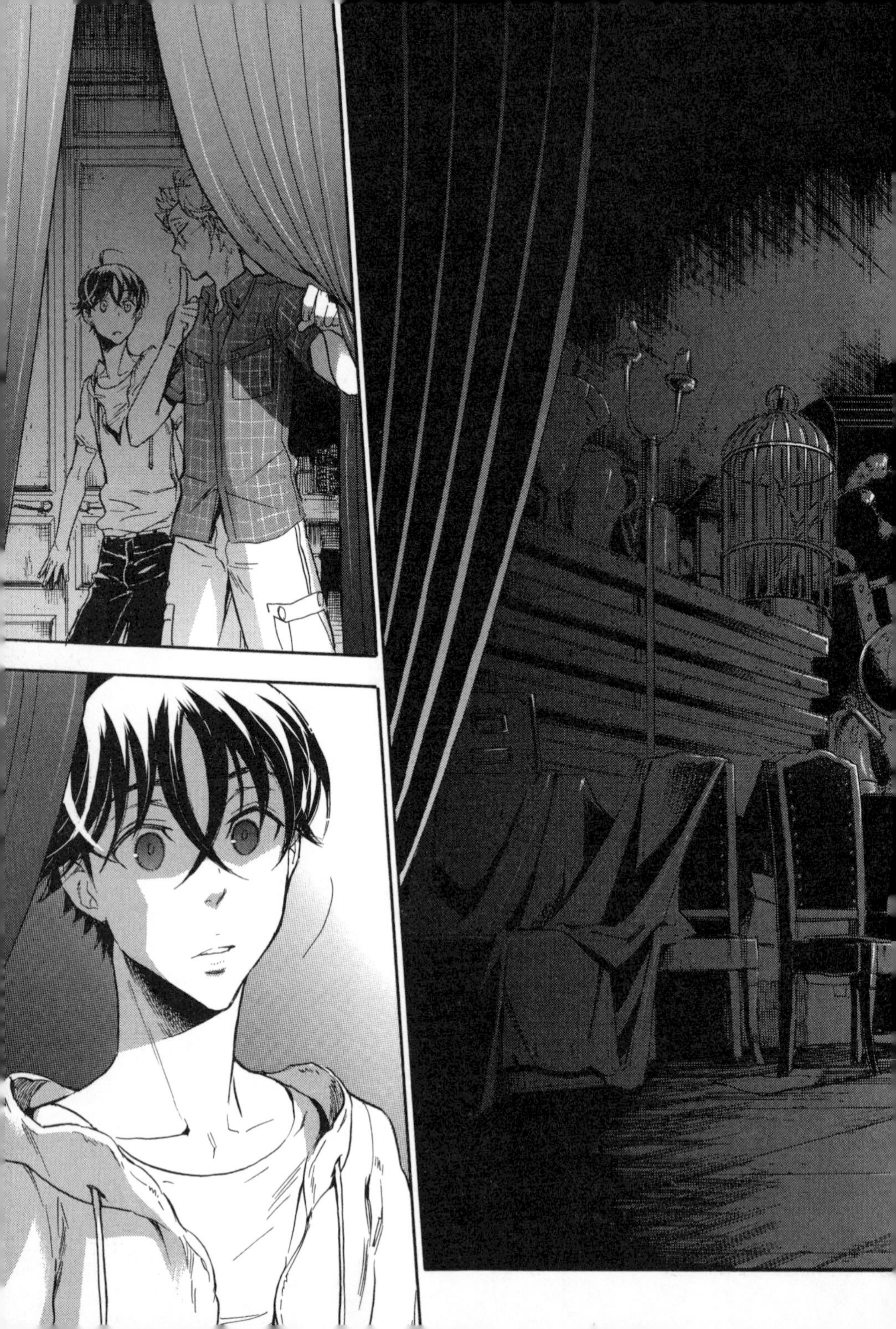

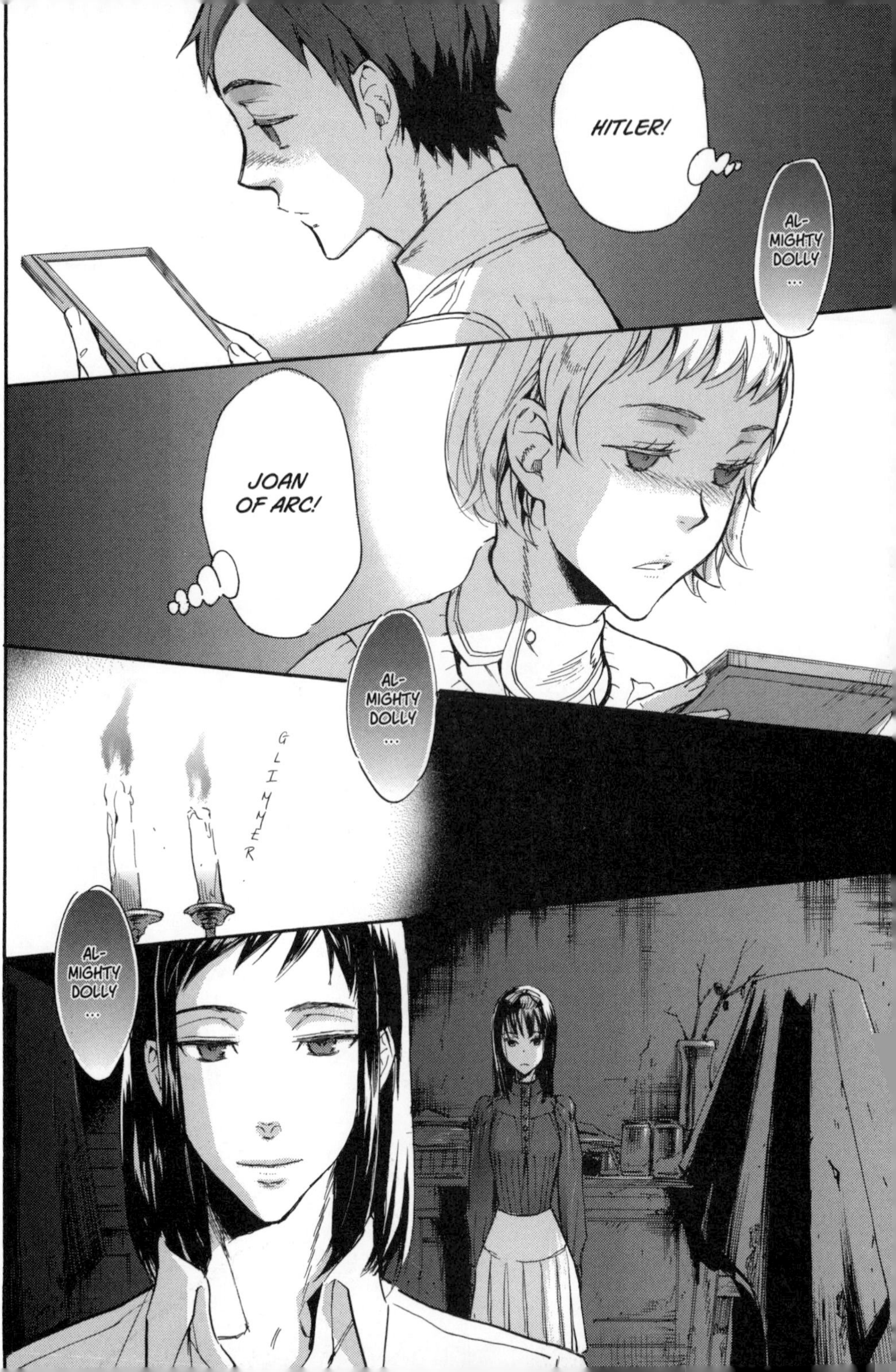
HITLER!
AL-MIGHTY DOLLY ...
JOAN OF ARC!
AL-MIGHTY DOLLY ...
GLIMMER
AL-MIGHTY DOLLY ...

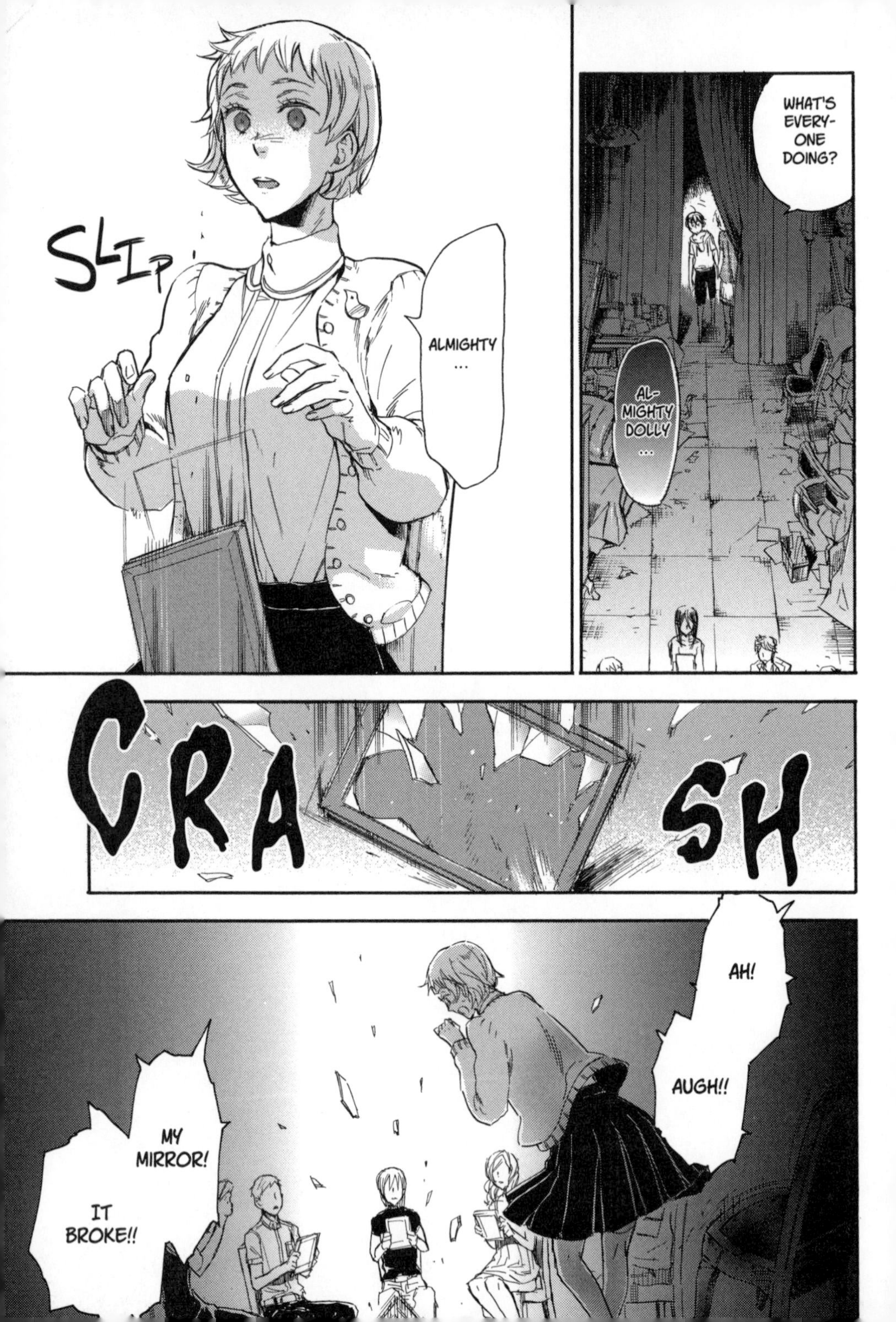
WHAT'S EVERY-ONE DOING?
AL-MIGHTY DOLLY ...
ALMIGHTY ...
SLIP
CRASH
AH!
AUGH!!
MY MIRROR!
IT BROKE!!

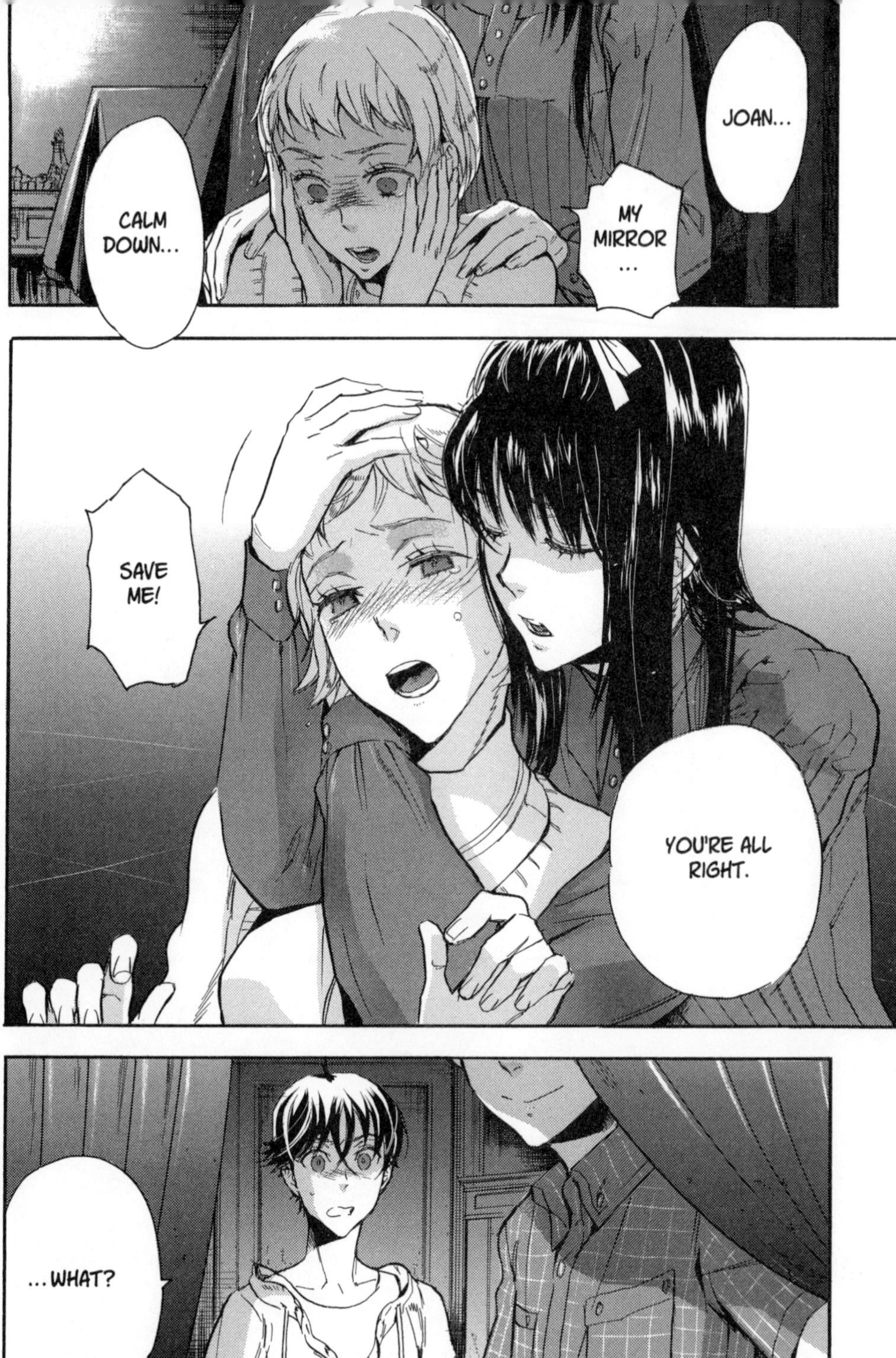
JOAN...
MY MIRROR ...
CALM DOWN...
SAVE ME!
YOU'RE ALL RIGHT.
...WHAT?

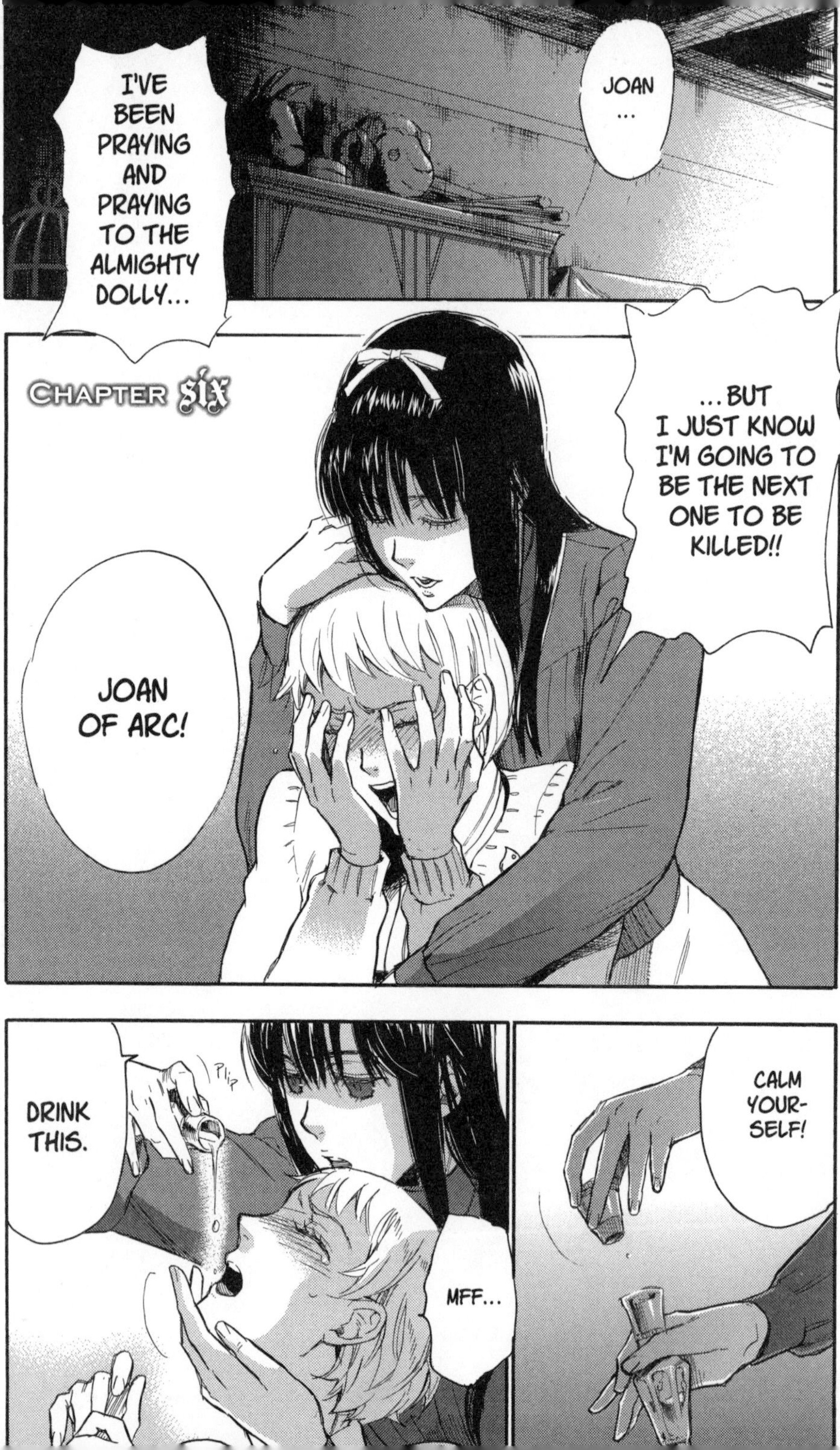
JOAN ...
I'VE BEEN PRAYING AND PRAYING TO THE ALMIGHTY DOLLY...
CHAPTER SIX
...BUT I JUST KNOW I'M GOING TO BE THE NEXT ONE TO BE KILLED!!
JOAN OF ARC!
CALM YOUR-SELF!
DRINK THIS.
Plip
MFF...

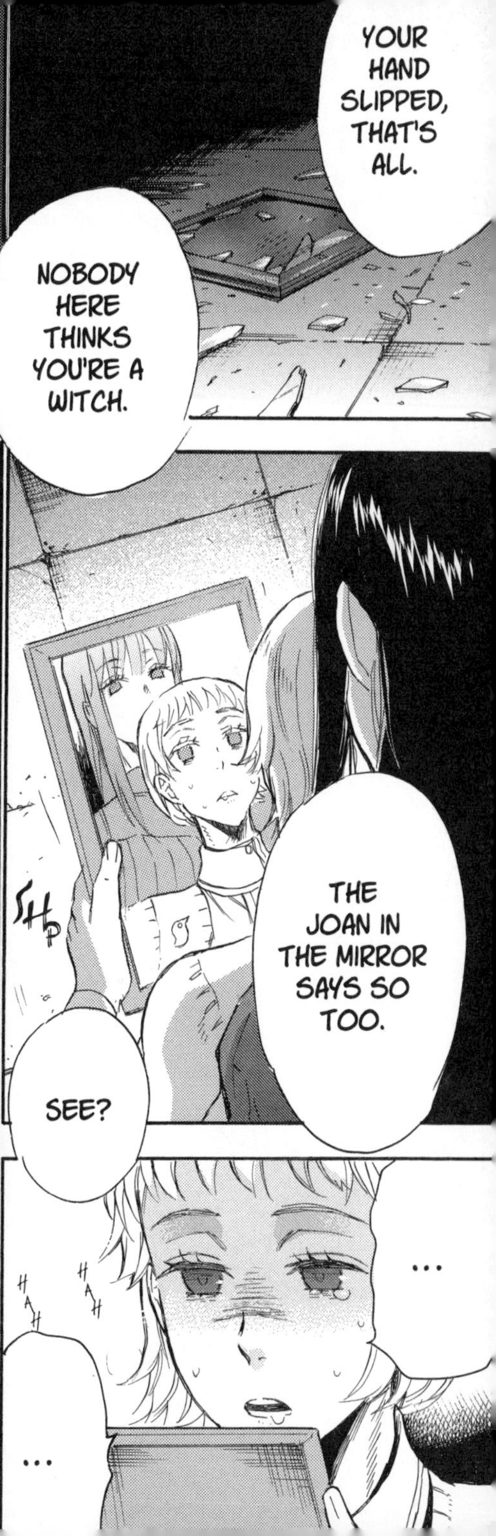
YOUR HAND SLIPPED, THAT'S ALL.
NOBODY HERE THINKS YOU'RE A WITCH.
THE JOAN IN THE MIRROR SAYS SO TOO.
SHP
SEE?
...
HAH
HAH
...
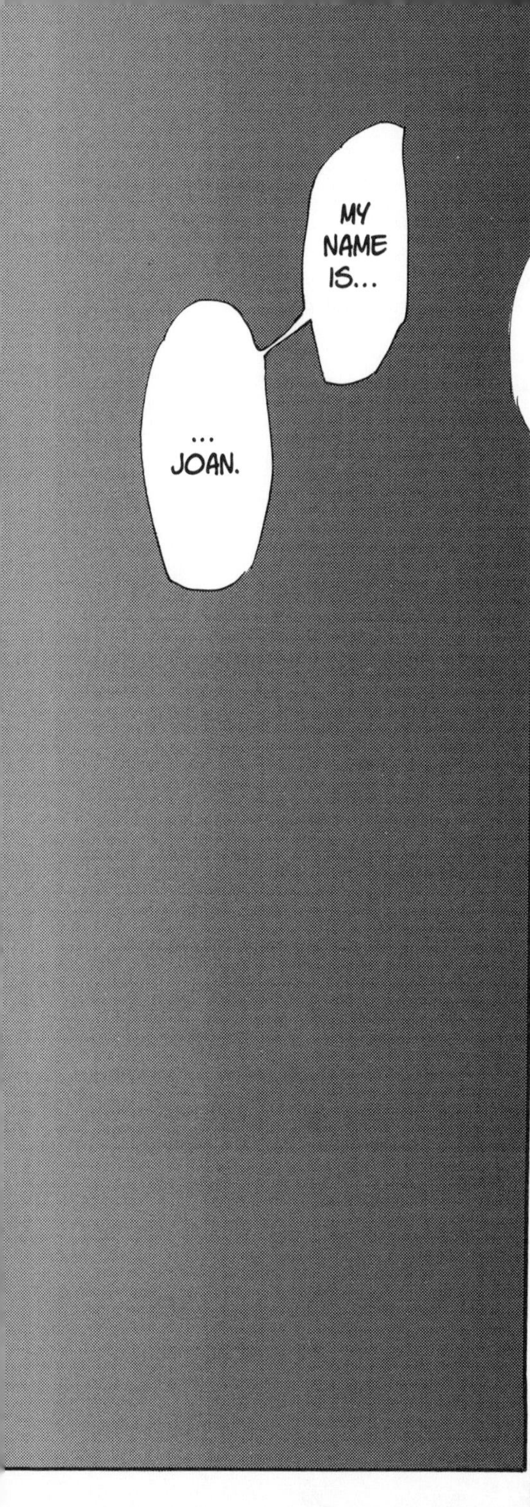
MY NAME IS...
... JOAN.

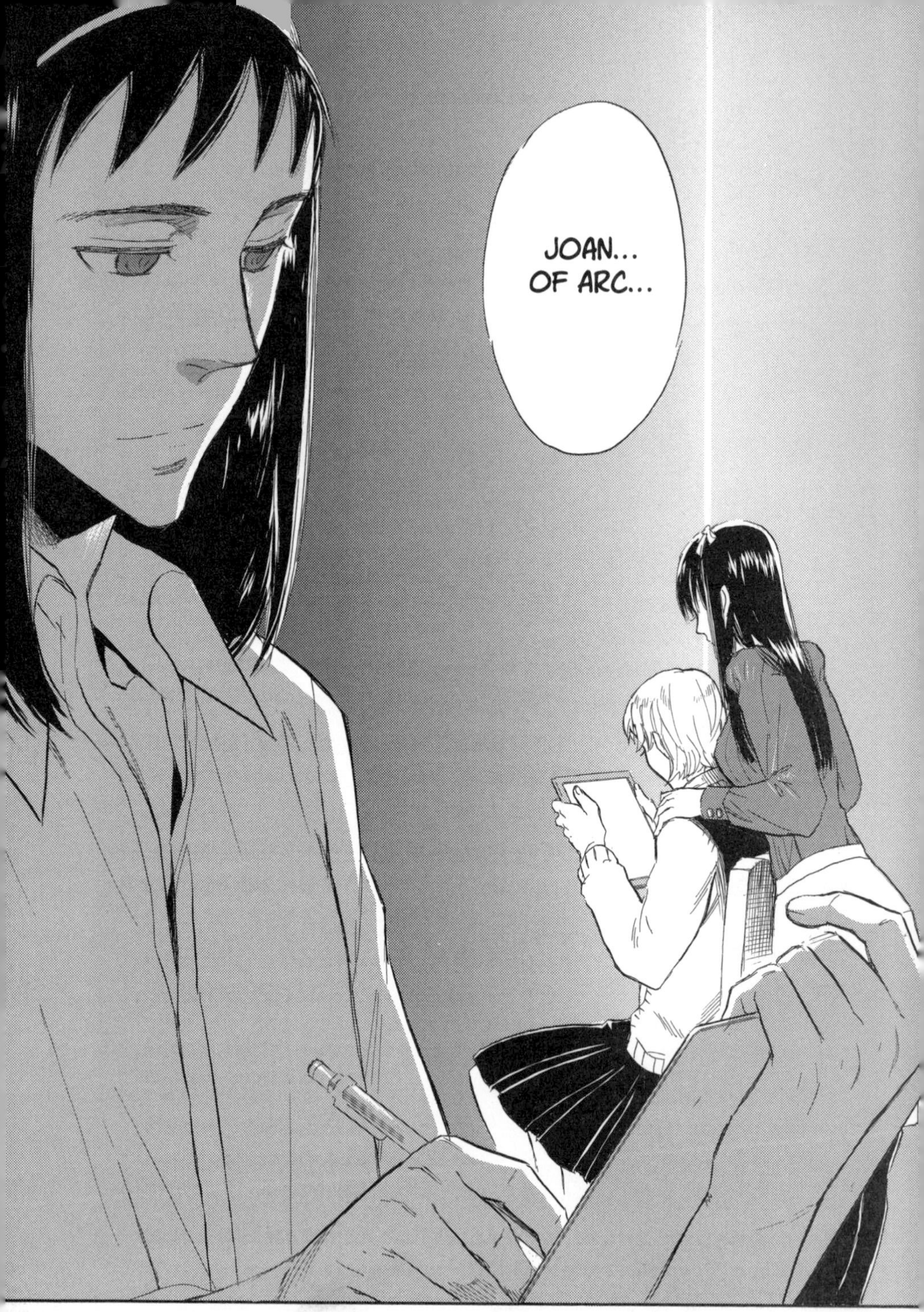
JOAN... OF ARC...

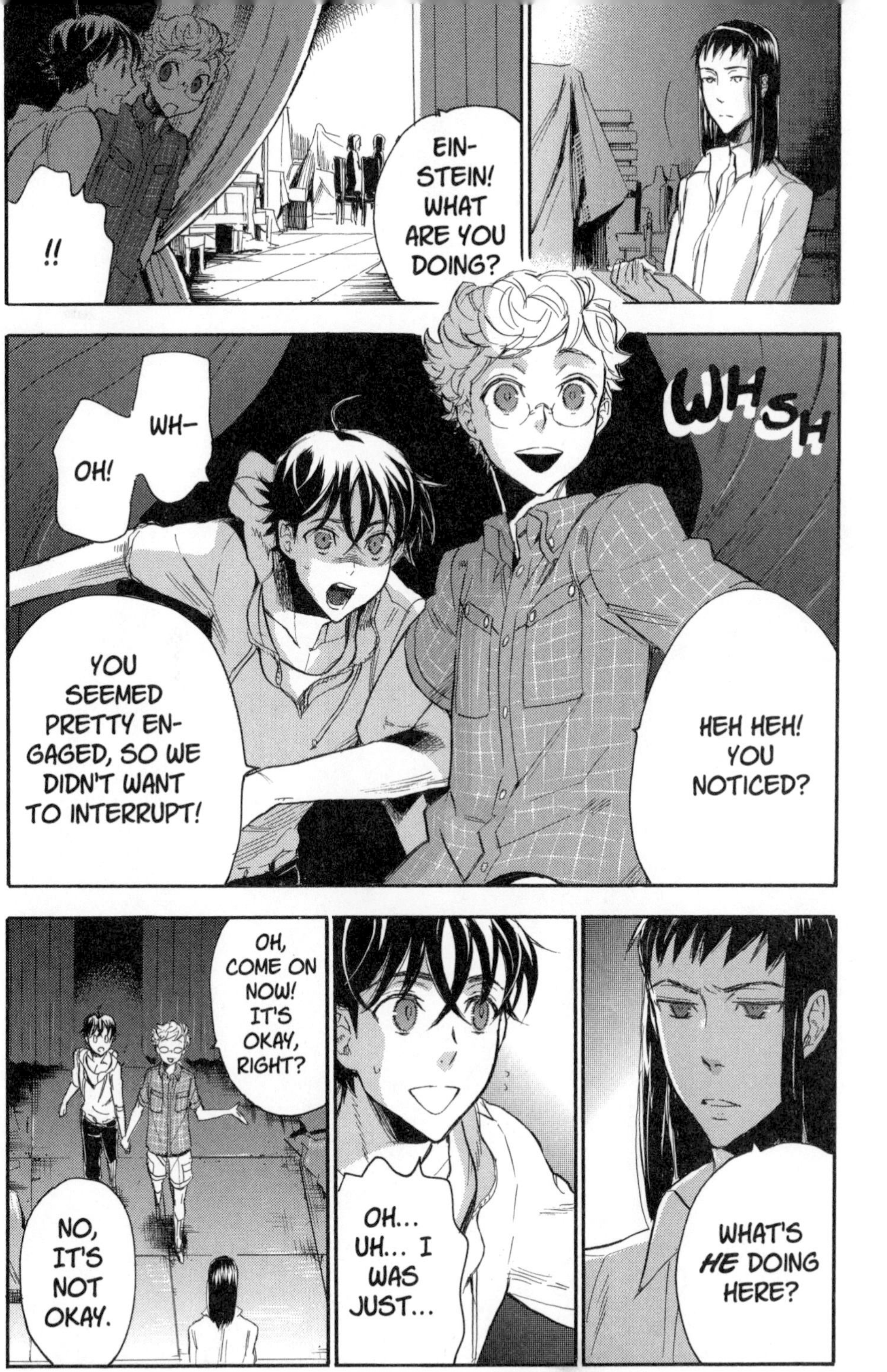
EIN-STEIN! WHAT ARE YOU DOING?
!!
WHSH
WH- OH!
HEH HEH! YOU NOTICED?
YOU SEEMED PRETTY EN-GAGED, SO WE DIDN'T WANT TO INTERRUPT!
WHAT'S *HE* DOING HERE?
OH... UH... I WAS JUST...
OH, COME ON NOW! IT'S OKAY, RIGHT?
NO, IT'S NOT OKAY.

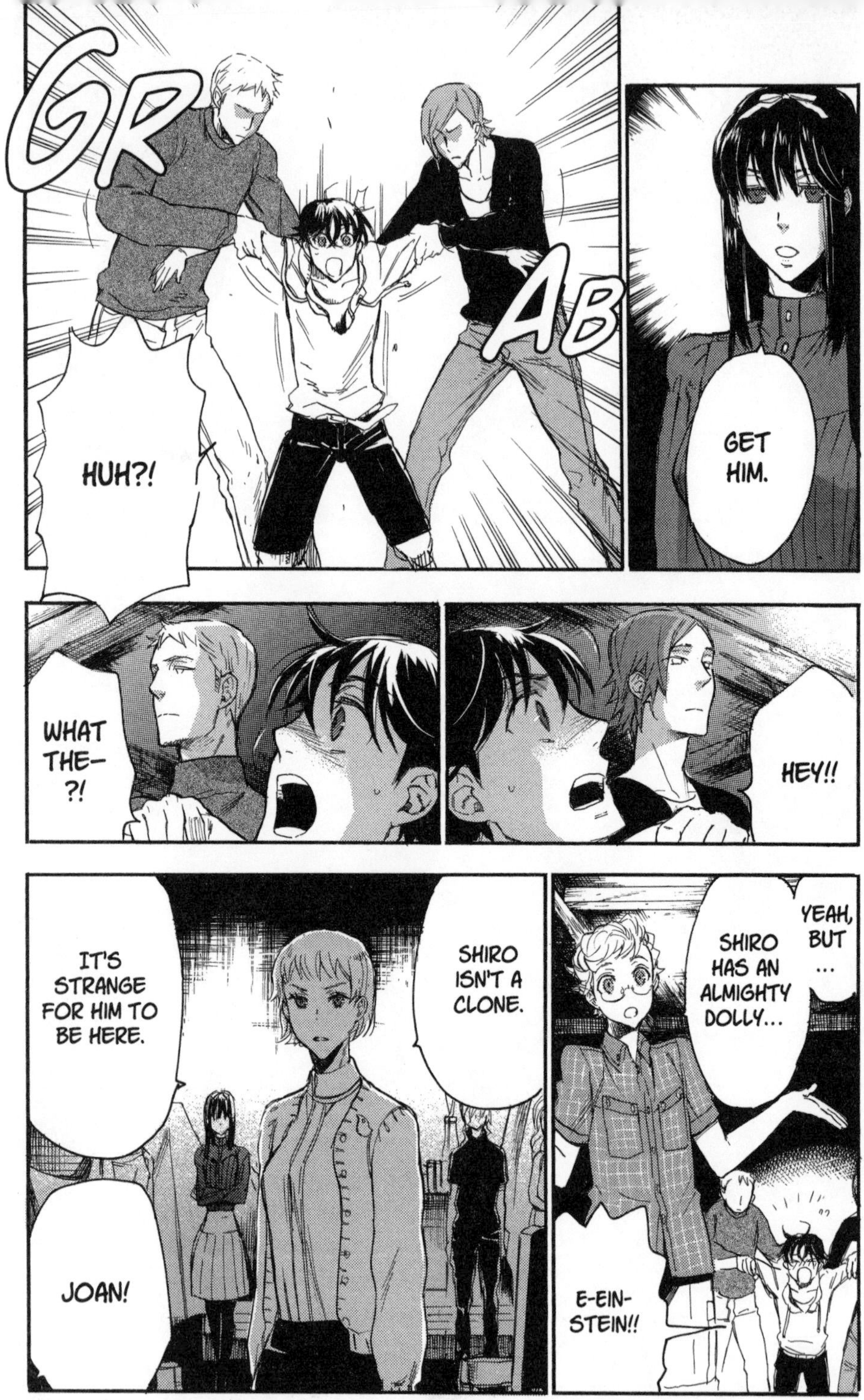
GET HIM.
GR
AB
HUH?!
HEY!!
WHAT THE— ?!
YEAH, BUT ...
SHIRO HAS AN ALMIGHTY DOLLY...
E-EIN-STEIN!!
SHIRO ISN'T A CLONE.
IT'S STRANGE FOR HIM TO BE HERE.
JOAN!

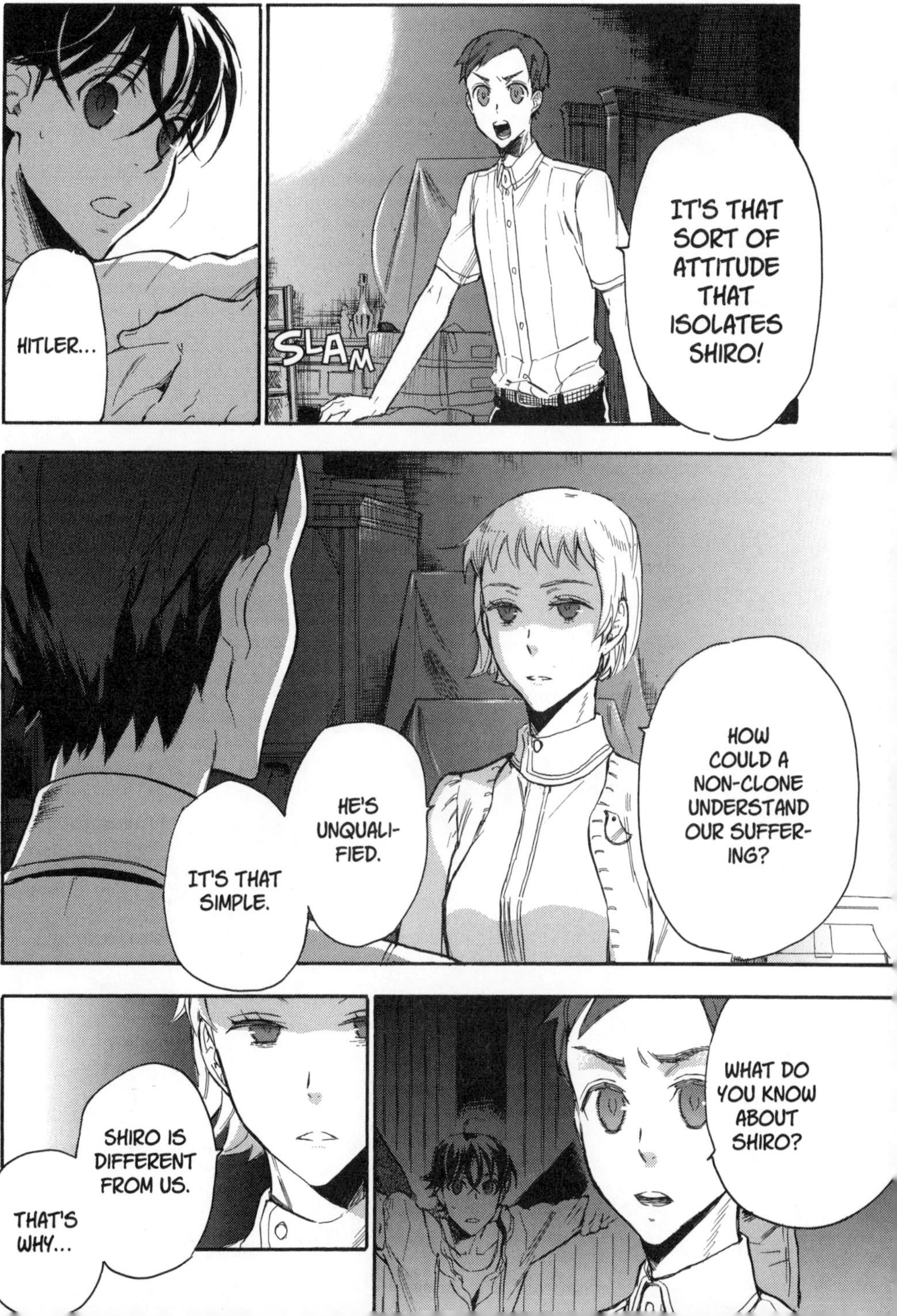
IT'S THAT SORT OF ATTITUDE THAT ISOLATES SHIRO!
SLAM
HITLER...
HOW COULD A NON-CLONE UNDERSTAND OUR SUFFERING?
HE'S UNQUALIFIED.
IT'S THAT SIMPLE.
WHAT DO YOU KNOW ABOUT SHIRO?
SHIRO IS DIFFERENT FROM US.
THAT'S WHY...

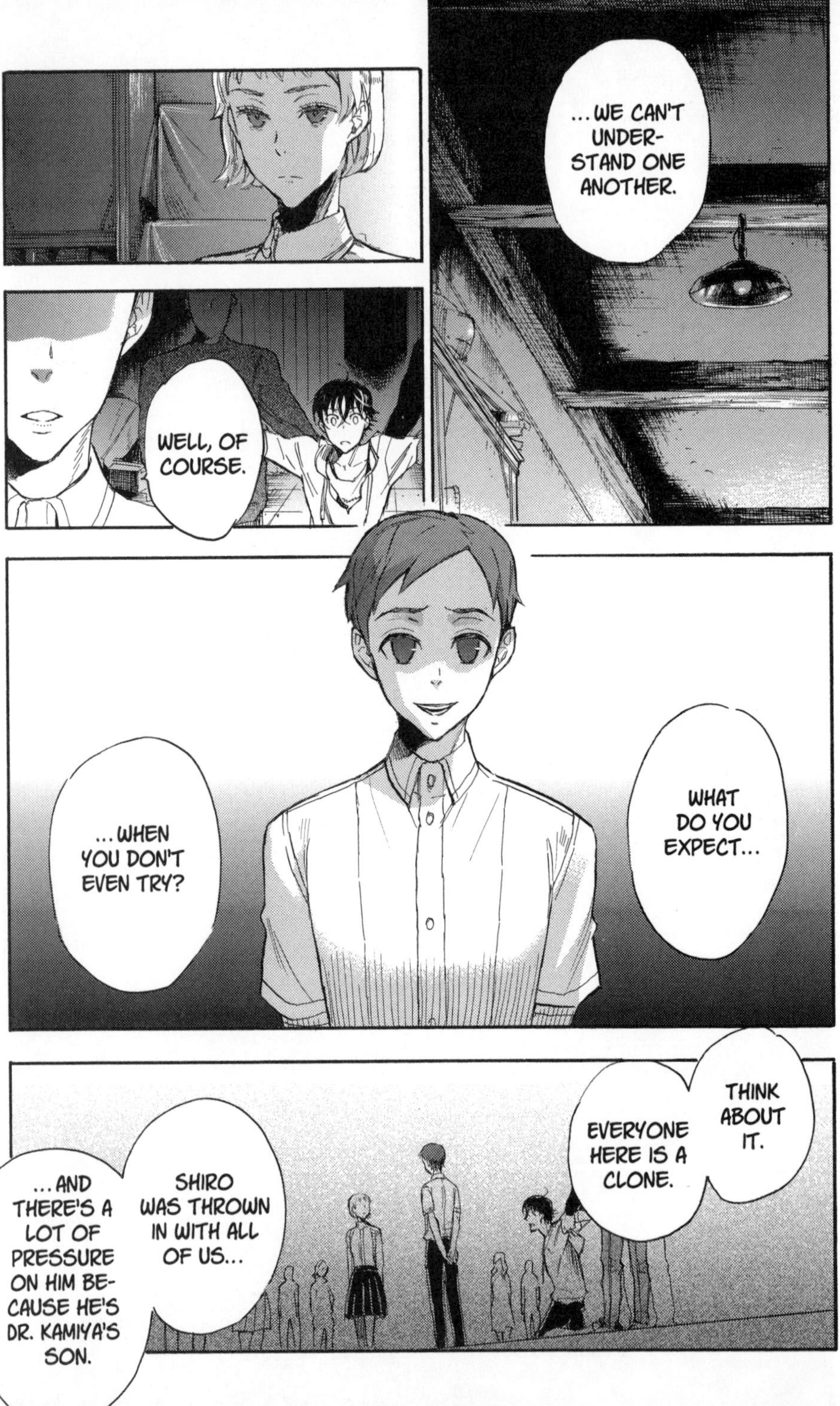
...WE CAN'T UNDER-STAND ONE ANOTHER.
WELL, OF COURSE.
WHAT DO YOU EXPECT...
...WHEN YOU DON'T EVEN TRY?
THINK ABOUT IT.
EVERYONE HERE IS A CLONE.
SHIRO WAS THROWN IN WITH ALL OF US...
...AND THERE'S A LOT OF PRESSURE ON HIM BE-CAUSE HE'S DR. KAMIYA'S SON.

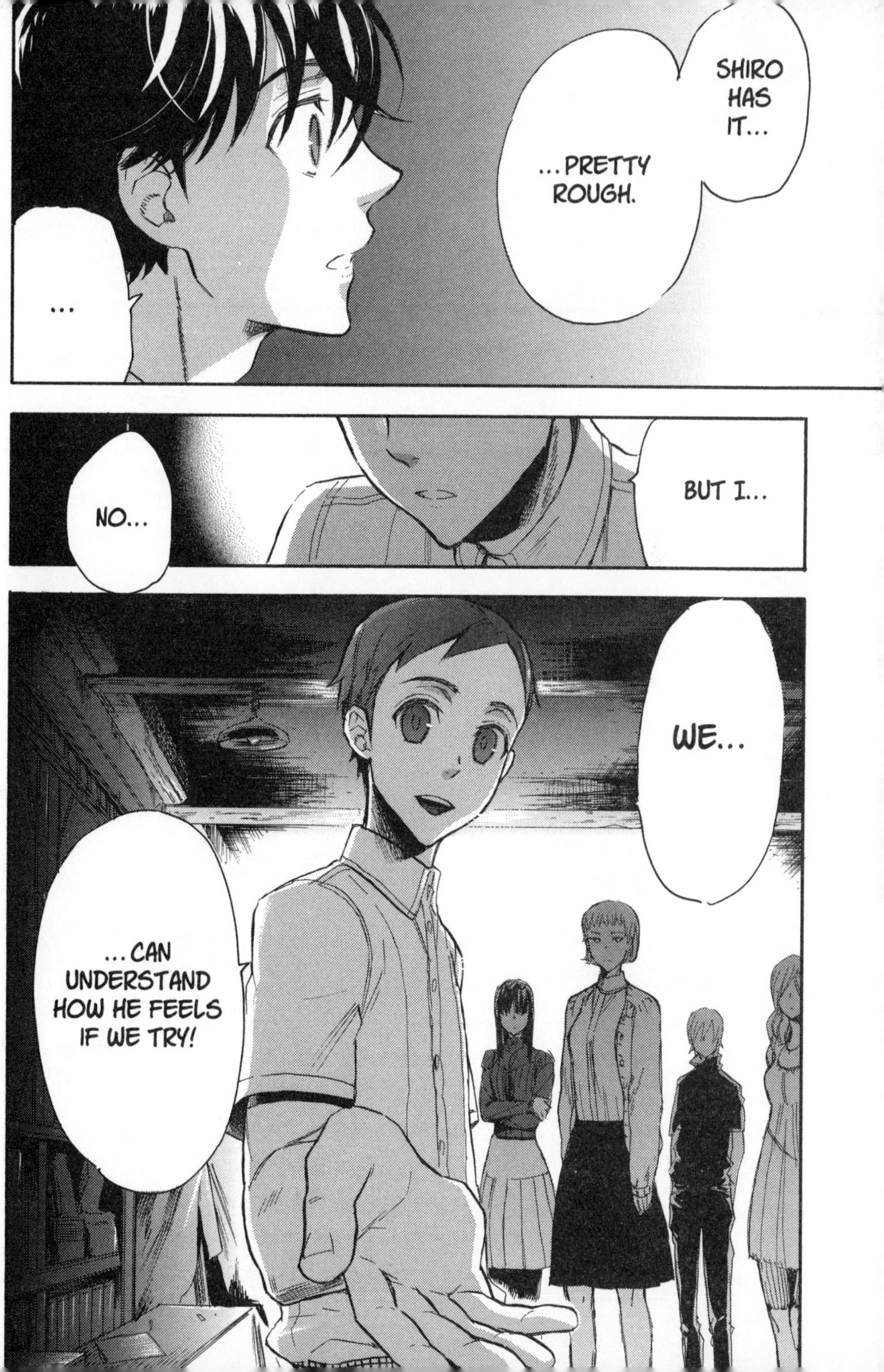
SHIRO HAS IT...
...PRETTY ROUGH.
...
BUT I...
NO...
WE...
...CAN UNDERSTAND HOW HE FEELS IF WE TRY!

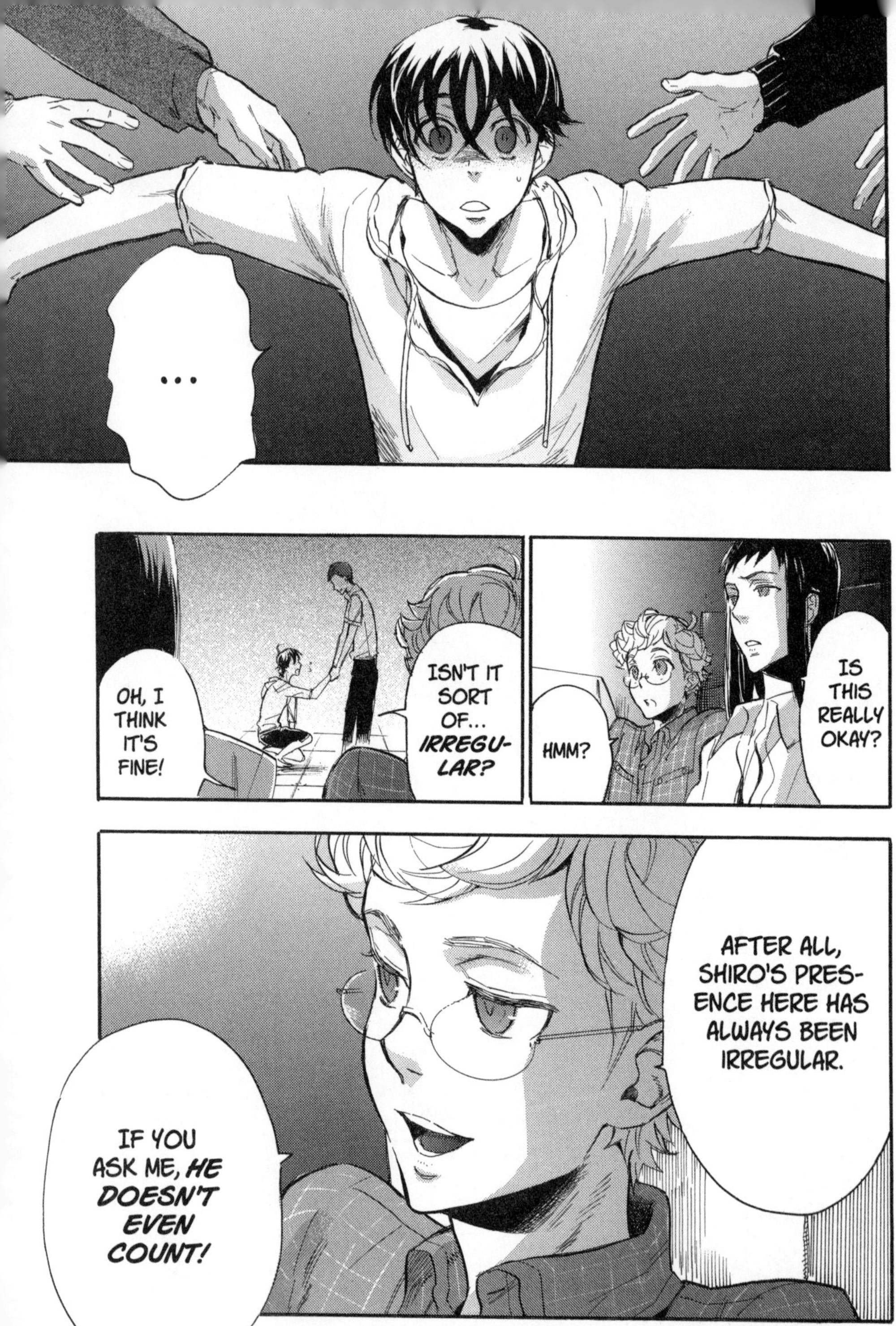
...
IS THIS REALLY OKAY?
HMM?
ISN'T IT SORT OF... *IRREGULAR?*
OH, I THINK IT'S FINE!
AFTER ALL, SHIRO'S PRESENCE HERE HAS ALWAYS BEEN IRREGULAR.
IF YOU ASK ME, *HE DOESN'T EVEN COUNT!*

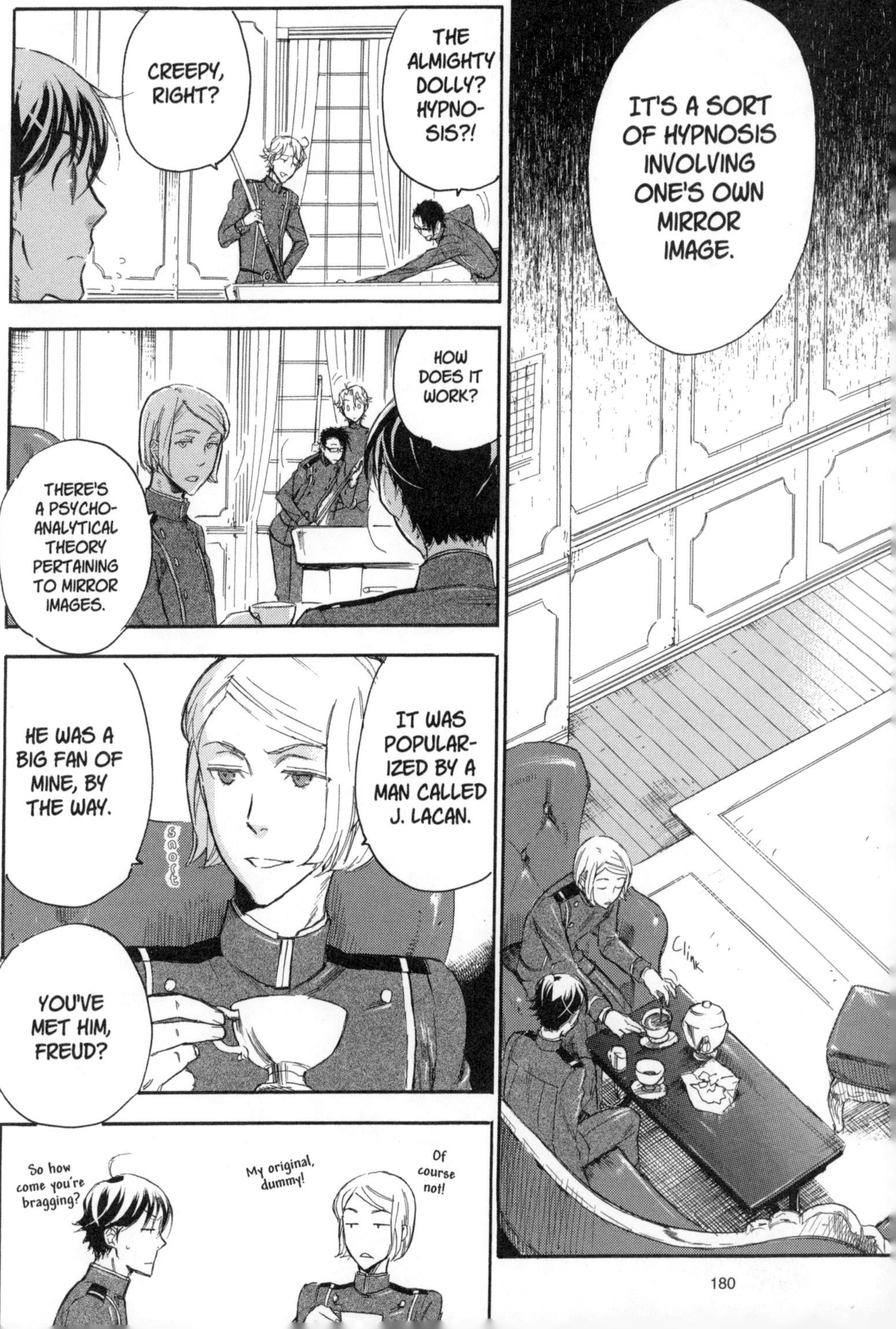
IT'S A SORT OF HYPNOSIS INVOLVING ONE'S OWN MIRROR IMAGE.
Clink
THE ALMIGHTY DOLLY? HYPNOSIS?!
CREEPY, RIGHT?
HOW DOES IT WORK?
THERE'S A PSYCHO-ANALYTICAL THEORY PERTAINING TO MIRROR IMAGES.
IT WAS POPULARIZED BY A MAN CALLED J. LACAN.
HE WAS A BIG FAN OF MINE, BY THE WAY.
snort
YOU'VE MET HIM, FREUD?
Of course not!
My original, dummy!
So how come you're bragging?

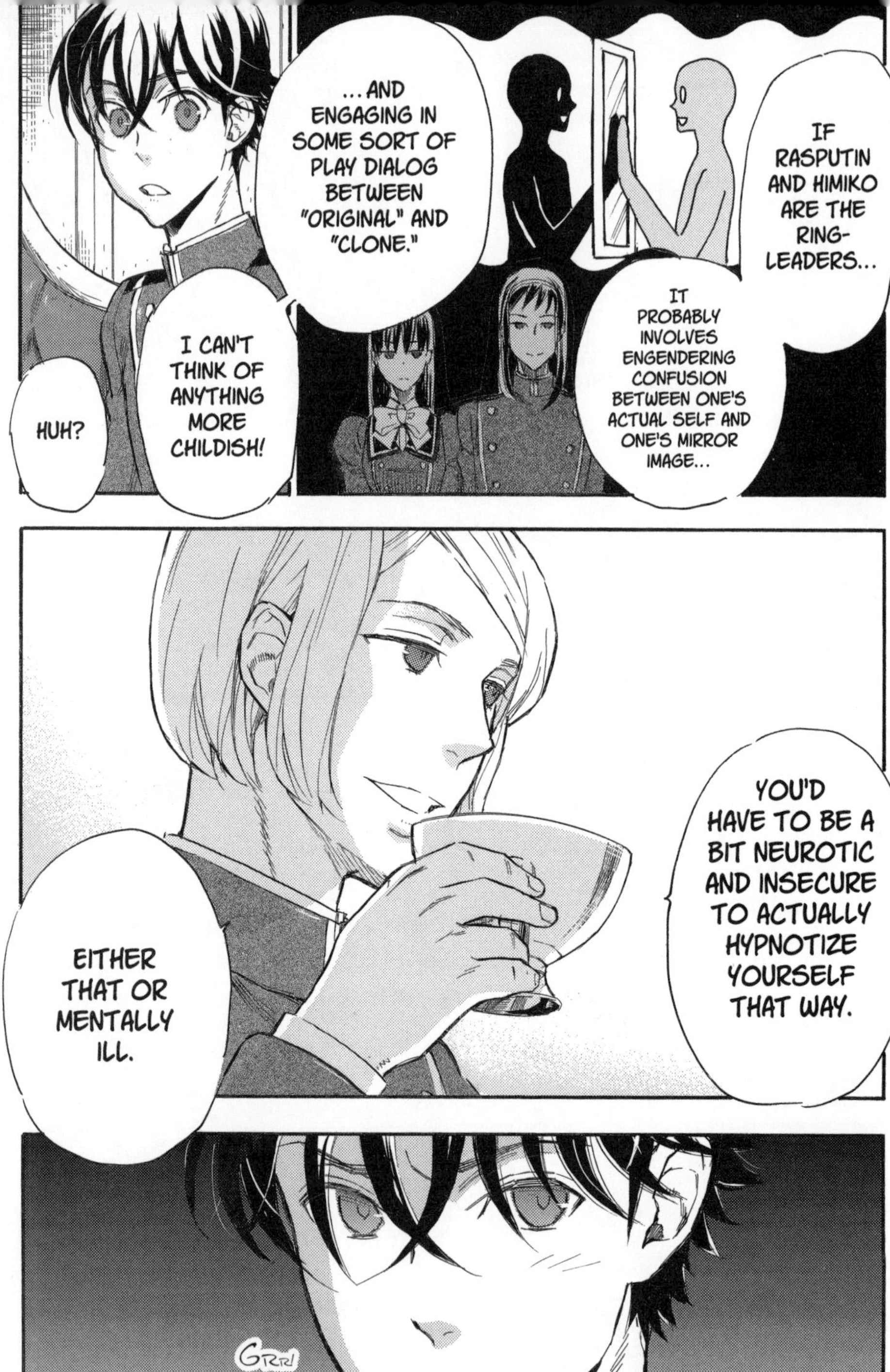
IF RASPUTIN AND HIMIKO ARE THE RING-LEADERS...
IT PROBABLY INVOLVES ENGENDERING CONFUSION BETWEEN ONE'S ACTUAL SELF AND ONE'S MIRROR IMAGE...
...AND ENGAGING IN SOME SORT OF PLAY DIALOG BETWEEN "ORIGINAL" AND "CLONE."
I CAN'T THINK OF ANYTHING MORE CHILDISH!
HUH?
YOU'D HAVE TO BE A BIT NEUROTIC AND INSECURE TO ACTUALLY HYPNOTIZE YOURSELF THAT WAY.
EITHER THAT OR MENTALLY ILL.
GRR!

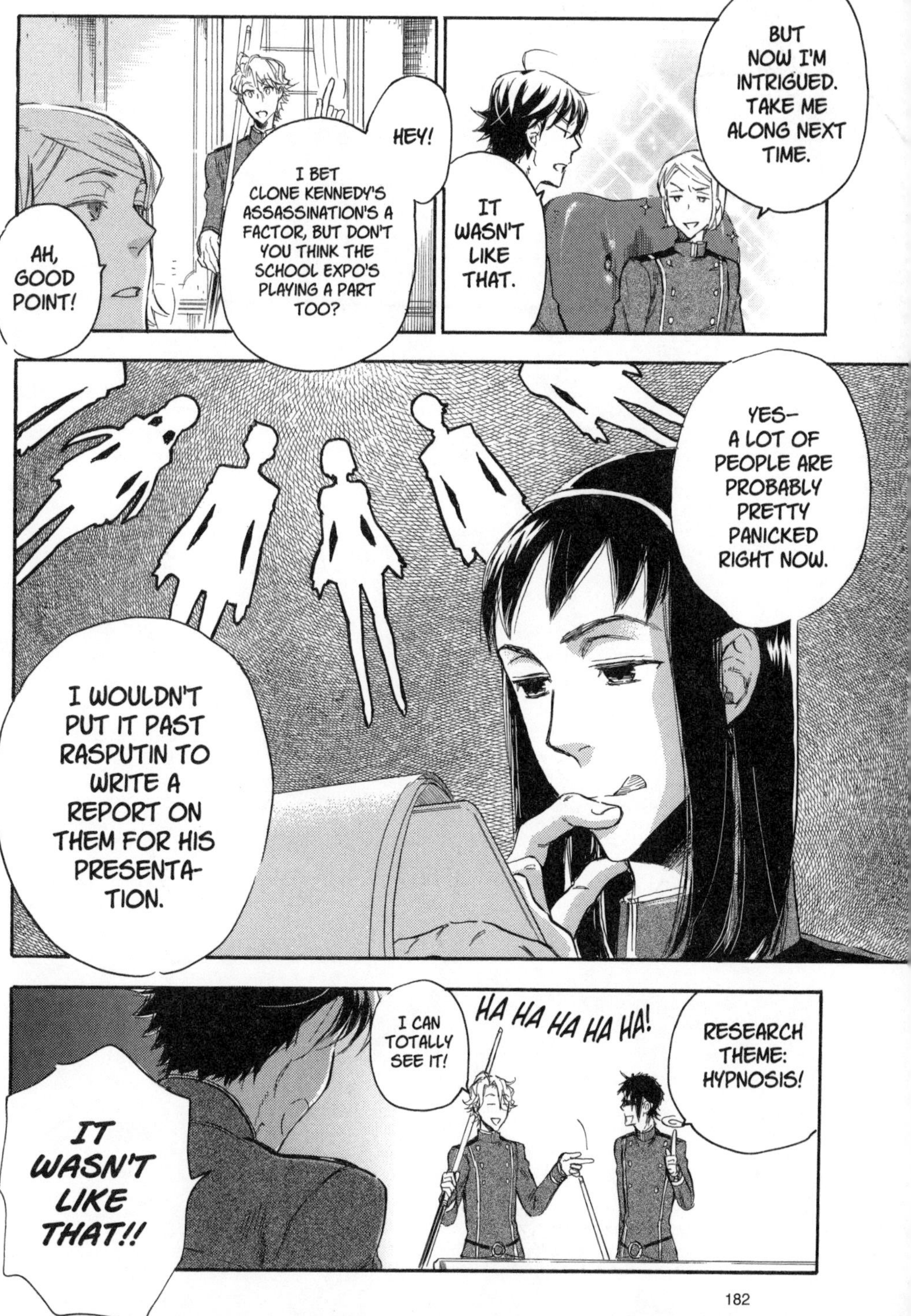
BUT NOW I'M INTRIGUED. TAKE ME ALONG NEXT TIME.
IT WASN'T LIKE THAT.
HEY!
I BET CLONE KENNEDY'S ASSASSINATION'S A FACTOR, BUT DON'T YOU THINK THE SCHOOL EXPO'S PLAYING A PART TOO?
AH, GOOD POINT!
YES— A LOT OF PEOPLE ARE PROBABLY PRETTY PANICKED RIGHT NOW.
I WOULDN'T PUT IT PAST RASPUTIN TO WRITE A REPORT ON THEM FOR HIS PRESENTA-TION.
RESEARCH THEME: HYPNOSIS!
HA HA HA HA HA HA!
I CAN TOTALLY SEE IT!
IT WASN'T LIKE THAT!!

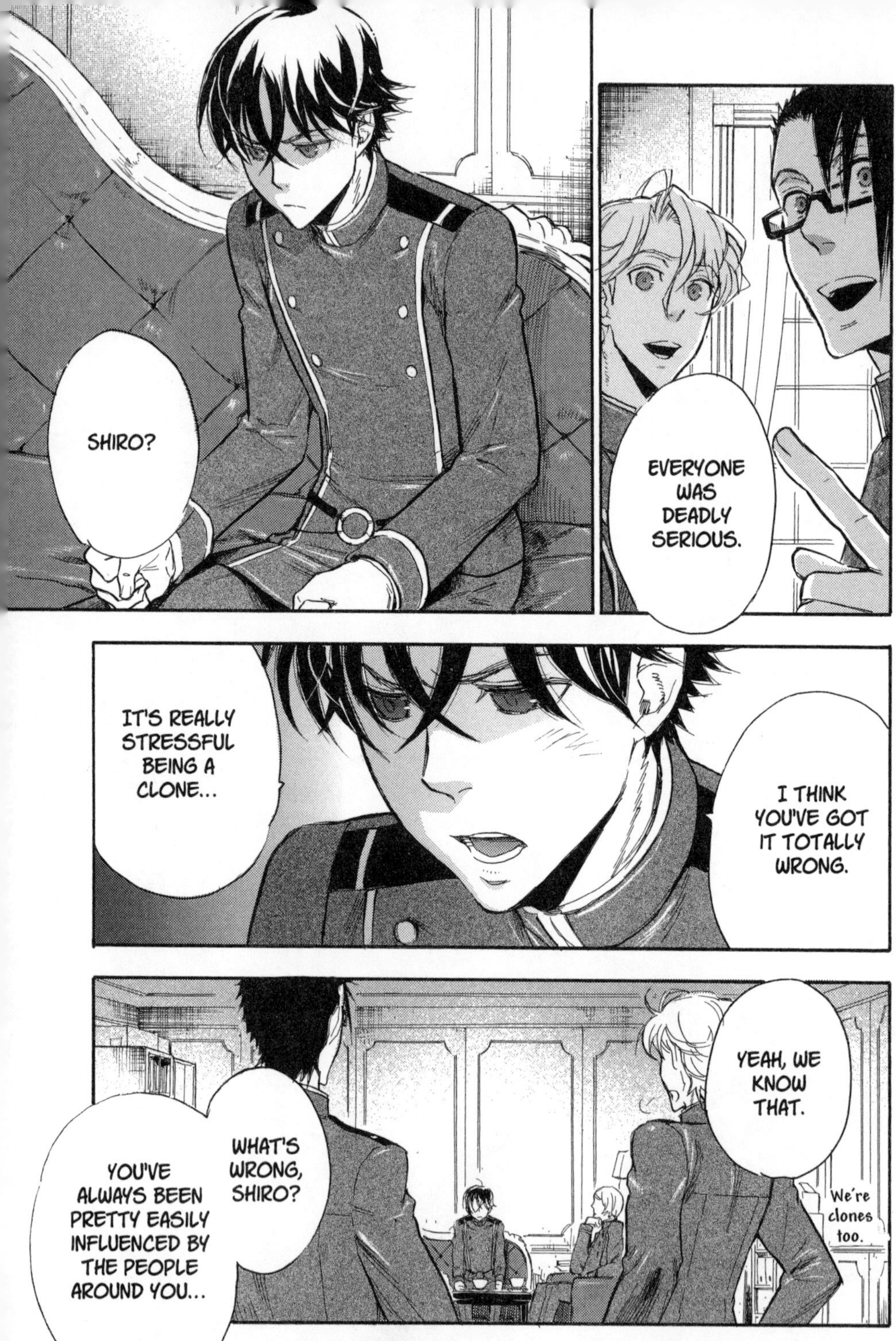
EVERYONE WAS DEADLY SERIOUS.
SHIRO?
I THINK YOU'VE GOT IT TOTALLY WRONG.
IT'S REALLY STRESSFUL BEING A CLONE...
YEAH, WE KNOW THAT.
We're clones too.
WHAT'S WRONG, SHIRO?
YOU'VE ALWAYS BEEN PRETTY EASILY INFLUENCED BY THE PEOPLE AROUND YOU...

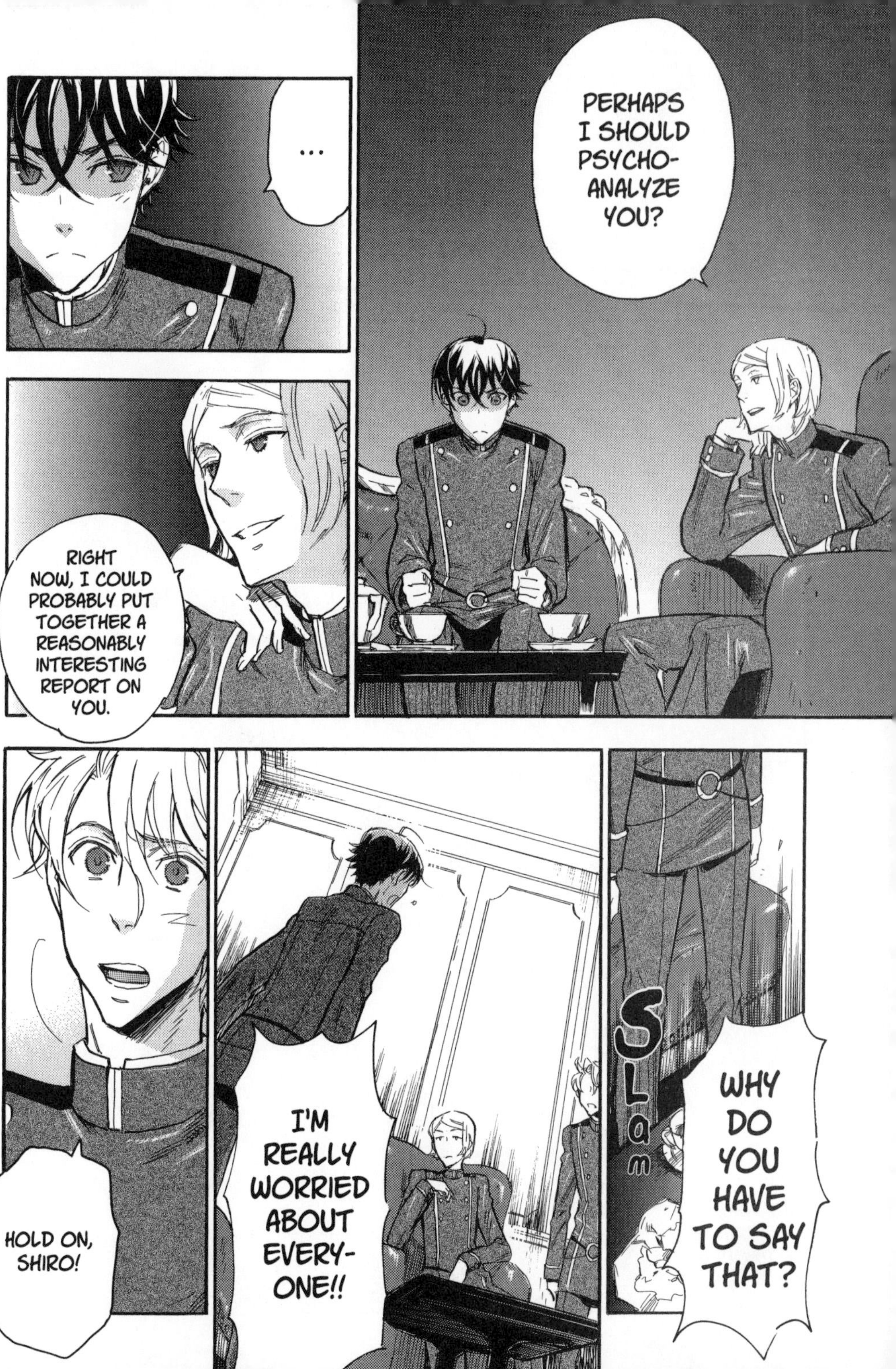
PERHAPS I SHOULD PSYCHO-ANALYZE YOU?
...
RIGHT NOW, I COULD PROBABLY PUT TOGETHER A REASONABLY INTERESTING REPORT ON YOU.
SLam
WHY DO YOU HAVE TO SAY THAT?
I'M REALLY WORRIED ABOUT EVERY-ONE!!
HOLD ON, SHIRO!

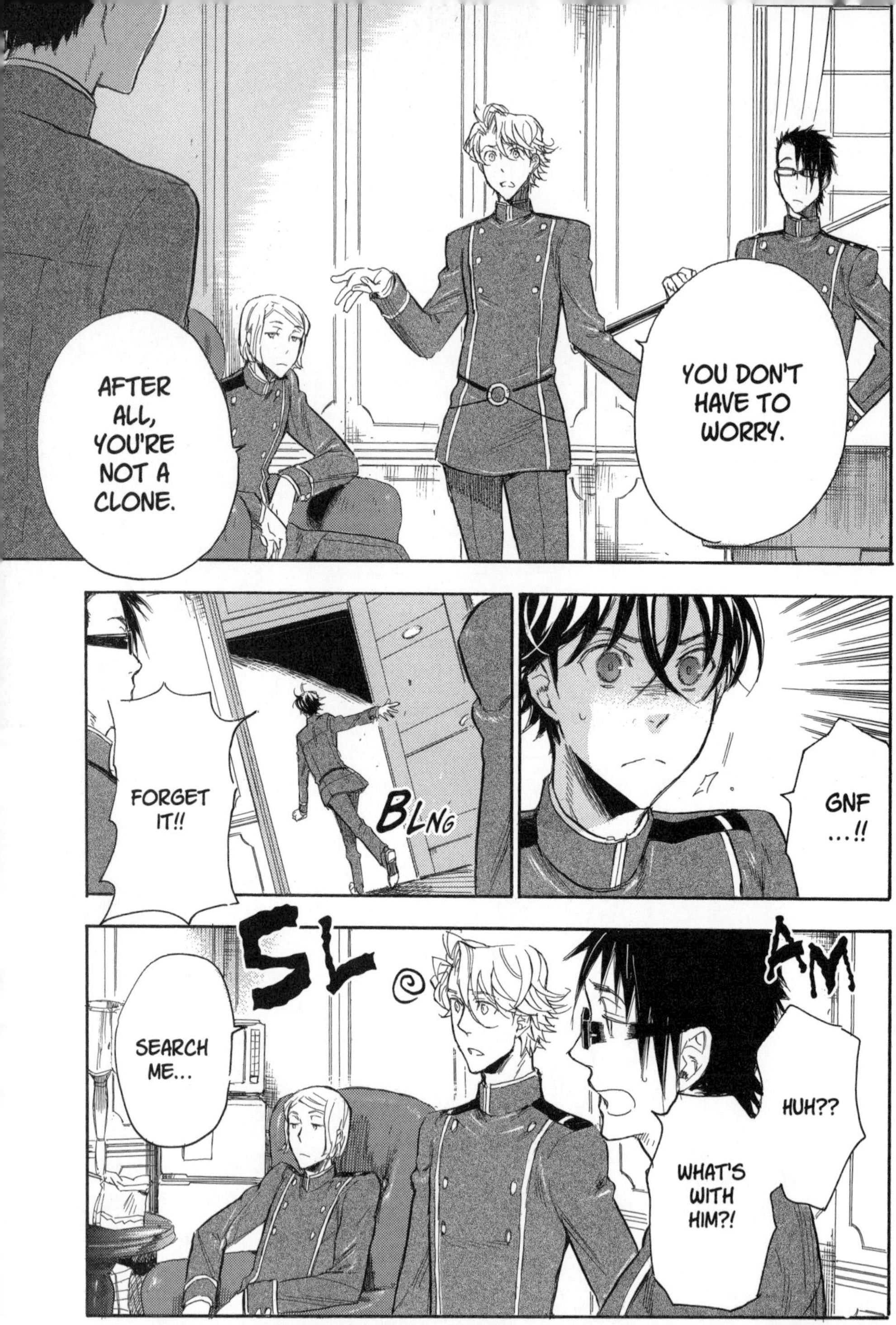
YOU DON'T HAVE TO WORRY.
AFTER ALL, YOU'RE NOT A CLONE.
GNF ...!!
BLNG
FORGET IT!!
SLAM
HUH??
WHAT'S WITH HIM?!
SEARCH ME...

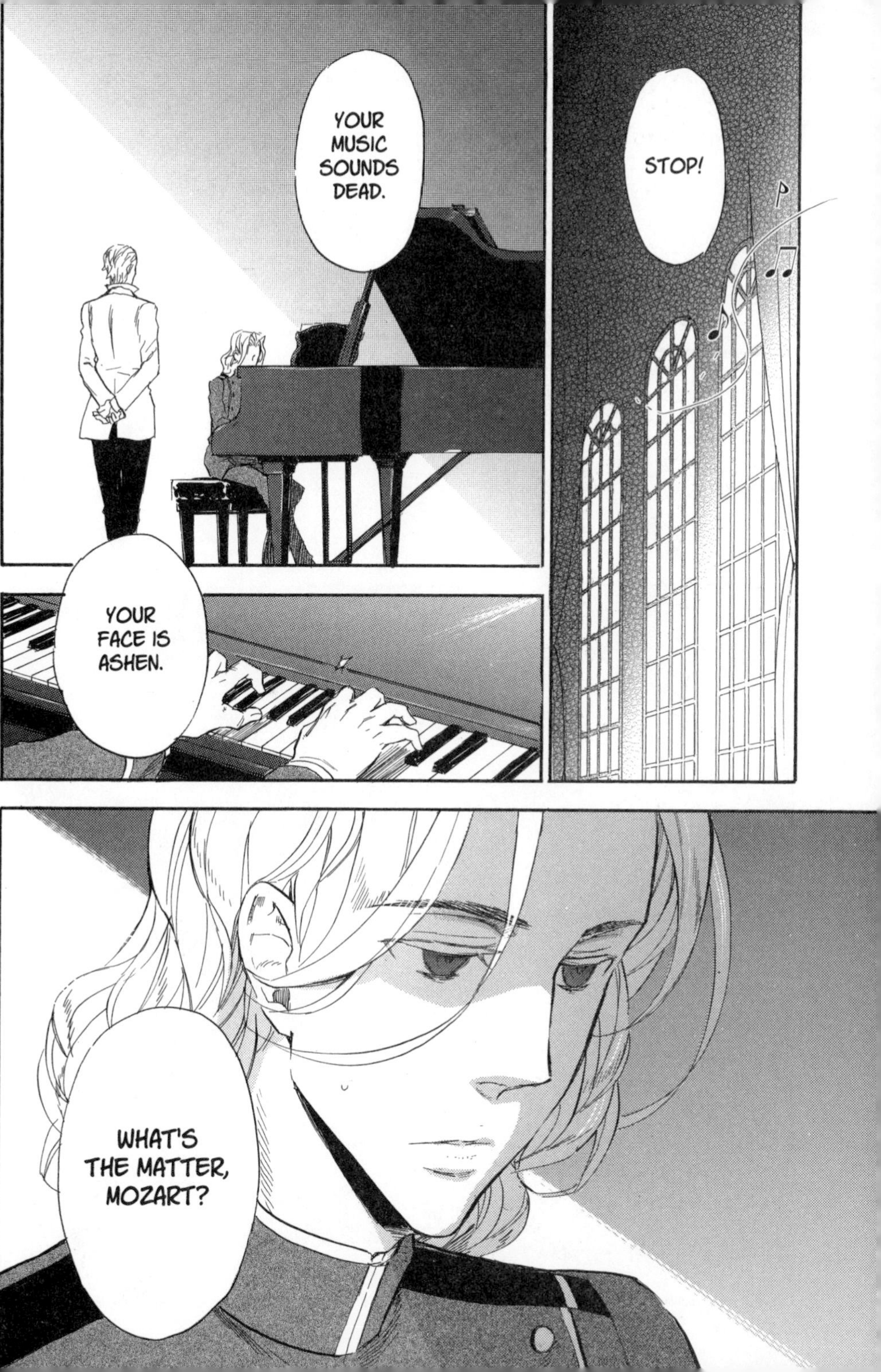
STOP!
YOUR MUSIC SOUNDS DEAD.
YOUR FACE IS ASHEN.
WHAT'S THE MATTER, MOZART?

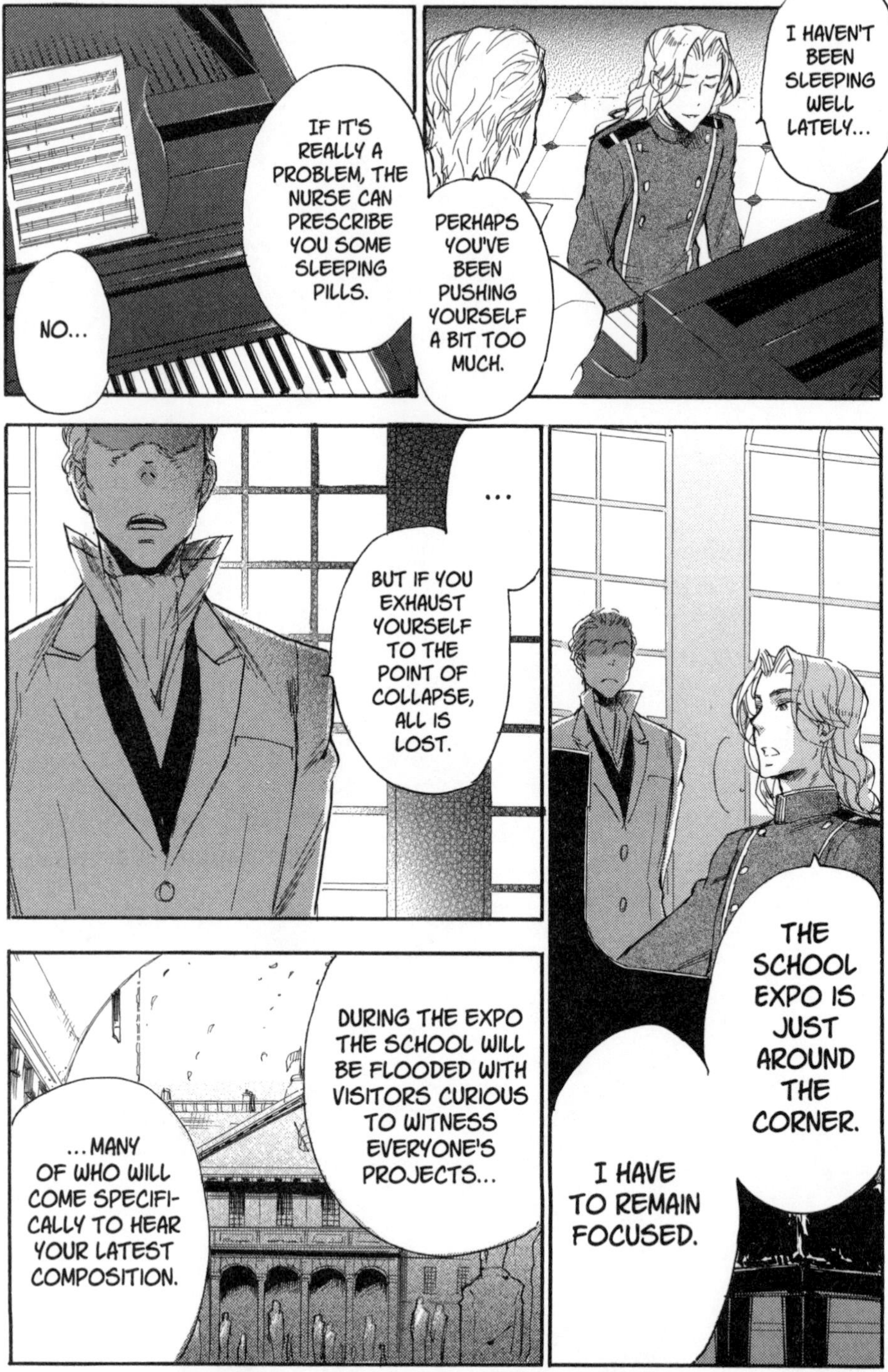
I HAVEN'T BEEN SLEEPING WELL LATELY...
PERHAPS YOU'VE BEEN PUSHING YOURSELF A BIT TOO MUCH.
IF IT'S REALLY A PROBLEM, THE NURSE CAN PRESCRIBE YOU SOME SLEEPING PILLS.
NO...
THE SCHOOL EXPO IS JUST AROUND THE CORNER.
I HAVE TO REMAIN FOCUSED.
...
BUT IF YOU EXHAUST YOURSELF TO THE POINT OF COLLAPSE, ALL IS LOST.
DURING THE EXPO THE SCHOOL WILL BE FLOODED WITH VISITORS CURIOUS TO WITNESS EVERYONE'S PROJECTS...
...MANY OF WHO WILL COME SPECIFICALLY TO HEAR YOUR LATEST COMPOSITION.

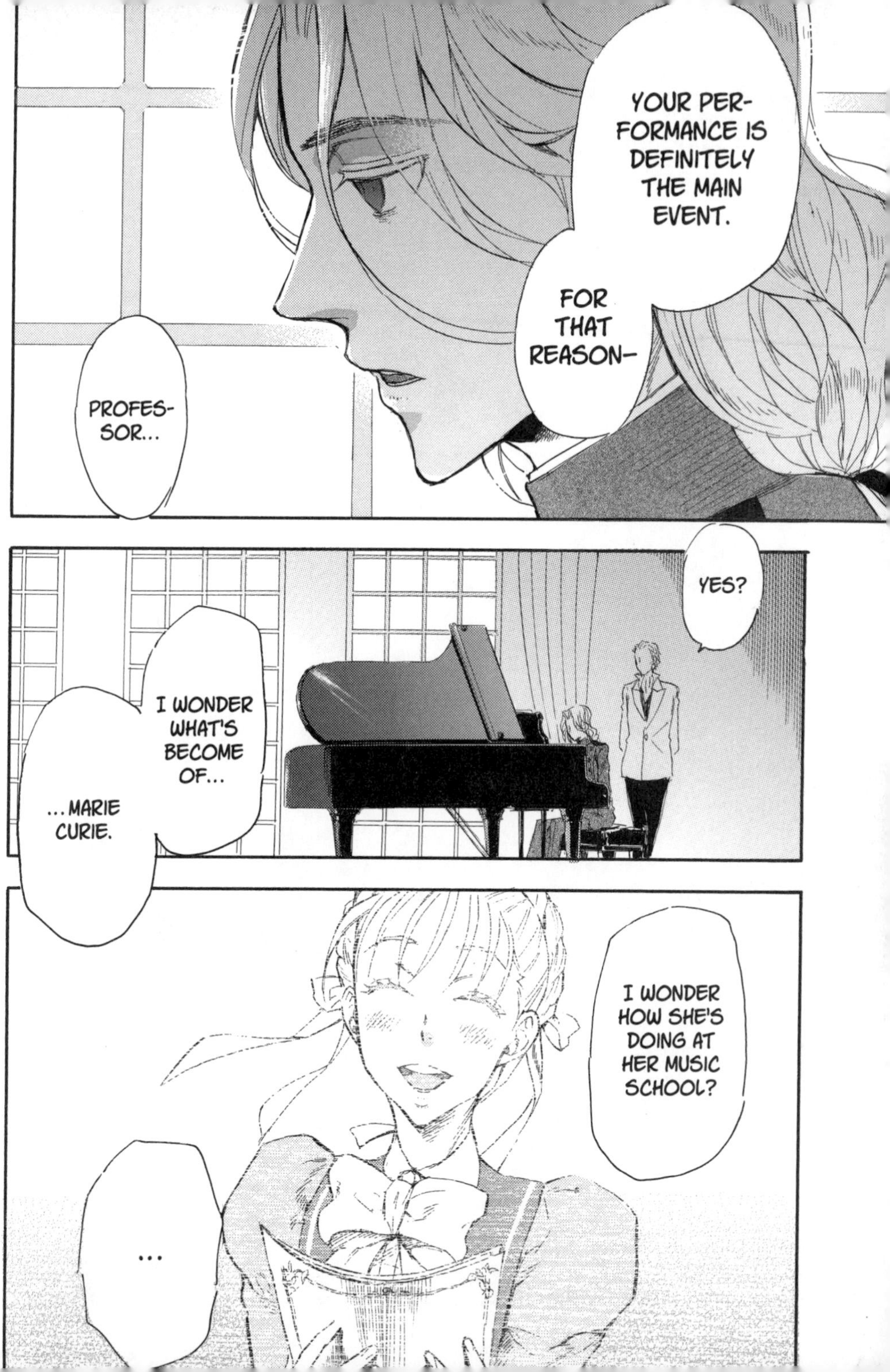
YOUR PER-FORMANCE IS DEFINITELY THE MAIN EVENT.
FOR THAT REASON—
PROFES-SOR...
YES?
I WONDER WHAT'S BECOME OF...
...MARIE CURIE.
I WONDER HOW SHE'S DOING AT HER MUSIC SCHOOL?
...

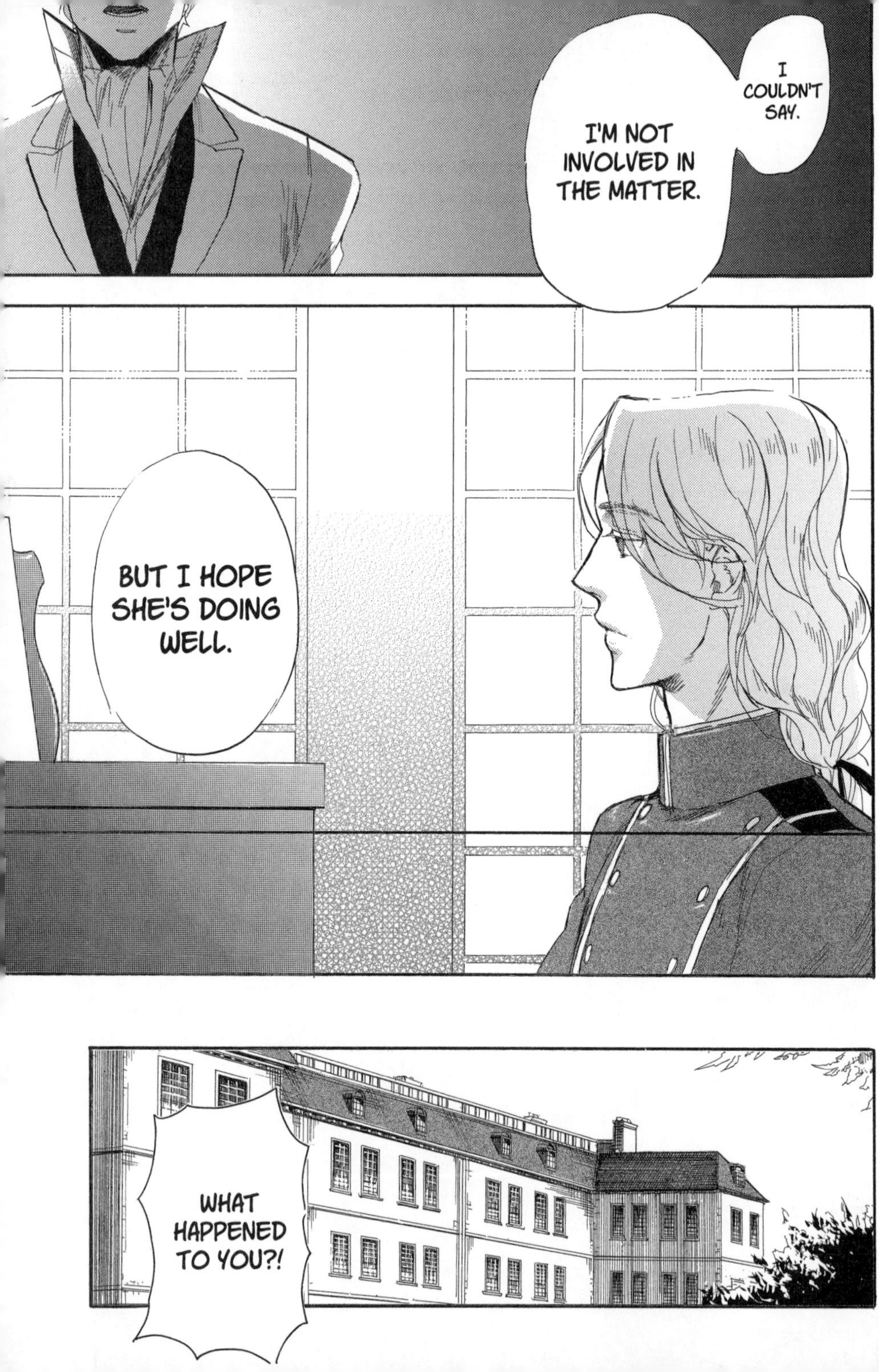
I COULDN'T SAY.
I'M NOT INVOLVED IN THE MATTER.
BUT I HOPE SHE'S DOING WELL.
WHAT HAPPENED TO YOU?!

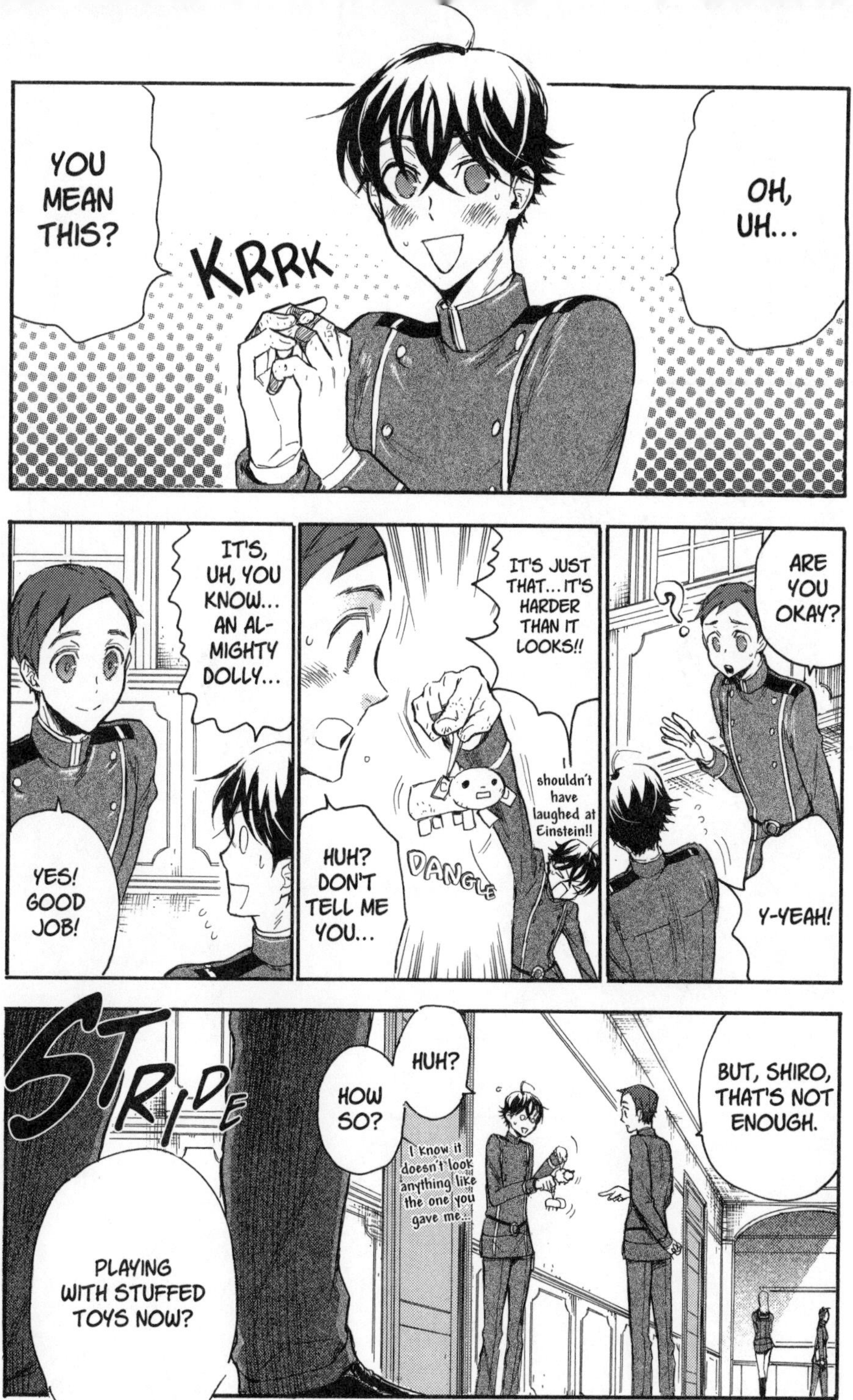
OH, UH...
KRRK
YOU MEAN THIS?
ARE YOU OKAY?
Y-YEAH!
IT'S JUST THAT... IT'S HARDER THAN IT LOOKS!!
I shouldn't have laughed at Einstein!!
HUH? DON'T TELL ME YOU...
DANGLE
IT'S, UH, YOU KNOW... AN AL-MIGHTY DOLLY...
YES! GOOD JOB!
BUT, SHIRO, THAT'S NOT ENOUGH.
HUH?
HOW SO?
I know it doesn't look anything like the one you gave me...
STRIDE
PLAYING WITH STUFFED TOYS NOW?

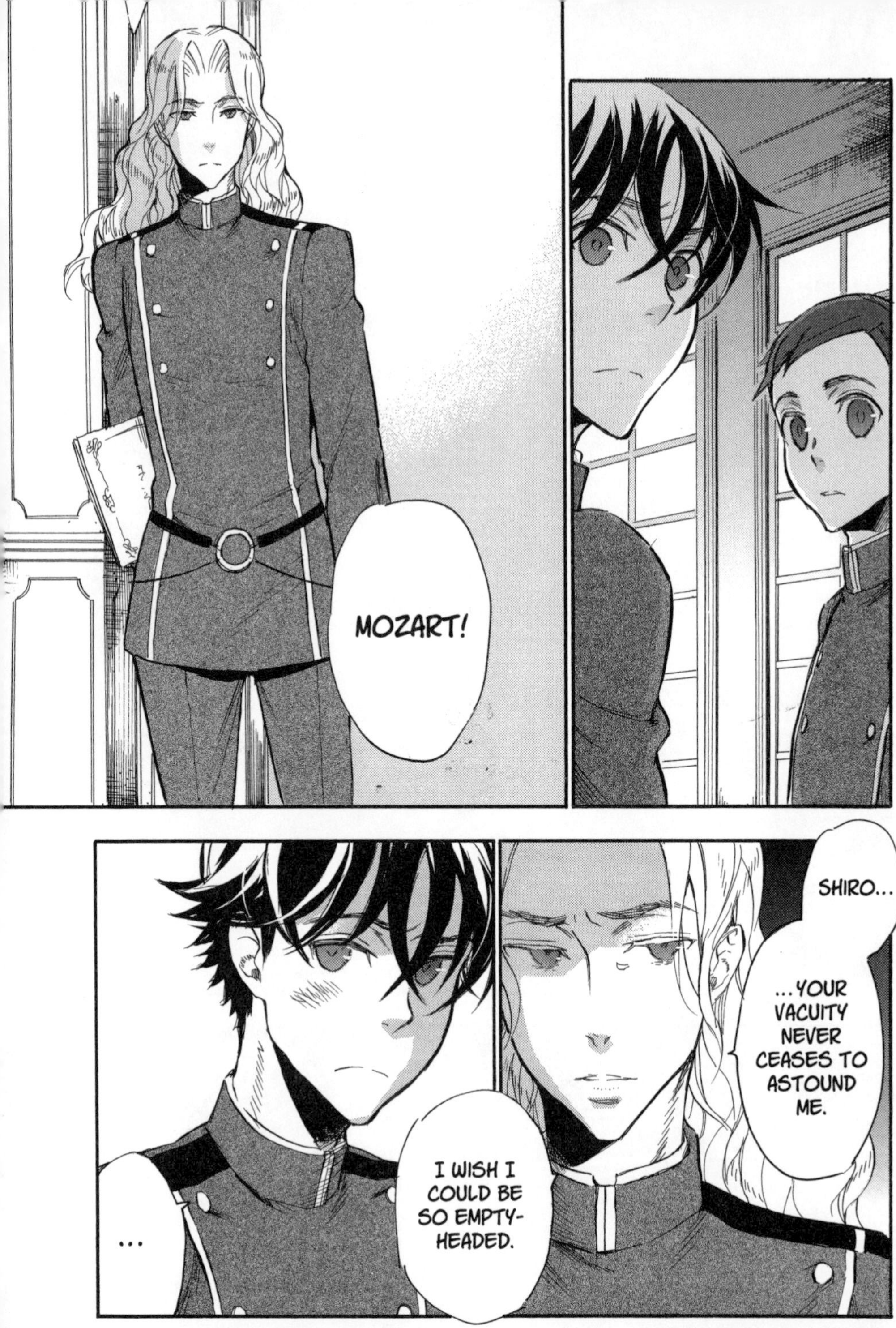
MOZART!
SHIRO...
...YOUR VACUITY NEVER CEASES TO ASTOUND ME.
I WISH I COULD BE SO EMPTY-HEADED.
...

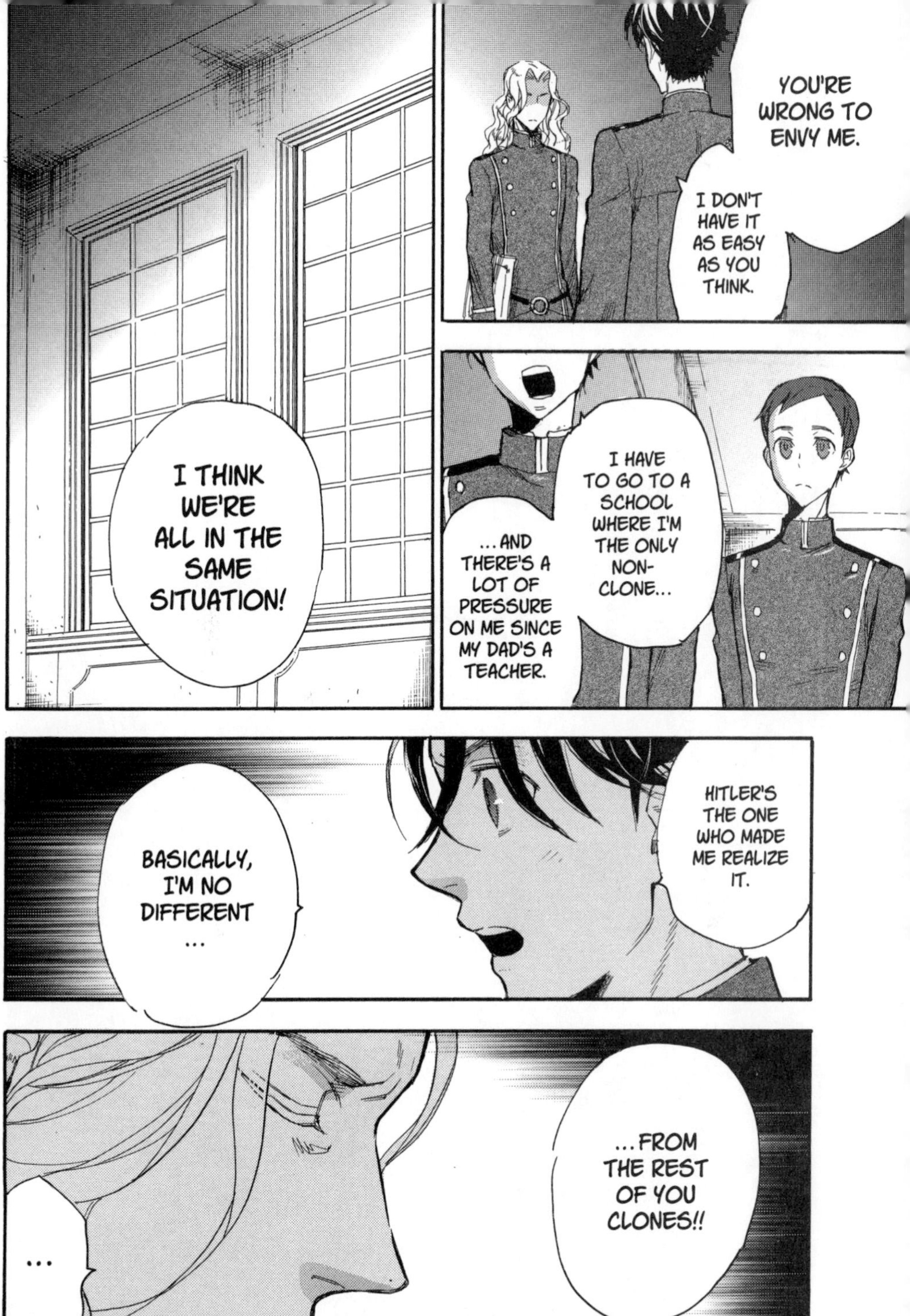
YOU'RE WRONG TO ENVY ME.
I DON'T HAVE IT AS EASY AS YOU THINK.
I HAVE TO GO TO A SCHOOL WHERE I'M THE ONLY NON-CLONE...
...AND THERE'S A LOT OF PRESSURE ON ME SINCE MY DAD'S A TEACHER.
I THINK WE'RE ALL IN THE SAME SITUATION!
HITLER'S THE ONE WHO MADE ME REALIZE IT.
BASICALLY, I'M NO DIFFERENT ...
...FROM THE REST OF YOU CLONES!!
...

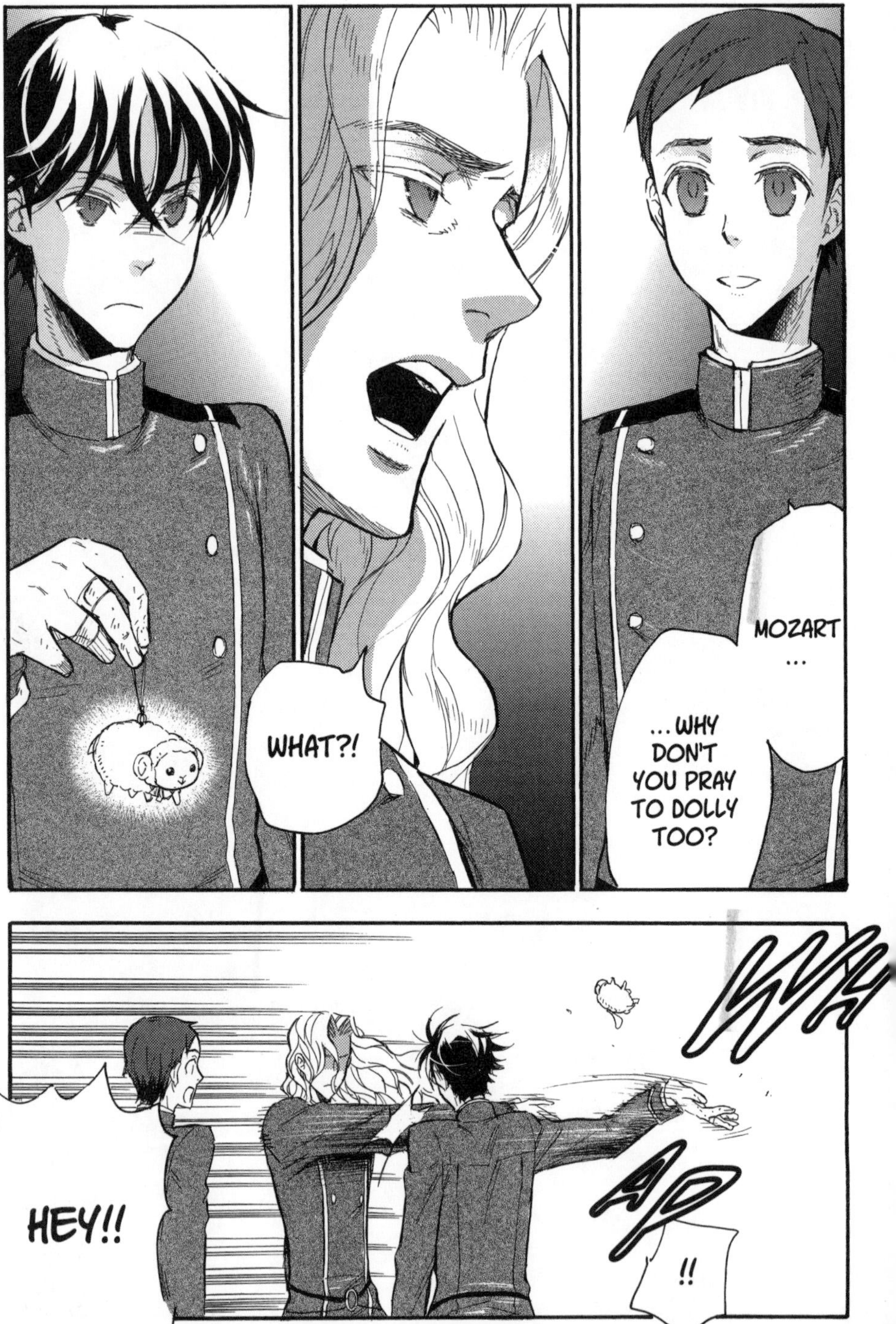
MOZART ...
...WHY DON'T YOU PRAY TO DOLLY TOO?
WHAT?!
!!
HEY!!

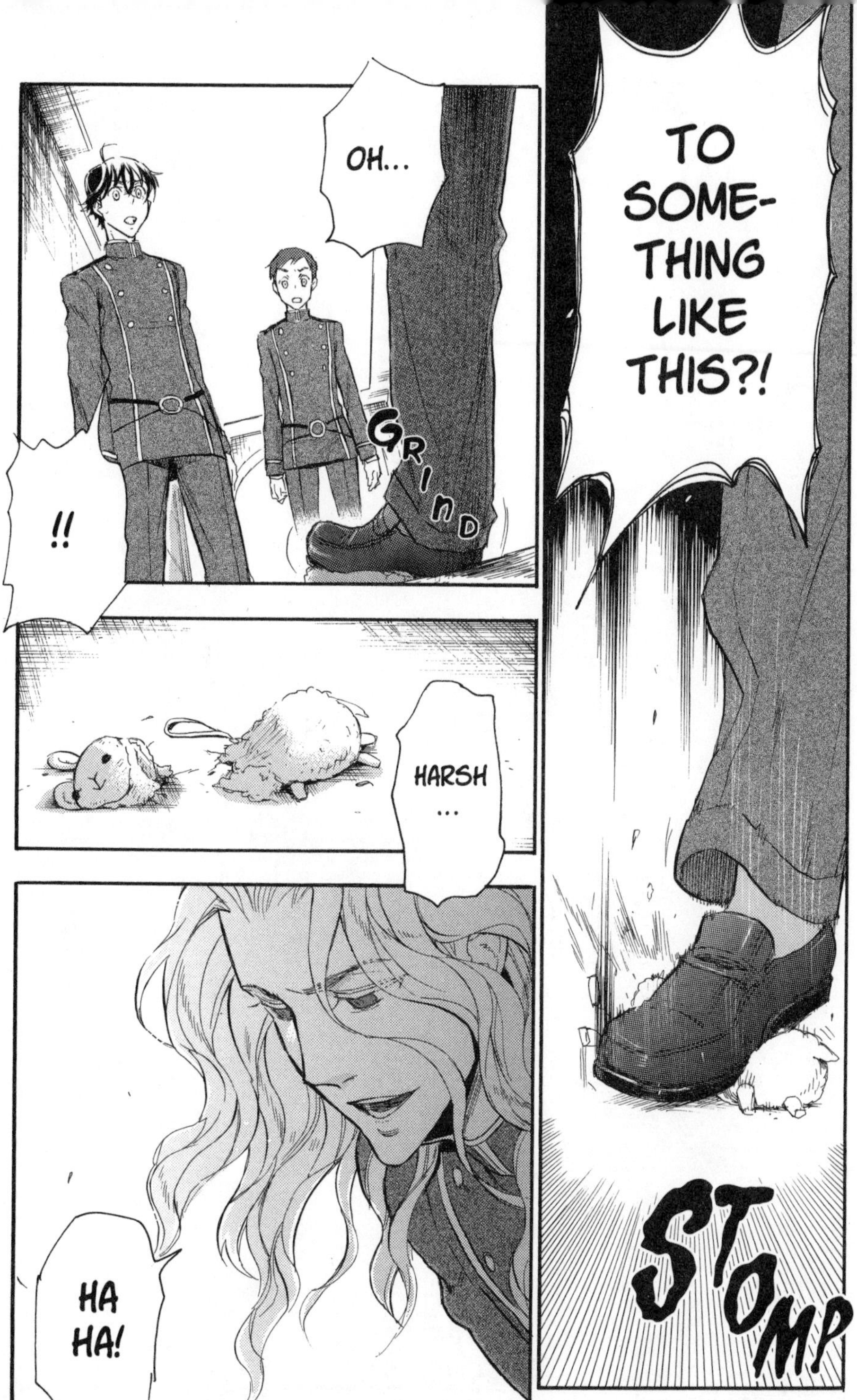
TO SOME-THING LIKE THIS?!
STOMP
OH...
GRIND
!!
HARSH ...
HA HA!

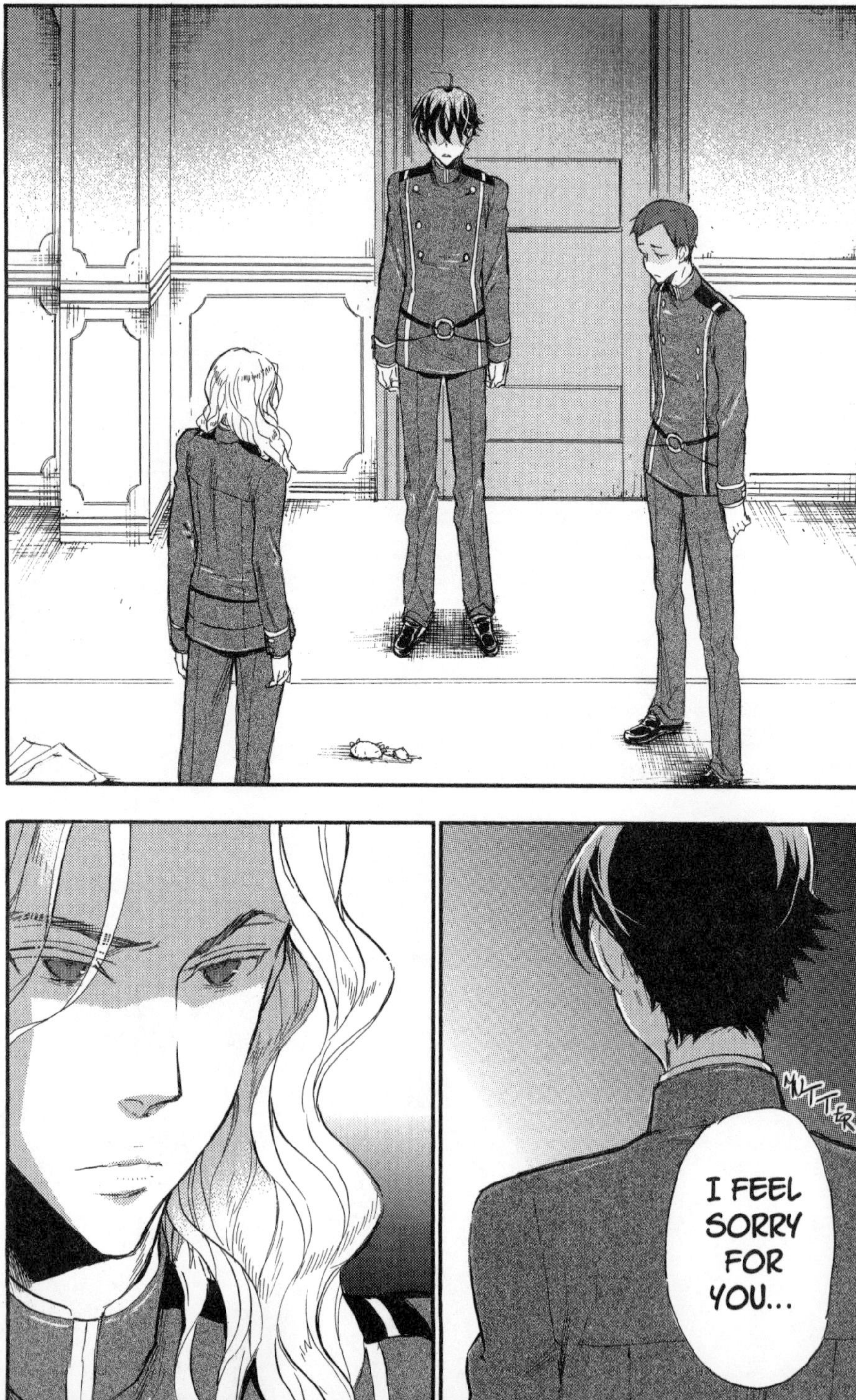
MUTTER
I FEEL SORRY FOR YOU...

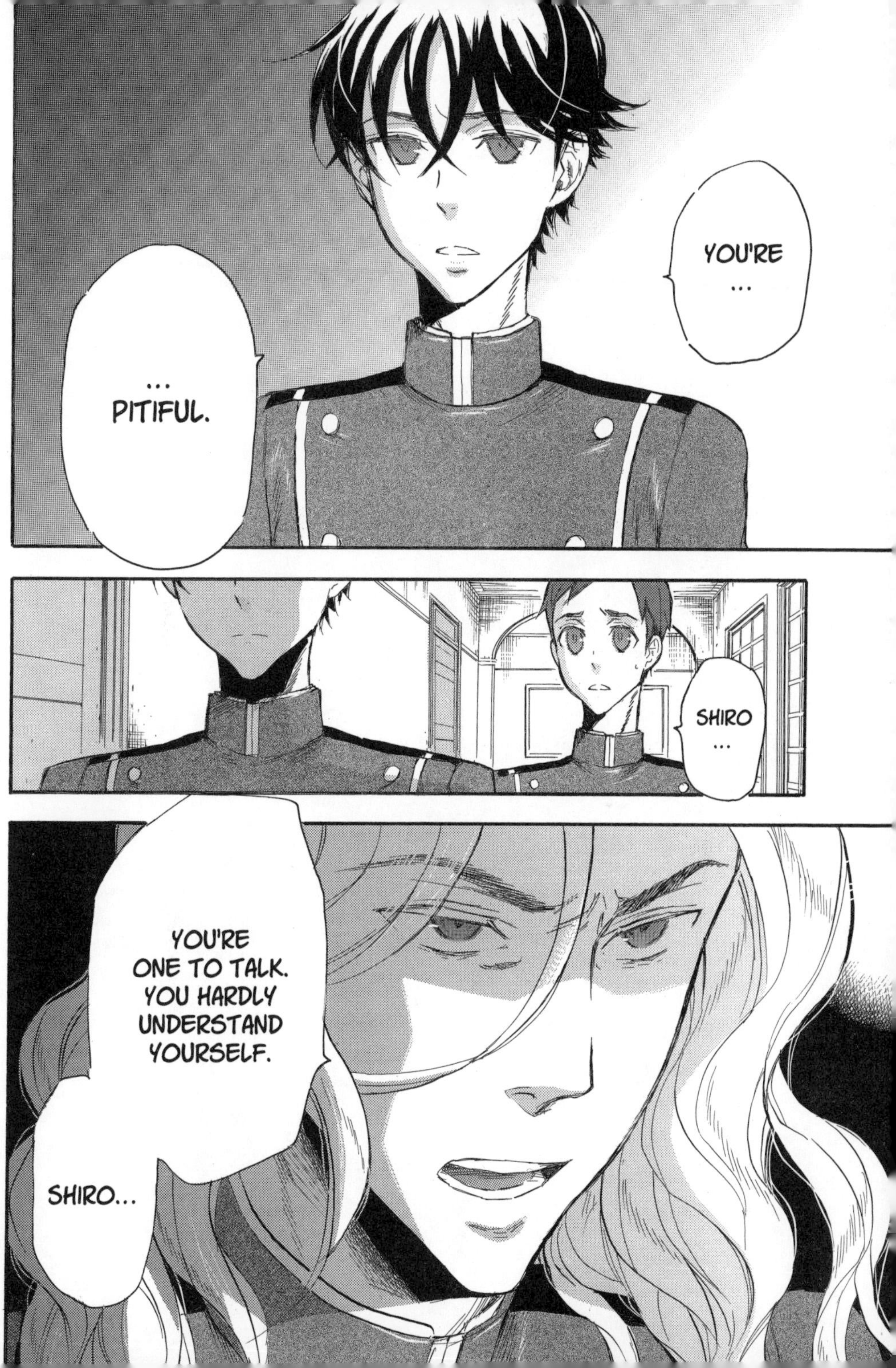
YOU'RE ...
... PITIFUL.
SHIRO ...
YOU'RE ONE TO TALK. YOU HARDLY UNDERSTAND YOURSELF.
SHIRO...

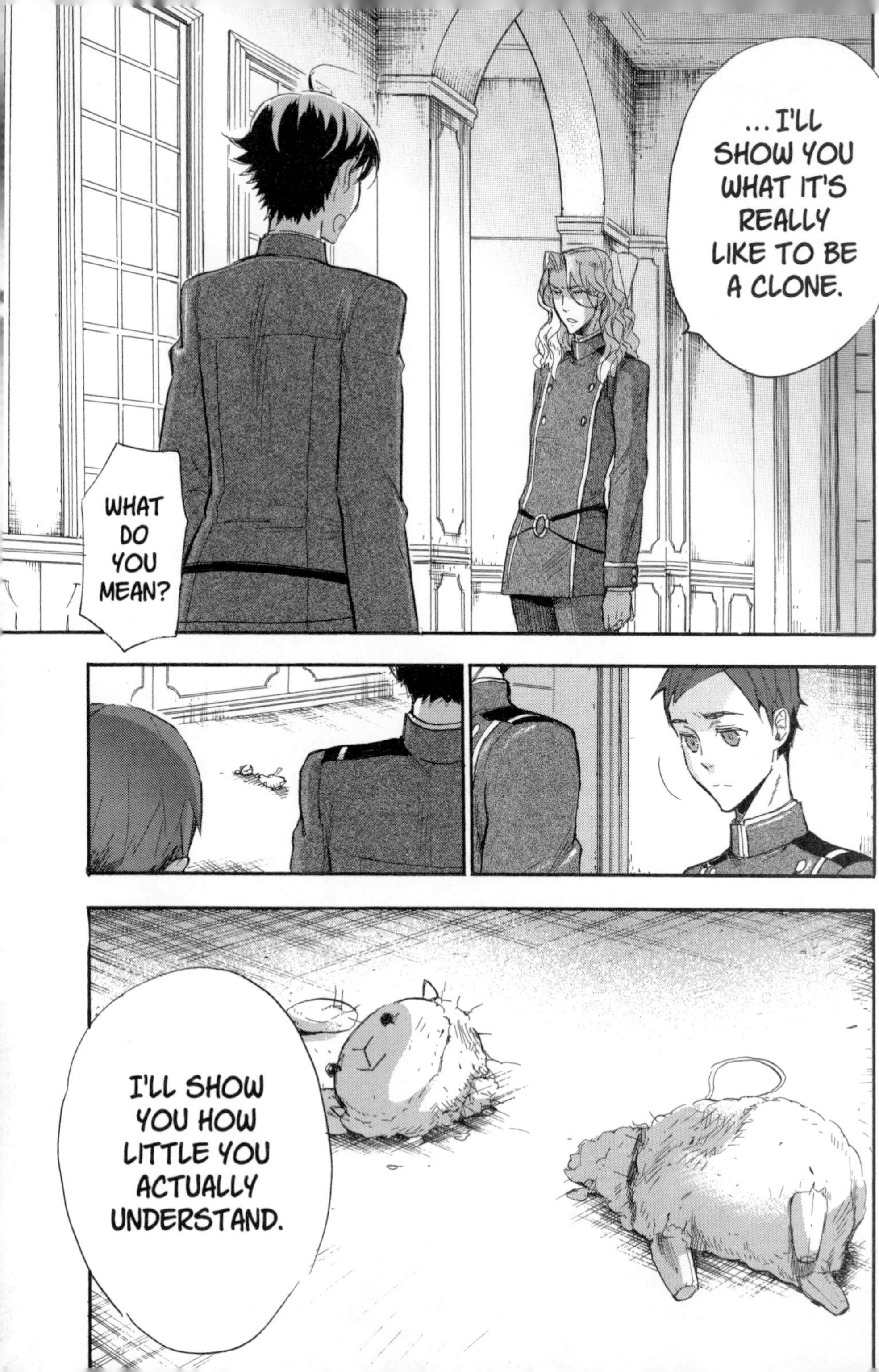
...I'LL SHOW YOU WHAT IT'S REALLY LIKE TO BE A CLONE.
WHAT DO YOU MEAN?
I'LL SHOW YOU HOW LITTLE YOU ACTUALLY UNDERSTAND.

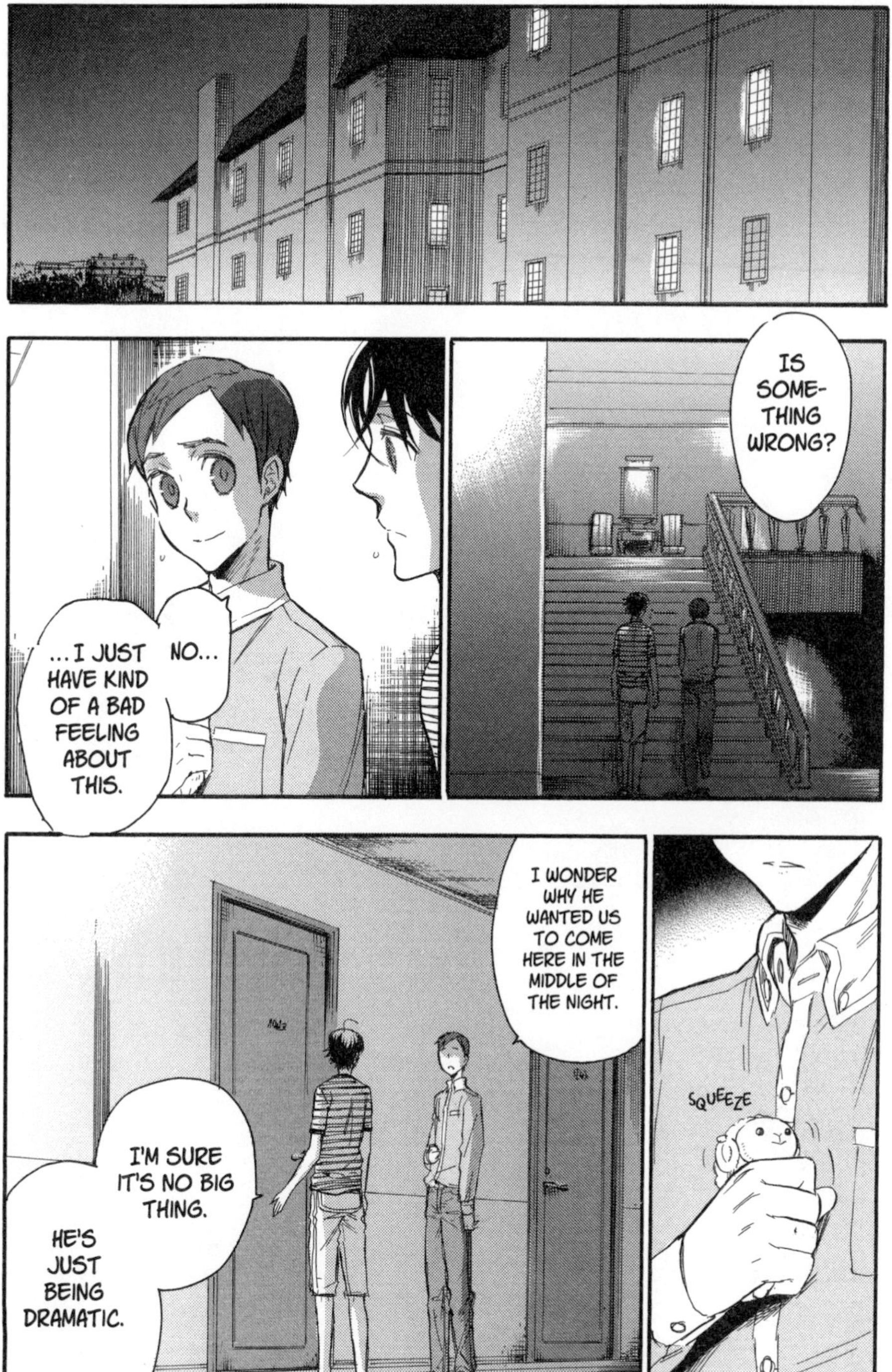
IS SOME-THING WRONG?
NO...
...I JUST HAVE KIND OF A BAD FEELING ABOUT THIS.
SQUEEZE
I WONDER WHY HE WANTED US TO COME HERE IN THE MIDDLE OF THE NIGHT.
I'M SURE IT'S NO BIG THING.
HE'S JUST BEING DRAMATIC.

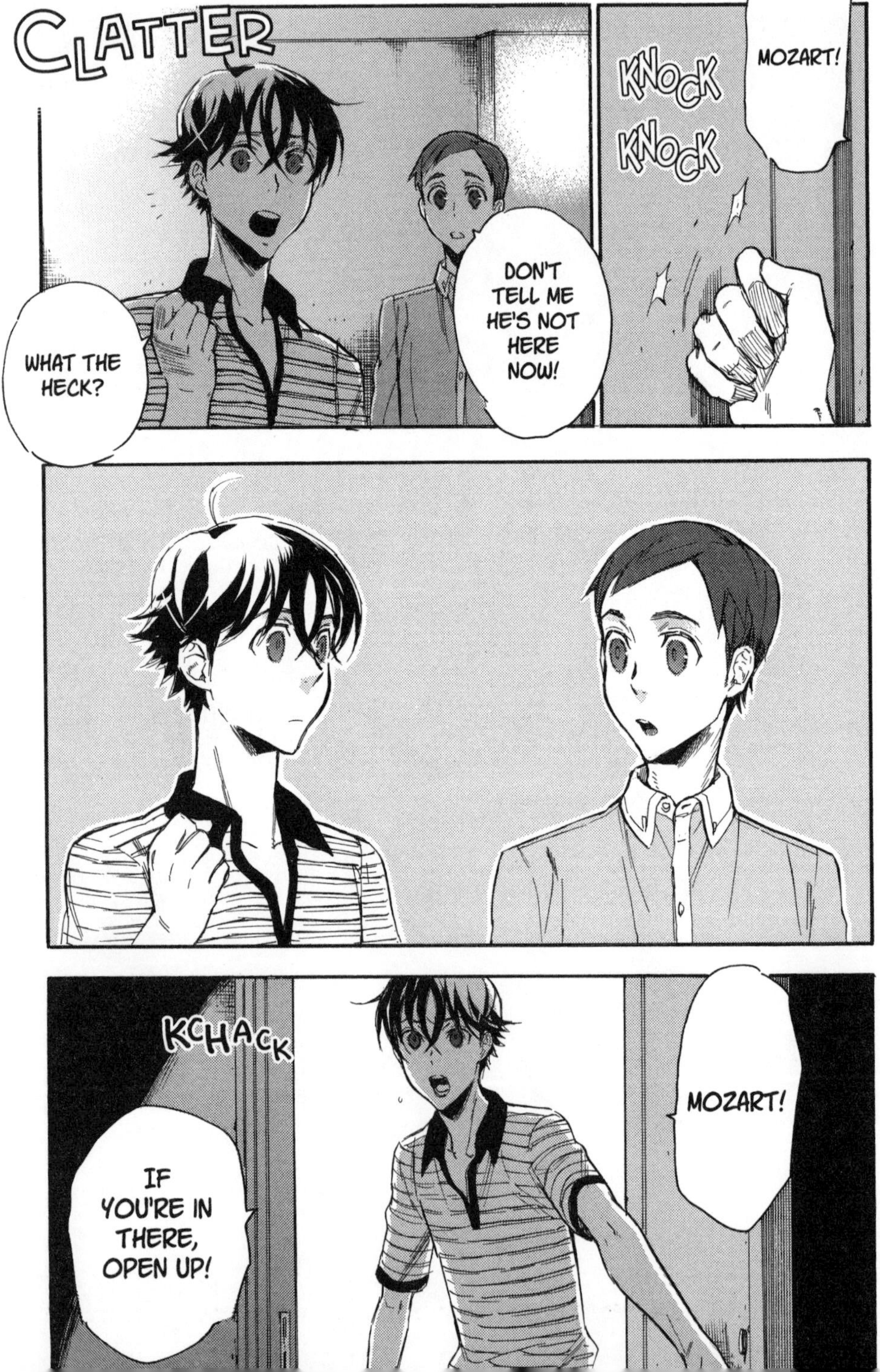
MOZART!
KNOCK KNOCK
CLATTER
DON'T TELL ME HE'S NOT HERE NOW!
WHAT THE HECK?
MOZART!
KCHACK
IF YOU'RE IN THERE, OPEN UP!

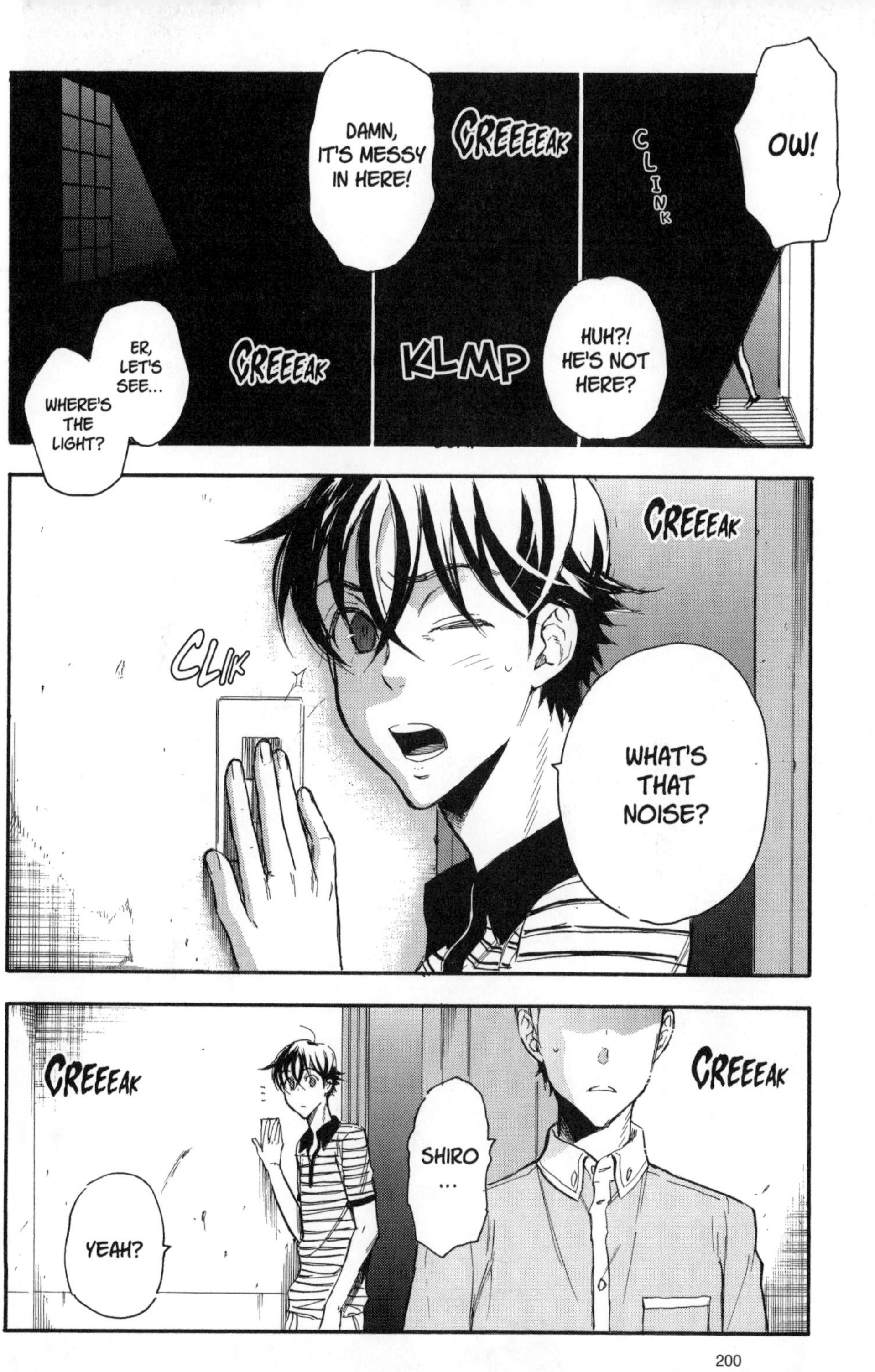
OW!
CLINK
HUH?! HE'S NOT HERE?
CREEEEAK
DAMN, IT'S MESSY IN HERE!
KLMP
CREEEAK
ER, LET'S SEE...
WHERE'S THE LIGHT?
CREEEAK
WHAT'S THAT NOISE?
CLIK
CREEEAK
SHIRO ...
CREEEAK
YEAH?

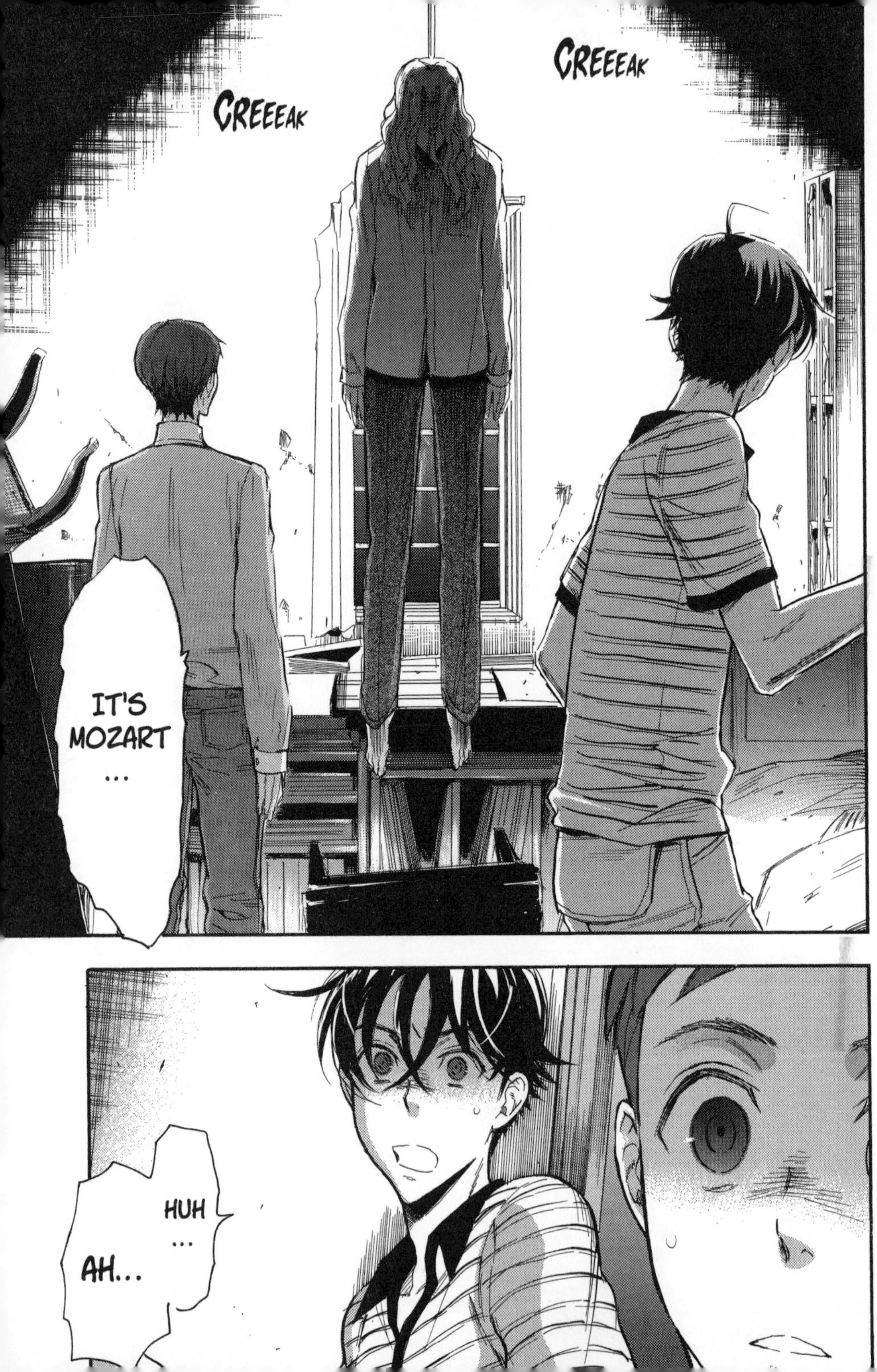
CREEEAK
CREEEAK
IT'S MOZART ...
HUH ...
AH...

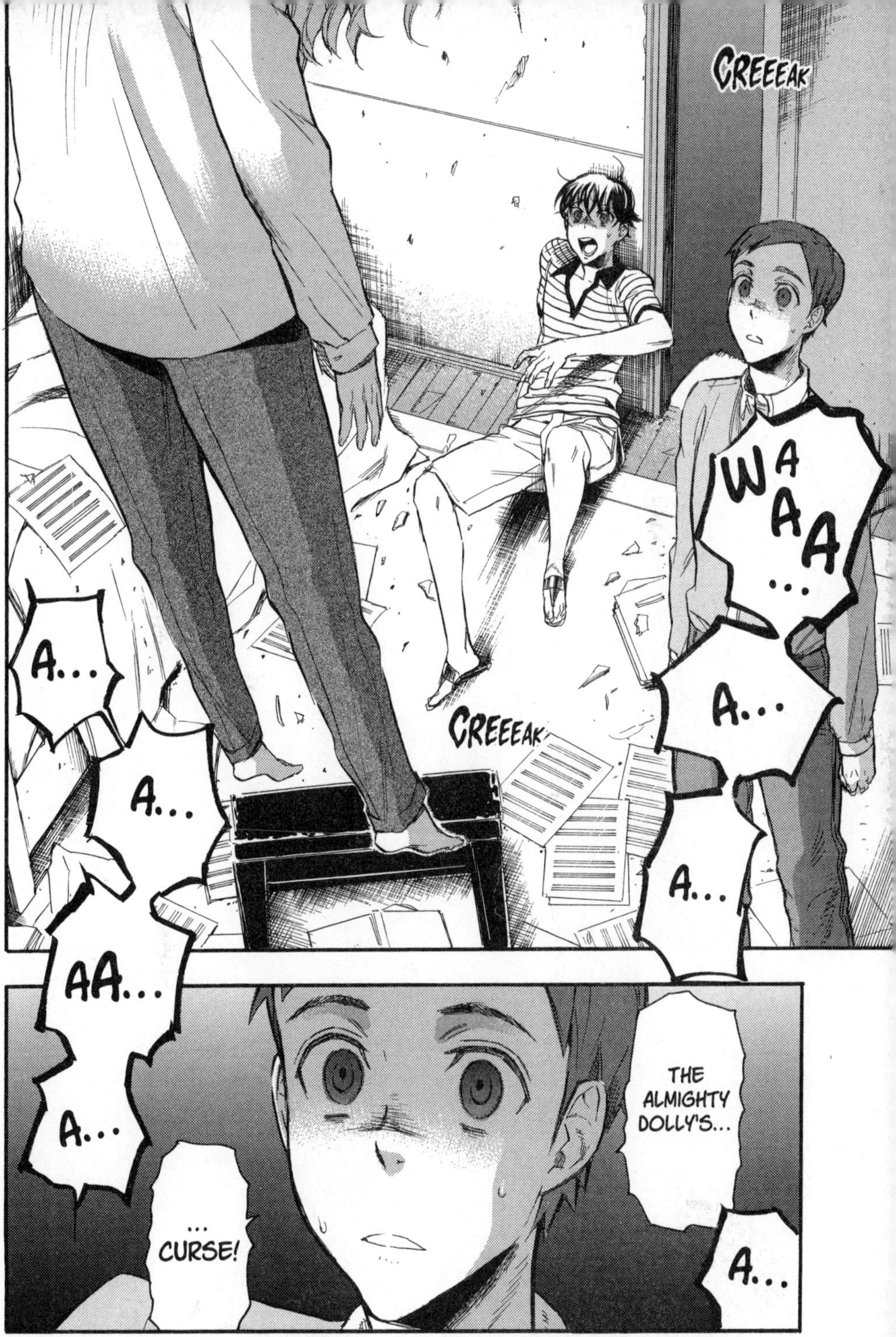
CREEEAK
WAAA...
A...
A...
CREEEAK
A...
A...
AA...
THE ALMIGHTY DOLLY'S...
A...
... CURSE!
A...

afterschool charisma

VOLUME ONE

end

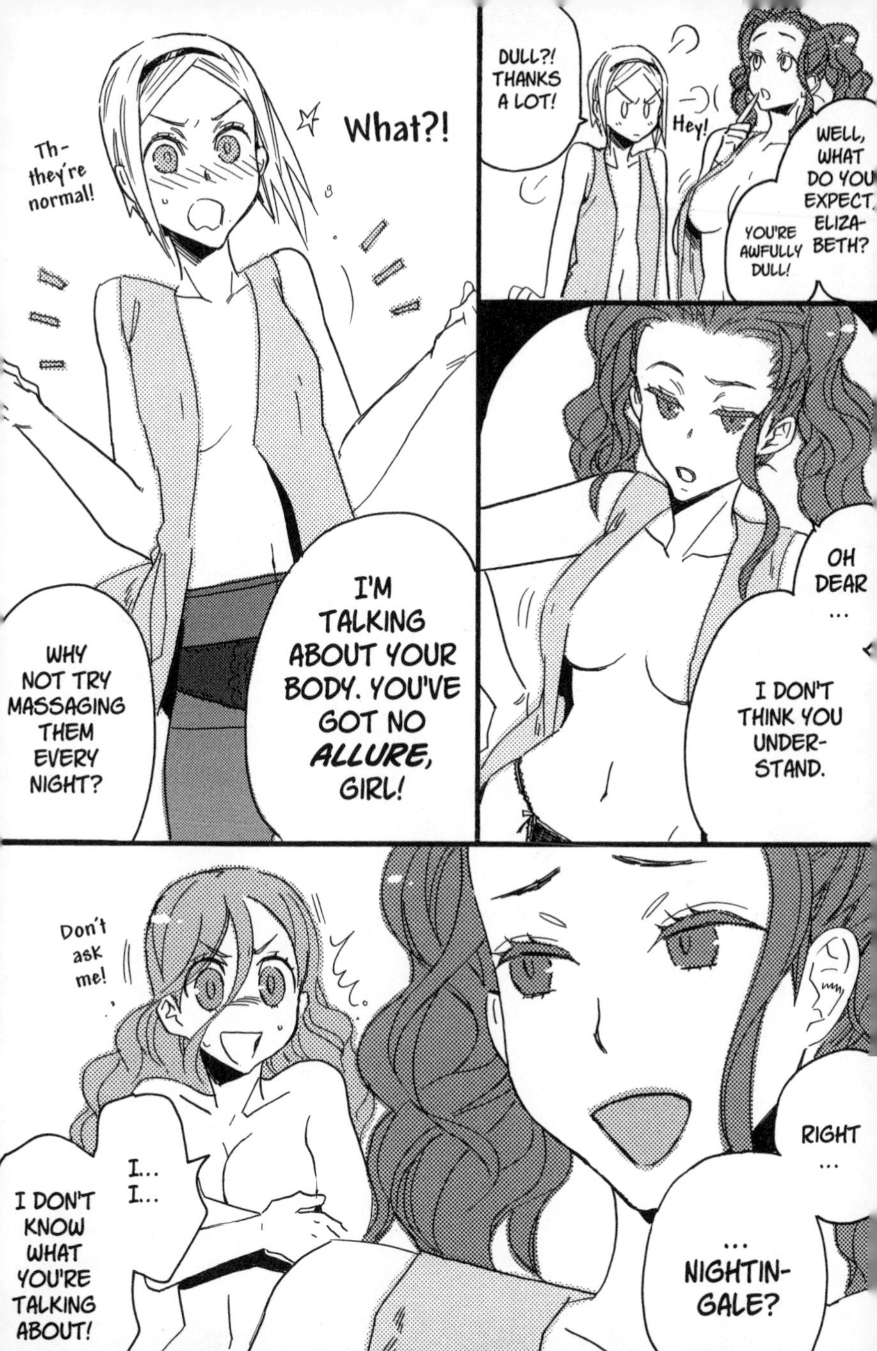
WELL, WHAT DO YOU EXPECT, ELIZABETH?
YOU'RE AWFULLY DULL!
Hey!
DULL?! THANKS A LOT!
OH DEAR...
I DON'T THINK YOU UNDERSTAND.
I'M TALKING ABOUT YOUR BODY. YOU'VE GOT NO ALLURE, GIRL!
What?!
Th-they're normal!
WHY NOT TRY MASSAGING THEM EVERY NIGHT?
RIGHT...
...NIGHTINGALE?
Don't ask me!
I... I...
I DON'T KNOW WHAT YOU'RE TALKING ABOUT!

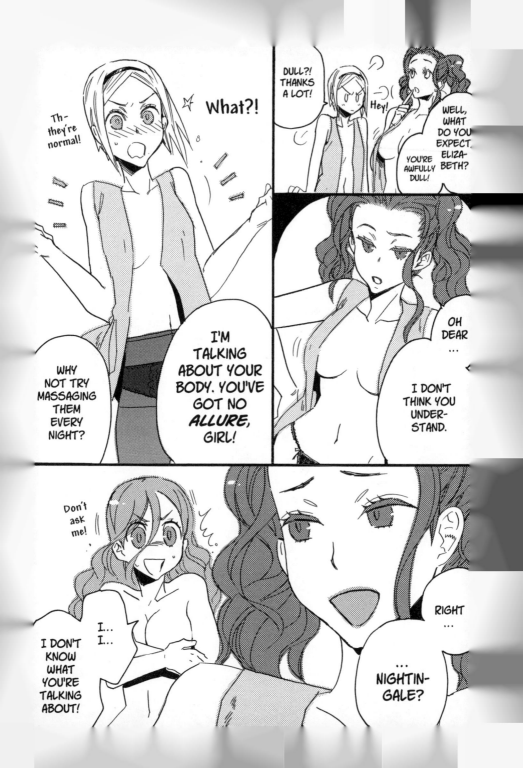

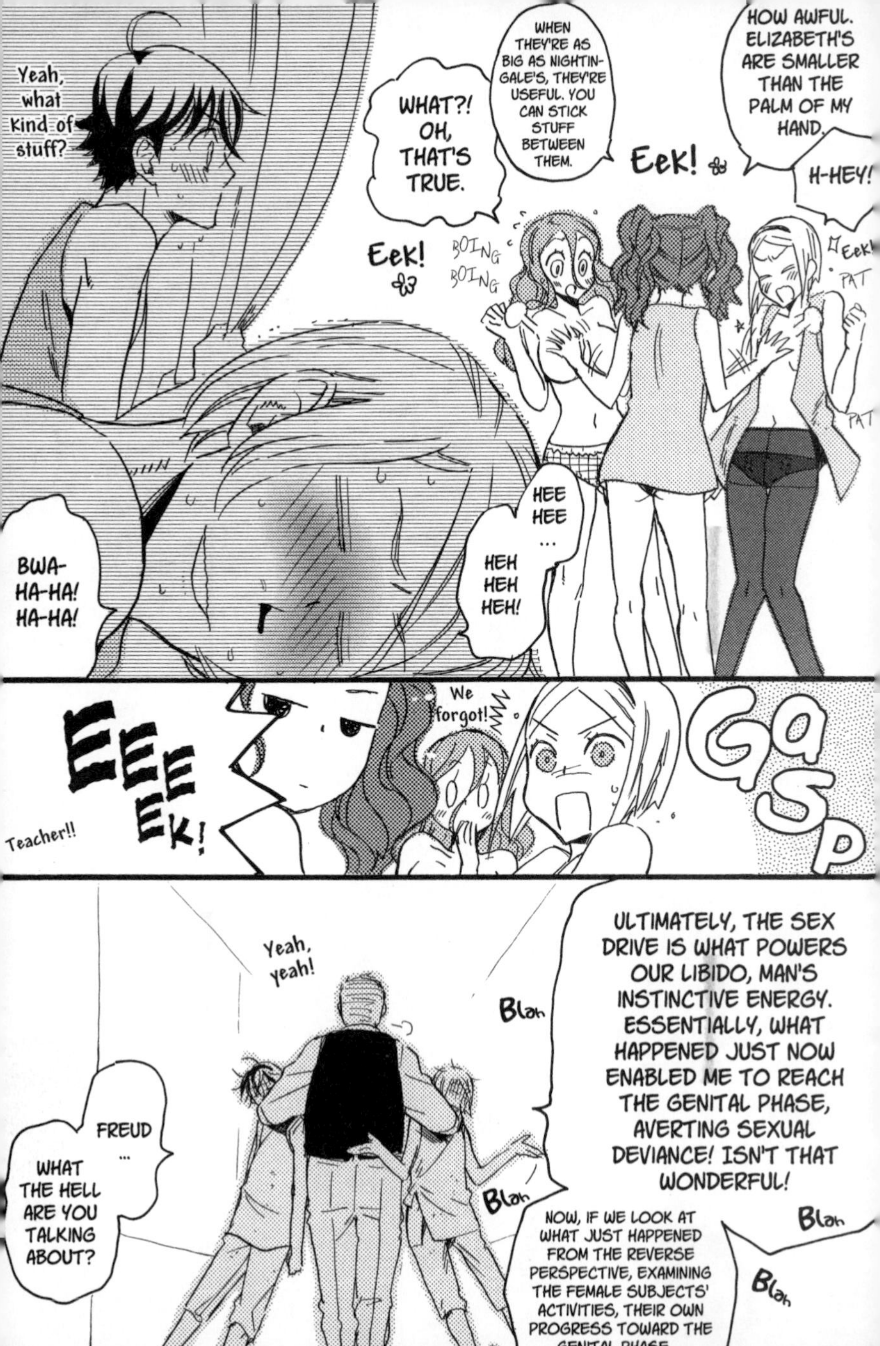
HOW AWFUL. ELIZABETH'S ARE SMALLER THAN THE PALM OF MY HAND.
H-HEY!
Eek!
PAT
PAT
WHEN THEY'RE AS BIG AS NIGHTIN-GALE'S, THEY'RE USEFUL. YOU CAN STICK STUFF BETWEEN THEM.
Eek!
WHAT?! OH, THAT'S TRUE.
BOING BOING
Eek!
Yeah, what kind of stuff?
HEE HEE ... HEH HEH HEH!
BWA-HA-HA! HA-HA!
GASP
We forgot!
EEEEEK!
Teacher!!
ULTIMATELY, THE SEX DRIVE IS WHAT POWERS OUR LIBIDO, MAN'S INSTINCTIVE ENERGY. ESSENTIALLY, WHAT HAPPENED JUST NOW ENABLED ME TO REACH THE GENITAL PHASE, AVERTING SEXUAL DEVIANCE! ISN'T THAT WONDERFUL!
Blah
Blah
NOW, IF WE LOOK AT WHAT JUST HAPPENED FROM THE REVERSE PERSPECTIVE, EXAMINING THE FEMALE SUBJECTS' ACTIVITIES, THEIR OWN PROGRESS TOWARD THE GENITAL PHASE...
Blah
Blah
Yeah, yeah!
FREUD ... WHAT THE HELL ARE YOU TALKING ABOUT?

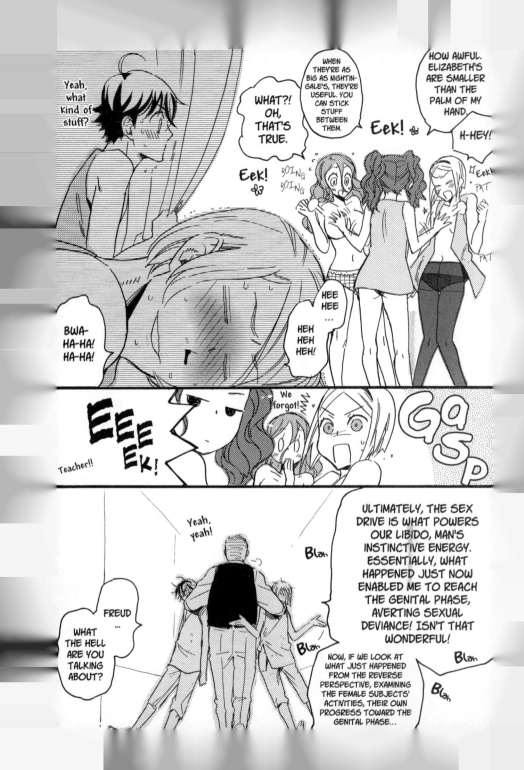

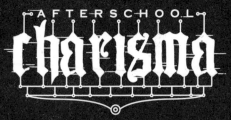

AFTERSCHOOL CHARISMA
VOLUME 1
VIZ SIGNATURE EDITION

STORY & ART BY **KUMIKO SUEKANE**

HOKAGO NO CHARISMA Vol. 1
by Kumiko SUEKANE
© 2009 Kumiko SUEKANE
All rights reserved.
Original Japanese edition published by SHOGAKUKAN.
English translation rights in the United States of America and Canada
arranged with SHOGAKUKAN.

Original Japanese cover design by Mitsuru KOBAYASHI (GENI A LÒIDE)

TRANSLATION ─○─ CAMELLIA NIEH
TOUCH UP ART & LETTERING ─○─ ERIKA TERRIQUEZ
DESIGN ─○─ FAWN LAU
EDITOR ─○─ ERIC SEARLEMAN

Printed in the U.S.A.

Published by VIZ Media, LLC
P.O. Box 77010
San Francisco, CA 94107

10 9 8 7 6 5 4 3 2
First printing, June 2010
Second printing, January 2014

www.viz.com

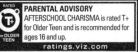
RATED **T+** FOR OLDER TEEN

PARENTAL ADVISORY
AFTERSCHOOL CHARISMA is rated T+
for Older Teen and is recommended for
ages 16 and up.
ratings.viz.com

www.sigikki.com

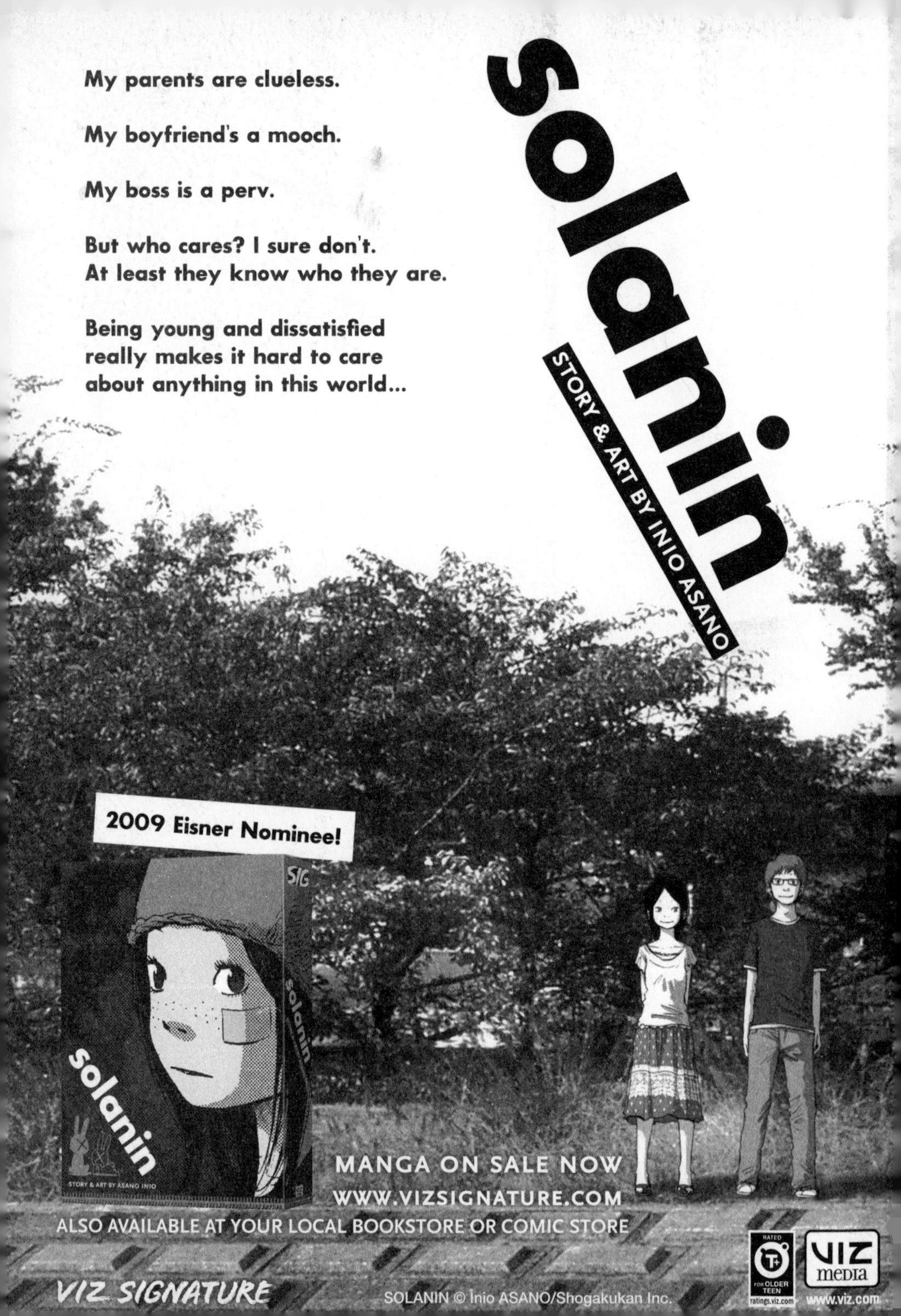
My parents are clueless.
My boyfriend's a mooch.
My boss is a perv.
But who cares? I sure don't.
At least they know who they are.
Being young and dissatisfied
really makes it hard to care
about anything in this world...
solanin
STORY & ART BY INIO ASANO
2009 Eisner Nominee!
SIG
solanin
solanin
STORY & ART BY ASANO INIO
MANGA ON SALE NOW
WWW.VIZSIGNATURE.COM
ALSO AVAILABLE AT YOUR LOCAL BOOKSTORE OR COMIC STORE
VIZ SIGNATURE
SOLANIN © Inio ASANO/Shogakukan Inc.
RATED T+ FOR OLDER TEEN
ratings.viz.com
VIZ media
www.viz.com

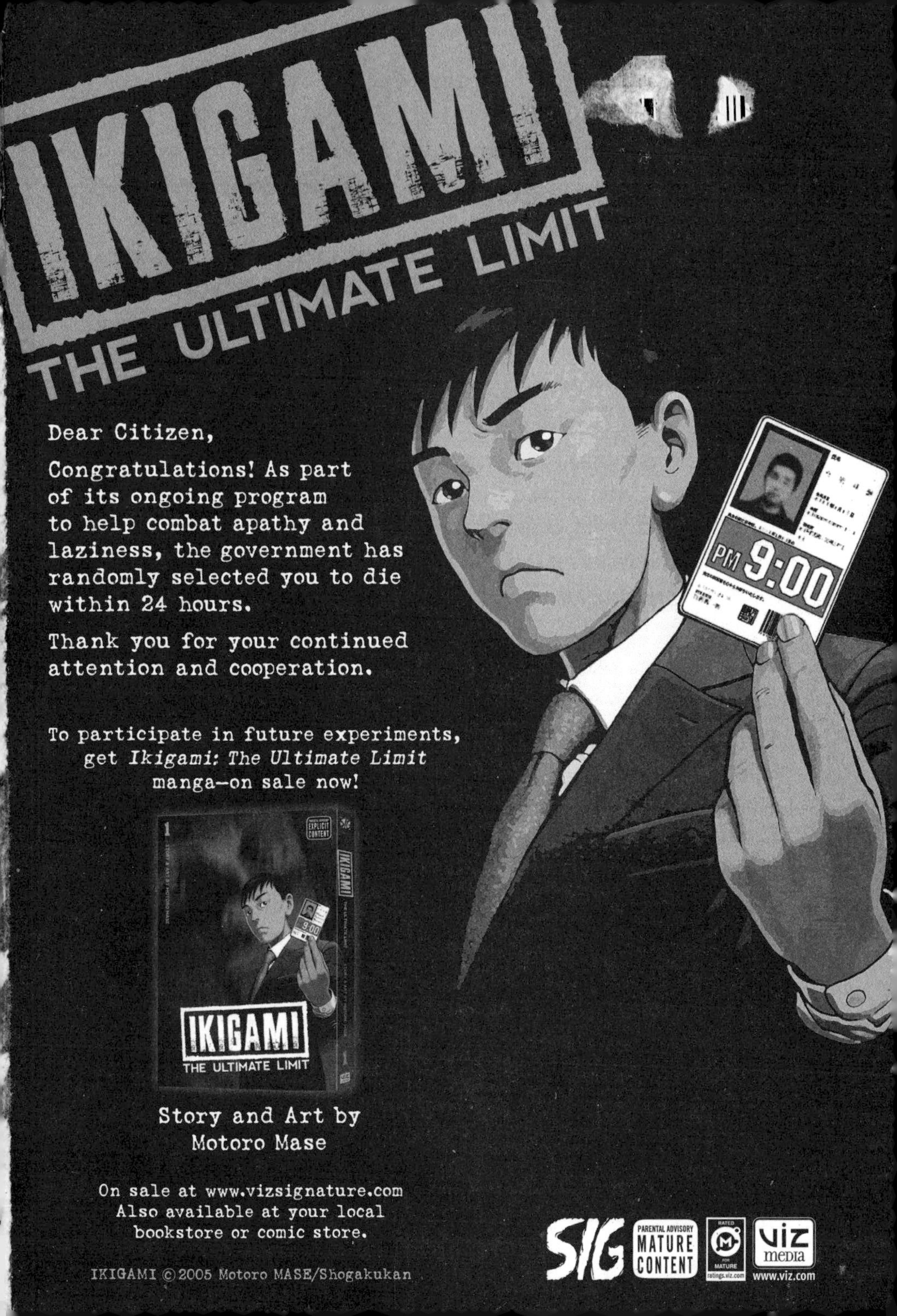

IKIGAMI
THE ULTIMATE LIMIT
PM 9:00
Dear Citizen,
Congratulations! As part of its ongoing program to help combat apathy and laziness, the government has randomly selected you to die within 24 hours.
Thank you for your continued attention and cooperation.
To participate in future experiments, get *Ikigami: The Ultimate Limit* manga—on sale now!
IKIGAMI
THE ULTIMATE LIMIT
Story and Art by Motoro Mase
On sale at www.vizsignature.com
Also available at your local bookstore or comic store.
IKIGAMI © 2005 Motoro MASE/Shogakukan
SIG
PARENTAL ADVISORY MATURE CONTENT
RATED M FOR MATURE ratings.viz.com
viz media www.viz.com